LITER
A

LITERARY RUSSIA
A Guide

ROSAMUND BARTLETT
and ANNA BENN

OVERLOOK DUCKWORTH
New York • Woodstock • London

In memory of Jenny Benn

To TPB and HB

First published in the United States in 2007 by
Overlook Duckworth Peter Mayer Publishers, Inc.
New York, Woodstock & London

NEW YORK:
141 Wooster Street
New York, NY 10012

WOODSTOCK:
One Overlook Drive
Woodstock, NY 12498
www.overlookpress.com
[for individual orders, bulk and special sales, contact our Woodstock office]

LONDON:
90-93 Cowcross Street
London EC1M 6BF
inquiries@duckworth-publishers.co.uk
www.ducknet.co.uk

Cataloging-in-Publication Data is available from the Library of Congress

Manufactured in the United States of America
ISBN 978 1-58567-444-2 (US)
ISBN 978-0-7156-3622-0 (UK)
1 3 5 7 9 8 6 4 2

Contents

List of Illustrations

Acknowledgements

We would like to thank the numerous people and institutions who have made the writing of this book possible, particulary Xa Sturgis. Also Peter Staus who first suggested the project and the Society of Authors and the K. Blundell Trust for their generous help in funding; Charlotte Hobson, Tanya Stobbs, Rose Baring, Katya Galitzine, John Dewey, Helen O'Connor and the Great Britain–Russia Centre, Olga Lawrence, Martha Gellhorn, Michael Makin, Margarita Nafpaktitis, Kelly Miller, Laura Kline, Stephanie Peters, Grigory Kruzhkov, Tom and Lucy Walker, Nigel Benn and Sebastian Benn, Venetia Scott and Elisabeth Gillies; Gerry Smith, Barbara Heldt, Ingo Seidler, Thomas Marullo, Peter James, Christine Kidney, Suzanne Dean and Rachel Lockhart.

In Russia we are especially grateful to: Ivan Movsesyan, Liliana Kerzhenevskaya, Marina Godlevskaya, Brook Horowitz, Alexander Fraser, Evgeniya Kompaneets; also to Marina Lyubimova, Russian National Library; Sergey and Ludmilla Vasiliev, Sasha Kozhin, Rostov-on-Don; Natalya Chernova, Dostoevsky Museum, St Petersburg; M. Chvanov, Aksakov Museum, Bashkortastan; M. Tagiltseva, Aksakov Museum, Ulyanovsk; Aksakov Museum, Orenburg; E. R. Shchemeleva, Blok Museum, Solnechnogorsk; N. M. Anokhina, Belinsky Museum, Penza; A. I. Ermolaev, Chekhov Museum, Moscow; G. P. Murenina, Chernyshevsky Museum, Saratov; Tatyany Stanislavovna, Dostoevsky Museum, Novokuznesk; M. V. Kurmyaeva, Esenin Museum, Saransk; Tamara Ryzhova, Gorky Museum, Nizhny Novgorod; Galina Kashigina, Gorky Museum, Krasnovidovo; I. A. Zhelbakova, Herzen Museum, Moscow; Tamara Melnikova, Lermonov Museum, Tarkhany; Anna Neverova, Lomonosiv Museum, Arkhangelsk; L. A. Ermolaeva, Nekrasov Museum, Chudovo; Solomon Kipniss, Novodevichy Cemetery, Moscow; E. V. Yanovskaya, Nekrasov Museum,

Yarolslavl; A. V. Dominyak, Pushkin Museum, Bolshie Vyazyomy; E. Bogatyrev, Pushkin Museum Moscow (Prechistenka); Alexandra Kalinina, Radishchev Museum, Penza; Sergey Savenko, Kislovodsk Local Museum; L. N. Samkhvalova, Saltykov-Shchedrin Museum, Vyatka; Olga Potapova, Saltykov-Shchedrin Museum, Tver; Larisa Kondrashova, Turgenev Museum, Spasskoe Lutovinovo; B. M. Shumova, Tolstoy Museum, Moscow (Prechistenka); R. N. Krylova, Tolstoy Museum, 'Lev-Tolstoy' (Astapovo); Olga Rubinchuk, Akhmatova Museum, St Petersburg (Fontanka); Svetlana Strizhneva, Mayakovsky Museum, Moscow; Nikolay Alexandrov, Bely Museum, Moscow; Valentina Bilichenko, 'Akhmatova: The Silver Age' Museum, St Petersburg; Esfir Krasovskaya, Tsvetaeva Museum, Moscow; Lyubov Klimenko, Nabokov Museum, St Petersburg; Zoya Atrokhina and Sofya Klepinina-Lvova, Tsvetaeva Museum, Bolshevo; Lilya Ryazanova, Prishvin Museum, Moscow; Natalya Portnova, A. N. Tolstoy Museum, Moscow; Anna Rudnik and Vladimir Krizhevsky, Literary Museum Moscow (Trubnikovsky per.); Ilya Komarov, Paustovsky Museum, Moscow; Veronika Akopdzhanova, Literary Museum, Moscow (Petrovka); Svetlana Shetrakova, Esenin Museum, Moscow.

Every effort has been made to contact all copyright holders. However, if any omissions have occurred the publishers would be happy to rectify them at the first opportunity. Grateful acknowledgement is made for permission to quote from the following copyrighted works: 'I don't have any special claims . . .,' by Anna Akhmatova, translated by Judith Hemschemeyer, is reprinted from *The Complete Poems of Anna Akhmatova*, (Expanded edition, 1992) with the permission of Zephyr Press of Somerville, Massachusetts. Copyright © 1990, 1992 by Judith Hemschemeyer. Tolstoy, *Childhood, Boyhood, Youth*, tr. Rosemary Edmonds, extract reprinted by permission of Penguin Books Lt. Translation © Rosemary Edmonds 1964. N. Zabolotsky, *The Life of Zabolotsky*, ed. R. Milner-Gulland, tr. R. Milner-Gulland & C. G. Bearne extract reprinted by permission of University of Wales Press. Translation © R. Milner-Gulland & C. G. Bearne 1994. Fyodor Dostoevsky, *Notes from the Underground and the Gambler*, tr. Jane Kentish, Oxford Univerisity Press, 1991, extract reprinted by permission of Oxford University Press. Osip Mandelstam, *The Noise of Time*, tr. Clarence Brown, Quartet Encounters, 1988, extract reprinted by permission of Quartet Books. Copyright © 1965 by Princeton University Press. Published by arrangement with North Point Press. Yevgeny Zamyatin, *A Soviet Heretic*, tr. Mirra Ginsberg, Quartet,

1991, extract reprinted by permission of Quartet Books, Extract from *The Collected Works of Velimir Khlebnikov*, edited by Charlotte Douglas. Copyright © 1987 by the Dia Art Foundation. Reprinted by permission of Harvard University Press. *A Reference Guide to Russian Literature*, edited by Neil Cornwell, London and Chicago: Fitzroy Dearborn, 1997. Extract reprinted by permission of Fitzroy Dearborn. Mayakovsky, *Love is the Heart of Everything*, ed. B. Jangfelt, tr. Julian Graffy, extract courtesy of Edinburgh University Press. *Leonid Andreyev: Photographs by a Russian Writer. An undiscovered portrait of pre-revolution Russia*, edited and introduced by Richard Davies. Copyright © Thames and Hudson 1989. Extract reprinted by permission of Thames and Hudson. *The Memoirs of Alexander Herzen*, Parts I and II, 1923, extract reprinted by permission of Yale University Press. Osip Mandelstam, *The Eyesight of Wasps*, tr. James Green, 1989, extract reprinted by permission of Angel Books. Osip Mandelstam, *The Moscow Notebooks*, 1991, and *The Voronezh Notebooks*, 1996, tr. by Richard and Elizabeth McKane, extracts reprinted by permission of Bloodaxe Books. Galina Visnevskaya, *Galina: A Russian Story*, extract reproduced by permission Hodder and Stoughton Limited. Copyright © 1984 by Galina Vishnevskaya and Harcourt Brace Jovanovich Inc. Fyodor Dostoevsky, *Poor Folk*, tr. C. J. Hogarth, 1915, extract reprinted by permission of J. M. Dent. Carl Proffer, *The Widows of Russia and Other Writings*, extract reprinted by permission Ardis Publishers. *My Life with Michael Bulgakov*, tr. Margareta Thompson, 1983, extract reprinted by permission of Ardis Publishers. *Mandelstam: The Complete Critical Prose and Letters*, ed. Jane Gary Harris, tr. Jane Gary Harris and Constance Link, 1979, extract reprinted by permission of Ardis Publishers. Thomas Seifrid, *Andrei Platonov, Uncertainties of Spirit*, 1992 Cambridge Studies in Russian Literature series, extract reprinted by permission of Cambridge University Press. Vladimir Nabokov, *Speak Memory*, extract reprinted by permission of Weidenfeld and Nicholson. Alexander Puskin, *Eugene Onegin*, tr. Charles Johnston (Penguin Classics 1977, revised edition 1979). Copyright © Charles Johnston, 1977, 1979. Fyodor Dostoyevsky, *The Gambler; Bobok; A Nasty Story*, tr. Jessie Coulson (Penguin Classics, 1966). Copyright © Jessie Coulson 1966. Ivan Goncharov, *Oblomov*, tr. David Magarshack (Penguin Classics, 1954). Copyright © David Magarshack, 1954. Fyodor Dostoyevsky, *Crime and Punishment*, tr. David McDuff, (Viking/Penguin Classics, 1991). Translation copyright © David McDuff, 1991. Fyodor Dostoyevsky,

The Idiot, tr. David Magarshack, (Penguin Classics, 1955). Copyright © David Magarshack, 1955. Fyodor Dostoyevsky, *The Brothers Karamazov*, tr. David Magarshack, (Penguin Classics, 1958). Copyright © David Magarshack, 1958. Nikolai Leskov, *Lady Macbeth of Mtsensk and Other Stories*, tr. David McDuff, (Penguin Classics, 1987). Translation copyright © David McDuff, 1987. Lermontov, *A Hero of Our Time*, tr. Paul Foote (Penguin Classics, 1966). Copyright © Paul Foot 1966. All Reproduced by permission of Penguin Books. Nadezhda Mandelstam: lines taken from *Hope Abandoned*. First published in Great Britain by Collins and the Harvill Press 1974. © Atheneum Publishers 1972. © in the English translation by Max Hayward, Atheneum Publishers, New York, and Collins Harvill, London 1973, 1974. Reproduced by permission of the Harvill Press. Anna Akhmatova: 'Voronezh' taken from *Poems of Akhmatova*, selected translated and introduced by Stanley Kunitz and Max Hayward. First published in 1973 by Little, Brown and Company. First published in Great Britain in 1974. © 1967, 1968, 1972, 1973 by Stanley Kunitz and Max Hayward. Reproduced by permission of the Harvill Press. Boris Pasternak: lines taken from *An Essay in Auto-biography*. First published in Great Britain by Collins and the Harvill Press 1959. © Giangiacomo Feltrinelli Editore 1959. © in the English translation by Manya Harari, William Collins and Co. 1959, 1990. Reproduced by permission of the Harvill Press. Evgeny Pasternak: lines taken from 'Waves' in *Boris Pasternak: The Tragic years 1930–1960*. First published in Great Britain by Collins Harvill 1990. © VAAP 1990. © in the English translation by Ann Pasternak Slater and Craig Raine, William Collins Sons & Co. Ltd 1990. Reproduced by permission of the Harvill Press. Aleksandr Solzhenitsyn: lines taken from *The Oak and the Calf*. First published in Great Britain by Collins Harvill 1980. © Aleksandr Solzhenitsyn 1975. © in the English translation by Harry Willetts, Harper & Row, Publishers, Inc., and William Collins, Sons & Co. Ltd. Reproduced by permission of the Harvill Press. Mikhail Bulgakov: lines taken from *The Master and Margarita*. First published in Great Britain by Collins and the Harvill Press 1967. © in the English translation by Harvill Press and Harper & Row Publishers 1967. Reproduced by permission of the Harvill Press.

Foreword

The Soviet Union collapsed in 1991, and within a decade, the Russian literary world was unrecognizable. There is no perhaps better symbol of the momentous changes which have transformed the face of Russian letters than the publishing phenomenon of Boris Akunin, whose detective fiction started to grip the national imagination at the beginning of the new millennium. Sales of his first novel, which appeared in 1998 with a print-run of 10 000, were initially slow. Two years later, however, there were already seven novels in print about the now legendary sleuth Erast Fandorin, and they had all become best-sellers. By the summer of 2001, new Akunin titles were selling out their initial print-runs of 100 000 copies in a matter of months and beginning to interest both Russian television producers and foreign audiences (an English translation of the first Fandorin novel, published as *The Winter Queen*, appeared in 2003). *The Collected Works of Lenin* were never so successful, even in the heyday of Bolshevik utopian propaganda. Over eight million detective novels by Akunin have been sold.

The Akunin phenomenon is interesting both for what it tells us about readers' tastes in early 21st-century Russia, and also about the general conditions for book publishing in the new post-Soviet market economy. In the good old, bad old days of the USSR, there was very little reading or writing for pure entertainment (and certainly no detective novels). But that does not mean that paid-up members of the Russian literary intelligentsia would not feel a sense of shame about abandoning High Art once it became permissible to do so. It was when Boris Akunin noticed his wife had furtively concealed the fact that she was reading detective novels in the metro by covering up the dustjackets (a tactic previously employed to conceal *samizdat*) that he came up with the idea of writing some himself. He was still not prepared to publish under his own name, Grigory Chkhartishvili, which he used in his career as a respected scholar and translator, but he wanted to write books his wife would not feel embarrassed to read in public. Within six weeks, writing in his spare time, he had crafted his first thriller. Alexandra Marinina and Viktor Dotsenko, best-selling authors and pioneers of the genre in Russia, set their detective novels in the gritty contemporary world of mafia violence. Drawing on their respective backgrounds as a high-ranking former police officer and ex-convict, Marinina's heroine is a dedicated and over-worked female detective, while Dotsenko's sleuth is a veteran of the war with Afghanistan. As a member of the intelligentsia, Akunin naturally drew on the best traditions of the Russian literature to create his much more upmarket hero: his 19th-century detective is a composite of characters from the novels of Tolstoy, Turgenev and Dostoevsky. Whereas Marinina and Dotsenko write fast-moving but formulaic thrillers with calculated mass appeal, Akunin's sophisticated, witty novels are stylistically far more ambitious. Having successfully made the detective novel a respectable literary genre in Russia, and himself a personal fortune along the way, Akunin was not too perturbed when his identity was blown. Smart readers had already twigged that B. Akunin spelt the name of famous Russian anarchist Bakunin; fewer appreciated that "Akunin" means "malefactor" in Japanese, one of Chkhartishvili's many languages.

As Russia became engulfed in violent crime in the 1990s, it is perhaps not surprising that readers wanted to read detective novels, either home-grown, or in translation. Just as sharp-witted former academics like Boris Berezovsky were able to acquire immense wealth when the Soviet Union collapsed by going into business, so have an increasing number turned to earning a good living by writing pulp fiction, albeit with a twist. It is encouraging to learn that Leonid Yuzefovich, one of the authors shortlisted for the Russian Booker Prize in 2003, is a writer with a doctorate in history who uses the traditionally low-brow genre of the detective novel as a means to a more high-brow end (eg., provoking his readers to think about the meaning of life). Where the line between literary and popular fiction should be drawn has become a perennial theme in discussions regarding Russia's most prestigious literary prize, whose history itself reflects the changing climate of national life. Another Western import, it was established in 1991 by the original British sponsors Booker plc, with a mind to commercial investments in Russia as well as philanthropic considerations. When the conditions for assisting with the modernization of Russian agriculture failed to materialize, the Smirnoff vodka company took over from Booker, and Smirnoff was in turn was replaced as chief sponsor in 2002 by Open Russia, the charitable arm of the oil company Yukos. In keeping with its aims to "help develop a liberal and democratic society, and support citizens striving to live, work and achieve success in Russia—and for Russia," Mikhail Khodorkovsky, the founder of Open Russia, fully supports the idea of an independent literary prize (the first such in Russia since 1917). It is a sign of the times that the winner of the 2003 Booker Prize, Ruben Gonzalez Gallego, who spent his childhood in Soviet homes for the disabled, is published by Limbus Press in St. Petersburg, the first independent publishing house to be established since 1917. It is also a sign of the times, however, that not only did President Putin jail the internationalist-minded, liberal Khodorkovsky, the country's richest man, in the autumn of 2003 for alleged financial improprieties, but the Russian Head of State has also reinstituted state literary prizes.

Although there is agreement that the wide range of works submitted for the Russian Booker Prize reflects the turbulent changes the country has gone through in changing from one socio-political system to another, there is much debate as to their quality. Even

members of the Booker Prize jury have been known to condemn
the overall standard of contemporary Russian prose as mediocre,
but as Alexei Kostanyan, editor-in-chief of leading publisher Vagrius
has commented, "Times of troubles do not bring forth master-
pieces." Compared with the twenty million copies of Dotsenko's
novels sold by the summer of 2004, the sales figures of 30,000 for
Gallego's *White on Black* seem small (Russia's overall population
is 150 million), but they are impressive when set against the fact
that serious literary works are generally considered to have done
well these days if they sell over 10,000 copies. Only literary fiction by Russia's top "highbrow" contemporary writers (such as
Viktor Pelevin, Tatyana Tolstaya or Lyudmila Ulitskaya) reaches
the 100,000 mark. The critic and scholar Igor Shaitanov, who
acts as Literary Secretary for the Russian Booker, has stressed the
importance of the prize in promoting serious writing nationwide, as
traditional subscriptions to once-popular literary journals continue
to plummet and bookshops in the provinces struggle to survive.
Bookshops in the major cities are filled with glossy new titles, but
there are still not that many of them. Travel outside the city limits, and you will appreciate that the era of the bookstore-café is a
long way off in Russia.

As an account of the author's tortured childhood separated
into what is essentially a collection of short stories, *White on
Black* is not exactly a novel, but it is, more importantly, a book in
which Russian readers might find something to "support them in
life", according to the head of the Booker jury Yakov Gordin,
himself a writer, and the editor of the prestigious literary journal
Znamya. Gonzalez was born with cerebral palsy, and writes while
lying on his back, typing with the only two fingers he can move,
so it is not surprising that his story of survival against the odds
has resonated so strongly with contemporary Russian readers.
They certainly have little time for the kind of prescriptive prose
traditionally provided by their native writers, as Alexander
Solzhenitsyn discovered to his cost after staging a triumphant
return from emigration in the early 1990s. Having anticipated

taking up his former position as moral scourge of the nation, he was forced to accept that his services were no longer required and had to beat a humiliating retreat.

Once Russian readers had grown accustomed to the excitement of being able to read thrillers and bodice-rippers after censorship was lifted in the late 1980s, they found that they still wanted to escape from the vicissitudes of coping with everyday life in the New Russia and be entertained. Since the 1990s they have also wanted to know more about what has really been going on in their country as they have become steadily poorer, while an army of ruthless so-called "New Russians" have carved up former state enterprises, creating unimaginable wealth for themselves and trailing a path of conspicuous consumerism and mobster violence in their wake. This thirst for knowledge is matched by a desire among writers to process recent history. The best possible example of this trend is the impressive and weighty novel *Big Slice*, published in 1999 by Yuly Dubov, sixty thousand copies sold, and well into its third printing in 2004. Billed by its publisher as the "first real novel about Russian business," *Big Slice* does more than tell an elaborately woven story about a group of research scientists who abandon their institutes at the end of the 1980s to go into car dealing together, eventually making vast profits. The novel (subsequently made into a film called *Oligarch* by the director Pavel Lungin) also reveals in vivid detail how Russian business came into being, from its lowly origins in the co-operative ventures first permitted under Gorbachev. The author is a former academic and the General Director of the automobile company LogoVAZ, headed by Boris Berezovsky, whom he joined in political exile in London in the autumn of 2003. It was only a matter of time before Mikhail Khodorkovsky's dramatic story inspired a thriller-writer. After Tatyana Ustinova watched Khodorkovsky being arrested and forced off his private jet at gunpoint on television in November 2003, she decided her next hero would be an oil tycoon who is jailed and bankrupted by the state. In her scenario, he is released after fourteen months, proceeds to defeat his enemies, fall in love with a beautiful woman and live happily ever after. When *The Oligarch and the Great Bear* was published in March 2004, Khodorkovsky was still sitting in jail.

Inevitably the classics have been rather overshadowed by such sensational fare in recent times. They have also come under attack by today's post-modernist avant-garde who wish to liberate Russian literature, loose it from its totalitarian moorings and "deconsecrate" it, as Moscow University Professor Vladimir Kataev put it in his 2002 book on the subject. The end of censorship in the late 1980s and the collapse of the USSR at one stroke removed late 20th-century Russian literature's central subject (opposition to Soviet power) and plunged it into a state of crisis, which writers have reacted to in different ways. Like the Futurists of the early 20th century, some have set out deliberately to shock, chief amongst them Vladimir Sorokin (b. 1955), whose full-frontal assault on Russian literature's hallowed traditions may most graphically be seen in his novel *Blue Fat* (1999), which, amongst other things, features steamy sex scenes between Khrushchev and Stalin. Other writers have subverted the Russian literary canon by in more anodyne ways. After Emil Dreitser wrote a sequel to Chekhov's *The Lady with the Little Dog* (1993), and Evgeny Popov wrote a prequel to Turgenev's novel *On the Eve*, entitled *On the Eve of On the Eve* (1994), Vasily Staroy concocted a "creative continuation" of *War and Peace* entitled *Pierre and Natasha* (1997), which follows the story of the couple's married life. The aforementioned Akunin has also made a successful essay in this genre by completing a new "detective play" sequel to Chekhov's *The Seagull* (1999), in which Treplev's apparent suicide turns out to be . . . murder. News that the complete works of Boris Pasternak are to be published for the first time to mark the 115th anniversary of the writer's birth in February 2005 is obviously not quite as headline-grabbing, but literary scholars continue to work with quiet dedication, often depending now on private and state grants for the publication of their research.

In the harsh new conditions of post-Soviet Russia in which historic buildings are being razed to the ground with scant regard for their cultural importance, the survival of the nation's literary museums seems more precarious than ever, and their legacy thus more precious. The August 2004 bulletin of the Moscow Architectural Preservation Society, the international lobby group which seeks to raise awareness about the present destruction of Moscow's historical buildings (http://www.gif.ru/eng/places/maps/), for example, reported on the threat to the estate of Fyodor Tyutchev, one of the Russia's most famous 19th-century poets, who is buried beside a tiny wooden church in enchanting surroundings in the Moscow countryside: "The poet chose to build his house in Muranovo for its view of a lake and rolling meadows, still enjoyed by thousands of visitors every year. Despite the vast areas of empty land nearby, these celebrated meadows are being sold to developers in contravention of the law. The museum has written a letter addressed to President Putin and the governor of the region". In January 2003, the clash between old and new Russia came to a head when Tolstoy's great-great-grandson Vladimir sued the architect who started building a red-brick mansion just outside the gates of the writer's ancestral estate for a wealthy businessman. Vladimir Tolstoy has been director of the family estate of Yasnaya Polyana since 1994, and has been instrumental in ensuring its reputation as one of the few state museums to make a profit. Like all Russian literary museums, however, the Yasnaya Polyana museum needs further funding, prompting the Tolstoy family to patch up their differences with the local business community. Perhaps it augurs well for the future of Russia's priceless literary heritage that in the spring of 2004, Tolstoy signed an agreement on cooperation in the Tula region with the local governor and representatives of industry and commerce, backed by the Ministry of Culture.

Introduction

The story of literary Russia is also the story of its cultural history. In no other country have creative artists played such a prominent role in their national life, and it is Russian writers above all who have traditionally occupied a position of pre-eminence among their fellow musicians and painters, with poets most hallowed of all. In Soviet times, the Union of Writers was the biggest and most important of all the artists' unions, and one of the most powerful political bodies in the country. Few nations appear to be as proud of their literary heritage. The fact that Russia has more literary museums than any other country in the world speaks volumes about the high esteem in which writers in that country have been held. In Moscow and St Petersburg, and throughout the provincial regions, extending to the far eastern parts of Siberia, houses of writers have been preserved as literary shrines, statues of writers stand in prominent locations, plaques commemorating literary associations have been fixed to walls, and scores of towns, streets and institutions have been named after the famous authors who had connections with them. This almost fetishistic idolatry of ideologically approved writers (along with the turning of repressed writers into martyrs by the intelligentsia), which went on chiefly during the Soviet period, has much in common with the cult of personality more usually linked to the worship of political leaders, but was not purely a Soviet phenomenon. Streets were named after writers even before the Revolution. But the absence until very recently, on the other hand, of any kind of permanent tribute to first-rank writers such as Nabokov, Tsvetaeva, Bunin and Zoshchenko also speaks eloquently of the peculiar relationship that has hitherto always existed between the writer and the state in Russia. Only since the demise of the Soviet Union has literature in Russia begun to play the marginal role it is allotted in the West, and become merely 'art'.

As Solzhenitsyn once asserted, writers in Russia were like a second government, and their inflated status as prophets and bearers of the Truth was only bolstered by a state which, in effect, treated them as such. For daring to tell things as they were, many writers in Russia paid with their lives, for only police states with no freedom of speech have held the written word in such high esteem. Russia has repressed its writers not only in the nineteenth and twentieth centuries. The tradition of exiling those who chose to disagree with official policies was begun in the seventeenth century, and identifying the roots of this tradition may help to explain why literature has always been so important in Russia, and why poets in particular, both before and after the Revolution, who either died tragically early, committed suicide or suffered or perished at the hands of the state (notably Pushkin, Lermontov, Blok, Esenin, Mayakovsky, Akhmatova, Mandelstam and Tsvetaeva), were accorded the status almost of saints. Russia, as the late Joseph Brodsky once commented, has always been a logocentric culture, and this has to do not only with the indisputable beauty of the Russian language, but also with the fact that the birth and early development of Russian literature were inextricably bound up with the adoption of the Greek Orthodox faith from Byzantium in the late tenth century. The cyrillic alphabet was created with the sole purpose of translating the scriptures into Russian, and for the next seven centuries Russian literary culture was predominantly a religious one. Hence one reason for the supreme importance traditionally bestowed on 'the word' in Russia.

The other main reason is of course political, and emerged as successive defensive Russian rulers refused to tolerate at first the truth being told about the barbaric conditions in which most of their subjects lived, and, in time, any kind of dissent or interest in democratic ideas. Whether they liked it or not, certain writers came to be championed by earnest critics such as Belinsky as representing the voice of moral righteousness, a noble tradition preserved throughout the Soviet regime by the intelligentsia. In pre-revolutionary times, writers who offended the tsar, such as Pushkin, were banished to remote corners of Russia, to their estate (if they were lucky enough to possess one), or to prison camps. Some writers, like Dostoevsky, were subjected to a tsar's strange sense of humour and taunted with mock executions. In Soviet times, the tradition of persecuting writers continued. Recalcitrant authors who refused to conform to the almost military strictures imposed on them by the government (writers were often described during these times as performing the role of the artillery in battle) were either sent to the gulag, expelled from the all-powerful Union of Writers, exiled to remote parts of the country or actually out of it (like Solzhenitsyn), or simply shot. And censorship continued to play a major role in the country's cultural life, forcing poets into silence or into hideous compromises with the regime, and rewriting the past to conform with the new orthodoxy.

For the traveller wishing to visit the major literary landmarks of Russia without specialist knowledge before the late 1980s, the topography would have been highly selective. The itinerary would have included the houses of Tolstoy and Chekhov, and the dozens of sites which have a connection with Pushkin, but no museum commemorating, say, Akhmatova or Bely. That topography is now changing radically, however. Not only is it now possible to travel in Russia to areas previously closed to foreign visitors, but scores of new museums are opening which are dedicated to honouring those authors repressed or neglected under the Soviet regime. One of the aims of this book is to make all the literary museums in Russia more accessible to the traveller, in the hope that those places which are in danger of extinction may be preserved. As well as the museums, there are countless surviving writers' houses throughout Russia which can be visited, many of which are beautiful ruins. This is the case with the magnificent house of Nabokov's uncle outside St Petersburg, for example, which burned down in 1995. There are no funds available to restore it. We hope that the guide will dispel some of the obscurity surrounding the lesser-known writers, while providing fresh information on literary giants such as Tolstoy and Dostoevsky.

At the same time we wanted to write a guide book that took the reader away from the over-indulgent, self-congratulatory Soviet attitudes of the past, which still tend to be reproduced in many literary museum brochures. Many visitors often encounter problems with the language barrier, and we hope the book will help non-Russian-speaking visitors navigate those museums which do not yet cater for foreigners. Because of lack of funding, many museums have been unable to reproduce their literature, and visitors are obliged to read a poorly translated Soviet version. The unveiling in St Petersburg in 1995 of a gargantuan granite nose in honour of Gogol's famous story, however, was a deliberate send-up of Soviet high seriousness, and is a healthy sign that some progress is being made in the abandonment of entrenched views.

It was during the Soviet period that most of the literary museums in existence were founded. Many writers' apartments and houses were turned into museums after being restored, while others were rebuilt from scratch after being destroyed in the Second World War. These sites became places of pilgrimage for many thousands of Soviet citizens, from school children to adults. Such museums were intended for a Russian public, but occasionally some of the bigger and more impressive ones such

as Tolstoy's Yasnaya Polyana and Turgenev's Spasskoe Lutovinovo were opened up to foreign visitors as well. While most of
the major nineteenth-century writers soon had commemorative
museums established in the places where they lived, the Soviet
authorities passed over in silence the lives of those who perished
in the purges. Meanwhile, vast resources were spent on confer-
ring privileges on the thousands of 'official' living writers and
their dependants. The Union of Writers went to great pains to
provide luxurious living conditions for its members, building
them huge apartment blocks and giving them dachas in the
country. Then came perestroika and it seemed that at last the
balance could be redressed. Hitherto banned literature by
authors such as Pasternak and Solzhenitsyn became available,
and repressed writers were now able to take their places in
Russian literary history. Dedicated enthusiasts were also now
able to found museums to writers such as Tsvetaeva and Akhmatova, and plaques began to go up on buildings to previously
proscribed poets such as Osip Mandelstam.

In the troubled post-Soviet era, however, the future of Russia's
literary museums hangs in the balance, as state funds rapidly dry
up. The fate of the Literary Museum of Sergey Esenin founded
by an enthusiast in the Mordovian village of Lukhovka, near
Saransk, is a case in point. A letter from its former director,
Mariya Kurmyaeva, sheds light on the situation:

> This literary museum was organized by the headmaster of
> the local school, Alexey Alexandrovich Kotlov. He was a
> great admirer of Esenin, and spent his whole life collecting
> 'Eseniniana'. The museum was wonderful, and on the
> ninetieth anniversary of Esenin's birth [in 1985] it acquired
> its own building. There were a great many exhibits, much
> to the envy of the larger museums. But alas ... along came
> perestroika, followed by 'democracy'. Culture has always
> dragged out a miserable existence in our country; well, it
> doesn't even bear thinking about in this day and age. The
> museum was part of the regional museum of the republic,

and when they decided to close it, there was no one who could prevent it happening. The local powers couldn't put it into their budget because they didn't have the money. As a result, it was dismantled; some of the exhibits (the most valuable ones) were put in the local regional museum, some were taken by the children of the collector, while the least valuable have stayed here. There is now a library in this building, and we do what we can to preserve things. Excuse me for going on at such length, but your letter touched a raw nerve. I loved the museum and its quietness...

The writers' abodes described here vary in grandeur. At one end are the manor houses of the nobility, with a park, stables, lakes and orangeries; at the other end of the spectrum are the small wooden huts and cramped apartments lived in by less affluent authors. Something that stands out about nineteenth-century writers is how nomadic most of them were. With the exception of authors like Tolstoy, who hated to leave his beloved country estate Yasnaya Polyana, and made forays into the city only with extreme reluctance, writers rarely stayed in one place all their lives. In the cities, impecunious writers changed flats continuously, usually renting accommodation in a *dokhodny dom* (apartment block) from a rich landlord who was usually from the merchant class. Huge areas of Moscow and St Petersburg were taken up by such lodging houses. Houses did not have numbers, so addresses took the form of the name of the street, followed by the name of the landlord. It is curious to note a similar pattern repeating itself in the twentieth century with the same combination of extremes: at one end of the scale official writers living in well-appointed, spacious flats and houses, and at the other writers who refused to compromise eking out a living in decidedly less glamorous surroundings – sometimes a tiny room in a communal flat – and forced to make frequent moves.

This book is intended as a practical guide to visitors wishing to acquaint themselves with the major literary sites in Russia; it is also to be hoped that it will be read with profit by those who intend to venture no further than their armchair. For it is not just a literary map of Russia that is sketched out here, but a social and political one as well. It will be noticed, for example, that the majority of writers chose to live in St Petersburg in the nineteenth century. When the capital moved back to Moscow following Lenin's death, however, most writers followed. The areas in which writers lived in both cities is also telling. It is the western part of central Moscow that boasts the most fashionable streets (Prechistenka, Arbat, Sivtsev-Vrazhek, for example). Accordingly, we find writers of noble birth (such as Tolstoy) residing here, whereas those from more humble origins, like the poet Esenin, lived in the Zamoskvorechie, the area immediately south of the Moscow river, traditionally inhabited by merchants, who comprised an altogether separate class in the hierarchical structure of Russian society.

Included in this guide are descriptions of all the major literary museums in Russia, not least a great number of houses and apartments once inhabited by famous authors, whose furnishings have been preserved as they were during their inhabitants' lifetimes, as well as permanent exhibitions housed in buildings that otherwise have no connection with the author they commemorate. The guide also lists the other main addresses of Russian authors, editorial offices, bookshops, publishers and other literary institutions, and the addresses of places with a significant literary association. Specific locales mentioned in literary works are also mentioned. This is particularly appropriate in the case of Dostoevsky's novel *Crime and Punishment*, but less so with the novels of Tolstoy, for example, who frequently sets his major works in Moscow and St Petersburg but comparatively rarely cites any particular building or street.

Not surprisingly, the visitor will find that each literary museum founded in a writer's former home possesses its own atmosphere, which more often than not reflects the spirit of its illustrious former inhabitant and his or her living conditions. The dour apartment of the classic Socialist Realist author and invalid Nikolay Ostrovsky, for example, with its standard-issue portrait of Lenin, is light years away from the bleak wooden NKVD dacha that Marina Tsvetaeva stayed in temporarily upon return from emigration, or the plush home of Alexey Tolstoy, yet only by visiting all three of these museums can the visitor hope to acquire a full picture of the literary spectrum of Soviet Russia in the 1930s and 1940s. The apartment of an author like Ostrovsky would have held little interest for most foreign visitors in Soviet times, but it too has now become an item of historical curiosity along with the regime which produced such a writer; as such, it merits attention. The atmosphere in each literary museum is also, it should be noted, to some extent determined by the auspices under which it is run. Some of the grander museums, which often seem the most 'official', are financed by the state, while others are run by local authorities, or by committed individuals, who are determined not to let the legacy of a cherished writer be forgotten. We have tried to cater for a wide range of literary tastes in this guide, and although some museums would seem to offer more attractions than others, the emphasis in this book, since it is the first comprehensive guide to literary places in Russia to appear in any language, has been to provide an accurate description rather than a biased account.

It has inevitably not been possible to mention all Russian writers in this book, nor have all the addresses of some of even the most famous writers been listed here. To list the address of every notable writer in a country where it has traditionally been the norm to write poetry rather than not do so is an impossible task, and some arbitrary choices have had to be made. In some cases, an author has been excluded or only briefly mentioned if information about where he or she lived has been scarce; in others the question of inclusion has been decided by the availability of translations of their works and general recognition outside Russia. Now that many authors, particularly female ones, are being published for the first time, it is to be hoped that some of the blank areas of the Russian literary map may soon be filled in, which will be reflected in any future edition of this book.

Addresses have for the most part been omitted from the guide if a particular author lived there for only a short time or if the relevant building has since been demolished, unless connected with a noteworthy literary event. Only two of the writers referred to here are still living, Solzhenitsyn and Anatoly Rybakov, in both cases only the locations of their earlier domiciles are described. Since the territory of Russia covers such a vast area, this guide has been divided into seven sections corresponding to the relevant geographical location: Moscow, Moscow region, St Petersburg, Leningrad region (local residents opted not to revert to the old name when asked to vote in 1992), European Russia (comprising all the various regions in this area), the Caucasus (that part of it which is still Russian territory) and Siberia. Literary places connected with Russian writers in Ukraine have not been included here, as Ukraine is now a separate country.

In the Moscow and St Petersburg sections, the guide is organized alphabetically by street. With very few exceptions, the entries are locations in the central parts of each city, and can be reached either on foot or by public transport. Where an address is listed with two numbers – for example, Bolshoi Nikolovorobinsky per., 9/11 – it means that it is a corner house. The first number is its street number at the address given, the second one its number on the next street. The streets on Vasilievsky Island in the St Petersburg section (see pp. 228–231) are numbered in lines rather than names and we have transliterated these accordingly; for example, Liniya, 8-aya, 20, means Eighth Line, number

20. The Glossary provides translations of necessary topographical vocabulary (ulitsa is the Russian word for 'street', for example), which is transliterated throughout the guide in abbreviated form; the abbreviations are indicated in the Glossary. Although inconsistencies are unavoidable, a simplified transliteration system has been followed wherever possible. Many streets reverted to their pre-revolutionary names after the demise of the Soviet Union (what was Ulitsa Gogolya in Soviet times, for example, is now known by its old name of Malaya Morskaya ulitsa), and although they are now listed as such in maps, they are sometimes cross-referenced with their Soviet appellations because many Russians still refer to them thus. The city of St Petersburg changed its name to Petrograd in 1915, and then to Leningrad in 1924, before reverting to its original name in 1992. The city is referred to in the text by the name appropriate for the given date. Maps of the areas covered in this guide have been included at the back of the book in order to give readers a general idea of the locations of the literary sites described. Each major literary museum is individually marked, but travellers will need to equip themselves with one of the many good city and regional maps that are now widely available to locate other sites. The index of authors at the back of the book provides a key to each entry, so that readers may follow writers as they move from place to place. Representative works are listed for each author mentioned.

Unless a site is specifically listed as being a museum, the houses and apartments mentioned here are not open to the public. Since opening hours vary enormously from museum to museum and are prone to change at short notice, only the days on which museums are closed are noted here wherever possible. As a rule of thumb, most museums are open between ten in the morning and six in the evening. Many are closed on Mondays and Tuesdays, and it is a common policy to close for one day at the end of each month for cleaning (known as the 'sanitary day' in Russian). Since 1992 admission charges have been much higher for foreign visitors, but still amount to little more than a nominal sum. A list of suggestions for further reading for Russian-speakers is included at the end of the book: the literature on Russian literary places is a vast one, and the bibliography compiled here is highly selective. All attempts to check accuracy have been made, but the authors would welcome corrections of any errors that appear here, as well as suggestions for additions, which can be incorporated into any revised edition.

Glossary

bulvar (abb. bulv.)	boulevard
dacha	cottage
dom	house
gorod	town
gymnasium	high school
izba	hut
korpus (abb. korp.)	building, block
krai	territory
kvartira (abb. kv.)	flat, apartment
most	bridge
naberezhnaya (abb. nab.)	embankment
oblast	region
ostrov	island
pension	private boarding school
pereulok (abb. per.)	lane, alley
ploshchad (abb. pl.)	square
proezd	passage
prospekt (abb. pr.)	avenue
reka	river
ryad	row
sad	garden
sazhen	1 *sazhen* is 2134 metres
selo	village
sezd	descent
tupik	alley
ulitsa (abb. ul.)	street
val	vale
verst	1 *verst* is two thirds of a mile or 1 kilometre

Moscow

Arbat, Ul.

The third part of Tolstoy's semi-autobiographical trilogy, *Youth* (1857), is set in the world of the Moscow aristocracy in the early part of the nineteenth century. Tolstoy occasionally gives us glimpses of the city, for example, at the point when Nikolay Irtenev, the fifteen-year-old narrator, decides to go and make a confession at the local monastery. He gets up shortly after dawn to leave his home in the Arbat area:

> Only a few loaded carts dragged slowly down the Arbat and a couple of bricklayers passed along the pavement chatting together. After I had gone about half a mile I began to meet people – women on their way to market with their baskets, watercarts going to fetch water and a pieman who appeared at the crossroads: one baker's shop was open and at the Arbat Gate I came across an old cabman dozing and swaying as he jolted along on his shabby, patched, bluish bone-shaker of a drozhky ... I climbed up into the lumpy, rickety light-blue seat and we went jolting along Vozdvizhenka street ...

Arbat, Ul., 2

The large yellow building at the end of Arbat houses the famous Prague Restaurant, which opened before the Revolution. It was here that Alexander Blok summoned Andrey Bely for a meeting in June 1906, having come up for the day from his family estate at Shakhmatovo. It was the first time that he had returned to Moscow since his visit in 1904. Since that time Blok's friendship with Bely had become complicated chiefly by the latter's growing affection for his wife, Lyubov Mendeleeva, who accompanied her husband on this day trip. Nothing was resolved on this occasion, and two days later Bely decided (somewhat absurdly) to summon Blok to a duel. Perhaps even more absurdly, two years later it was Blok who summoned Bely to a duel, and once again took a day trip up from Shakhmatovo to await Bely at the Prague Restaurant, although he was forced to go home again when his messenger did not find Bely at home. A week later the meeting finally took place, and the friends' differences were resolved after a conversation which lasted from seven in the evening to the following morning.

Arbat, Ul., 4

In pre-revolutionary times the first floor of this long yellow three-storey building used to house the Hotel Stolitsa, which offered reasonably priced furnished rooms to writers such as Ivan Bunin and Konstantin Balmont.

Arbat, Ul., 7

In 1908 the building which used to stand here became one of the first cinemas in Russia, and was called Le Grand Parisien in honour of the Lumière brothers. In September of that year the eighty-year-old Tolstoy made his first – and last – visit to the movies here, totally unable to understand how people could derive enjoyment from such an activity. After the Revolution, the building became a meeting place for writers such as Maya-kovsky and Esenin; the latter read his long poem 'Pugachov' for the first time here.

Arbat, Ul., 15

The writer Anatoly Rybakov, author of the glasnost classic *Children of the Arbat*, a semi-autobiographical novel about a group of young people who live on the Arbat in the 1930s, was a pupil at the school located here.

Arbat, Ul., 17

At the turn of the century, Chekhov's and Tolstoy's doctor Vladimir Shchurovsky used to live in this building, and between 1912 and 1913 it became a temporary home for Tsvctaeva's great friend, the writer Max Voloshin, whose principal home was in Koktebel in the Crimea.

Arbat, Ul., 36

From 1892 to 1920 this building housed the editorial offices of the publishing house Posrednik (The Intermediary), which was founded by Tolstoy and his disciple Chertkov in 1884 (and survived until 1935), with the aim of distributing inexpensive mass editions of morally edifying literature. Tolstoy first published stories such as 'Captive of the Caucasus' and 'God Sees the Truth But Waits' through Posrednik.

Arbat, Ul., 51

Alexander Blok stayed here with friends in 1920 when he came to Moscow to give three readings to packed audiences at the Palace of Arts (POVARSKAYA UL. 52, see p. 98), and at the Polytechnic Museum (NOVAYA PL., 3/4, see p. 84). He stayed here again in 1921, three months before his death, when he visited Moscow for the last time. During this visit he gave five readings, but by this time the poet was already gravely ill, and the readings were less successful. In the late 1980s this house became famous because it was where Anatoly Rybakov, author of *Children of the Arbat*, grew up.

Arbat, Ul., 53

— *Pushkin Museum* As the plaque on this turquoise building tells us, 'Alexander Pushkin lived here from February to May

1831.' On the second floor is the only flat in Moscow which Pushkin rented as an adult and it was here that the thirty-two-year-old poet started his married life with the eighteen-year-old Natalya Goncharova. On 17 February, the eve of his wedding, Pushkin held his stag night here; the poets Vyazemsky, Baratynsky and his uncle Lev Pushkin were among the guests. Reports suggest Pushkin was in an uncharacteristically melancholy mood that evening as he read farewell poems to his youth, but the following day he was in high spirits for his wedding, holding a large party with Natalya at the flat.

The Pushkins' five-room apartment is now a museum and has been furnished to recreate its appearance at that time. The flat evokes a brief but happy period in Pushkin's life: 'I am married – and happy,' he wrote in a letter; 'My only wish is that nothing will change in my life – I could not expect better. This condition is so new to me that I feel reborn.' A few months later his tone had changed, caused by the demands made upon him by his new wife's family: 'I do not like Moscow life – you live here not as you want to live – but as old women want you to. Such an old woman is my mother-in-law.' Three months after their wedding the couple left Moscow for TSARSKOE SELO (see p. 317) near St Petersburg.

Closed Mondays and Tuesdays and the last Friday of the month

Arbat, Ul., 55

— *Andrey Bely Museum* The third-floor apartment with the balcony in the former Rakhmanov Building (constructed in 1878) on the corner of the Arbat and Denezhny per. was the birthplace and childhood home of the Symbolist writer Andrey Bely, the pen-name of Boris Bugaev. It now houses a small museum dedicated to the writer.

It was in this building that Bely spent his childhood, adolescence and early adulthood, which he later evoked in typically idiosyncratic and elliptical fashion in his memoirs and autobiographical novels *Kotik Letaev* and *The Christened Chinaman* (1922). His father was Nikolay Bugaev, the distinguished Professor of Mathematics at Moscow University, and it was in order not to embarrass him that Bely began publishing his writings in 1902 under a pseudonym. Bely's upbringing was neither conventional nor particularly happy, due chiefly to the tug of war his scientifically minded father and artistic mother fought over their only child. Bely would spend the rest of his life trying to resolve and overcome the deep contradictions of his character he felt emanated from those early battles.

He was exposed to Moscow intellectual life from a young age. Not only did he come into contact with his father's colleagues from the university, and with other acquaintances from the scholarly and literary world (Tolstoy was known to have made visits here), but his parents formed a strong association with the family of Mikhail Solovyov (brother of the famous philosopher and son of the well-known historian), who moved into the flat below in 1893. It was through them that Bely first made contact with his fellow poet Alexander Blok, whom he met for the first time here in 1904. Both Blok and Bely, who had already been in correspondence, were to become major figures in the Symbolist movement. From the start intense, their relationship was often fraught.

During Soviet times the Bugaev apartment became part of the Ministry of Foreign Affairs, which remodelled it extensively for office use. In 1989 work was begun to restore the apartment to its original state, as far as was possible, with a view to it becoming a permanent museum dedicated to Bely's memory. While it has not been possible to restore the hall, kitchen and back staircase leading to the apartment of Bely's neighbours the Solovyovs, the dining room and sitting room (opening out on to the balcony), his parents' bedroom, the nursery, his father's study and the corridor have all been decorated according to the

detailed descriptions in Bely's memoirs (which describe even the colour of the wallpaper). Not many of Bely's possessions or furnishings have been preserved, but the museum does contain items such as the writer's desk and chair, his watch, some of the pens he wrote with, a selection of his father's books and several photographs. One of the most interesting exhibits is the 'Line of Life', one of many intricate charts Bely created to show intellectual heredity, in this case the major influences on his own work.
Closed Mondays and Tuesdays and last Friday of the month

Armyansky Per., 2

In 1822 the Turgenev family left their country estate of Spasskoe Lutovinovo in the Orel province, in order to educate their three sons in the capital. They bought a town residence at the former Bolshoi Spassky per., now Ermolovoi ul., from where Turgenev's father hoped to oversee his sons' education.

The pension which Turgenev entered in 1829, at the age of twelve, was housed in an early-nineteenth-century building. The school prepared its pupils for entrance to Moscow University. Within a few months, Turgenev's father removed his son, disagreeing with the school's teaching methods, and deciding that he would receive a better education under private tutelage at home.

Armyansky Per., 11

The poet Tyutchev spent his childhood in the earlier part of the nineteenth century at this house, which his parents rented from Prince Gagarin. The family usually passed their winters here, living the rest of the year on their country estate at OVSTUG (see p. 335) in the Bryansk region. A typical residential house of the nobility, it was built by the famous nineteenth-century Russian architect, Kazakov.

It was in this house that Tyutchev was educated by private

tutors until he was seventeen. Chief among these was the young minor poet Raich, who more than anyone else nurtured the young poet's talents – giving him an impressive grounding in Classical and Russian literature and encouraging him to write his first poems. When he was only fifteen, Tyutchev's early neo-Classical poem 'The Nobleman (an Imitation of Horace)' was read to the Society of Lovers of Russian Literature and his public career as a poet was launched. The following year he entered Moscow University, where he studied until 1822, when he left the city to join the Russian legation in Munich. He was to spend most of the next twenty-two years in the West before returning to St Petersburg.

Avtozavodskaya Ul.

The metro station Avtozavodskaya, to the south of the Simonov Monastery, stands on the site of the Lizin Prud (Liza's Pond) which was named after the heroine of Karamzin's short story 'Poor Liza', who drowned herself here. In the nineteenth century, this spot was a favourite walking place for Muscovites.

Baumanskaya Ul., 40

At number 40 is School No. 353, named after Alexander Pushkin. It was built on the site of Pushkin's birthplace. A memorial plaque reads, 'Here stood the house where Alexander Pushkin was born on 26 May [6 June] 1799.' In the small square in front of the house is a bust of Pushkin, erected in 1967 by the sculptor Belashev.

Although Pushkin was to spend most of his adult life away from the city, Moscow retained a special place in his heart. As he wrote in his draft of *Eugene Onegin*, 'In exile in grief in separation, Moscow! how I loved you, my sacred birthplace.'

For many years the exact spot of Pushkin's birth was disputed. His birth certificate was discovered only in 1879; it

The house (now demolished) where Pushkin was born in 1799

stated that he was born at the house of Ivan Vasiliev Skvortsov. As Skvortsov had been the steward to a certain Countess Golovkina, it was assumed that he had lived at her address. In 1880 a plaque was put up at Baumanskaya ul., 55, where her house would have stood. In fact Skvortsov had lived not with the Countess but near by. The plaque was moved to the correct spot – number 40 – in 1927, but debate over the exact address continued. Only in 1980 was Skvortsov's exact address unearthed and Pushkin's birthplace confirmed.

When Pushkin was born the street was called Nemetskaya ul. (German street) and it stood in the Nemetskaya Sloboda (German suburbs). Although today *Nemetskaya* means 'German', in the seventeenth century the word meant 'mute' and it was an adjective used to describe all those who did not speak the Russian language. All foreigners were ordered to move to this area from the city in 1652 and it became their quarter. Soon after, the area was favoured by Peter the Great, and by the time Alexander Pushkin's parents moved here it had become an area lived in by the nobility. Although the richer among them had large mansions, the lesser nobility such as Pushkin's family lived in or rented smaller wooden houses, such as Skvortsov's. The church where Pushkin was christened stands at nearby SPARTA-KOVSKAYA UL., 15 (see p. 115).

It was in the Nemetskaya Sloboda that the thirteen-year-old Nikolay Karamzin attended the school of Matthias Schaden, Professor of Moral Philosophy at Moscow University between 1777 and 1781. Its exact street address is unknown.

Bersenevskaya Nab.

The large apartment block overlooking the Moscow river is the fabled House on the Embankment, which was immortalized in Yury Trifonov's 1976 novella of the same name. Built in 1931 to house the party elite and other privileged citizens, it became notorious for the number of night-time arrests made here during the purges. Trifonov himself was witness to some of those arrests; he lived here as a child, and stayed on in the family apartment with his grandmother after his father, a former Red Army commander and loyal Bolshevik, fell from grace and was taken away in one of the NKVD's trademark black cars.

Bolshaya Cheryomushkinskaya Ul., 14, Kv. 41

In the 1960s Novye Cheryomushki was built as a new suburb in the south-west of Moscow. It was here in 1964 that Osip Mandelstam's widow, Nadezhda Yakovlevna, moved when she was at last given permission to reside in Moscow again. Since her husband's death in the gulag in 1938 she had lived in many different areas of Russia. With a loan from her friend, the writer Konstantin Simonov, she was able to buy a small apartment in this building, part of a co-operative housing project. Her memoirs, *Hope against Hope* and *Hope Abandoned*, were first published abroad in the 1970s. It was in this tiny flat that she received many Russian and foreign visitors until her death here in 1980. One of her visitors, the American Slavist Carl Proffer,

Nadezhda Mandelstam at home in her apartment

recorded visiting her here in his book *The Widows of Russia and Other Writings*:

> Her apartment consisted of an entrance hall – with bathroom and toilet doors directly to the right – and two real rooms ahead: her bedroom through the left-hand door and kitchen through the right. Both of these rooms faced out onto the street and the trolley tracks. The kitchen was roughly 7' × 14' (arms outspread, I could almost touch both walls) and the bedroom 12' × 17'. Although the building was fairly new, everything already looked old and battered ... On the walls were paintings by Vaisberg and Birger, among others – all hung, in the Russian style, very high. The plug-in telephone was moved from room to room as convenience dictated, but usually ended up in the bedroom. Vases full of dried flowers, cattails, etc. were always in the bedroom. Bare bulbs and bare wood floors did nothing to lend warmth to the place. N. M. recognized that it was uncomfortable, but said that it had taken working her whole life to get even this in retirement – and it had running water and other things she had done without

much of her life, so while she scorned its style, she was glad to have it. Since leaving her father's home, she had never really had a place of her own, a true 'home'. During her life with Osip Mandelstam finding a room, never mind an apartment, had been difficult. Her time spent teaching in various provincial schools had been no less nomadic, so this apartment was the summit of her material accomplishments.

Bolshaya Dmitrovka Ul., 1

At number 1 is a Classical building with six columns, built by the Russian architect Kazakov in the 1770s for Prince Dolgorukov. In Soviet times this was the House of Unions, but it was known as the Hall of the Nobility before the Revolution. The front of the building looks out on to Okhotny Ryad, but it stretches back quite some way on to Bolshaya Dmitrovka ul. In 1784 both the house and its gardens were acquired by the Club of the Nobility and they organized balls, concerts and receptions here. Between 1780 and 1790 a huge columned hall was built over the former courtyard with twenty-eight Corinthian columns and crystal chandeliers to accommodate the large gatherings. Alexander Pushkin frequented the Club in his youth, and wrote that 'Moscow was the assembling place for all the Russian nobility who gathered here in the winter from all the provinces – the shining young guards came here from St Petersburg. The music thundered out to all corners of the ancient capital and there was a crowd everywhere. In the hall of the Club of the Nobility five thousand people would meet twice a week. Young people would meet each other here; marriages were arranged. Moscow was as famous for its brides as Vyazma for its honeycakes.' Pushkin exaggerated the numbers, but the hall could accommodate up to 3,000. In *Eugene Onegin*, Tatyana Larina is brought here by her matchmaking aunt whom she obliges by meeting her future husband.

Mikhail Lermontov also came here to a masquerade in 1830 during his winter holiday from his Moscow University pension. In the same year he attended a concert given by the Irish pianist John Field, whom he was later to mention in his novel *Vadim*. The concert was a major event, attended by Tsar Nicholas I. On 31 December 1831, Lermontov attended a New Year's Eve masquerade dressed as an astrologer, carrying a huge book under his arm. On each page, under Chinese lettering cut from black paper, lay verses dedicated to some of his friends who he knew would attend the ball. Dostoevsky later made a famously impassioned speech here on the evening of 8 June 1880, at the ceremony surrounding the unveiling of Pushkin's statue, on Tverskoi Bulv. (the statue was later moved to PUSHKINSKAYA PL., see p. 102) in which he described Pushkin as a prophet.

In Soviet times the Hall of Columns was used for large congresses, and it was where Soviet leaders traditionally lay in state. Lenin lay in state on 23–24 January 1924, and in *Hope Abandoned* Nadezhda Mandelstam describes how she queued up with her husband Osip to pay their last respects, together with thousands of other Soviet citizens, including the Pasternaks, from 'somewhere near the Bolshoi Theatre'. In 1934 the Hall of Columns was the setting for the first congress of the Union of Soviet Writers, which was opened by Gorky, its first president. After his death in June 1936, Gorky's body also lay in state here before his cremated remains were placed in the Kremlin wall.

Bolshaya Dmitrovka Ul., 15

In 1905 this pale-green three-storey building (since remodelled) became the permanent home of the Literary–Artistic Circle, which had started up in 1898. The Tuesday evening meetings, which continued until the First World War, when the building became a military hospital, were a focal point of literary life for the Moscow Symbolists; among the poets who gave readings here were Konstantin Balmont, Andrey Bely, Vyacheslav Ivanov and Valery Bryusov; the last named was one of the directors.

Bolshaya Nikitskaya Ul., 15

This is the site of a famous bookstore on the former Gertsena ul. founded in the early 1920s by Esenin and fellow Imagist poet Anatoly Mariengof, who would both sometimes serve behind the counter in order to attract customers. The first floor housed the 'manager's office', with a large round table, couch and armchairs, and was used by Esenin and Mariengof as their own kind of private literary club.

Bolshaya Nikitskaya Ul., 23

Ogaryov's house on the site of number 23 was where, in the early 1830s, Herzen's and Ogaryov's circle of fellow Moscow University students met. Here they debated the progressive socialist ideas then current in Europe. The nature of these meetings was remembered by Herzen in his memoirs *My Past and Thoughts*:

> As before our chief meeting place was Ogarëv's house. His invalid father had gone to live in the country, and he lived alone on the ground floor of their Moscow house, which was near the University and had a great attraction for us all ... In his bright cheerful room with its red and gold wallpaper, amid the perpetual smell of tobacco and punch and other – I was going to say eatables and drinkables, but now I remember that there was seldom anything to eat but cheese – we often spent the time from dark till dawn in heated argument and sometimes in noisy merriment.

Herzen left the university in 1833 and the following year he and other members of the group were arrested and sent into internal exile.

Bolshaya Nikitskaya Ul., 46, Kv. 12

In the late 1840s this typical Moscow mansion with mezzanine and central columns – one of the rare houses to escape the Moscow fire of 1812 – became the rented winter home of the Vasilchikov family, to whose children Gogol had been tutor in 1831 (during the time that he lived with their *babushka*, he had written his story 'May Night'). In the early 1850s Gogol renewed his acquaintance with the hospitable Vasilchikovs, and was remembered later for his long hair and red velvet waistcoat. Other frequent guests included their relative, the writer Count Sollogub, as well as Aksakov, Samarin (another prominent Slavophile), Pogodin and the painter Aivazovsky.

The house was later to become a temporary home in 1924 for Mikhail Bulgakov, who had just married his second wife, Lyubov Belozerskaya. The building was by this time a school, and it was where Bulgakov's sister Nadya Zemskaya lived and worked. Bulgakov and his new wife spent the summer here, sleeping in the staff room on a slippery oilskin couch. They had to move out in the autumn when the school term began.

Bolshaya Nikitskaya Ul., 53

The modern building of the Central House of Writers on Bolshaya Nikitskaya connects to the nineteenth-century mansion with an entrance on POVARSKAYA UL., at number 50 (see p. 98), and in Soviet times was the location for writers' receptions, poetry readings, film showings and meetings. Entrance to these events was always restricted to members of the Union of Writers and their guests, and they would often attract huge celebrity audiences.

Bolshaya Ordynka Ul., 17, Kv. 13

An apartment on the first floor of this building was the home of the writer Viktor Ardov and his actress wife Nina Olshevskaya, friends of Anna Akhmatova, who would often stay here on visits to Moscow. It was during one of these visits in June 1941 (made on this occasion on behalf of her son, who had just been arrested again) that Akhmatova met Marina Tsvetaeva for – astonishingly – the first and only time. She spent several hours in conversation with her over the next two days. Akhmatova never revealed the content of her discussions with Tsvetaeva, who committed suicide two months later. Russia's two greatest women poets, linked by their close relationships with Osip Mandelstam and Boris Pasternak, and by age, were nevertheless utterly different in temperament. Akhmatova recognized Tsvetaeva's gift and importance as a poet, but did not share the latter's mercurial nature and highly charged emotional response to the world. Tsvetaeva had first addressed poems to Akhmatova in 1915, but the adulation was not mutual.

It was here that Lev Kopelev took Alexander Solzhenitsyn to meet Akhmatova in October 1962 during his brief visit to the capital from Ryazan to check the page proofs of *One Day in the Life of Ivan Denisovich*. Solzhenitsyn had great admiration for Akhmatova's work (he called her 'the soul of Russia'), and knew her 'Poem without a Hero' by heart. For her part, Akhmatova strongly believed that every citizen should know *One Day in the Life of Ivan Denisovich* by heart.

Bolshaya Pirogovskaya Ul.

It was in a building on this street which no longer stands that Mikhail Bulgakov lived from 1927 to 1934. These were the final years of his marriage to Lyubov Belozerskaya, whom he left in 1932 for his third wife Elena Shilovskaya (he found accommodation for his ex-wife in the same block). The couple lived a few hundred yards from the cupolas of the Novodevichy Convent in what Bulgakov described as a 'monstrous pit', but Lyubov Belozerskaya describes it more affectionately in her memoirs:

> One must go up two steps from the dining room to reach M.A.'s study through an oak door. It is a very beautifully carved door of dark oak. The doorhandle is a bird's foot made of bronze; the claws grasp a ball ... A little landing was formed in front of the entrance to the study. We loved this unique elevated place ...

It was here that in 1928 Bulgakov started work on his masterpiece, the fantastical, satirical and mystical novel, *The Master and Margarita*. But these were also the years of the greatest crisis in Bulgakov's life. By March 1929 all of his plays had been banned by the authorities. The following year his play *The Cabal of Hypocrites*, about Molière, was read to the Drama Union and banned before rehearsals could commence. In despair and maybe with a degree of self-dramatization Bulgakov burned the manuscripts of all his work in progress, including the early drafts of *The Master and Margarita*. He then wrote a famous letter to Stalin, asking for permission to leave the country: 'All my literary works have perished as have my literary plans. I am condemned to silence and, quite possibly, to complete starvation.' The response was a telephone call from Stalin himself. Lyubov Belozerskaya was in the house when the phone rang, and later recorded the conversation in her memoirs:

> 'We have received your letter. And read it with our comrades. You will have a pleasing answer. Perhaps we really should let you go abroad. What is it, have we bored you so very much?'
>
> 'I have thought very much recently about whether a Russian writer can live outside his motherland, and it seems to me that he cannot.'

'You're right. I don't think so either. Where do you want to work? At the Arts Theatre?'

'Yes, I would like to. But I asked about it – they refused me.'

'Well you submit a request there. It seems to me that they will agree . . .'

Stalin was magnanimous – the suicide of Mayakovsky had just taken place and the dictator probably wished to avoid a similar embarrassment. Bulgakov was allowed to join the Moscow Arts Theatre as assistant director and with this new guarantee of safety he resumed work on *The Master and Margarita*.

Bolshaya Pirogovskaya Ul., 2

It was here that Professor Ostroumov ran a famous clinic to which the ailing Chekhov was brought in 1897 following the lung haemorrhage he suffered during his lunch with Suvorin at the Hermitage Restaurant (PETROVSKY BULV., see p. 90). Tolstoy, who lived near by, came to visit his friend during his ten-day sojourn here, and coerced the ailing writer into a discussion on the subject of immortality (after which Chekhov apparently suffered another haemorrhage).

Bolshaya Sadovaya Ul., 10, Kv. 34, 38, 50

In the 1920s, apartment number 38 on the top floor of this building was the studio of the avant-garde artist Georgy Yakulov, and it was famously where in 1921 Esenin met the dancer Isadora Duncan, who had come to Russia to teach dance. Esenin was seduced by her glamour, she by his winsome looks, and within a short time he had moved into her luxurious accommodation at PRECHISTENKA UL., 20 (see p. 101).

The building also contains the two flats in which Mikhail Bulgakov lived between 1921 and 1924. In the absence of an official Bulgakov museum the staircase leading to the top flat has in recent years become a place of pilgrimage for the author's devotees, much to the annoyance of the present inhabitants. The walls of the staircase are covered in often very beautiful graffiti which celebrate Bulgakov and his novel *The Master and Margarita*. Handwritten slogans jostle with depictions of black cats, witches, images of Christ and the beautiful Margarita. In fact Bulgakov did not start work on *The Master and Margarita* until after he had left the building, but it is the prototype for 'House 302bis' in the novel, 'the mysterious flat' with 'its vanishing lodgers'.

Built in the Moscow Art Nouveau style, the building was divided into cramped communal flats, one of which became home to Bulgakov and his first wife, Tatyana Nikolaevna Lappa. They found living conditions extremely difficult. After the Civil War Moscow was a city struggling to survive with galloping inflation brought on by the introduction of the New Economic Policy, which allowed a small amount of private enterprise. This caused widespread famine. Bulgakov writes of it being 'the fifth-floor nightmare ... the room is terrible, the neighbours too'. Struggling to survive was 'an all-consuming task'. He was beginning to make progress as a writer and wrote a number of satirical sketches based on communal life. But it was on his journalism that he subsisted, working for *Gudok* (the Whistle), the official organ of the Railway Workers' Union. It was only in the evening that he was able to turn to his writing. For the most part he was working on plays during this period, although half of the novel *The White Guard* was written here. In 1924 Bulgakov met his second wife, Lyubov Belozerskaya, and moved into another flat in the same block.

Sadovaya ul., 1, is where the Rubansky Chemist described in *The Master and Margarita* stood. At number 16 are the 'Aquarium' Gardens, also described in the novel, which now stand in front of the Mossovet Theatre. At number 18 is the building of the former Nikitin Circus, built in 1911, which then

Graffiti on the staircase in the building where Bulgakov lived between 1921 and 1924. The house is the model for 'House 302bis' in The Master and Margarita

became the Moscow Music Hall, and later the Theatre of Satire. The circus is mentioned in Bulgakov's novellas *The Fatal Eggs* and *Heart of a Dog* and in *The Master and Margarita* it is described as the Variety building where the fantastical show of black magic takes place which starts with the lines, 'A little man with a crimson pear-shaped nose, in a battered yellow bowler hat, check trousers and patent leather boots pedalled on to the Variety stage on a bicycle.'

Bolshaya Sadovaya Ul., 20

This was the site of the former Meyerhold Theatre, which was based here in the 1920s. It was here that Mayakovsky's play *The Bedbug* was first performed in 1929. His play *The Bath-House* was premièred in Leningrad, but had its first Moscow performances here in 1930. The Tchaikovsky Concert Hall, initially designed as Meyerhold's new theatre, now stands in its place.

Bolshaya Yakimanka Ul., 45

The twenty-five-year-old Anton Chekhov and his family settled into the ground floor of this old columned house on the former Dmitrova ul. in 1885, having spent six weeks living in a damp apartment in a house up the road. This was not an ideal location either: the upstairs rooms were used for wedding receptions and dinners, which meant there was much noise to compete with, and it was also a long way from the centre of town and the editorial offices of the journals to which Chekhov contributed. In addition to his activities as a doctor he was now beginning to make a name for himself as a writer. The family were thus very glad to escape to a dacha at the Babkino estate near Voskresensk the following summer, where they had enjoyed an idyllic holiday the year before, mushroom picking, fishing and hunting. It was to this address, in March 1886, that the respected writer Dmitry Grigorovich sent Chekhov a famous letter heralding him as a major talent, and exhorting him to take his writing more seriously.

It was in apartment 8 in this building that Osip Mandelstam and his wife Nadezhda spent the winter of 1923–4. Their rented accommodation has been described by Nadezhda Mandelstam in her memoir *Hope Abandoned*:

> Old Moscow houses can look cozy and charming enough on the outside, but we now saw how poor and dilapidated they are inside, in every room a whole family presided over by some old woman – worn out but still as tough as nails – who constantly scrubbed, cleaned, and scoured everything, trying to keep the place spick and span in country fashion as it fell more and more into decay ... In those days the Yakimanka was at the end of the world, and in the

streetcars people hung from the straps in clusters, like bunches of cherries.

In a letter, Osip Mandelstam described the street as quiet, and their house as a mansion with columns. He describes the area – Zamoskvorechie (behind the Moscow river) – in his essay *Journey to Armenia*: 'Nowhere have I experienced so strongly the watermelon emptiness of Russia; the brick-coloured sunsets over the Moscow River, the tile-coloured tea, brought to mind the red dust of the blast furnace on Mount Ararat.' While the houses may have looked cheerful on the outside they had 'mean little souls' and 'cowardly windows'.

Bolshoi Afanasievsky Per., 12

Gogol first came to Moscow in June 1832, on his way to spend the summer at his parents' estate in the Ukraine. He was twenty-three years old, had lived in St Petersburg for the last four years, and had just begun to achieve success as a writer with his recently published and wildly successful tales, *Evenings on a Farm near Dikanka*. Although the address of the hotel he stayed in on this occasion is not known, we do know that Sergey Aksakov (who would later achieve renown as a memoirist and author of detailed books on fishing and hunting) was one of the many writers Gogol became acquainted with during his ten-day stay. Aksakov, whose sons became prominent Slavophiles, had worked as a bureaucrat in St Petersburg and was currently living here in this large two-storey house off the Arbat. Gogol met up with Aksakov later that October, when he stopped off again in Moscow on his way back to St Petersburg.

Gogol visited Aksakov at his new house at Novaya Basmannaya ul., 3, during his next visit to Moscow in 1835 (when he was again on his way to his family home). On this occasion he met the young critic Vissarion Belinsky, who was just beginning to attract attention, and championed his fiction in the two important articles he wrote about him that year.

Bolshoi Gnezdnikovsky Per., 10

It was at the house of his friends the Moiseenkos that Mikhail Bulgakov met Elena Sergeyevna Shilovskaya, the woman who was to become his third wife, in 1929. At the time both were married and it was Bulgakov's second wife Lyubov who seems to have been most struck by Elena on this first meeting: 'An interesting well-coiffed lady sat at the table [Elena]. She quickly became my friend and would often drop by our house.' Bulgakov's friendship soon developed into romance and had important consequences on his work. He had recently started on his masterpiece, *The Master and Margarita*, and apparently early drafts contained no heroine – it was only after the appearance of Elena that Margarita entered the novel.

The house, built by the architect Nirenzee in 1912, had earlier been the offices of the journal *Nakanune* (On the Eve), to which Bulgakov was a contributor, and it makes a fictional appearance in the stories 'Forty Times Forty' and 'Diaboliad'. In 'Diaboliad' the hero commits suicide by jumping from one of the tallest buildings in Moscow, which may well have been intended for the Nirenzee house with its ten storeys.

Bolshoi Karetny Per., 12

The spot where house number 12 meets Sadovaya Samotyoch-naya, 24, is where a small town estate belonging to Ivan Turgenev's parents once stood. Turgenev's parents bought the house in 1827 and brought their son here from provincial Orel to educate him in Moscow. However, after sending Ivan to two different pensions, his father decided that his son would receive a better education from visiting tutors in their Moscow home.

Bolshoi Karetny Per., 17, Kv. 22

This was the distinguished critic Prince Dmitry Svyatopolk-Mirsky's last official address. He was forty-five when he moved here in September 1935 to a fifth-floor room which he had to reach without the aid of a lift, but which had a fine view of the north of Moscow. Mirsky, author of the best-known and best-written history of Russian literature (1926 and 1927), had emigrated after the Revolution to England, where he taught from 1922 at the University of London's School of Slavonic Studies. In 1931 he became a member of the Communist Party, however, and returned to Soviet Russia the following year, with help from Gorky. In Moscow, he continued his work as a writer and critic, becoming a member of the newly founded Union of Writers, and contributing, for example, to the multi-authored book about the construction of the notorious White Sea Canal in 1934. His outspoken views soon got him into trouble, however. Already in 1934 it had become anathema to criticize such officially venerated authors as Alexander Fadeev, and Mirsky's uncompromising stance, coupled with his aristocratic background and a past as an émigré and former White Army officer, led to his denunciation and arrest in 1937. Mirsky was sentenced to eight years' hard labour for alleged espionage and sent to the camps at Kolyma, where he died two years later.

Bolshoi Kharitonevsky Per.

A statue of the poet Nekrasov stands opposite number 12 on this street.

Bolshoi Kharitonevsky Per., 21

It was in the grounds of this late-seventeenth-century palace with eccentric medieval detailing and a steeply pitched chessboard roof that the Pushkin family rented accommodation between 1801 and 1803 and where Pushkin spent the early years of his childhood. The contract between Pushkin's father and his landlord Prince Yusupov stated that the flat was to be taken 'with all its appurtenances, that is: the carpentry, joinery, metal and plasterer's work, the floors, panels, doors, windows, the furniture that there is ...' Yusupov, the owner of the estate Arkhangelskoe outside Moscow, was a highly eccentric character who wore a pale-blue smock coat with velvet trimmings and used to drive about Moscow in a landau pulled by two pairs of horses. He wore a powdered wig with plaited braids tied with black bows, while his Borzoi dog, dressed in a gold collar, would sit on a cushion next to him. Pushkin was later to describe such Moscow eccentrics in his *Journey from Moscow to St Petersburg* and Yusupov also figures in Herzen's memoir *My Past and Thoughts*, where he is described as 'a Tartar prince, a grand seigneur of European reputation, and a Russian grandee of brilliant intellect and great fortune'.

Yusupov's neo-Gothic palace still stands on this quiet Moscow backstreet. Pushkin remembers the street with affection in *Eugene Onegin*; it is where he brings his heroine Tatyana Larina on her arrival in Moscow from the country.

Bolshoi Nikolopeskovy Per., 11

From 1913 to 1915, this was the home (and is now the museum) of Alexander Scriabin, a composer with close links to writers such as the Symbolist poets Vyacheslav Ivanov (who lived near by at ZUBOVSKY BULV., 25, see p. 138), Konstantin Balmont (who lived up the road) and Boris Pasternak, all of whom came to call here. The street takes its name from the church which used to stand opposite the house.

Bolshoi Nikolopeskovy Per., 15

The poet Konstantin Balmont lived here in the years immediately before the Revolution.

Bolshoi Nikolovorobinsky Per., 3–9

The Ostrovsky family moved to this street in 1840. The playwright's father had married Baroness Emiliya von Tessin (who came from Swedish aristocratic stock) in 1836, and acquired nobleman's status through her two years later. He had become increasingly wealthy by this time, and bought five houses on this street from his brother-in-law. In 1841 he retired from his position in the civil service (although continuing his private practice as a lawyer), and moved his family to the main house on this street. The two-storey house which used to stand here was constructed in stone and wood, and had a large garden and pond. It was situated at the end of the lane near the church (pulled down in the 1930s), at the corner of Serebryanichesky per. It was in this area that Moscow's most successful merchants lived, for the most part in houses with tall fences and guard dogs on chains. The young Ostrovsky lived here until 1849. At the behest of his father he had started work in the courts as a clerk in 1843, but at the same time had also embarked on his real career, which was writing. His first play, about Moscow business life, was published in 1847, but it was not until several years later that he had a work performed on stage. Wary censors submitted his first play to Tsar Nicholas I, who found it subversive and banned it, subjecting Ostrovsky to police surveillance which resulted in dismissal from his civil service post.

Bolshoi Nikolovorobinsky Per., 4, Kv. 3

Isaak Babel lived on this small street in a wooden two-storey house in the 1930s. He shared this spacious accommodation with an engineer, who was the representative of an Austrian electronics firm. Their one rule was that no women were allowed to stay on the premises, but it was relaxed when Babel's mistress moved in.

Bolshoi Nikolovorobinsky Per., 9/11

In 1850 Alexander Ostrovsky was forced to move into the wing of his father's house, which stood here formerly, when he refused to give up the romantic association he had formed with a girl who lived on the same street, and who came from a distinctly inferior social background. When the playwright's father also cut him off, Ostrovsky was forced to depend on his meagre literary earnings to support himself and his burgeoning family (he had three children by 1857). His position began slowly to improve after 1853, when his first play was performed on stage, but the family situation was for a long time one of hardship, both financial and emotional (four of his children died).

In 1853, when his father died, Ostrovsky inherited the house. An unprepossessing yellow wooden building, with five windows looking out on to an empty yard where a public bath-house had previously stood, it was his home for twenty-eight years. Visitors to the house included many notable literary figures of the time, including Goncharov and Turgenev, whose arrival at the gate would be announced by the barking of the family dog.

Bolshoi Palashevsky Per.

The Church of the Birth of Christ, where Tsvetaeva married Sergey Efron in January 1912, used to stand at the corner of Bolshoi Palashevsky and Maly Palashevsky lanes, a few minutes' walk from the Tsvetaev family home at TRYOKHPRUDNY PER., 8 (see p. 122). In Soviet times, the church was demolished and replaced by a school.

Bolshoi Strochenovsky Per., 24, Kv. 6

— *Esenin Museum* Esenin had made his first visit to Moscow from his native Ryazan in 1911, and returned the following year initially to live here in the Zamoskvorechie area. He shared lodgings with his father, who for thirty years rented one of the four flats in this small wooden house from the merchant he worked for. In 1995, on the centenary of Esenin's birth, a museum commemorating the poet opened on the ground floor of the house, which has been extensively remodelled.

The sixteen-year-old Esenin had received an elementary education in his village school before moving to Moscow, and his family tried to persuade him to continue his studies so that he could become a teacher himself, but to no avail. Esenin began a clerical job in the office of his father's employer, but the discovery that he spent most of his time writing poetry rather than working led to some sharp disagreements. As a result, Esenin decided to move out of the family apartment after a week and set up on his own. Now without any kind of support, he was forced to find himself a job. He worked for a while in a bookshop on Pushkinskaya pl., and then decided to abandon Moscow for a while after the business closed down. When he returned in March 1913, his father found him work at the Sytin printers, one of the oldest such firms in Russia, then located at the southern end of Pyatnitskaya ul., at number 71, at the corner with Vtoroi (2nd) Monetchikovsky per., 2. It was through literary friends that Esenin made here that he was able to publish his first poem in 1914. He also took time to enrol at the People's University at Miusskaya pl., 6, founded in 1908 by the democratically minded philanthropist Shanyavsky with the aim of offering education to anyone who wanted to study (after the Revolution the three-storey building became a Communist Party school attached to the Central Committee, and is now part of the Russian State University for the Humanities).

Esenin left his job in May 1914, and worked for almost a year at another firm of typographers at Bankovsky per., 10, during which time he lived somewhere in the vicinity of the Pl. Serpukhovskoi Zastavy with his first wife, before deciding to try his luck with forging a literary career in St Petersburg. When he returned to live in Moscow again in 1918, he stayed first with his father again here on Bolshoi Strochenovsky per.

The design of the Esenin Museum (which stands set back from the road in the left-hand corner of the courtyard) has been imaginatively conceived and executed by a Moscow artist. Green carpeting and dried flowers serve to remind the visitor of the poet's rural background and of the important theme of nature in his work, while facsimiles of his poems, many of which are written in purple ink, are displayed in frames resembling icon cases. To the right of the front door is Esenin's father's room, complete with icon, samovar and humble furniture, which has been restored to look as it did at the beginning of the century. The museum's two other rooms contain contemporary photographs, early editions of Esenin's poetry, press cuttings, drawings, icons and manuscripts.
Closed Mondays and Tuesdays

Borisoglebovsky Per., 6, Kv. 3

— *Tsvetaeva Museum* From 1914 until 1922, a first-floor flat in this yellow two-storey nineteenth-century building was the home of Marina Tsvetaeva and her family. It became a communal flat housing as many as forty people after she emigrated, and only in the 1980s, when the tenants began to be found new accommodation, and the era of glasnost officially restored Tsvetaeva to her rightful place among Russia's greatest writers, was it possible to restore the building and create a permanent museum dedicated to her memory. It opened in 1992, the centenary of her birth.

Despite the odd shape of some of its rooms, and uneven light, Tsvetaeva was very attached to this flat, where she wrote some of her most famous poems, and received visits from her friends and acquaintances, including Konstantin Balmont, Osip Mandelstam and Sofia Parnok, the poet with whom she began a two-year affair in 1914. Yet she also endured great hardship here. The years following the Revolution, which brought privation to millions, were no less difficult for Tsvetaeva, whose second daughter Irina was born in April 1917. She was separated from her husband Sergey Efron for almost five years after he joined the White Army, and her impractical nature only compounded the problems she faced in eking out a living during the Civil War, during which time four of the rooms of her once-spacious flat were taken over by other people and her possessions gradually sold. Tsvetaeva's elder daughter Ariadna, who was five years old at the time of the Revolution, recalled their home looking as if it had been involved in a shipwreck. In his memoirs, Tsvetaeva's friend Prince Sergey Volkonsky recalls her flat as bare and unheated, and sometimes even without light: 'the stairs were dark and cold, the banister did not go all the way down, and there were three treacherous steps at the bottom. The dark and cold came in from the street as if they owned the place.' Tsvetaeva's inability to fend for herself, let alone her daughters, led her to place them in an orphanage in Kuntsevo, then a distant suburb to the west of Moscow, where Irina died of starvation in 1920, a few months short of her third birthday.

The building originally housed four spacious apartments. The Tsvetaeva Museum consists of the six rooms that she and her family moved into in 1914, while the rest of the house has been turned into a Tsvetaeva centre. Although it has not been possible to restore most of the apartment's original furniture, much of its character has been recreated through careful research and the preservation of its original architecture. The dining room, which features an enormous skylight situated over the table Tsvetaeva and Efron used to eat at, leads into the drawing room, which has no windows at all, and has as its centrepiece the grand piano, brought from the family's summer home in Tarusa. Tsvetaeva's study, where she worked at a desk in front of the window which overlooks the courtyard at the back of the house, is unusual in that it has eleven corners. Tsvetaeva never liked beds very much, and slept on the narrow divan here, in front of which is a wolf-fur provided by the Moscow Zoo, to replace the one which originally lay here. Next to Tsvetaeva's study is the nursery, with its three large windows, on whose ledges used to stand cages with squirrels inside, to accompany the other wildlife kept here: a parrot, a hedgehog, a cat and a tortoise.

Upstairs is Sergey Efron's large study, complete with stuffed eagle perched over the divan and windows on two levels (later on, as many as eleven people lived in this room alone). It was on the upper floor of the flat that guests were accommodated, and where the servants had their quarters in the more affluent times before the Revolution.

Open Sunday through Friday.

Bryusov Per., 2a, Kv. 27

Upon returning from his trip to America in 1922 with Isadora Duncan, from whom he was now divorced, Esenin once again led a nomadic and turbulent life in Moscow, but settled here temporarily in 1924 with his friend Galina Benislavskaya, who had a flat here on the seventh floor (the street was known as Ul. Nezhdanovoi in Soviet times). The following year Esenin married Tolstoy's granddaughter, and moved into her large quiet flat on Pomerantsev per., 3, flat 8. This was another short-lived marriage, however, and Esenin moved out a few months later, and departed for Leningrad, where he would shortly afterwards commit suicide.

Chekhova Ul. (*See* MALAYA DMITROVKA UL., p. 56)

Chernyshevskogo Ul. (*See* POKROVKA, UL., p. 95)

Chistoprudny Bulv.

The statue of Griboedov which stands here was erected in 1959.

Chisty Per., 9

The writer Varlam Shalamov lived here in this yellow and white two-storey house with his wife and daughter from 1934 to 1937, when he was arrested again. Shalamov had been arrested for the first time in 1929, when he was a twenty-two-year-old law student at Moscow University. As punishment for his unidentified crime he had been imprisoned for five years in the notorious concentration camp in Solovki, a former monastery in the far north of Russia. Now he was sent to do hard labour in the camps at KOLYMA (see p. 443), in the remote north-eastern part of Siberia. Shalamov's wife lived across the street at number 8 when she returned from exile in 1946, and the writer visited her when he himself returned from the seventeen-year sentence in Kolyma in 1953, but was not allowed to stay overnight.

Bulgakov lived on this street between 1924 and 1926 in an outbuilding of house number 9 that no longer survives. The outbuilding, situated in a garden full of lime trees, was nicknamed 'The Dovecote' by Bulgakov and his new wife, Lyubov Belozerskaya, who later recalled it vividly in her memoirs:

> We are living in the ramshackle little addition in the court-yard of no. 9 Obukhov Pereulok, now Chisty Pereulok. On the building next door, no. 7, a commemorative plaque is displayed: 'The outstanding composer Sergei Ivanovich Taneev and the eminent scholar and statesman Vladimir Ivanovich Taneev lived and worked in this building.'

What unsightly homes these famous people chose for
themselves! ... We live on the second floor. The entire
upper floor is divided into three apartments, two along the
front, one on the side. In the middle is a corridor, and in
the corner of the corridor there is a stove.

Denezhny Per., 9/5

— *Lunacharsky Museum* The first Soviet Minister of Culture
lived in this building from 1923 to 1933 and a museum was
opened here in 1964, but it is currently closed to visitors. Its
three rooms contain personal items, autographs, paintings,
photographs and other memorabilia relating to the life of this
important figure, who intervened to help writers in the hungry
years of the Civil War.

Dmitrova Ul. (*See* BOLSHAYA YAKIMANKA UL., p. 22)

Dolgorukovskaya Ul.

It was in a house on this street that the writer Maximilian
Voloshin, born in Kiev in 1877, lived from the age of four to
sixteen with his widowed mother, having spent the early years
of his childhood in Taganrog and Sevastopol. Voloshin was first
a pupil at the famed Polivanov Gymnasium at PRECHISTENKA
UL., 32 (see p. 102), then transferred to High School No. 1
on nearby Volkhonka. When Voloshin was sixteen, he and
his mother moved to the Crimea, and the remainder of his
secondary education was completed at a school in Feodosia,
before he returned to Moscow to enter the law department
of Moscow University. In 1899, after two years of study,
Voloshin was exiled to Feodosia, having been arrested for
organizing student riots, and soon afterwards made his first trip
abroad to France, Italy, Germany and Switzerland. His return to
Moscow to complete his law degree was followed by another

arrest, and exile this time to Tashkent in Central Asia. Thereafter, Voloshin led a relatively itinerant life, dividing his time between Paris, his house in Koktebel in the Crimea (famous for the writers who used to come and stay), and Moscow and St Petersburg.

Donskaya Ul.

The graves of Chaadaev and Sumarokov lie in the monastery cemetery.

Dostoevskogo Ul., 2

— *Dostoevsky Museum* Although associated above all with St Petersburg, it was in Moscow that Fyodor Dostoevsky was born in 1821 and spent the first fifteen years of his life. The ancient quarter where his family lived, traditionally associated with the poor, was known then as Bozhedomka, after a nearby cemetery called the 'home for the wretched' where beggars, suicides, criminals, murderers and their victims were buried.

The Dostoevsky Museum, established in 1928, is situated in the left wing of the huge Empire-style building designed by the architect Zhiliardi, the former Marinsky Hospital for the Poor, where Dostoevsky's father was employed as physician. Dostoevsky was born in another wing of the hospital building, but the family moved to this ground-floor flat in 1823.

Dostoevsky was the second son in the family of eight children. His younger brother Andrey wrote a vivid memoir, describing the exact appearance of the flat, and the interior of the museum matches his description very closely. Andrey described the space as cramped and dark, rarely seeing the sun. As well as reconstructed rooms such as the nursery with its scattered toys, the various stages of Dostoevsky's life are illustrated in photographs and documents. As a boy, Dostoevsky, who played in the hospital grounds, would often meet the inmates of the hospital, his first experience of the 'Poor Folk' whom he was to describe in his novel of that title.

A statue of Dostoevsky by S. D. Merkurov was unveiled in the hospital courtyard in 1918.

Closed Mondays, Tuesdays and the last day of the month

Gagarinsky Per., 8a

Situated near the Gogolievsky Bulv., this was Baidengammer's pension where the ten-year-old Ivan Turgenev received his first schooling in Moscow. Two years later, he was sent to another pension at ARMYANSKY PER., 2 (p. 8).

Gertsena Ul. (*See* BOLSHAYA NIKITSKAYA UL., p. 15)

Glinishchevsky Per., 6

A famous Moscow hotel used to stand here, first called the Sever (North) and, from 1829, the Angliya (England). Pushkin often stayed here when visiting Moscow. A contemporary guide book praised its comforts: 'the rooms are peacefully situated, the wine and food are good'. Adam Mickiewicz came to see Pushkin at the hotel in the spring of 1829 and a high relief depicting the two figures commemorates their meeting. Beneath are engraved the lines Pushkin dedicated to Mickiewicz: 'He spoke about a future, when people, forgetting their differences, would join together as one great family.' Underneath are Mickiewicz's words, written in Polish: 'They knew each other for a short time, but well. In the space of a few days they became friends.'

Gogolievsky Bulv.

In Soviet times, Prechistenky Bulv. was renamed after Gogol, who lived near by on NIKITSKY BULV. (see p. 80) in the last years of his life. The statue of Gogol which now stands in the courtyard at that address was originally unveiled here, at the beginning of the boulevard, on 26 April 1909, the 100th anniversary of the writer's birth. Stalin apparently found the statue too gloomy, however, and had it transferred to the courtyard of the house on Nikitsky Bulv. in 1952. The new statue which was commissioned to stand at the northern end of Gogolievsky Bulv., universally known by its nickname 'the soldier', attempts (and fails rather dismally) to fit Gogol into the heroic Socialist Realist mould.

Gogolievsky Bulv., 10

Ivan Turgenev often stayed in a flat here on visits to Moscow in the 1860s. This grand, Classical building with a six-columned façade, was owned by Turgenev's friend Ivan Maslov. Turgenev described 'a comfortable room, with, outside my window, a garden buried under a snowy feather-bed; and above the trees is a red Byzantine church with a green roof; its bell wakes me every morning'.

One of Turgenev's many guests, Suvorov, briefly described the main room's interior: 'To the right of the door stood a sofa with an oval table in front of it and a few armchairs. On the table towered an ancient lamp. At the other end of the room, against the wall, was a massive desk. Various papers were strewn across it.' Turgenev often came to Moscow at this time to oversee publication of works such as *On the Eve* and *Fathers and Sons* in the journal *Russkii vestnik* (Russian Messenger). However, in 1867 he quarrelled with the editor Katkov over his new work *Smoke*, so decided to publish it elsewhere.

Gorkogo Ul. (*See* TVERSKAYA UL., p. 125)

Gorokhovsky Per., 4

The family of Dostoevsky's favourite sister, Vera Mikhailovna Ivanova, lived in a flat here belonging to the Konstantinov Institute of Land Surveyance. Dostoevsky was a frequent visitor and the Zakhlebinin family in *The Eternal Husband* were based on the Ivanovs.

Granatny Per., 12, Kv. 3

Nikolay Klyuev moved to this address from Leningrad in 1931. He had by this time become disillusioned with Bolshevik politics and spoke openly in his poetry about his (well justified) fears for the extinction of Russian village life. His outspoken views and defence of Russian peasant culture brought him the unwelcome attention of the authorities, and during the years of industrialization and collectivization the campaign against him intensified. He was arrested at this address in February 1934, and exiled to Siberia, where he was later shot.

Kachalova Ul. (*See* MALAYA NIKITSKAYA UL., p. 61)

Kalayevskaya Ul., 33

In 1908–9, Mayakovsky lived in an annexe in the yard of the main building here.

Kamergersky Per., 3

This famous building was from 1902 until 1973 the main home of the Moscow Arts Theatre (MKHAT), and was where Chekhov's last play *The Cherry Orchard* was premièred (his other plays having been performed in the theatre's first building, in the Hermitage gardens, on Karetny ryad, 3). Formerly a private residence dating from the eighteenth century, the theatre was used in the 1880s (by private entrepreneurs, once the Imperial Theatres monopoly was lifted, including F. Korsh and the railway magnate Savva Mamontov, founder of the Moscow Private Opera company).

In 1902 the theatre's interior was extensively remodelled (at the expense of another of Russia's great merchant patrons, the art collector Savva Morozov) in the Modernist style by Russia's leading Art Nouveau architect Fyodor Shekhtel, a friend of Chekhov, who took a serious interest in the building and was brought plans and sketches for approval. Shekhtel designed the theatre's emblem of the seagull, inspired by Chekhov's play. It was in 1902 that the theatre also acquired its present Art Nouveau doorway, featuring a bas-relief by Anna Golubkina.

Mikhail Bulgakov was closely associated with the theatre for eleven difficult years and later described it satirically in his *Theatrical Novel*. His early impressions, however, were of awe and wonder: 'We found ourselves in a small auditorium which could seat about three hundred spectators. Two lamps burned faintly in the chandelier hanging from the ceiling, the curtain was open, and empty. Darkness filled its edges, but in the centre, faintly gleaming, was the figure of a golden horse, prancing on its hind legs ... this is my world.' After having many changes imposed upon it his play *The Days of the Turbins* was premièred here on 5 October 1926 and the following three years marked the peak of Bulgakov's career as a playwright, despite attacks from the Soviet press. In 1929 all his plays were banned. After sending a begging letter to the government Bulgakov was telephoned by Stalin and attached to the theatre as assistant director and actor. Bulgakov continued to write for the state, but his play *A Cabal of Hypocrites*, following four years of rehearsals and six years after it was written, was banned after only seven performances in 1936, and Bulgakov left the Arts Theatre for the Bolshoi Opera, where he worked as a librettist. His last play written for the theatre, *Batum*, was banned before rehearsals began.

Kamergersky Per., 4

This is the site of the nineteenth-century Hotel Chevalier, where Tolstoy stayed in 1850 (it features in his short novel *The Cossacks*), and where Nekrasov stayed in 1855.

Khlcbny Per., 2

In Tolstoy's *Anna Karenina*, this elegant two-storey, yellow house with central columns is the home of the Shcherbatsky family, and is where Levin comes to propose to Kitty.

Kievskogo Voksala, Pl.

The Kiev Station, known in the early 1920s as the Bryansk Station, was where, in 1921, Mikhail Bulgakov first arrived in Moscow from his birthplace, Kiev. Having trained as a doctor, he had spent his early career practising in hospitals in the Smolensk province, and then in the city of Vladikavkaz in the Caucasus. Having made the decision to abandon medicine and become a writer, he settled in Moscow, where he was to live for the rest of his life. He records his impressions of the station in the story 'Forty Times Forty' and it features frequently in his works: 'It was the end of September in 1921. Till the day I die I will remember the dazzling light at the Bryansk Station, and the two street lights of Dorogomilovsky Bridge which showed the way to my native capital. For no matter what happens, no matter what they say, Moscow is the mother, Moscow is the native city: and that was the first panorama. A block of darkness and three lights.'

Kotelnicheskaya Nab., 1/15

An apartment in this building downriver from the Kremlin, one of the famous 'wedding cake' skyscrapers built by Stalin in the late 1940s, was the home of prose writer Konstantin Paustovsky from 1950 to 1955. Its current residents, members of Paustovsky's family, have kept the apartment exactly as it was when the writer was alive. It may one day open as a museum.

Kozitsky Per.

Esenin led a fairly itinerant life in Moscow during the turbulent years of the Civil War. For a while in 1919 he shared a suite in the Hotel Luxe, on Tverskaya, 10 (which in Soviet times became the Hotel Tsentralnaya), then in January 1919 took up residence on this street. In a five-room flat in the former house of the wealthy theatre-lover A. Bakhrushin situated on the corner of Tverskaya and Kozitsky per., he created a writers' commune which was inhabited by several other writers and their friends.

Krasnaya Pl.

Moscow's famous Red Square has been a source of wonderment and inspiration for Russian writers ever since it was built. An untitled poem written by Mandelstam in 1935, for example, evokes the curiously rounded appearance of Russia's most famous square, as if one is looking at the globe:

> The earth is at its roundest on Red Square.
> And its unchained curve is hard,
> On Red Square the earth is at its roundest
> And its curve, rolling all the way down to the rice fields...

In *Hope against Hope* Nadezhda Mandelstam writes that 'Mandelstam quite liked to live in Buddhist Moscow, in the unseemly capital and even came to see a certain charm in it – because of its sprawling, scattered character, its Buddhist inertness, its air of having been outside history for a thousand years.'

Krasnaya Presnya, Ul., 36, Kv. 24

Mayakovsky and his family lived in this flat from 1913 to 1915. The area, named after the Presnya river, had become one of the city's main industrial districts by the beginning of the twentieth century, and a hotbed of revolutionary activity. This was not something one could judge from Mayakovsky's reference to his home in his poem 'I and Napoleon', however ('I live on Bolshaya Presnya street / 36, 24 / A peaceful little place / Very quiet').

It was in 1913 that the twenty-year-old poet published his first book of verse, and had his verse-drama *Vladimir Mayakovsky: A Tragedy* staged in St Petersburg by fellow Futurists, whose ranks he had joined some years earlier while a student at the Moscow Academy of the Study of Painting, Sculpture and Architecture. The Futurists were renowned for their deliberately scandalous behaviour, and it was also in 1913 that Mayakovsky outraged scores of well-heeled Muscovites who had turned up at midnight to the opening of a cabaret called the Pink Lantern in Mamonovsky per. by publicly insulting them.

The family's former abode was turned into a museum in 1978 by friends and relatives, who attempted to restore the flat to how it looked when Mayakovsky was living there, but it is no longer open to visitors. The apartment is now used as a book-storage facility for part of the Mayakovsky archive.

Krasnykh Vorot, Pl. (*See* LERMONTOVSKAYA PL., p. 49)

Kremlin

Lermontov's poem 'Panorama of Moscow' describes the ancient capital from the height of the Ivan the Great Bell Tower in the Kremlin. Standing at 270 feet, the belltower was then the highest building in Moscow. The poem was written while Lermontov was in St Petersburg, but it contains vivid sketches of the Moscow of his childhood and youth.

Tolstoy was married in the Church of the Nativity of Our Lady in the Kremlin in 1862 (his father-in-law was a court doctor and had a state apartment).

Krivokolenny Per., 4

This was the poet Venevitinov's house. A plaque decorates the side of this building where Venevitinov's friend Alexander Pushkin gave a reading of his new work *Boris Godunov* in 1826.

Krivokolenny Per., 12

Persuaded to leave his native Simbirsk, Nikolay Karamzin was given accommodation in a house which used to stand here by the masonic society to which he belonged, the Druzheskoe Uchenoe Obshchestvo (Friendly Learned Society), in 1784. He spent just over four years in his 'blessed dwelling by Chistie Prudy', mainly translating for the Society, and editing a journal for children, the *Detskoe chtenie dlya serdtsa i razuma* (Children's Reading for the Heart and Mind). His own short story 'Evgeny and Julia' was published in the journal in 1789. He later admitted jokingly that he had 'wasted a great deal of paper' at this address. He lived here until his trip to Europe in 1789–90.

Kropotkinskaya Ul. (*See* PRECHISTENKA UL., p. 99)

Kurskogo Vokzala, Pl.

The literary associations of the Kursk Railway Station begin with *Anna Karenina*; it is from here that Tolstoy's heroine sets out on her last, fatal journey.

It was on the platform of Kursk Railway Station that Boris

Pasternak met the German poet Rainer Maria Rilke in 1900. He was with his father, who had made Rilke's acquaintance at the Academy of Painting, Sculpture and Architecture, where he taught. Rilke was on his way to visit Tolstoy, whom he hoped to find at home on his estate at Yasnaya Polyana. Leonid Pasternak wrote of their meeting: 'My son Boris, then a ten-year-old schoolboy waiting with me for the train to leave, saw my young German friend for the first and last time in his life. Little did he or I dream that the great German poet was to wield such an influence over him in the future, and that Boris in his turn, through his translations, was to bring Rilke's poetry to Russia's new literary circles.'

The Kursk Station is where the drunken hero of Venedikt Erofeev's *Moscow–Petushki* finds himself at the beginning of his journey down the line to Petushki: 'It always works out that when I'm looking for the Kremlin I end up at the Kursk Station. In fact, I really did have to go to the Kursk Station and not the centre of town, but I set out for the centre all the same in order to see the Kremlin at least once, meanwhile thinking, "I won't see the Kremlin anyway and I'll end up at the Kursk Station."' *Moscow–Petushki*, written in 1969, but only first published in Russia in 1987, is now recognized as a classic of modern Russian fiction.

Kutuzovsky Pr., 1/7

The poet Alexander Tvardovsky lived here from 1950 to 1961. It was in 1950 that Tvardovsky first became editor of *Novy mir* (New World), Soviet Russia's most prestigious literary journal.

Kuzminsky Park, 17

— *Paustovsky Museum* The museum about the Soviet prose writer Konstantin Paustovsky is located in the middle of Kuzminsky Park (formerly part of the Golitsyn estate before the

Revolution), in the south-western part of Moscow. It is housed in an attractive wooden building which used to be the residence of Count Golitsyn's gardener, a few minutes' walk from Ul. Yunikh Lenintsev, but otherwise has no connection with the writer. Founded in the 1970s by a Paustovsky enthusiast, a local school teacher called Zoe Kvitko, the museum spent the first years of its existence as an itinerant exhibition until moving into the current premises, and acquired status as a national museum only in 1994. Now also a centre for the study of Paustovsky's writings, the museum's staff publish regular journals and articles.

With the aid of photographs, maps and various other memorabilia, the museum's four small rooms trace Paustovsky's life and works, from his childhood in Kiev to his last years in Moscow and TARUSA (see p. 340). Exhibits include editions of his works and the writer's grand piano.

Closed Mondays, Tuesdays, Thursdays, Fridays

Kuznetsky Most

In the eighteenth century this street was a very fashionable shopping centre where according to a contemporary guide book 'everything can be bought, from the latest hats, jewellery, lamps, vases – even nail brushes'. In the nineteenth century, at number 9, on the corner of Kuznetsky most and Neglinnaya ul., stood the famous restaurant Yar. It was here that Baratynsky, Pushkin, Yazykov and Vyazemsky met in 1831, following the death of their friend Delvig. The restaurant was often patronized by Pushkin, who mentions it in many of his letters, and remembers it for its truffles in his poem 'Travel Complaints'. The restaurant was later fictionalized by Tolstoy in the third part of his semi-autobiographical trilogy *Childhood, Boyhood, Youth*, in which the narrator celebrates passing the entrance examinations to Moscow University at Yar's with his friends. The self-conscious Nikolay Irtenev also goes shopping on Kuznetsky most beforehand,

Chekhov's funeral procession on Kuznetsky most in 1904

wearing his new uniform. His brother had bought lithographs of horses, pipes and tobacco when he had got into university and he decides he has to do the same:

> With several people looking at me from all sides, with the sun shining on my gilt buttons, on the cockade of my hat and on my sword I drove up to Kuznetsky Bridge and stopped at Dazziaro's picture shop. With a glance all around me I stepped inside. I did not want to buy any Victor Adam horses, so as not to be accused of copying Volodya, but hurrying to make my choice as quickly as possible (I was embarrassed at the trouble to which I was putting the obliging shopman) I took a female head painted in gouache, which was in the window, and gave twenty roubles for it . . .

In the twentieth century, a former shop at number 5, Kuznetsky most became the location for the avant-garde Café Pittoresco, decorated by Tatlin, Rodchenko and Yakulov, which opened in January 1918. Rather more elegant than the Poets' Café on Tverskaya, it was also a popular haunt with writers such as

Vyacheslav Ivanov and Valery Bryusov. There was no heating when the Pittoresco opened, so customers had to sit in their fur coats. In more recent times the street has been better known for its profusion of bookshops.

Lavrushinsky Per., 17

In 1935 *Literaturnaya gazeta* (Literary Gazette), the newspaper of the Union of Writers, announced a plan to build an apartment block specially for writers. When completed, in 1937, it was twelve storeys high, containing its own bank and even a barber's shop. Boris Pasternak was allotted two small rooms on the seventh and eighth floors, joined by an inner staircase.

During the Second World War Pasternak performed fire-watching duties on the roof and his experiences are recalled in the poem 'Lines in Haste'. He also recalls the period in a letter to his wife: 'I was in Moscow on the roof ... of our house, together with Vsevolod Ivanov, Khalturin and others ... with high-explosive bombs coming down and bursting on every second or third house, and incendiaries setting entire street blocks almost instantaneously alight ...' Among the many other writers who lived here was Paustovsky, who had an apartment in the 1940s.

Leningradsky Pr., 40

At number 40 is the famous Petrovsky Palace, a huge pseudo-Gothic building designed by the Russian architect Kazakov in 1775–82 as a stopping-place for the Imperial family on their journeys between Moscow and St Petersburg. In 1812 it was occupied by Napoleon, who came here to escape the Moscow fire. The Palace is described in Pushkin's *Eugene Onegin* as one of the first major Moscow landmarks seen by Tatyana on her first visit to Moscow:

> *Here stands, with shady park surrounded,*
> *Petrovsky Castle; and the fame*
> *in which so lately it abounded*
> *rings proudly in that sombre name.*
> *Napoleon here, intoxicated*
> *with recent fortune, vainly waited*
> *till Moscow, meekly on its knees,*
> *gave up the ancient Kremlin keys:*
> *but no, my Moscow never stumbled*
> *nor crawled in suppliant attire.*
> *No feast, no welcome-gifts – with fire*
> *the impatient conqueror was humbled!*
> *From here, deep-sunk in pensive woe,*
> *he gazed out on the threatening glow.*

Lermontov stayed at the Castle with his friend Baron Rozen in April 1841, his last visit to Moscow before his death.

After the Revolution the building became the Zhukovsky Air Force Engineering Academy and in 1922 Bulgakov worked in its editorial section. This was one of his first Moscow jobs after he settled here in 1921.

Leningradsky Pr., 44

Another branch of the famous Kuznetsky most restaurant Yar opened at this site in the middle of the nineteenth century, when the nearby Petrovsky Park became very popular with Muscovites for outings during the summer. Gogol was one of the diners here in 1849.

Lenin Hills (*See* VOROBYOVYE GORY, p. 134)

Leontevsky Per., 24

Chekhov came to Moscow from Yalta for the final time on 3 May 1904, when he and Olga Knipper rented an apartment at this address, just off Tverskaya. By this time, however, Chekhov was so ill with tuberculosis that he was forced to stay in bed. Two days before his departure for Badenweiler on 2 June, however, he went for a last drive round Moscow with his wife. Following his death in Badenweiler on 2 July 1904, Chekhov's body was brought back to Moscow, and carried on foot through the city from the Nikolaevsky (now Leningrad) Station to the Novodevichy Cemetery, accompanied by a huge crowd of mourners.

Lermontovskaya Pl.

The square is named after Mikhail Lermontov, who was born here on the night of 2/3 October 1814. Lermontov's grandmother insisted that her grandson should be born in Moscow to be in the hands of the best doctors. Once he had been christened in a nearby church and spent his first winter in Moscow, he returned to his grandmother's estate, TARKHANY (see p. 375) in the Penza region, where he spent his childhood and youth. The house where Lermontov was born no longer exists, and a giant multi-storey Stalinist building stands on its site. A small memorial plaque and a picture of the poet's head are on its wall. In the square in front stands a large statue of Lermontov by the sculptor Brodsky, which was unveiled in 1965. An iron railing behind it depicts a scene from Lermontov's poem 'Mtsyri', showing a demon and Mtsyri's skirmish with a snow-leopard. By the entrance to the square are engraved some lines from Lermontov's poem 'Sashka': 'Moscow, Moscow ... I love you as a son, as a Russian – strongly, fierily and tenderly.'

In 1742, the square was named Pl. Krasnykh Vorot (Square of the Beautiful Arch) after the triumphal arch built for the entry of the Empress Elizabeth (now replaced by a modern version).

Lubyanskaya Pl.

The massive building which dominates the north-eastern side of this square is the Lubyanka, headquarters of the Russian secret police, known during Soviet times as the KGB. The cavernous building also houses a prison, to which thousands of Soviet citizens were brought for interrogation and sometimes execution, particularly in the 1930s. Among them were countless prominent writers, including Babel, Mandelstam and Solzhenitsyn, to name just three.

Lubyansky Proezd., 3/6, Kv. 12

— *Mayakovsky Museum* When Mayakovsky moved back to Moscow from Petrograd in 1919, he obtained a small room in a communal apartment at this address, which he found with the help of the scholar and linguist Roman Jakobson, also resident here. Mayakovsky himself never lived here very much – after Osip and Lili Brik moved to Moscow from Petrograd in 1919, his permanent home for the next few years was with them (see SECHENOVSKY PER., 5, p. 109; TURGENEVSKAYA PL., p. 124; and MAYAKOVSKOGO PER., 15, p. 69), but he retained his Lubyansky proezd address as a place of work. It was where he shot himself in 1930, at the age of thirty-seven, and it is now the location for the main Mayakovsky museum in Russia. Until the early 1970s, the museum was based at number 15, MAYAKOVSKOGO PER. (see p. 69, the former Gendrikov per.), where Mayakovsky lived from 1926, but it was moved here for political reasons, namely squeamishness about the poet's relationship with Lili Brik, which literary officialdom believed did not enhance his status as a Soviet poet.

Some of Mayakovsky's best poetry, including 'About This', 'Vladimir Ilyich Lenin', 'Good' and 'At the Top of My Voice', was written here. By the 1920s, he had become Russia's most famous living poet, and was giving readings to enormous audiences. He had thrown himself into revolutionary politics with all the exuberance and extravagance that had characterized his association with the Futurists, but his larger-than-life public persona masked a deep unhappiness which came increasingly to the fore as the political scene grew more difficult. It eventually led to his suicide.

The Mayakovsky Museum was reopened in 1989, following innovative renovation by theatre designers. The Futurist-style exhibition follows the course of his life from his childhood in Georgia, and leads upstairs to the top floor, to the sparsely furnished room where the poet shot himself. On display are some of Mayakovsky's notebooks, sketches and propaganda posters he created during the Civil War for ROSTA, the Russian Press Agency, as well as photographs, letters and manuscripts, all culled from the museum's vast archive.

Closed Wednesdays and the last Friday of the month

Luzhnetsky Proezd, 2

The cemetery which lies behind the south wall of the Novodevichy Convent is the best known in Russia, and contains the graves of many leading writers, including Gogol, Chekhov, Bulgakov, Bely, Ilf, Mayakovsky, Bryusov and Aksakov. The large and sprawling cemetery has been given a sense of order by a central path and ten numbered sections. The writers buried here lie in the first three.

Bulgakov, Gogol, Chekhov, Aksakov, Bedny and Ilf lie buried in section 2. During the 1930s, when many churches and burial sites were being destroyed, Gogol's, Chekhov's, and Mayakovsky's graves were transferred here from their initial burial sites. The sarcophagus and railing have remained from Gogol's original tomb, while his headstone and cross were replaced by a pedestal with his statue. When Gogol's body was moved his coffin was opened and he was found to be lying on his side. This was eagerly seized upon as confirmation of old rumours that the author of *Dead Souls* had been buried while he was asleep.

But it was thanks to Gogol's reburial that Bulgakov's grave bears a headstone at all. The black slab of granite which once stood at the head of Gogol's grave at the Danilovsky Monastery now stands at the head of Bulgakov's own grave. Known as the Golgotha Stone, recalling the place of Christ's execution, it was originally brought to Moscow from the Crimea. Bulgakov's wife Elena Shilovskaya found it in a stone-cutter's shed when she was looking for a suitable marker for her husband's grave. The coincidence is a fitting one given that Bulgakov had always loved Gogol and once wrote, 'Teacher, cover me with your iron overcoat.' Elena Sergeyevna is buried alongside him.

The decoration on the railings of Chekhov's grave represent the stage curtains of the Moscow Arts Theatre, where his plays were performed, together with the emblem of a seagull. The graves of Mayakovsky, Nikolay Ostrovsky and Olesha lie in section 1. Bely and Bryusov lie buried in section 3.

Lva Tolstogo Ul., 21

— *Tolstoy Museum* Although Tolstoy's main home was at YASNAYA POLYANA (see p. 402) in the Tula Region, he bought this house in Moscow in the former Dolgo-Khamovnichesky per. in 1882 due to his wife's concern for the education of their eight children. Their eldest son Sergey was now a student at Moscow University, and their daughter Tanya was studying at the Academy of Painting and Sculpture and Architecture at MYASNITSKAYA UL., 21 (see p. 77). The Tolstoys from this time on spent their winters here until 1901, when they moved back permanently to Yasnaya Polyana. Sergey continued to live in the house with his family, and Sofya always stayed here on subsequent visits to Moscow. Tolstoy himself last set foot in the house in 1909, when he came up from Yasnaya Polyana on his way to visit his friend and disciple Vladimir Chertkov in Krekshino, in the Moscow region. The house is now the main Tolstoy landmark in the city.

The main building of the house was built in 1808, and survived the 1812 fire following the French occupation of Moscow because of the number of trees in the area. Indeed it was the spaciousness of the estate and its sprawling, unkempt garden which attracted Tolstoy to the house in the first place. After it was purchased, Tolstoy spent three months supervising repairs and the addition of an extra storey, during which time he lived in the wing (dating from the 1830s), which was later used as a publication office for his writings. He also took great interest in furnishing the house, and scoured local antique shops and markets for mahogany chairs and other pieces of furniture.

Following Tolstoy's death in 1910, Sofya sold the house to the Moscow city authorities, and its contents were either put into storage or taken to Yasnaya Polyana. The house then gradually fell into disrepair until 1921, when Lenin decreed that it should be turned into a museum. With the help of Tolstoy's children, contemporaries, former servants and Sofya's notes, the house was restored to its former condition, and most of the furniture reinstated (the walnut chest in his bedroom even contains his linen). The sixteen rooms that have been restored include the family dining room, the workroom where Tolstoy made his own boots, and the writer's study, where he wrote much of his last novel *Resurrection*, as well as stories and plays such as *The Death of Ivan Ilych, The Power of Darkness, The Kreutzer Sonata* and *Father Sergius*.

Tolstoy was constantly inundated with visitors during the periods he was resident here. He received not only fellow writers, including Chekhov, Bunin, Garshin, Gorky, Leskov, Ostrovsky, Solovyov and Fet, but also thousands of people from all walks of life, from professors to peasants, artists and aristocrats. So famous was Tolstoy by this time that the young Diaghilev, for example, felt he could not leave Moscow without setting eyes on the great man, and with characteristic boldness simply turned up one day to pay his respects. Numerous musicians also came to call, and sometimes perform, among them Chaliapin, Rachmaninov, Rimsky-Korsakov and Skryabin. As many as twenty people (the ten members of the family, plus guests) would sit down to dinner here; Tolstoy had become a strict vegetarian by this time (as had his daughters), so there would always be two soup tureens on the table. Food was brought to the house along the narrow wooden walkway from the kitchen, which was housed in a separate building.

In front of the house is a lawn, used for croquet in the summertime, and flooded in winter to make a skating rink for the children. Tolstoy remained active until the end of his days. As well as taking to the ice with his children, he also developed an enthusiasm for bicycle riding (the bicycle he purchased in 1898 is on view here), and remained a keen rider; in the mornings he would often mount his horse Krasavchik, later Tarpan, to go and fetch water from the river. In Yasnaya Polyana, Tolstoy was used to working in the fields, cutting wood, carrying water and making bread, and he tried to maintain his spartan and self-sufficient lifestyle in Moscow as well, several times making the 120-mile journey to his estate in the summer on foot. Understandably, Tolstoy was particularly fond of the garden at his Moscow house. 'What a pleasant place the garden is,' he wrote in a letter to Sofya; 'You sit at the window overlooking it and all is pleasant and peaceful.' The garden also makes a disguised appearance in Chapter 28 of the first part of *Resurrection*, where the family's summer house, in which he corrected the proofs of the novel, becomes a coach-house:

Tolstoy skating in the grounds of his Moscow house in 1898

He felt hot. He went to the window and opened it. It looked out on to the garden. It was a fresh quiet, moonlit night; the rumble of wheels on the street could be heard, and then everything became quiet. Directly beneath the window could be seen the shadow of the branches of the tall bare poplar tree clearly outlined on the swept gravel of the driveway.

To the left was the roof of the coach-house, which looked white under the bright light of the moon. In front were the interwoven branches of the trees, behind which could be seen the black shadow of the fence. Nekhlyudov looked at the garden and the roof, and at the shade of the poplar tree and breathed in the life-giving fresh air.

In 1892 Tolstoy transferred ownership of the Moscow house to his son Lev, and also gave up the rights on his creative works, much to the chagrin of Sofya, who had painstakingly made fair copies of all his manuscripts, and had taken charge of their publication. His relations with his wife had grown increasingly strained by this time. Following his spiritual crisis in the late 1870s, Tolstoy had begun to devote himself increasingly to humanitarian causes, and during his winters in Moscow he spent much time acquainting himself with the depressing conditions in doss houses, factories, prisons and tenements, and campaigning on behalf of the oppressed population who were forced to put up with squalid working and living conditions. His forthright indictments of all tsarist institutions brought him worldwide fame (such that it was difficult for him to walk down a street in Moscow without being recognized and greeted ecstatically by well-wishers), but also the wrath of the Russian government and, in 1901, excommunication from the Russian Orthodox church. *Closed Mondays and the last Friday of the month*

Malaya Dmitrovka Ul.

This street has so many associations with Chekhov, who lived along it at various points in his life, that it was renamed Chekhov street in 1944, on the fortieth anniversary of his death, but has now reverted to its original name.

Malaya Dmitrovka Ul., 1

This yellow three-storey building was the location of the editorial offices of the lowbrow comic journal *Zritel'* (the Spectator), to which Chekhov began contributing humorous anecdotes and sketches in 1881. He was then a medical student at Moscow University, and at the very beginning of his literary career. The editor of *Zritel'* was, by all accounts, a jovial character, and Chekhov (as well as three of his four brothers, who were also involved in varying ways with producing the journal) tended to spend more time here drinking tea and telling jokes than conducting the business of publishing a journal.

Malaya Dmitrovka Ul., 11, Kv. 14

Chekhov spent about four months here in a modestly furnished flat in this four-storey building on the corner of Degtyarny per. in the spring of 1899, while he was waiting for his house in Yalta to be finished. During his stay, he was given a private performance of his play *The Seagull*, which the Moscow Arts Theatre had successfully staged the previous December. He now entered into negotiations with the theatre about the production of his play *Uncle Vanya*, which he had withdrawn from consideration by the Imperial Theatres (who wanted him to rewrite it). During his time in Moscow, Chekhov led, as always, a very active social life. Among the many visitors he received while he was staying here was Tolstoy, although on the occasion that the great writer came to pay a call there were so many other people sitting round the samovar that Chekhov ended up going for dinner at Tolstoy's house the following day so that they could have a proper conversation. It was at this time that Chekhov also pursued his nascent relationship with the Moscow Arts Theatre leading lady Olga Knipper (she had played Arkadina in *The Seagull*), who was later to become his wife. Chekhov spent another couple of months in this flat the following autumn before leaving to spend the winter in Nice. At the time he was in the middle of writing *The Three Sisters*, and was able to read the first draft to the Moscow Arts Theatre company before his departure.

Malaya Dmitrovka Ul., 12, Kv. 10

Chekhov stayed for a short time with his family in this two-storey pale-green building in April 1899 while his villa in Yalta was being built (ill health having forced him to leave his house at MELIKHOVO (see p. 151) in the Moscow region, which was sold that summer). He soon afterwards found a flat of his own, however, in the house opposite, on the corner of Degtyarny per.

Malaya Dmitrovka Ul., 17

Nikolay Karamzin moved here in 1802 with his daughter Sofya after the death of his wife, Elizaveta Ivanovna Protasova, to whom he had been married for only one year. The original house is now demolished. Struck down by grief, Karamzin invested all his energies in work. While living here he founded the literary–historical journal *Vestnik evropy* (Herald of Europe), one of the most distinguished journals of its time, which published both foreign and Russian works and to which he also contributed, making his name for the first time as a historian as well as a writer.

Malaya Dmitrovka Ul., 29

Chekhov moved into a flat in the annexe at the back of this six-storey building which his family had rented upon his return from Sakhalin in December 1890. Living quarters were so cramped here that his brother Mikhail was forced to sleep on the floor when he came to stay. He thereby ran the risk of having his feet bitten all night by the mongooses Chekhov had brought back with him from his travels in India, where he had stopped off on the way back from Sakhalin. Although the two male mongooses adapted well to domestic life (in letters Chekhov describes them fondly sleeping on people's beds, purring like cats), the animals were eventually donated to the Moscow Zoo a year later, after the family had grown tired of them jumping up on to the table all the time. It was then discovered that the female 'mongoose', which had spent most of its time hiding under the furniture, and had the greatest propensity for biting people, was actually a palm civet, a wild and ferocious creature not suited for domestication at all.

Chekhov was not particularly happy to be back in Moscow ('boredom is already looking through the window and wagging its finger at me,' he wrote in a letter soon after his return), and leaped at the opportunity to leave again. In March 1891 he went on his first trip to Western Europe with his friend Suvorin, editor of the conservative newspaper *Novoe vremya* (New Time). The family moved out of the house in 1892, when the estate at Melikhovo was purchased.

Malaya Molchanovka Ul., 2

— *Lermontov Museum* The Lermontov Museum is located in the small wooden house lived in by the poet and his grandmother between 1829 and 1832. Lermontov's grandmother, who had decided to take complete charge of the boy's education, brought him to Moscow at the age of fifteen, from the country estate of TARKHANY (see p. 375) in the Penza province to enrol him at the Moscow pension at TVERSKAYA UL., 7 (see p. 127). The museum was opened in 1981 after the whole building had been refurbished and redecorated to reflect its appearance when Lermontov lived here.

Lermontov, who was to become Russia's successor to Alexander Pushkin, wrote poetry from a very early age. Despite his extremely short life – he died in the Caucasus in a duel at the age of twenty-six – he left a substantial volume of work, including his major novel *A Hero of Our Time*. His mother had died when he was a child, and he was to hear of the death of his father in 1831. It was in response to this untimely death that he wrote the poem 'The Appalling Fate of a Father and Son'. At this address he also wrote 'Menschen und Leidenschaften', the drama *A Strange Man*, the tragedy *The Spaniards* and the poem 'Confession' and continued his work on 'Demon'.

It was while living here that Lermontov met and fell in love with the sixteen-year-old Varvara Lopukhina. Lopukhina was to inspire the creation of Lermontov's character Vera, who appears in the drama *Two Brothers*, the unfinished novel *Princess Ligovskaya* and *A Hero of Our Time*. Lopukhina's marriage in 1837 to Bakhmetev was to cause Lermontov much grief, but he nevertheless presented her with his own self-portrait after the

The house where Lermontov lived between 1829 and 1832, now the Lermontov House Museum

marriage. This portrait now hangs in the museum, having been rediscovered in Germany.

In Lermontov's own low-ceilinged room in the mezzanine hang portraits of his literary heroes Byron and Pushkin. There is a bust of Napoleon, an engraving of the Caucasus, journals from that time and volumes of the works of Pushkin. Although the Moscow museum is dedicated in particular to the Moscow period of Lermontov's short life, it also draws attention to his other talent, for painting, and many of his works hang throughout the museum.

Closed Mondays and Tuesdays and the last day of the month

Malaya Molchanovka Ul., 8

The prose writer A. N. Tolstoy lived in a flat in this six-storey building from 1915 to 1918.

Malaya Nikitskaya Ul.

Opposite the Ryabushinsky House at number 5 on the former Kropotkinskaya ul. is the Tserkov Bolshogo Vozneseniya or Church of the Great Ascension. The church was completed in 1840, and while it was being built the old five-domed Church of the Ascension with its tall belltower still stood alongside. Alexander Pushkin married Natalya Goncharova here on 18 February 1831, but it is not clear whether the wedding service was held in the old church or in one of the chapels of the new one.

Pushkin had obtained the hand of Natalya Goncharova with some difficulty as her family, particularly her mother, were unwilling to give immediate consent. She was not yet eighteen when she married the thirty-two-year-old Pushkin. Two years passed between the day that he met her at a ball in Moscow and the day of the wedding, and Pushkin was continually worrying that the event would never take place at all. He was refused permission to marry in his local church, and the wedding was watched by the police, who stood at the doors of the church.

Natalya Goncharova was universally regarded as a woman of outstanding beauty, a fact which has been confirmed by many of Pushkin's contemporaries, although not borne out by her surviving portraits. At the wedding ceremony one of the wedding rings was dropped, and the candles blew out, all signs which the superstitious Pushkin took as bad omens. The couple were married for six years, before Pushkin died in a duel over his wife's alleged affair with D'Anthès.

Malaya Nikitskaya Ul., 6/2

— *Gorky Museum* The former Ryabushinsky House, which became the residence of Soviet writer Maxim Gorky in 1931, when he returned from Italy after a seven-year absence, was built at the turn of the century by Fyodor Shekhtel, and is one of the best-known Art Nouveau landmarks in Moscow. The yellow-brick house with its ornately curved iron railings, stained-glass windows and mosaic frieze of irises was originally built for the industrialist Stepan Ryabushinsky, an early collector of icons. After Gorky's death, its interior was preserved as it had been during the writer's lifetime, and it was opened as a museum in 1965, giving visitors the chance also to see the immaculate Art Nouveau decor, which features a magnificent carved stone staircase at its centre.

According to the critic Vitaly Shentalinsky, author of an important book about the literary archives of the KGB, Stalin himself picked out this house for Gorky when he returned to Russia. It was conveniently near the Kremlin, and could be used as a place for informal meetings between writers and members of the government, who could report back to the Soviet leader on what was going on in the literary world, and also take a hand in its events. Due to his political commitment and previous close association with Lenin, Gorky had been a pivotal literary figure immediately before and after the Revolution, and his return to Russia now was trumpeted with much fanfare, not so much because of his literary achievements as because Stalin realized how useful Gorky could be to him in the propaganda war. He required a prominent writer to approve his policies and keep up the smokescreen of lies. Gorky was also the ideal figurehead to play a leading role in the regimentation of Russian writers, whom Stalin needed to serve the party cause as it went into the second five-year plan, and as collectivization and industrialization continued.

Gorky was a talented man, who had done a great deal to help writers in the early revolutionary years, but he was also weak. He chose to ignore the countless letters he received abroad from loyal Soviet citizens who tried to warn him about what was going on in their country. And his integrity was forever compromised by the tacit pact he made with Stalin when he returned to Russia. As well as his luxurious Moscow residence, Gorky was given a large dacha in the village of Gorky-10, to the west of Moscow, on the road to Zvenigorod (the name of the village has nothing to do with the writer). He was also allocated a resort house in the Crimea, a brigade of servants, cooks and secretaries, critical impregnability and the kind of status never before accorded to a living writer. Not only was Moscow's main street, Tverskaya, named after Gorky, but also the former town and region of Nizhny Novgorod, where he was born, the Moscow Arts Theatre (to Stalin it was irrelevant that the theatre had a closer association with Chekhov), and numerous other theatres, institutes, libraries, streets, parks, factories, collective farms and schools all over the country. In return, Gorky had to do as he was told, and close his eyes to the atrocities being carried out under his nose, which included the suppression and arrest of many of his fellow writers. The party also played a role in trying to ensure that Gorky was kept in a state of ignorance about what was going on. The orthodox daily newspaper *Pravda* (Truth) was sometimes censored and an individual doctored copy printed especially for Gorky's consumption, which was carefully hand-delivered to his door. By the end of his life, the house on Malaya Nikitskaya had become, as Shentalinsky has revealed, a veritable annexe of the NKVD, and Gorky a sick and broken man, a prisoner in his own house, and isolated from the country at large.

Of the five rooms which make up the Gorky Museum, it is the wood-panelled dining room, to the left of the front door, which is most important from the point of view of literary history. It was here, in the autumn of 1932, that Stalin and his chief henchmen met with the Soviet literary elite and dreamed up the theory of Socialist Realism, which was later championed by Gorky when he became the first president of the Union of Soviet Writers in 1934 (its headquarters were situated in nearby BOLSHAYA NIKITSKAYA UL., at number 53, see p. 15). Needless to say, neither Akhmatova nor Mandelstam, Babel nor Pasternak, was present; those who attended were writers who later became 'official' like Fadeev and Sholokhov, as well as less talented hacks and functionaries, more interested in furthering their careers than in questions of literary craft. The Bechstein grand piano in the dining room was played during Gorky's day by Kabalevsky, Khachaturian, Yudina and Neuhaus.

Of all the rooms in the house, it is the study, to the right of the front door, which most reflects Gorky's tastes. The writer is known to have disliked the house's interior decor and most of the furniture chosen for him. He would usually spend a minimum of eight hours a day sitting at the large green-topped desk by the window while he was living here. The fountain pen he used to write with can still be seen here, as well as his spectacles, an assortment of coloured pencils and a neat pile of papers. Gorky was an extremely organized person with a phenomenal memory, it is said, which allowed him to dispense with keeping notebooks and diaries. He would generally work on his fiction from eleven until two every day (he worked on his novel *The Life of Klim Samgin* here), and then deal with correspondence and editorial matters after five in the afternoon. Also of interest in Gorky's study is his collection of Japanese netsuke above the fireplace (during his lifetime he also collected paintings, coins and medals, which he gave away before moving here) and a copy of the Da Vinci *Madonna* kept at the Hermitage. Next to Gorky's study is his bedroom, whose furniture he felt was more suitable for a ballerina (it was bought for him before his arrival), and the office of his secretary, whose job it was to deal with the writer's voluminous correspondence. A small part of Gorky's equally vast library is also on display here, which was surpassed in size only by Tolstoy's collection at Yasnaya Polyana.

The only other room in the house open to visitors is the tiny chapel at the top of the house built for Ryabushinsky, a fervent Old Believer. It is doubtful Gorky ever visited it, however. By the time he moved back to Moscow he was too ill to climb the stairs, and he lived and worked on the ground floor. His overcoat, walking cane and boots can still be seen by the front door, next to his study; everyone else entered the house from the back, so as not to disturb the great writer while he worked.

Closed Mondays and Tuesdays and the last Thursday of the month

Malaya Ordynka, Ul., 9

— *Ostrovsky Museum* Russia's famous nineteenth-century playwright was born in this two-storey wooden house in the Zamoskvorechie area of Moscow in 1823. The Ostrovsky family rented only two rooms on the ground floor, but the whole house has now been turned into a museum dedicated to his memory. It is well preserved and full of period detail.

The house, in the heart of what used to be the merchant quarter of Moscow, belonged to Nikifor Maksimov, deacon of the small church next door which was pulled down in 1929. It is a typical example of Moscow architecture dating from after the great fire of 1812, and has now been restored to its original state. Alexander Ostrovsky spent the first three years of his life at this address. His father was an ambitious business lawyer, and within a few years was able to build a house on land he had bought in the nearby area of Monetchikovsky per. The family moved to the new house at the beginning of 1826, where Ostrovsky enjoyed a fundamentally happy childhood, marred only by the death of his mother in 1831.

The museum contains six rooms. The three rooms downstairs recreate the modest surroundings Ostrovsky grew up in, while the three rooms upstairs trace the stage history of his plays. None of the furniture in the study or bedroom downstairs where the family lived ever belonged to the Ostrovskys, with the exception of a portrait of the dramatist's father and a travelling writing case, but it has been carefully selected to evoke the atmosphere of the period. The drawing room reflects Ostrovsky's early adulthood, when he began writing plays, and among the exhibits here are portraits of the editorial staff at the journal *Moskvityanin* (the Muscovite), which published his first play in 1850.

The decor of each of the rooms upstairs reflects the lifestyle of the different characters of Ostrovsky's plays (merchants, gentry and civil servants). Visitors can inspect some of Ostrovsky's personal effects here, including his black velvet cap, tobacco tin, wooden workbench and a letter opener of intricate design that he himself carved. Also on display are materials relating to the productions of his plays at the Maly Theatre. Ostrovsky worked at the Maly from 1853 until his death in 1886, by which time he had written forty-seven plays, most of which are set in the kind of Moscow milieu he himself grew up in, and all but one of which were staged during his lifetime at the Maly. The theatrical exhibits include such paraphernalia as make-up cases and props, as well as set designs by Golovin, models of the Maly Theatre and sets of Ostrovsky productions (particularly interesting are those designed by the Stenberg brothers and directed by Meyerhold in the early 1920s), posters and photographs of the actors who performed in productions of Ostrovsky's plays.
Closed Monday and Tuesday and the last Friday of the month

Malaya Polyanka Ul., 12, 3

Afanasy Fet lived at number 12 from 1839 to 1844 during his student days. In the cosy, dark entresol, he was visited by many of his friends, including the future poet and critic Apollon Grigoriev. His poem 'The Sad Birch Tree by My Window' was inspired by the view from his bedroom window, and his poem 'Student' describes these years.

After his marriage in 1857 to the wealthy Mariya Botkina,

Fet returned to the street, living in the spacious house with a coach-house and stables at number 3. It was during this time that his friendship grew with Lev Tolstoy, who was then living near by at PYATNITSKAYA UL., 12 (see p. 104). Tolstoy was among those who attended musical evenings organized by Fet and his wife at their home. In November 1858 Ivan Turgenev stayed for a few days. In his memoirs, Fet writes, 'With the exception of S. T. Aksakov who did not leave his house because of a torturous illness, the entire Moscow intelligentsia visited Turgenev.' In 1861, Fet left the house to live on his country estate, Stepanovka, in the Orel region, and stopped writing poetry for almost two decades.

Maly Levshinsky Per.

The building on the street where Mikhail Bulgakov lived with his wife Lyubov Evgenievna Belozerskaya in 1926–7 no longer remains; she later recalled their apartment here in her memoirs: 'We slept in the blue room and spent the day in the yellow one. The fashion then was to paint the walls with glossy paint in the colours that were used in the 1840s and 50s. We shared a kitchen without gas; primus stoves hummed on the tables and kerosene lamps blinked. The house was spacious but crammed to overflowing. Just who didn't live here?'

Maly Putinkovsky Per., 1/2

This building houses the editorial offices of *Novy mir* (New World), Russia's most prestigious monthly literary journal. *Novy mir* was founded in 1925, and, like all other periodicals, later came under the jurisdiction of the Union of Writers, founded in 1932. Before then it was able to publish the work of diverse writers, including Mayakovsky and Pasternak, Babel and Gorky, but in the 1930s it became a mouthpiece for Socialist Realism. Its most famous editor was Alexander Tvardovsky, in charge of the journal during the 'Thaw' years under Khrushchev. In 1962 Tvardovsky published Solzhenitsyn's *One Day in the Life of Ivan Denisovich*. The journal again rose to prominence during the glasnost years, when it began to publish the works of suppressed writers like Brodsky. In 1988 Pasternak's *Doctor Zhivago* was published for the first time in Russia in *Novy mir*, and the journal's circulation for a time soared into the millions. Like all other highbrow publications in the post-Soviet climate, however, its situation is precarious.

Maly Tolmachevsky Per., 8

The eccentric prose writer Alexey Remizov was born in this two-storey brick house in 1877. The house belonged to his father, a merchant, who owned two haberdashery shops in the centre of town. Remizov lived here only at the very beginning of his life. Before he was two years old his mother left her husband, taking their fours sons with her, and went to live with her brothers at Zemlyanoi val, 53. Remizov returned here only when his father died.

Mansurovsky Per., 9

The basement of this small wooden building is thought by some to be the prototype for the master's basement in Bulgakov's *The Master and Margarita*. It was part of a small estate owned by two brothers, Sergey and Vladimir Topleninov, friends of Bulgakov from the theatrical world. Bulgakov stayed in the basement for a while, writing *The Master and Margarita* by candlelight, as well as by the light of the stove. This house fits the description of the master's house very well, and you can imagine the master waiting here for the woman he loves, Margarita: 'She only came through the gate once a day, but my heart raced at least ten times every morning with false alarms. Then, when both hands were pointing to twelve, my heart continued to pound until her shoes with their black patent-leather straps and steel buckles drew level, almost soundlessly, with my basement window.' In the novel exact topographical references are never given. Perhaps Bulgakov himself did not want to give the master's abode an address, preferring to leave it as material for Moscow legend. Another possible prototype for the master's basement is at PLOTNIKOV PER., 10 (see p. 91).

Marksa, Pr. (*See* MOKHOVAYA UL., p. 73)

Mashkova, Ul., 10

Turgenev was given an overwhelming reception at a dinner here held on 15 February 1879 by his friend Professor Kovalevsky, who had invited a circle of Moscow professors to come and meet the famous writer, who was visiting Russia from France. During the dinner, Kovalevsky raised a toast to Turgenev, which apparently reduced him to tears. Turgenev's reply was to propose a silent toast to the memory of his friend Belinsky. Turgenev, then sixty-one years of age, had written most of his major works, and the enthusiasm of Kovalevsky's circle, together with the rapturous reception Turgenev was to receive a week later at the Hall of the Nobility among a crowd of 1,000 students, was a clear indication of his enormous popularity in Russia.

Mayakovskogo, Per., 15, Kv. 5

A first-floor flat in this two-storey yellow and white house in former Gendrikov per., located in the Taganka area of Moscow, became home to Mayakovsky and the Briks in 1926. They shared the house with three other families. Mayakovsky and Lili Brik had ceased to be lovers by this time, but still wanted to live together, which was also fine with Osip, who continued to be Mayakovsky's close friend. Their living conditions here were later described by Lili:

The statue of Vladimir Mayakovsky in Mayakovsky Square

At that time ... there was a dining room and three identical cabin-rooms. The only difference was that in mine the writing-desk was smaller and the wardrobe was bigger, and all the books were in Osip's room. There was a bath, which we had been deprived of for so long, and which we loved as if it were a living creature. It was so small that it's amazing that Vladimir Vladimirovich could get into it. We had 'our own kitchen', which was tiny but full of life ... There was no pretty garden with a fence around it. Instead there were trees and sheds for the inhabitants' firewood ... It was interesting to buy everything for the new flat and to order furniture. The first thing Volodya did was to order a copper plate for the entrance door – 'like people have' ... The principle according to which the flat was decorated was the same one that had been used for the printing of the first edition of 'A Cloud in Trousers' – nothing superfluous. No beautiful objects – no mahogany, no pictures, no decorations. Everything was new, even the knives and forks, everything was essential. Bare walls.

Mayakovsky was by this time a major celebrity and travelled a great deal all over Russia giving hundreds of readings. He was also, of course, a central figure in the Russian avant-garde, and a driving force behind the association LEF – the Left Front of the Arts – which had formed in 1923. LEF regrouped in 1927, and its journal *Novy Lef* (New Lef), edited by Mayakovsky, was contributed to by such diverse figures as Rodchenko, Shklovsky, Eisenstein, Pasternak and Meyerhold, who would come to meetings at the flat on Gendrikov per. on Tuesday nights. Shklovsky liked the bathroom so much here that he made a point of shaving in it before the meetings each week. It was here that Mayakovsky read his plays *The Bedbug* and *The Bath-House* for the first time.

After the poet's death, the street was renamed in his honour, and the first Mayakovsky Museum opened here in 1937, after Lili Brik's appeal to Stalin. In the 1970s, however, it was transferred to Lubyansky proezd, where the poet kept a study, in order to minimize any connection with her. The unconventional relationship that the couple had was seen as decadent and bourgeois and was viewed with opprobrium by the Soviet literary establishment.

Merzlyakovsky Per., 16, Kv. 27

Having initially lived in an NKVD dacha at BOLSHEVO (see p. 144) outside Moscow following her return from Paris in the summer of 1939, Marina Tsvetaeva and her son stayed temporarily in a flat in this green and beige five-storey building in the centre of town following her husband's and daughter's arrest later that year. The flat belonged to her sister-in-law Lilya Efron. Because of the appalling conditions at Bolshevo, Tsvetaeva had made a plea for help with accommodation to Fadeev, a senior functionary at the all-powerful Union of Writers, but to no avail. 'He said there wasn't a metre free. At the dacha it became completely unbearable, we were just freezing ...' As a result Tsvetaeva locked up the dacha and took her son to Moscow, where she put herself at the mercy of her sister-in-law. There was so little room here, however, that they ended up sleeping in the hall on trunks, and had to walk the streets after breakfast because Lilya gave lessons here during the day. Tsvetaeva spent much of this time meeting with friends such as Pasternak and Arseny Tarkovsky in a futile attempt to find work.

Milyutinsky Per., 14

An annexe of this house was the birthplace of the Symbolist writer Valery Bryusov, whose grandfather, a former serf, had set up a business trading in cork. For a time the family later lived at Yauzsky bulv., 10, but at the end of the 1870s they moved to TSVETNOI BULV., 22 (see p. 123), which remained the poet's home until 1910.

Mira, Pr., 30

Bryusov moved to a flat in this building in the autumn of 1910, and it remained his residence until his death here on 9 October 1924. The flat opened as a museum after his death, but is now closed. Preparations are currently under way to reopen the museum, and also to found a new museum about the 'Silver Age' of Russian culture in this building.

After the demise of Symbolism as a literary movement in 1910, Bryusov continued to write poetry and prose while living at this address, but also worked as a translator (of Virgil's *Aeneid*, for example), and, after 1917, became involved with the Soviet literary establishment, becoming a member of the Communist Party in 1920. Among the writers who came to visit Bryusov here were Mayakovsky, Blok, Esenin and Gorky.

Mokhovaya Ul., 3

The imposing Classical building on the hill here at the corner of Znamenka and Manezhnaya streets, built by V. Bazhenov in the 1780s, is known as the Pashkov House, after the man who commissioned it.

In August 1851, on the anniversary of the coronation of Nicholas I, Gogol stood here on the belvedere (reconstructed in the 1830s), watching the illumination of the Kremlin opposite, and being reminded of Rome, where he had lived for most of the preceding decade. At the time the building housed the 4th Moscow Gymnasium, and one of the pupils later recalled seeing the emaciated Gogol (this was less than a year before his death) striking an unprepossessing figure in his black frock-coat and with his famous long nose.

In 1862, the Pashkov House became home to the Rumyantsev Museum, whose library (the basic collection of which was later to become the Lenin Library housed next door) was used extensively by Tolstoy when he was doing historical research for *War and Peace*, and later in the 1880s, after he had become a Moscow resident. After the Revolution the museum became home to the Lenin Library's manuscript division. Bulgakov became a regular reader at the Lenin Library when he moved to Moscow in the 1920s, and it is ironic that all his forbidden manuscripts, letters and editions of his novel *The Master and Margarita* were later to be deposited here. One of the scenes from that novel takes place on its roof: 'At sunset, high above the town, on the stone roof of one of the most beautiful buildings in Moscow, built about a century and a half ago, stood two figures – Woland and Azazello. They were invisible from the street below, hidden from the vulgar gaze by a balustrade adorned with stucco flowers in stucco urns, although they could see almost to the limits of the city.'

Mokhovaya Ul. 9, 11

This complex makes up part of the 'old buildings' of Moscow University. They still belong to the university, although the main campus – dominated by a skyscraper – is now in the southwestern part of the city. Predictably, the university has numerous literary associations.

Moscow University was founded by the scientist and man of letters Mikhail Lomonosov in 1755, in a building on Red Square. In Pushkin's words, Lomonosov was 'a great man. He created the first university – or it's best to say he was our first university.' A statue of Lomonosov now stands outside number 9. The university was moved to Mokhovaya ul. in the 1780s into a building designed by Kazakov. After the fire of Moscow in 1812, Kazakov's building was rebuilt by the architect Zhiliardi. 'The significance of Moscow University grew with Moscow after the fire of 1812,' wrote Alexander Herzen in his famous memoirs, *My Past and Thoughts*; 'A new epoch began for her. Her university became more and more the focus of Russian education. The conditions for its development were a combination – of historical significance, geographical position and the absence of the Tsar.' Herzen also describes it as 'the bastion of democracy'. A statue of Herzen and his lifelong friend and fellow student Ogaryov (by N. Andreev, 1922) stands in front of the building. They were the leading figures of a circle of students who fiercely debated the French utopian socialist ideas then prevalent in the West.

Herzen and Lermontov attended the university at the same time, but did not know each other. They did, however, share a lecturer, Malov, who used to describe his students as little boys or horses. When Malov once claimed that they expressed their thoughts as horses did, by stamping their feet, the indignant students chased him out of the classroom, as far as the university gates, throwing their galoshes after him. Lermontov recalls the university in his poem 'Sashka': 'A sacred place. I remember, like a dream, your departments, auditoriums, corridors, your sons' arrogant debates.'

Gogol never had any scholarly connection with the university during his lifetime, but it was to the church here that his body was carried through the deep snow of February 1852 from his last residence on Nikitsky bulv. For two days it was impossible to go up Bolshaya Nikitskaya ul. owing to the crowds of people who wanted to come and pay their last respects, even at night. Some people did not know who Gogol was, and thought only the death of a prince could cause such a commotion. The writer was initially buried at the Danilovsky Monastery (in 1931 his remains were transferred to the Novodevichy Cemetery), with much police vigilance, as the government still regarded Gogol as a dangerous individual. There was also strict censorship about what was printed about Gogol in the press; it was only in 1855 that the four-volume edition of Gogol's collected works was completed, to which a further two volumes were added in 1856. As a result of the long obituary Pogodin published in his journal *Moskvityanin* (the Muscovite), which was surrounded by a black border and described the writer's illness, he was placed under police surveillance. The famous 'Letter from St Petersburg' about Gogol by Turgenev was published in *Moskovskie vedomosti* (Moscow News) on 13 March 1852. For daring to call Gogol 'great', Turgenev was arrested and exiled to his country estate at Spasskoe Lutovinovo.

Turgenev had studied here for only a year in 1833 before moving to St Petersburg. Despite the brevity of his enrolment, the university plays an important role in his novels and Turgenev's literary characters such as Rudin and Lezhnev in *Rudin* and Litvinov in *Smoke* are loosely based on some of Turgenev's

Moscow University at the turn of the century

fellow students. In 1879, towards the end of his life, he was given an impressive welcome here (the auditorium was unable to accommodate all those who wished to attend) by the Society of Lovers of Russian Literature, an organization through which he was to play a large part in the Pushkin celebrations of 1880, an unparalleled literary event in Russia.

Numerous other authors have studied at Moscow University, including Griboedov, Fonvizin, Goncharov, Fet, Tyutchev, Pasternak, Andreyev and Vyacheslav Ivanov.

Myasnitskaya Ul., 7

There was a famous bookshop in this now rebuilt house run by I. V. Bazunov and the Salayev brothers. As well as booksellers, they were the publishers of some of the first editions of Turgenev's work. Turgenev frequently complained of the misprints they contained.

Myasnitskaya Ul., 21

The pale pink Yuzhkov house stands opposite the main Post Office. (Only this saved it from getting lost in Moscow, according to Mayakovsky.) In 1844, it became the Academy of Painting and Sculpture, a college under the patronage of the Imperial Court. The three-year-old Boris Pasternak came to live here with his family when his father was appointed as a teacher at the school in 1894, and the family lived in two flats in the school building for twenty years. The building of the Institute has an impressive balcony and from it Pasternak saw the funeral procession of Emperor Alexander III in 1894, as well as the ceremony for the coronation of the new Tsar Nicholas II two years later. These years are recalled in his *Essay in Autobiography*, in which he remembers the building as:

> old, beautiful and remarkable in many ways. The fire of 1812 had spared it. A century before our time under the Empress Catherine, it had been the secret refuge of a Masonic Lodge. One corner, at the intersection of Myasnitskaya and Yuzhkov Lane, had a pillared, semi-circular balcony; part of it formed a recess and communicated with the College hall. From it, you could have a clear view of Myasnitskaya running into the distance towards the railway stations.

One of Pasternak's earliest memories, also recorded in his *Essay in Autobiography*, is of a musical recital given here by his mother, an extremely accomplished pianist. Lev Tolstoy was in the audience:

> The air was filled with cigarette smoke; the candles blinked as if it stung their eyes. They shone on the red varnished wood of the cello and of the violin. The piano loomed black. The men were in black frock coats. Women leaned out of their shoulder-high dresses like flowers out of flower baskets. Like smoke rings, the grey-ringed heads of two or

three old men drifted together. One of them was the painter Gué, whom I was later to know well and see often. The image of another has been present to me, as to most people, all my life: to me especially because my father illustrated his work, went to see him, honoured him, and indeed our whole house was permeated by his spirit ... This was Lev Nikolayevich.

Tolstoy became a friend of Pasternak's father Leonid, when he was commissioned to illustrate his last novel *Resurrection*, and the young Boris later remembered the illustrations being dispatched from the kitchen.

It was while studying here in 1911 that Mayakovsky met the painter David Burliuk, already a key figure in the artistic avant-garde, and the founder of Russian Futurism, with whose ranks Mayakovsky soon joined forces. The institute was reopened in 1918 as the Higher Technical–Artistic Studios (Vkhutemas), and became a centre of the revolutionary avant-garde. The Cubo-Futurist poet Alexei Kruchonykh lived for a while in a room on the seventh floor in the early 1920s.

Myasnitskaya Ul., 42

It was here, in this grand house built in the Classical style in the late eighteenth century, that Alexander Griboedov worked on his famous play *Woe from Wit*, while on leave during the winter of 1823/4. Later known as the Baryshnikov Mansion, during Griboedov's time the house belonged to his friend Stepan Begichev. Küchelbecker, Chaadaev and Odoevsky were among the literary figures who visited here.

Nashchokinsky Per., 5

Earlier this century this building had a special wing in which writers were housed. Osip and Nadezhda Mandelstam, as well as Bulgakov and his wife Elena Shilovskaya, were given accommodation here by the Union of Writers. It was demolished in 1976.

The Mandelstams first came here in 1933. Osip Mandelstam's poem 'The flat is quiet as paper' written here evokes the horror of Stalin's Russia, concluding, 'It's not the ancient spring of Hippocrene, / which will burst through the cardboard walls, / but the gush of age-old terror / which will flood this evil Moscow home.' On 13 May 1934, agents of the secret police came at night and arrested the poet. He was then interrogated and tortured in the Lubyanka prison, where he spent two weeks before being sentenced to a three-year term of exile at Cherdyn in the Urals.

The Mandelstams returned in 1937, by which time it had changed considerably: 'The writers had gone wild at having so much money for the first time in their lives ... It was like Doomsday, with some being trampled underfoot by demons, and others having their praises sung,' wrote Nadezhda Mandelstam in her memoir *Hope against Hope*.

The Bulgakovs lived in flat 44 from February 1934 until Bulgakov's death in 1940. They enjoyed a higher standard of living here than at any other time of their lives. This period of greater security was a result of Bulgakov's letter to Stalin. Embarrassed by the publicity surrounding Mayakovsky's suicide, Stalin arranged for Bulgakov to be given employment by the Moscow Arts Theatre. In May 1935 Bulgakov wrote to his brother: 'It's light and dry and we have gas. God, how delightful! I call down a blessing on the person who thought of putting gas into apartments.' Ermolinsky, a friend of Bulgakov, was amazed by what he found on entering the flat: 'Instead of Bohemian disorder he was surrounded by comfortable and tasteful furnishings ... My irrepressible and bold Bulgakov is lost – he's gone bourgeois.'

Bulgakov completed *The Master and Margarita* here, and was still revising the final version three days before his death.

Neglinnaya Ul., 4

The Hotel Europa once stood here. Dostoevsky twice stayed here in 1878.

Nemirovich Danchenko Ul. (*See* GLINISHCHEVSKY PER., p. 36)

Nikitsky Bulv., 7

— *Gogol Museum* It was in an apartment here that Gogol spent the last few years of his life. The two rooms which became his main home in 1848 have now been turned into a museum. The statue of the writer which stands in the courtyard was moved here in 1952 (see GOGOLIEVSKY BULV., p. 36).

When Gogol returned to Russia in the autumn of 1848, having lived mostly abroad for the previous twelve years, he decided to settle in Moscow. He stayed initially with S. P. Shevyryov, an editor of the conservative journal *Moskvityanin* (the Muscovite), at his house at Degtyarny per., 4, and then went to stay with Pogodin, the friend he used to stay with in Moscow, and with whom he had fallen out in 1840. Although Gogol held his nameday party in Pogodin's garden again in 1849, it was not the festive occasion it had been in 1840. Good relations were not fully restored with Pogodin, and in December 1848 Gogol moved in with a new patron, Count A. P. Tolstoy, whom he had met in Rome in 1843, and who lived in this large detached house in the area of Moscow traditionally inhabited by the aristocracy. It was here that Gogol now stayed on all his subsequent visits to Moscow (as commemorated in the memorial plaque on the outside of the building) and where he died in 1852. By and large, he would spend his winters here, and then leave the city in the summer, going on several occasions to Abramtsevo to visit his friends the Aksakovs, the first visit taking place in 1849.

The house looks slightly different from its appearance in Gogol's day, owing to a later extension to the side of the building looking out on to the street, which was the part Gogol lived in. During his time, the façade of the first floor was still wooden (it was replaced by a stone one in the late 1870s). Gogol occupied two small rooms on the ground floor of this two-storey house, whose Classical construction was typical for moderately well-off landowners of that time. His reception room was to the right of the front door, with a green carpet, two couches along the walls, a stove with a furnace, and a table covered with a green cloth. It was here, surrounded by piles of books, that Gogol would receive his friends, who were mostly writers like himself, or critics, scholars and actors. The house was usually very quiet, and Gogol would spend his mornings working on the second volume of *Dead Souls*, after which he would read over what he had written to himself several times (according to Tolstoy, who used to hear his tenant doing so) in order to hear how the words sounded. Afterwards, he would make corrections to his manuscript and, before lunch was served, would go for walks, stick in hand, along the boulevard.

It was here that Turgenev came in October 1851 with the actor Mikhail Shchepkin to pay a visit. Then at the beginning of his literary career, Turgenev was a great admirer of Gogol and knew his works almost by heart (Gogol also admired Turgenev's writings). The visit clearly left an indelible impression on Turgenev, for the observant writer later described it in detail in his *Literary Reminiscences*:

> We entered and I saw Gogol standing in front of a bureau with a pen in his hand. He was wearing a dark coat, a green velvet waistcoat and brown trousers ... I was astonished by the change that had taken place in him since 1841 ... At that time he was a stocky, thick-set Ukrainian; now he seemed a thin and worn out person whom life had dealt some severe blows. Some kind of hidden pain and anxiety,

a sort of sad restlessness hovered over the always perceptive expression on his face.

Turgenev returned one evening in November to listen to Gogol's reading of *The Government Inspector* to an assortment of friends sitting round a table. It was his last public reading, and took place in the room to the left of the entrance hall. Gogol had been disappointed by the recent performance of his play at the Maly Theatre, which he had attended, and was keen for the actors to come and hear his suggestions for improving their interpretations. He was as offended by their absence as they had been by his criticisms.

Gogol spent the last few years of his life preparing his collected works for publication (permission for which was given by the censor in October 1851), and finishing the second volume of *Dead Souls* (the first volume of which had been published in 1842). While he was in the middle of writing it he had read most of it to his friends, but then in February 1852 he burned the manuscript in the midst of a great spiritual crisis, which was the culmination of years of depression and self-doubt that had been far from assuaged by a pilgrimage to Jerusalem. Returning to Russia had not made Gogol any happier, and his last years were dominated by an increasingly misguided religious paranoia. His state of mind was certainly not improved by living in the gloomy house of Count Tolstoy, an ultra-conservative and pious civil servant who worked for the Holy Synod. It was through him that Gogol became acquainted with Father Matthew, another resident, who only intensified the writer's obsession with the purging of his soul. Following intense fasting, Gogol died on 21 February 1852 at 7.45am, and the house was immediately besieged by crowds wanting to come and pay their last respects to the great writer, whose body was laid out in the reception room.

The Gogol 'memorial rooms' opened in 1972, having previously provided communal housing for several families. Although none of the furniture is original, it dates from the period and evokes well the atmosphere of Gogol's living conditions. Visitors can see the fireplace where the manuscript of *Dead Souls* was burned in the drawing room, as well as a death mask of the writer, and pages filled with tiny writing from his notebooks. Father Matthew's room and the room where Gogol read aloud *The Government Inspector* are now part of the library which occupies the rest of the ground floor of the building.

Closed Tuesday, Wednesday, Saturday and Sunday (schedule subject to alteration during the winter months), and the last working day of the month

Nikolskaya Ul., 17

A hotel in tsarist times, the Slavyansky Bazar, gutted by fire in the early 1990s, is Moscow's oldest restaurant, and best known for being the location of the marathon meeting Stanislavsky had with Nemirovich-Danchenko in 1897 which resulted in the foundation of the Moscow Arts Theatre. The hotel also appears in Chekhov's writings several times; in 'The Lady with a Dog' it is where Anna always stays on her visits to Moscow to see Gurov, in 'Peasants' it is where the waiter Nikolay Chikildeyev falls with his tray of ham and peas, and in *The Seagull* it is where Trigorin invites Nina to an assignation.

Nizhny Tagansky Tupik, 3

— *Vysotsky Museum* A museum dedicated to the poet, singer, actor and composer Vladimir Vysotsky opened in 1989. Vysotsky's fame rests chiefly on his guitar-accompanied songs, which, when his public performances were banned, circulated in hundreds of thousands of copies (*magnitizdat*) throughout the Soviet Union and made him the most popular Russian poet ever. The poignant and often political words of his songs had immediate appeal to a Russian audience. However, none of his work was published in the Soviet Union during his lifetime.

The museum contains autographs, photographs, personal possessions, a plastercast death mask and Vysotsky's left hand. Before they became part of the museum, some of the rooms in the building were used to breed animals for the nearby pet market.

Novaya Basmannaya Ul., 20

This was the site of the home of Pyotr Chaadaev, one of Russia's leading nineteenth-century philosophers. Chaadaev settled in Moscow in 1826 after serving in Alexander I's campaign against Napoleon and living for a spell in Western Europe. He was a friend of both Pushkin and Baratynsky, and is best known for his *Philosophical Letters*, published in 1836, which contained a damning indictment of Russia, and for which he was pronounced insane and placed under house arrest for a year. His Monday and Wednesday soirées were attended by Pushkin and Turgenev among others.

Novaya Basmannaya Ul., 31

Dostoevsky studied in L. I. Chermak's pension, situated here, between 1834 and 1837. Considered one of the best schools of its type, it prepared its pupils for entry to Moscow University. But Dostoevsky's father had other intentions for his son, and in 1838 took him away from the pension and sent him to the Engineering College in St Petersburg, to follow a career for which he was wholly unsuited.

Novaya Pl., 3/4

The auditorium of the Polytechnic Museum has long been a venue for poetry readings. Most major twentieth-century Russian poets, including Blok, Esenin and Mayakovsky, have given readings here, usually to huge audiences. The auditorium was a particularly popular venue in the 1960s, when Yevtushenko, Akhmadulina and Vosnesensky attracted a wide following.

Novinsky Bulv., 11

A. N. Tolstoy lived in an apartment in this Classical mansion from 1912 to 1914.

Novinsky Bulv., 17

This large house, built on the site of a previous residence destroyed in the 1812 fire, was the home of the distinguished Griboedov family, resident in Moscow since the sixteenth century. It is supposedly where the dramatist and diplomat Alexander Griboedov was born in 1795. His parents having separated soon after their marriage, Griboedov was brought up by his mother, who had decided her husband should reside in the countryside and look after the family estates. She spared no expense with her son's education and engaged the composer John Field to teach him and his sister. In 1803, when he was eight years old, he was enrolled in the Blagorodny Pension, the best school in Moscow, which used to be located on the site of the Central Telegraph Office at TVERSKAYA UL., 7 (see p. 127), and was attended by the children of the nobility. Three years later, Griboedov enrolled as a student at Moscow University, where he rapidly became one of the most educated people in Russia, fluent in several languages, and well versed in both Latin and Greek. In 1808 he began studying law, graduating two years later with honours.

After the fall of Smolensk to Napoleon in 1812, Griboedov's family abandoned their house while Griboedov himself joined the Hussars, leaving Moscow for St Petersburg after the war's conclusion, and subsequently travelling to the Caucasus, where he was to pursue a career as a diplomat. He returned to the family home in 1823 while on leave, and spent much time during his visit working on his masterpiece, *Woe from Wit* (he finished the play at the estate of Dmitrovskoe, in Efremovsk province, to the south of Tula). He had no desire to go back to the Caucasus, and asked for his leave to be extended so that he could spend more time with his friends, among whom were the writers Vyazemsky, Küchelbecker and Odoevsky, and the composers and musicians Alyabev, Vielgorsky and Verstovsky. It was Vielgorsky's accidental discovery of Griboedov's play that marked the real beginning of his fame.

Novodevichy Monastyr (*See* LUZHNETSKY PROEZD, 2, p. 51)

Okhotny Ryad, 20

Formerly a building of Moscow University, this was where Afanasy Fet studied in 1838, as a student in the philological faculty. He found the courses he took dull, however, preferring to study ancient and modern literature. Already writing poetry, Fet published his first collection *Lirichesky Panteon* (The Lyrical Pantheon) at the age of nineteen. His lyrics were also published in the *Moskvityanin* (the Muscovite), a leading journal of its time.

Oruzheiny Per.

Meaning literally 'Gun' or 'Armoury' street, Oruzheiny per. runs behind the Sadovoe koltso (Garden Ring). Boris Pasternak was born in 1890 in a house (now demolished) just opposite the late-eighteenth-century Ostermann Mansion, which was then a seminary. He describes his 'two-storeyed stone house' and neighbourhood most clearly in his *Essay in Autobiography*; the area he knew as a child was taken up to the north by the

Tverskaya Yamskaya streets, the coach service streets for Tver, and to the south-east by Tsvetnoy (Flower) boulevard and Trubnaya (Pipe) square where there was a fleamarket. Pasternak calls it a 'sordid' neighbourhood, where you 'rubbed shoulders with beggars and pilgrims'. At the beginning of *Doctor Zhivago* Lara stays at the Hotel Montenegro on Oruzheiny per., when her mother brings her to Moscow from the Urals. The quarter is also evoked in Pasternak's autobiographical novel, *The Last Summer*.

Ostozhenka Ul., 37

Turgenev often stayed here in the 1840s with his mother, who had sold their previous town house at Ermolovoi per. An attractive one-storey house with six columns and pediments, it had a mezzanine on the courtyard side. Recently, the house's original wallpaper, dating back to 1827, was uncovered and is of some fascination to experts as a fine example of neo-Classical wallpaper. The short story 'Mumu', about a fierce landlady's tyrannical treatment of one of her servants, is closely based on Turgenev's mother and the way she ran this household. It was while Turgenev lived here that he became acquainted with Alexander Herzen.

Patriarshie Prudi

The large rectangular pond, forming the centre of a large square called Patriarch's Ponds, is one of Moscow's most famous literary sites and is named after the Patriarch of the Russian Orthodox Church. The pond owes its fame to being the scene of the opening of Bulgakov's *The Master and Margarita*: 'One spring, at the time of an unusually hot sunset, in Moscow at Patriarch's Ponds there appeared two citizens ...' Bulgakov was a frequent visitor to the pond and used to sit on the bench where the novel's opening scene takes place while wooing both his second and his third wives. Early on in his relationship with his third wife, Elena Sergeyevna Shilovskaya, Bulgakov took her to the pond on the night of a full moon in 1929. There, she later recalled, he began to discuss his new novel: 'Just imagine, there are two literary men sitting on the bench, just as we are, and from a neighbouring bench wearing a gray beret over one ear, with a cane under his arm, an amazing gentleman rises and addresses a courteous question to them ...' After describing his novel to her, Bulgakov led her down numerous backstreets to the flat of an old man. The man asked if he could kiss Elena Sergeyevna and then pronounced the word 'witch', to which Bulgakov responded 'how did he guess?' Bulgakov never told Elena Sergeyevna who their host was and would simply put his finger to his lips and say 'shhh' whenever she quizzed him about it.

In *The Master and Margarita* the chain of events is set in motion by the death of Mikhail Berlioz, who slips on some spilled olive oil and falls under the wheels of a tram as he turns into the square from Ermolaevsky per.

Pervaya Tverskaya Yamskaya Ul.

Tverskaya ul., the road which leads to the city of Tver, becomes Pervaya Tverskaya Yamskaya after the Sadovoe koltso or Garden Ring road. When Boris Pasternak was born in nearby ORUZHEINY PER. (see p. 86) in 1890, this was the coach service area for Tver, and it is mentioned rather disparagingly in *Doctor Zhivago*: 'It wasn't only in Moscow or in Russia that there existed these Tverskaya Yamskaya Streets ... the dirt and the heroism, the vice and the slums, and the proclamations and the barricades...'

Petrovka, Ul., 1

Originally built as the palace of Prince Gagarin, this Classical building designed by Kazakov in 1775 used to house the English Club, an elite institution for select nobility, described in *War and Peace*. After the Napoleonic wars, the club moved to TVERSKAYA UL., 21 (see p. 131). Nikolay Karamzin used to come here to read the newspapers and play cards. The building now houses a hospital.

Petrovka, Ul., 5

There is now a square at the spot where the Hotel Frantsiya used to stand. Ivan Turgenev often stayed here in the 1850s and 1860s on his journey between St Petersburg and his estate, Spasskoe Lutovinovo, in the Orel province.

Petrovka, Ul., 19

Although Chekhov was based in Yalta for the last few years of his life, he was so bored there that he came back as often as possible to Moscow, staying at various addresses. In the spring of 1902 he lived at Zvonarsky per., 2, with his wife Olga Knipper for about a month, and then took a flat here on nearby Petrovka in April 1903. It was in this large four-storey grey building, dating from 1899, that the first reading of his last play *The Cherry Orchard* took place. He returned to this apartment in December when the play was already in rehearsal, and left soon after its première on 17 January 1904.

Petrovka, Ul., 28

— *Literary Museum* The State Literary Museum, now housed in a building which before the Revolution was part of an eighteenth-century monastery, was founded in 1934 by the critic

Bonch-Bruevich, who became its first director. Its first exhibition, about Pushkin, was held on the centenary of the poet's death in 1937. The Literary Museum became the first state repository for the archives of Russian writers when it acquired the papers of Chekhov and Esenin, and went on to gather other rich holdings. In 1939 its most important manuscripts found more permanent homes in the newly founded state literary archives of Moscow and Leningrad, which were setup for that purpose, while the Literary Museum continued to organize exhibitions about pre-twentieth-century Russian writers, which give visitors the opportunity to see rare first editions, autographed manuscripts, drawings and portraits. Exhibitions about Soviet writers are held at the Museum's other branch, at TRUB-NIKOVSKY PER., 17 (seep. 123). The building on Petrovka is now an administrative centre, in charge of seven other literary museums in Moscow and the Moscow region.

Closed Mondays and Tuesdays and the last day of the month

Petrovsky Bulv.

The Hermitage was reputed to be the best restaurant in pre-revolutionary Moscow and was located on the south-west corner of Petrovsky bulv. and Neglinnaya ul. It was here that Chekhov first started coughing up blood seriously while having lunch with Suvorin on 24 March 1897, having come up to Moscow from his country house at Melikhovo. It was now impossible to ignore the fact that Chekhov had contracted tuberculosis, and the writer was forced to spend some time recuperating at the Ostroumov Clinic on Bolshaya Pirogovskaya ul.

Petrovsky Park

In Karolina Pavlova's novel *A Double Life* (1849), the heroine's mother rents for the summer one of the 'nice pseudo-gothic –Chinese buildings' which used to stand here, so that her daughter might go riding with eligible young bachelors.

Petrovsky Per., 3

Now an annexe of the Moscow Arts Theatre, in the late 1880s this red neo-Russian-style building housed the Korsh Theatre, where Chekhov's first plays were staged, including his first successful full-length drama *Ivanov* in 1887 and his most popular one-act vaudeville *The Bear* in 1888.

Petrovsky Per., 5, Kv. 36

From 1918 to 1923, Esenin lived in a communal flat here on the third floor of the former Bogoslovsky per. (Ul. Moskvina in Soviet times) with his friend the poet Anatoly Mariengof. In order to be able to write, they often stuck a note on the door with he words: 'The poets Esenin and Mariengof are working. They ask not to be disturbed.'

Plotnikov Per., 10

The basement of this building is considered by some to be the master's basement in Bulgakov's *The Master and Margarita*. Bulgakov often came here to visit his friend and biographer P. S. Popov, and Bulgakov's second wife Lyubov Belozerskaya suggested that the master lived here. But the six-storey house built at the beginning of the century, does not seem to fit the description in the novel and a better candidate for the house is at MANSUROVSKY PER., 9 (see p. 68).

Plotnikov Per., 21, Kv. 7

In 1906, following his father's death, Andrey Bely moved here with his mother. Their new address was not far from where they had previously lived on the ARBAT (see p. 6), at number 55. Bely was twenty-six years old, had graduated from Moscow University in 1903, and had published his first fiction, the experimental *Second Symphony*, the previous year. The publication of his first collection of poetry, *Gold in Azure*, in 1904 established him as a leading writer in the Symbolist movement, then in its ascendancy. From the per-

sonal point of view, Bely's life at this point was rather less successful. When he moved to this address he was in the middle of what
would proved to be an abortive affair with the wife of his friend and
fellow Symbolist Alexander Blok, whom he hoped to rescue from
an unsatisfactory marital situation.

Plyushchikha Ul.

It was at the Church of the Exaltation of the Cross in this quiet
back street that Chekhov married Olga Knipper on 25 May 1901.
Chekhov had told no one about his plans, including his family, and
they were shocked to receive a telegram on the day, by which time
the happy couple were already en route for their honeymoon.
They were married by the priest who had officiated at Chekhov's
father's funeral a year and a half earlier. The church was threatened
with demolition on numerous occasions after the Revolution, and
was turned at one point into a button factory. Only the fact that
Chekhov had got married there saved it for posterity, and it has
now been lovingly restored by its devoted congregation.

Plyushchikha Ul., 11

Tolstoy was nine years old when his father brought his family from
Yasnaya Polyana to live in this one-storey house with a mezzanine he
had rented for them in 1837. It was the first time he had left his family home. The house was always full of guests – for the most part
friends and relatives from Moscow aristocratic society – and Tolstoy
later drew on his memories of life here when he came to write
Childhood, his first piece of published fiction. As a result either of his
exhibitionist tendencies or of an intense need to be accepted, Tolstoy
decided to surprise everyone one day be jumping out of a window on
the mezzanine. He was lucky to escape without injuries, but slept
eighteen hours afterwards. The Tolstoy children were forced to move
out of this house a year and a half after moving in due to straitened
circumstances following the death of their father in 1838. For the
next year or so, they lived on Bolshoi Kakovinsky per., now

Kakovinsky proezd, a small street off what is now Kompozitorskaya ul. in the Arbat area. The poet Vladislav Khodasevich lived in this building in flat 4, in the years leading up to the revolution.

Plyushchikha Ul., 36

In the 1880s, towards the end of his life, the poet Afansy Fet bought a house on the site of number 36 which he had seen advertised in a Moscow journal. 'This house is pinned to my heart, just as a colourful butterfly in pinned on to cork,' wrote Fet in his memoirs. It was during this time that his poetry became fashionable, and four collections of his *Evening Fires* were written and published before his death in November 1892.

Plyushchikha Ul., 53, Kv. 1

This was Andrey Bely's last address, which he shared with his second wife Klavdiya Bugaeva. Bely had experienced great problems in finding somewhere to live after 1917, having spent the preceding years in Germany at Rudolf Steiner's anthroposophical headquarters in Dornach, and then the first two years after the Revolution in Berlin. Bely returned to Russia in 1923, and lived at a variety of locations before moving here in 1932. Before the Revolution he had produced his great novel *Petersburg*; now he dedicated himself to the composition of three novels about Moscow. Artistically, Bely now found himself in an inhospitable and lonely environment where it was difficult to publish. He died here in 1934.

Pogodinskaya Ul., 10–22

A wooden dacha with attractive carvings is all that remains of the estate of M. P. Pogodin, writer, historian, collector of rare books and friend of Nikolay Gogol, who stayed here many times during his visits to Moscow. The main house burned down in 1941

Gogol had got to know Pogodin in St Petersburg. In 1835 he gave a reading of his play *The Marriage* at Pogodin's house, and worked on the first volume of *Dead Souls* during his stay in

1839. Pogodin's spacious one-storey house with a mezzanine in the Deviche Pole (Maiden's Fields) area of Moscow, at that time on the outskirts of the city, was surrounded by a large garden with a pond. Gogol lived and worked upstairs on the mezzanine, in a large room with five windows overlooking the street. He would stay upstairs all morning to write, breaking for lunch and then remaining alone again upstairs all afternoon until seven in the evening, when he would join his host for dinner.

It was during his stay in October 1839 that Gogol saw his dramatic masterpiece *The Government Inspector* performed at the Bolshoi Theatre. Following a trip to St Petersburg, Gogol came back to stay with Pogodin until April 1840, and in March of that year was visited by his mother and sister Olga. On 9 May, the first of many subsequent nameday parties in honour of Gogol took place in Pogodin's garden. The first was undoubtedly the most successful and was attended by his various Moscow friends and acquaintances, including the writers Lermontov, Vyazemsky, Aksakov and Chaadaev. After dinner, Lermontov read to the assembled party his poem 'Mtsyri'. Sergey Aksakov later wrote that 'the dinner was cheerful and noisy. After dinner everyone formed a small circle in the garden. Lermontov recited his poem "Mtsyri", and they all said how beautifully he read.' Gogol was to rank Lermontov's prose higher than his poetry, stating that 'before Lermontov no one had written such correct, beautiful and fragrant prose'.

Following his trip to Rome in 1840, Gogol returned to Moscow at the end of the year to stay with Pogodin again, and now completed the first volume of *Dead Souls*. By this time he was in huge financial debt to his friend, and was forced to sell his writings to Pogodin's conservative journal *Moskvityanin* (the Muscovite), which was a disappointment to Belinsky, who thought he should publish in the radical journal *Otechestvennye zapiski* (National Annals), of which he had become chief critic. In October 1841 copyists started writing out the first volume of

Dead Souls in preparation for publication, which was inevitably hampered by problems with the censor, who objected to Gogol's title by asking how a soul could be dead. The novel was finally passed for publication in April 1842, at which point Gogol decided to go back to Rome. By this time his relations with Pogodin had soured. The former friends lived under the same roof but did their best to avoid each other. The situation had not much improved by 1848, when Gogol returned to Moscow from his travels abroad and once again stayed here for a short while.

The estate has many other literary associations. Alexander Ostrovsky read his first play *A Family Affair* here, which led to Pogodin inviting him to edit *Moskvityanin* in 1850, and other visitors to the house included Pushkin, Tyutchev, Tolstoy and the actor Shchepkin (who was also a good friend of Gogol). The poet Afanasy Fet studied in the pension Pogodin ran here in the grounds of the estate. The house was also fictionalized by Tolstoy as Shcherbatov's house in *War and Peace*; it is where Pierre Bezukhov is taken for interrogation. A statue of Tolstoy stands in the nearby triangular-shaped park, where Pierre sees the French executing a group of Russian prisoners.

Pokrovka, Ul., 22

The so-called Trubetskoy House at number 22 was built between 1766 and 1769 for Count Apraksin. It has an extravagant Baroque façade, decorated with Corinthian columns, mouldings and pediments, and was nicknamed the 'Trubetskoy Chest of Drawers' by Muscovites as it bears a resemblance to a Regency chest of drawers. The Trubetskoys, distant cousins of the Push-kins, lived here from the 1770s. Alexander Pushkin came here as a child for dance lessons and apparently would entertain his classmates by taking them into a corner and reading them his epigrams. Near by, at the bottom of the street, on the same side of the road, is a statue of Chernyshevsky.

Pokrovsky Bulv., 14/5

A room in a communal flat on the seventh floor of this building was the poet Marina Tsvetaeva's last Moscow address. Tsvetaeva and her son Georgy ('Mur') took up residence here in October 1940, following the arrest of her husband Sergey and her daughter Ariadna. The room, formerly inhabited by a polar explorer, was found for Tsvetaeva by Litfond, the pre-revolutionary organization taken over by the Union of Writers to help writers in need, and the poet was able to stay here (eking out a living by selling her luggage, when it eventually arrived from Paris) until July 1941, when Russia entered the Second World War. Tsvetaeva and her son were evacuated to Elabuga, in Tatarstan, where the poet committed suicide a month later. They had left Moscow by boat from the Northern River Port Passenger Terminal in August 1941, where they were seen off by Pasternak.

Povarskaya Ul., 3

In pre-revolutionary times, this used to be the 5th Moscow High School, and it was where Mayakovsky became a pupil in 1906.

Povarskaya Ul., 11

In Soviet times, this building housed the editorial offices of *Sovetsky pisatel* (Soviet Writer), the most important literary publishing house for prose writers and poets.

Povarskaya Ul., 25a

— *Gorky Museum* This imposing Classical mansion, set back from the road, was built by Zhiliardi in 1820, and is the headquarters of the Institute of World Literature. It also houses a museum on the first floor about Maxim Gorky, the hallowed

Soviet writer. The museum opened in 1937, the year after Gorky's death, and by 1977 had been visited by over two million people. Formerly one of the most important literary museums in the country, with over 42,000 items in its archive, its condition is rather moribund now that Gorky can no longer be seen as the exemplary human being and writer of genius he was fêted as for so long.

Its five rooms trace Gorky's career, from his humble beginnings in Nizhny Novgorod to the final years of his life as the Soviet Union's most important literary figure. On display are numerous autographs, handwritten letters from writers such as Chekhov and Bunin, paintings (including a portrait of Gorky by Serov), photographs and personal items such as the writer's desk, brought from his state dacha at Gorky-10, in the western suburbs of Moscow.

A statue of Gorky by the Soviet sculptor Vera Mukhina stands in the front courtyard. It is a copy of the statue which stands in Nizhny Novgorod.

Closed Monday, Tuesday, and the last Friday of the month.

Povarskaya Ul., 26

This street is named Cook street, after the Tsar's cooks who lived here in the seventeenth century. Lermontov and his grandmother stayed at a mansion house (now demolished) at the site of number 26 between 1827 and 1829 before they moved to MALAYA MOLCHANOVKA UL., 2 (see p. 59). This was one of their first Moscow addresses after their arrival from the country estate of Tarkhany, where Lermontov grew up. Lermontov's grandmother had brought him to Moscow to be educated at the Nobility Pension for entrance to Moscow University.

In 1917 and 1918, prior to his emigration to Paris, Ivan Bunin lived in a flat in this building.

Povarskaya Ul., 50

This nineteenth-century mansion houses part of the Central House of Writers, and extends through to the modern building on Bolshaya Nikitskaya ul. It is this part of the House of Writers, usually known by its acronym of Ts-D-L, which housed the plush oak-panelled restaurant much frequented by the luminaries of Soviet literary life. An elite private establishment, like all the other restaurants attached to professional associations, it offered a plentiful supply of good food and alcoholic beverages to its members, regardless of their availability for general purchase in the shops.

Povarskaya Ul., 52

In the nineteenth century this was the grand Moscow home of the writer Count Vladimir Sollogub. In 1856, he was made official court historiographer, and it is known that Tolstoy visited Sollogub while he was writing *War and Peace* in the 1860s (a statue of Tolstoy was erected here in 1956 in front of the house which many have thought was his model for the house of the Rostov family).

In 1920, the mansion became the Palace of Arts, and housed many starving writers, who suddenly found themselves unable to earn any kind of living. One of those writers was Andrey Bely, who lived in a room full of books and manuscripts, and very little furniture except, curiously, a blackboard, on which he would sketch circles and spirals to explain his arcane thought processes. In a letter he never actually sent to his wife Asya, he explained that he survived during the cold winters of the Civil War by using his manuscripts to light the stove. This did little to relieve the cold, however: 'Everywhere heaps of old junk were piled up, and my room resembled the room of a junkman. Amidst the debris and garbage, with the temperature between 6°

and 9°, in winter gloves, with a hat on my head, legs numb to the knees, I would sit in the very dim light of a burned out lamp.'

In the 1930s, the building became the headquarters of the newly formed Union of Writers. Mikhail Bulgakov's civic funeral was held here in 1940.

Prechistenka Ul., 11

— *Tolstoy Museum* The Tolstoy State Museum on the former Kropotkinskaya ul. was founded the year after the writer's death in 1911 by the Tolstoy Society with the help of Bunin, Gorky, Bryusov and other literary figures, and is one of the oldest such institutions in Russia. It is housed in the yellow Classical building (1817) which was the former Lopukhin mansion in pre-revolutionary times, and opened in 1920. The building has otherwise no connection with Tolstoy.

There are nine rooms in the museum, the first of which contains famous portraits of Tolstoy by Repin, Gué, Pasternak and Nesterov and the ninety-volume jubilee edition of his collected works, a publishing project which spanned thirty years. The remaining rooms follow a chronological plan. The second room, for example, explores Tolstoy's family background and childhood, and includes his first literary compositions among the exhibits, while the third documents his tour of duty in the Crimea, his travels abroad and educational activities in the second half of the 1850s. The museum contains a huge collection of Tolstoy's manuscripts, first editions and photographs, a selection of which are on display in each room, and give an overview of the author's creative process at each stage of his life. One can see in the fourth room, for example, the fifteen successive drafts for the opening of *War and Peace* (each page densely covered with Tolstoy's inimitable scrawl), proofs marked up by both the author and the censor, and a copy of the novel when it was first published as a separate volume. Other rooms are devoted to the composition of *Anna Karenina*, Tolstoy's relationships with other writers and with his many correspondents (he received over 50,000 letters over the course of his lifetime). Among the more curious exhibits here are a model of the room in which Tolstoy died at the stationmaster's house in Astapovo and the list of things he needed which he made on a scrap of paper shortly after leaving Yasnaya Polyana for the last time ('soap, notebook, socks').

Closed Mondays and the last Friday of the month

Prechistenka Ul., 12

— *Pushkin Museum* At number 12 is the Pushkin Memorial Museum, a yellow and white mansion built between 1814 and 1816, by the Russian architect A. G. Grigorevich, a pupil of D. I. Zhiliardi. Pushkin never lived here, but it is possible that he paid visits to its owner, the war veteran A. P. Khrushchev. It has ten halls with more than 4,000 exhibits including portraits of the poet, his friends and acquaintances; his personal belongings; pictures of places he visited; manuscripts and editions of his work.

Closed Mondays and the last Friday of the month. Entrance on Khrushchovsky per.

Prechistenka Ul., 16

It has been claimed that the gates of house number 16 are those described at the beginning of Bulgakov's novel *Heart of a Dog*. Bulgakov attended literary evenings here in the former TSEK-UBU (the Commission for the Improvement in the Living Conditions of Scholars); the house later became the Moscow House of Scholars.

Prechistenka Ul., 20

Formerly the home of the ballerina Balashova, built by the millionaire Ushakov, this opulent mansion became home to Isadora Duncan when she arrived in Moscow in 1921 to teach young working-class children how to dance, and subsequently also to Sergey Esenin, whom she married in 1922. Isadora spoke almost no Russian, and Esenin spoke no English, but he managed, so the story goes, to scrawl 'I love you' in lipstick on the mirror here. The couple lived an extravagant life, fuelled by champagne and late-night parties. When Nikolay Klyuev came to visit one afternoon he was bemused to find Esenin, the son of a Ryazan peasant, in a strange red and black striped outfit, which he assumed was prison uniform, having never encountered pyjamas before.

Prechistenka Ul., 22

Alexander Herzen was held under arrest in the house 'under the watch-tower' in July 1834 before he was exiled to Perm. He was arrested a year after he left Moscow University, where he had mixed in revolutionary student circles.

Prechistenka Ul., 31

An annexe in the courtyard at the back of this building once housed the editorial offices of the Symbolist publishing house Musaget, which was founded in 1910 by Emil Medtner (a close friend of Andrey Bely and brother of the composer). Many writers congregated here. Blok came up from Shakhmatovo towards the end of 1910 to discuss the publication of his three-volume collected works, and other regular visitors included Vyacheslav Ivanov and Andrey Bely (both closely involved with Musaget's activities), as well as poets such as Marina Tsvetaeva.

Prechistenka Ul., 32

In pre-revolutionary times, this building housed the prestigious Polivanov Gymnasium, where numerous Russian writers, including Andrey Bely and Valery Bryusov, received their education. Tolstoy's sons Ilya and Lev were pupils in the 1880s. In Soviet times the building continued to be used as a school.

Prechistenskaya Nab.

Until the middle 1930s, in front of houses 19–21, there were double-sided granite steps as well as a bath-house. This is where Ivan Bezdomny in Bulgakov's *Master and Margarita* is supposed to have taken his swim in the Moscow river after having chased two strangers and a cat through the Moscow streets. Bulgakov used to swim here himself; his friend Lyamina Ushakova recalls how he swam in the black, oily water, washing it off later in the bathroom at her house.

Pushkinskaya Pl.

The statue of Pushkin which stands in the square is a major Moscow landmark. It took some two decades to raise the funding to commission it, and it was the first monument to a literary figure to be put up in a prominent position in Russia. The statue originally stood on Tverskoi bulv. and was moved to its present position of prominence in 1950.

The ceremony of the unveiling of the statue took place in 1880, and was a huge public event lasting three days. After his speech on Pushkin at the Hall of the Nobility at BOLSHAYA DMITROVKA UL., 1 (see p. 13), Dostoevsky laid a large laurel wreath at the foot of the statue. The sculptor, chosen in a competition, was Alexander Mikhailovich Opekushin, the son of a Yaroslavl peasant. His model was chosen for 'the simplicity, ease and calm of its pose'.

Not surprisingly, the Pushkin monument has always been something of a focal point for writers in Moscow, most notably Marina Tsvetaeva, who devotes pages to it in her essay 'My Pushkin'. In her childhood, it was the destination point of one of the two daily walks she took with her sister Asya and their nurse from their home on nearby Trekhprudny per., and the preferred one:

> The Pushkin monument was not the monument to Pushkin (dative case) but simply the Pushkin-Monument, one word containing two equally incomprehensible notions, the one never found without the other, of a monument and of Pushkin. That which is eternal, under the rain and under the snow – oh, how I can see those shoulders loaded down with snow, the African shoulders loaded down and over-whelmed with all the Russian snows! – it stands, shoulders into the sunset sky or into the snowstorm, whether I am coming or going, running away or running up to it, it stands with the eternal hat in hand, is called 'The Pushkin Monument'.

The statue is also described in Bulgakov's *The Master and Margarita*, through the envious eyes of the poet Ryukhin as he travels past it in the back of a lorry:

> Ryukhin lifted his head and saw that he was in the middle of Moscow, that day had dawned, that his lorry had stopped in a traffic-jam at a boulevard intersection and that right near him stood a metal man on a plinth, his head inclined slightly forward, staring blankly down the street. Strange thoughts assailed the poet, who was beginning to feel ill. 'Now there's an example of pure luck ...' Ryukhin stood up on the lorry's platform and raised his fist in an inexplicable urge to attack the harmless cast-iron man. '... everything he did in life, whatever happened to him, it all went his way, everything conspired to make him famous! But what did he achieve? I've never been able to discover ... What about the famous phrase that begins "A

storm of mist …?" What a load of rot! He was lucky, that's all, just lucky!…'

The satirists Ilf and Petrov describe an absurd scene on the square in their short story 'Football Fans' where a crowd of thousands are on their way to the nearby Dinamo Stadium. In the crush, they manage to run over a car. 'We repeat. It wasn't a car that ran over a pedestrian, but the pedestrians that ran over a car.'

Pushkinskaya Ul. (*See* BOLSHAYA DMITROVKA UL., p. 13)

Pyatnitskaya Ul., 12

— *Tolstoy Museum* Tolstoy lived in this unassuming one-storey house in the Zamoskvorechie area of Moscow from 1857 to 1858 with his brothers and sister. The building is now an annexe of the main Tolstoy museum at PRECHISTENKA UL., 11 (see p. 99), and currently contains an exhibition about his wife Sofya. Among the exhibits in its two rooms are portraits of the family (by artists such as Leonid Pasternak), many interesting contemporary photographs, letters, pages from Sofya's famous diaries and a chronicle of her husband's illness in 1902, as well as curiosities such as the visiting cards of various distinguished acquaintances, the manuscript of a poem by Fet, and some of Sofya's drawings.
Closed Mondays and Tuesdays and the last Friday of the month

Rakhmanovsky Per., 4

The critic Vissarion Belinsky lived in a house which used to stand at this address from 1832 to 1834 and also in 1835 and 1837. Downstairs there was a blacksmith, and next to his flat a laundry, so that there was a permanent smell of wet linen and soap in the air. Belinsky had come to Moscow in 1829 from his native town of Chembara, in the Penza region, to attend Moscow University, but was expelled two years later for writing a play which criticized the institution of serfdom. In 1833 he began writing for Nadezhdin's journal *Teleskop* (the Telescope) which was closed down three years later when Pyotr Chaadaev's *Philosophical Letter* was published. Belinsky edited another journal for a while, until it too was shut down, and in 1839 moved to St Petersburg to work as a critic for the distinguished journal *Otechestvennye zapiski* (National Annals).

Red Square (*See* KRASNAYA PL. p. 41)

Revolyutsii, Pl., 1

It was where approximately the Hotel Moskva stands today that the Grand Moscow (Bolshaya Moskovskaya) Hotel used to be situated in pre-revolutionary times. After Chekhov bought his country estate at Melikhovo, he used to stay in this hotel on his visits to Moscow, and always took room number 5. The character of Nikolay Chikildeyev, the waiter in his story 'Peasants' (1897), who is forced to go back to his village after slipping with a tray of ham and peas was inspired by a waiter who used to serve Chekhov in his hotel, and who used to write him letters.

Rozhdestvensky Bulv., 12

This large house, now part of the archive of the State Literary Museum, was the last Moscow residence of the poet Demyan Bedny. A writer of peasant background, Bedny (his name is a pseudonym and means 'poor' in Russian) became a member of the Communist Party in 1912, at the age of twenty-nine. His satirical verse was very popular during the Civil War and afterwards, and much favoured by Lenin and Trotsky.

Rozhdestvensky Bulv., 14

Although significantly altered in the 1870s, earlier in the century this elegant two-storey building with ornate carvings on its façade was the home of Nikolay Pavlov. His German-born wife, the poet Karolina Pavlova, was author of the most important nineteenth-century novel by a woman, *A Double Life*, which is set in Moscow. Following their marriage in 1837, the Pavlovs were hosts to a famous literary salon on Thursday nights, attended by both Westernizers (including Alexander Herzen) and Slavophiles, who would sit until the small hours debating Russia's destiny. Lermontov made an appearance here in 1840 just before he departed on his second period of exile to the Caucasus.

Rozhdestvensky Bulv., 15

The property of eighteenth-century playwright Fonvizin's family lay on the territory now occupied by house number 15. It was a one-floored wooden house, surrounded by gardens. At that time the wall of the 'White town', the old Kremlin walls, stood where the boulevard is now. The street was formerly called Pechatnitskaya ul., as it stood near the printers' suburb. Moscow features heavily in Fonvizin's plays, particularly in his comedy *Nedorosl* (The Adolescent).

Sadovaya Kudrinskaya Ul., 6

— *Chekhov Museum* Between 1886 and 1890, this small pink two-storey house on the Sadovoe koltso (the Garden Ring road) was the home of Anton Chekhov, and is now the location of the principal museum in Moscow dedicated to the memory of the writer. Now an extremely busy thoroughfare with large volumes of traffic, it is difficult to imagine this street in the 1880s, when it was still lined with trees (they were removed by Stalin), and there were neither cars nor buses (the first trams began to run here only at the turn of the century). Electric lighting, which was first installed in Moscow in the Kremlin in 1883, was also some way off. The eight-room house, which Chekhov rented for 650 roubles a year from a Dr Korneyev, was built in 1873. Although the front garden has long since disappeared, the house itself, including its colour (which Chekhov once described in a letter as 'liberal, that is to say, red'), has essentially not changed since then.

Chekhov was twenty-six years old, and had been working as a doctor for two years when he, his parents, sister and younger brother moved into the house on Sadovaya Kudrinskaya; it was the first time they were able to afford to live in a whole house, rather than a flat, and the family lived here far longer than in any other accommodation they rented. It must still have been cramped, however – Chekhov used to refer to the house as a 'chest of drawers'. Patients were received by him in the ground-floor study (the nameplate you can still see on the door today reads 'Dr A. P. Chekhov'). It was at this time that Chekhov was beginning to enjoy some degree of success as a writer of short stories. Having started out as an author of humorous sketches and vignettes of Moscow life, published in various lowbrow comic journals, as a way of supporting his impoverished family, he was now devoting more and more time to literary pursuits. The year 1886 marked his emergence as a more serious writer, as his stories now began to be published in daily newspapers for the first time, and he began to eschew his favourite pseudonym of Chekhonte for his real name, an indication that he was starting to take himself seriously as a writer. By 1888 he had made his debut in *Severny vestnik* (the Northern Messenger), one of Russia's leading literary journals, with the story 'The Steppe', which has traditionally been regarded as the turning point of his career. Other stories written here include 'The Kiss', 'A Dreary Story', 'The Nameday Party' and 'An Attack of Nerves'.

Chekhov also wrote a number of plays while living here, including *Ivanov*, successfully produced at the Korsh Theatre on Bogoslovsky (now PETROVSKY 3, see p. 91) per. in 1887, and the one-act comedy *The Bear*, which also enjoyed a riotous success the following year.

The house was turned into a museum in 1954, when it was restored to look as much like it did in Chekhov's time as possible. The unpretentious decor features typical furniture of the period, and many of Chekhov's personal effects from various periods of his life. Chekhov worked and slept downstairs. His study to the left of the hall was furnished very simply with a desk (kept uncluttered), bookshelves, an oval table and soft chairs. Lighting was provided by a kerosene lamp, although Chekhov preferred to work by candlelight. He would generally work on his writing from nine in the morning until lunchtime and then from evening tea to bedtime (the regularity of his regime caused him to regard himself as a functionary). Patients would be received in the afternoons, but his medical duties decreased over time, as his writing career developed.

The drawing room, on the first floor, was where visitors were received. The actors, musicians, artists and writers who came here included Leskov, the great landscape artist Isaak Levitan, who became a good friend of the family and lived near by on Tverskaya, and Tchaikovsky, whose music Chekhov greatly admired (he dedicated a collection of his stories to the composer, who was so delighted he decided simply to turn up and pay a visit one day). Another frequent visitor was the great Russian Art Nouveau architect Fyodor Shekhtel, also a good friend of the family, who designed the cover of Chekhov's first book, *Motley Tales*, which appeared in 1886. Guests would congregate on the couch, and would sometimes spend lively evenings playing the piano, singing or engaging in amateur dramatics.

Chekhov and his brother had bedrooms downstairs, while

There were a number of rooms in the flat, but it was difficult to heat them at the same time. To keep warm we all huddled together in the smallest room. We covered the walls and floor with carpets to make sure there were no draughts. In the corner there was a stove and fireplace. We lit the stove rarely, but we lit the fire morning, noon and night, using old newspapers, broken boxes, anything we could get hold of.

Sivtsev-Vrazhek Per., 19, Kv. 11

This house was built in 1911 by N. Zherikhov. Marina Tsvetaeva and Sergey Efron, her fiancé, moved here in October of that year and stayed in a 'huge, uncomfortable flat' on the sixth floor with Efron's sisters and Voloshin's mother until March 1912. Tsvetaeva and Efron had just met at Voloshin's dacha in Koktebel that summer and were deeply in love. She was eighteen, he was seventeen.

Tsvetaeva's first collection of poetry had just been published and had been highly praised by Voloshin (although less so by Bryusov). While she lived here, Tsvetaeva wrote poetry for her second book, published in 1912.

Sivtsev-Vrazhek Per., 27

— *Herzen Museum* Alexander Herzen moved into this property with his wife and child in 1843 soon after his return from exile. He was not to stay here for long as he emigrated to Europe in 1847, where he set up an anti-tsarist press. While living here he wrote *Letters on the Study of Nature* and the stories 'Forty Thieves' and 'Doctor Krupov', establishing his reputation as a major political writer.

The exhibition in the museum covers the many stages of Herzen's life, both abroad and in Russia. The house contains many of Herzen's own belongings and reflects the aristocratic milieu in which he lived. Among the guests were other political writers such as Belinsky and Chaadaev.

Herzen had earlier lived on this street at number 25 during his student days and it was here that he was arrested for his activity in revolutionary circles just after he had graduated from Moscow University.

Closed Mondays and last day of the month

Sivtsev-Vrazhek Per., 30

— *Aksakov Museum* Sergey Aksakov and his family lived in this eighteenth-century Classical-style mansion in 1848–9. The house, which was renovated after a fire in 1823, had a ballroom, large dining room and study. The museum here is not, however, dedicated solely to the Aksakovs but calls itself 'An Almanac of Literary Life in the 1840s–1880s'. Of the writers represented in the exhibition apart from Aksakov are Gogol, Turgenev, Goncharov, Dostoevsky, Ostrovsky, Tolstoy and Tyutchev. One of the aims of the display is to show how the literary heroes may have lived and it includes pictures of old estates and household interiors. Part of the exhibition is devoted to the opening of the Pushkin Monument in Moscow in 1880, a literary event of great importance.

Closed Mondays, Tuesdays and the last day of the month

Sivtsev-Vrazhek Per., 34

Tolstoy came to Moscow from Yasnaya Polyana for a relatively lengthy stay in 1850. He first stayed in the Hotel Chevalier, which used to stand at KAMERGERSKY PER., 4 (see p. 40), then rented a flat here in this small one-storey house with five windows looking on to the street. Tolstoy was twenty-two years old. He had left Kazan University in the middle of his course, his agricultural and educational experiments at Yasnaya Polyana had not led anywhere, and he now came to Moscow to play cards, go into high society and find someone to marry. He was also beginning to read a great deal, however, particularly the writings of Sterne and Rousseau, and it was while he was living here that he made his first attempts at writing fiction. The house makes a fictional appearance in *War and Peace*: it is where Nikolay Rostov and his mother and Sonya move after the French invasion of Moscow. Tolstoy stayed here until April 1851, when he set off for the Caucasus with his brother.

Sivtsev-Vrazhek Per., 38

The house which stands on the corner of this street and Plotnikov per. is thought to be the Gromeko House in Pasternak's novel *Doctor Zhivago*.

Smolensky Bulv., 19

In 1862 this became the residence of the writer and critic Prince Vladimir Odoevsky, who was born and grew up in Moscow, but who had spent most of his adult life in St Petersburg, as deputy director of the Public Library. He was also director of the Rumyantsev Museum, which he followed to Moscow when it was transferred there in 1862. An immensely cultured man, who knew Schelling, and was host to Richard Wagner during his visit to Moscow in 1863, Odoevsky held regular soirées on Friday evenings attended by writers including Tolstoy and Turgenev.

Sokolniki

The Sokolniki area, on the north-eastern outskirts of Moscow, has for centuries been a place of recreation for Muscovites, and among the many visitors who have come here during the summer months have been numerous writers, including Gogol, who attended the fête traditionally held here on 1 May in 1842, and a nameday party for one of his friends held here in a marquee in

1849. One of the seventy guests remembered overhearing a conversation which took place at a card table between a group of bilious officials dressed in full military uniform who all regarded Gogol as a dangerous and revolutionary figure, although by this time he was probably as obscurantist as they. One of this party had taken particular exception to Gogol when he had been a municipal governor; during performances of *The Government Inspector*, so he related, everyone sitting in the stalls would turn their heads towards his box after every joke or reference to the government, which irritated him so much that he simply banned the play from further performances.

Chekhov was another writer who came to Sokolniki. In 1885 he wrote a piece for the comic journal *Budilnik* (Alarm Clock) about the ubiquitous drunkenness of Muscovites at the 1 May fête here, and Mayakovsky actually lived in this area for a while in 1924 with the Briks when they lost one of their two rooms in the communal apartment they lived in on Vodopyanny per. (now part of Turgenevskaya pl.). The four-room winter dacha they rented was larger than any other place they had lived in since leaving Petrograd, but the accumulation of furniture (which included, as well as a table and sofa, a grand piano and a billiard table) soon made it rather cramped. Their cook Annushka stayed on at Vodopyanny per., but travelled out each day to prepare their meals. Mayakovsky did not spend very much time here, since he was at that point travelling a great deal (to Paris, Mexico and the United States), and he and the Briks found it too far out to be convenient. In 1926, they moved back into central Moscow, to Gendrikov per. (now MAYAKOVSKOGO PER., see p. 69).

Solyanka, Ul., 12

The main façade of this building, the former Palace of Labour, faces on to the Moscow river. It housed the offices of the newspaper *Gudok* (the Whistle), a journal for railway workers, which is published to this day. Mikhail Bulgakov worked here from 1922 to 1926. Also on the staff were the satirists Ilf and Petrov, who like Bulgakov came to Moscow from Odessa. The two met for the first time while they were working on *Gudok*; acting on the suggestion of Petrov's elder brother Valentin Kataev, they decided to form a writing partnership which lasted for ten years. Together they wrote two highly successful novels, *The Twelve Chairs* (1928) and *The Golden Calf* (1931), as well as many short stories. Their works were found to be 'ideologically pernicious' in their satire of the Soviet regime and were later banned from publication. At number 7a was a hall of residence lived in by the *Gudok* staff, Ilf and the writer Yury Olesha. Their accommodation is described by Bulgakov in the feuilleton *Moscow in the 20s*, which portrayed the horrors of communal living.

Soymonovsky Pr., 5

The satirists Ilf and Petrov lived at this address in the 1920s.

Sparrow Hills (*See* VOROBYOVYE GORY, p. 134)

Spartakovskaya Ul., 3

The Classical building of the former house of Count A. I. Musin-Pushkin on the former Yelokhovskaya ul. was famous in the eighteenth century for its unique library and collection of antiquities. The most valuable item in this collection was the only copy of the epic twelfth-century poem *The Lay of Prince Igor*, which Musin-Pushkin purchased in 1795 from the Archimandrite of the Spas-Yaroslavl Monastery. It was preserved in a single sixteenth-century copy. Nikolay Karamzin was often a guest here and in his *History of the Russian State* describes the manuscript as a unique treasure. The manuscript was destroyed by fire in 1812. Luckily it had already been copied for Catherine the Great's public library in 1795–6.

Spartakovskaya Ul., 15

Near Pushkin's birthplace stands the Church of the Epiphany, *Tserkov Bogoyavleniya v Yelokhove*, also known as the Yelokhovsky Cathedral. Pushkin was christened here on 8 June 1799 in one of the chapels. The church has been rebuilt since Pushkin's day, although the refectory and part of the old belltower remain. A plaque to Pushkin is on the right of the main doors.

Spiridonevsky Per., 12

The thirteen-year-old Mayakovsky moved to Moscow from Kutaisi in July 1906 with his mother and two elder sisters soon after the death of his father. The family rented a small flat on the second floor of this building in the centre of Moscow, and struggled to make ends meet. Renting out rooms to students was one way of making money, and it was through his contacts with the Marxist students who lived in their flat that Mayakovsky came to be arrested for the first time on 29 March 1908. Several spells in prison followed over the next couple of years, which were relatively brief due to Mayakovsky's youth, during which time the family changed addresses several times. They lived for a time in a dacha with a garden on the western outskirts of the city, at Novoe Shosse, 14, then on Dolgorukovskaya ul., 33. Intending to become an artist, in 1911 Mayakovsky enrolled at the Academy of Painting and Sculpture (at MYASNITSKAYA UL., 21, see p. 77). After he met the Futurist David Burlyuk, however, he changed direction. Burlyuk heard him read some of his poetry and pronounced him a genius. Mayakovsky now joined Burlyuk, Kamensky, Kruchonykh and Khlebnikov and became a Futurist. It was at this point that he started to don his famous yellow shirt and to lead an extremely flamboyant lifestyle. His first poetry was published in the notorious 1912 anthology *A Slap in the Face of Public Taste*, which proclaimed that past culture should be thrown overboard from the steamship of modernity.

Spiridonovka, Ul., 2/6

— *A. N. Tolstoy Museum* It was at this address that the historical novelist Alexey Tolstoy spent the last years of his life, from 1941 to 1945. The spacious first-floor apartment overlooking the courtyard which he inhabited with his wife had been divided into communal flats before they moved in. Originally it was part of a building designed as accommodation for the servants at the grand house next door, built by Shekhtel in 1903 for Ryabushinsky (MALAYA NIKITSKAYA UL., 6/2, see p. 61), and now more famous as Gorky's last residence. The interior of the flat was preserved exactly as it was during the author's lifetime by his widow, who in turn bequeathed it to the state in 1982. Following renovation work, the Alexey Tolstoy Memorial Museum opened here in 1987.

There are essentially two rooms to visit here: the author's study and the drawing room. The third room, once the Tolstoys' bedroom, is now used for meetings and concerts. It is immediately apparent to the visitor that Tolstoy liked to live elegantly – his apartment is well appointed, and full of beautiful antiques and comfortable furniture. In contrast to those of his contemporaries who were unable to publish and were forced to eke out a living in squalid conditions, Tolstoy certainly led a charmed existence. But this of course was only fitting for an author awarded the Order of Stalin prize in 1942 (for his novel *Road to Calvary*). As a Deputy of the Supreme Soviet, indeed, Tolstoy was very much part of the literary establishment of his time.

The organization of Tolstoy's study in this flat resembled

that in all his other previous abodes. The writer liked to have four different desks to work at his fiction. First he would stand at the tall bureau by the window, writing out the initial draft of his manuscripts in longhand (with his favourite Parker pen). Then he would transfer to the small desk in front of the door, where he would type up what he had written. The small round table by the fireplace was where, pipe in hand, he would make corrections. The large desk in front of the bureau was where he would write his letters and read newspapers and journals. Tolstoy worked on his novel about Peter the Great while he lived here, and his study is filled with portraits of the tsar, and also with rare books, paintings, ornaments and furniture dating from the eighteenth century. Tolstoy's study was thus also a kind of workshop, in which even the eighteenth-century inkwells had some meaning for his work. If anything, the historical value of all the precious objects in this room outweighed their aesthetic qualities.

After working for five or six hours each day, Tolstoy would retire to the drawing room, whose furnishings are also testament to his refined tastes; a grandfather clock stands in one corner, a cabinet of exquisite porcelain in another. It was in this room, at the oval table beneath the chandelier, that Tolstoy would entertain his many guests in the evening, among them writers such as Fedin, Ehrenburg, Tvardovsky and Chukovsky.

Also on display in the museum are bookcases with editions of Tolstoy's writings, as well as the works of his favourite Russian writers. A statue of the writer is to be found in the square near by.

Closed Mondays and Tuesdays

Spiridonovka, Ul., 6

In January 1904, Blok stayed here with his wife, Lyubov Mendeleeva. The ground-floor flat in the annexe of the two-storey building which used to stand here belonged to his mother's relatives. A statue of the poet marks the spot.

This was Blok's third visit to Moscow. The first had taken place in 1898, just after he had graduated from his gymnasium in St Petersburg, when he made a day trip to the city from his family estate at Shakhmatovo together with a friend. In 1902 he returned for a lengthier stay, during which time he visited the Solovyov graves in Novodevichy Cemetery, the Kremlin, the Tretyakov Gallery and the Pushkin statue on Tverskoi bulv. By 1904 Blok had already begun to make a name for himself as a poet, and was shortly to publish his first collection of verse. Upon arrival from St Petersburg, he went with Lyubov Dmitrievna straight to the Arbat, to the flat of his cousin Sergey Solovyov. It was here that he first met his fellow poet Andrey Bely, who lived in the same building (ARBAT UL., 55, see p. 6), and with whom he had already struck up a close friendship through correspondence. Strangely, they had both decided to write to each other at the same time and their first letters had crossed in the mail. The fact that they were also born in the same year (1880) also seemed to be of mystical significance to them at the time, and suggested their fates were bound together. During his visit, Blok met with other Symbolist writers such as Balmont and Bryusov.

Starokonyushenny Per., 32

A restless man who was always on the move, Ivan Bunin never had a fixed address in Moscow. On one of his early visits he stayed in 'furnished rooms' near the Nikitsky Gates, on another he stayed at the National Hotel, and sometimes he stayed with his elder brother in the small two-storey brick house which used to stand here. Bunin had first visited Moscow in 1889, and started to make regular visits to the city in the 1890s, as he began to acquire a reputation as a writer. His first volume of poetry had been published in 1891, and his first story in a major journal appeared in 1894. In 1895 Bunin first met Tolstoy and Chekhov in Moscow, and over the years got to know Bryusov and Balmont. It was in 1906 in Moscow that Bunin met Vera Muromtseva, who became his lifelong partner, following the failure of his first marriage. It was in Moscow that Bunin wrote many of his best-known works, including the story 'The Gentleman from San Francisco' (1911).

Starosadsky Per., 9

After Dostoevsky's mother died in 1837 and his father in 1839, Dostoevsky's aunt, Alexandra Fyodorovna Kumanina, became the guardian of the family. The wife of a wealthy Moscow merchant, she lived on this street in a house that has now been demolished. The old Moscow grandmother described in *The Gambler* and the old Rogozhin woman in *The Idiot* are both based on Kumanina.

Strastnoy Bulv., 10

In the early nineteenth century, the ground floor of this building used to house Shiryayev's bookshop, often frequented by Lermontov.

Sverdlova Pl. (*See* TEATRALNAYA PL. below)

Teatralnaya Pl., 2

In the middle of the eighteenth century the area which now forms one of the most magnificent Moscow squares was an unclean marshy swamp on the banks of the Neglinnaya river. The original theatre built here, called the Maddox Theatre, after the English entrepreneur who founded it, was burned down in 1805 and replaced in 1821–4 by the present theatre, which forms part of an ensemble of buildings designed by the architect O. I. Bove. Until the Revolution, the Mariinsky Theatre in St Petersburg was Russia's premier showcase for opera and ballet, but the Bolshoi Theatre was always popular with its Moscow audience. Pushkin regularly attended the theatre when he was in the city (when it was called the Petrovsky Theatre). His first visit took place on 12 September 1826, when he came to see a comedy by A. A. Shakhovskoy, and was rapturously greeted by the public. Lermontov also came here often, while studying at the pension for Moscow University, as did Tolstoy and countless other writers in following decades.

The chief association of the Maly Theatre (1821), also in Theatre square, is with Alexander Ostrovsky, who worked here from 1853 to 1886, the year of his death. There is a statue of the great dramatist in the front of the building. It was here that all the great Russian plays were produced in the nineteenth century, including Gogol's *The Government Inspector* and Griboedov's *Woe from Wit*.

Teatralny Pr., 1/4

Across the way from the Bolshoi Theatre is Moscow's grandest hotel, the 400-room Metropol. Built in the Art Nouveau style by the British architect William Walcott at the turn of the century, it features a magnificent mosaic frieze by Mikhail Vrubel. The hotel also rented out office space in pre-revolutionary times. In 1904, the year after it opened, the hotel was home to the editorial office of the important Symbolist journal *Vesy* (the Scales), which was edited by Valery Bryusov, and the first Symbolist publishing house Skorpion (Scorpio). The hotel, along with its rival, the National, continued to be a famous gathering place for members of the literary intelligentsia after the Revolution.

Teatralny Pr., 3

This building on the site of the former Hotel Dussot is where Dostoevsky stayed in June 1866 and 1867. Tolstoy also stayed here, as do his characters Vronsky, Levin and Karenin in *Anna Karenina*.

Trekhprudny Per., 8

It was in a one-storey wooden house with large windows which stood here formerly that Marina Tsvetaeva was born in 1891. The house (which had been the dowry of her father's first wife, and technically belonged to her stepbrother and sister) was quite elegant, although it still lacked electricity when Marina left home in 1911. It had eleven rooms, and stood in a yard surrounded by poplar, acacia and lilac trees. Besides the main house, there was an outbuilding with seven rooms (let to a family who kept a cow, which was driven to Petrovsky Park every morning), a coachhouse, two cellars, a shed, a separate kitchen across the way, a laundry and a well. A wooden boardwalk led from the front gate to the house. Inside the house was quite spacious, with high ceilings and parquet floors.

Tsvetaeva came from an affluent and cultured family. Her father Ivan Tsvetaev was an academic. As well as teaching art history at Moscow University, however, he was curator of the Department of Fine Arts and Classical Antiquities at the Rumyantsev Museum, and he achieved his dream of founding a fine arts museum in Moscow in 1912, when the Alexander III Museum of Fine Arts on Prechistenka (later renamed the Pushkin Museum) was opened by the Tsar in 1912.

Tsvetaeva and her sister had a very strict upbringing, but the grey house and its yard filled with doves was 'magical and adored' because it was linked to her childhood, which she idealized both in her poetry and in the prose pieces she wrote in the 1930s. Like her sister Anastasia, Marina began her education at home, with governesses, and began to attend school only at the age of eleven. She also began her ill-fated musical studies at home, at the insistence of her mother, a talented pianist, who desired for her daughter a career she herself had been unable to pursue. Marina's interests lay in literature, however, and from an early age she loved to shut herself up in her room (in which she had hung a portrait of Napoleon rather than the customary icon, much to the consternation of her father) and immerse herself in books.

Tsvetaeva spent the early years of her adolescence at a boarding school in Germany, after her mother contracted tuberculosis, but returned to this house in 1906 following her mother's death, and attended other schools until 1910. She lived here until the summer of 1911, the year that she met her husband Sergey Efron. The house was pulled down after the Revolution for firewood, and replaced by a six-storey building.

Trubnaya Ul., 23

When Chekhov first came to Moscow from his native Taganrog in 1879 after leaving school, he lived with his family in a cramped and damp basement flat attached to the church which used to stand near by. The house stood at the top of this street near the corner of Sadovaya Sukharevskaya ul. in a very poor area of the city, near what used to be Moscow's red-light district. Chekhov's father had been forced to flee Taganrog in 1876 to escape debtors' prison, and took a series of poorly paid jobs, which left the family in very straitened circumstances. They had already moved twelve times in three years, and Chekhov (who had to share a room with two of his brothers) soon started part-time work as a contributor to various lowbrow comic magazines to supplement the family income. This was in addition, of course, to his main occupation as a student of medicine at Moscow

University. It was at this point that the family moved to a first-floor flat in a building at number 23 on the same street, then known as Grachevka street, best known for the number of criminals who hung out there. The notorious Sobolev alley near by, now Bolshoi Golovin per., where most of Moscow's brothels were located, was later to feature in Chekhov's story 'A Nervous Breakdown' (1888), which describes the reaction of a sensitive young student to the social evil of prostitution. Chekhov's facility for producing comic anecdotes to order meant that his family were able gradually to move to more salubrious quarters.

Trubnikovsky Per., 17

— *Literary Museum (Soviet Literature branch)* Since 1984, this branch of the State Literary Museum has held temporary exhibitions about Russian literature of the Soviet period. Its eleven rooms are housed in the attractive nineteenth-century house of Ilya Ostroukhov, artist and icon collector (Matisse was known to have visited here). Like the museum's pre-twentieth-century branch at PETROVKA UL., 28 (see p. 89), it draws its exhibits from its large archive of manuscripts and literary memorabilia, but in the case of twentieth-century writers these are amplified by photographs, posters and recordings of poets such as Mayakovsky and Esenin reading their works.
Closed Mondays, Tuesdays and the last day of the month. Entrance from the back garden

Tsvetnoi Bulv., 22

The future leader of the Moscow Symbolists, Valery Bryusov, moved to this attractive yellow and white two-storey house at the end of the 1870s with his family when he was a child, and lived here until 1910. Bryusov was taught at home here by his father until he was eleven years old, after which he was sent to a private gymnasium. By the time that he graduated from the famous Polivanov School, where he finished his secondary education, he was already writing poetry. In 1892 Bryusov entered Moscow University, but had already decided he was going to make his name as a writer. This was achieved with the publication in 1894 of a scandalous collection of decadent verse which immediately established his notoriety. Bryusov was visited here by Blok and Bely, and by other writers linked to the Symbolist school.

Tsvetnoi Bulv., 30

This seven-storey modern building is home to the editorial office of *Literaturnaya gazeta* (Literary Gazette), a weekly newspaper with a wide circulation whose journalism focuses on literary news and reportage. An important publication, it was founded in 1929.

Turgenevskaya Pl.

From 1920 to 1924, two low-ceilinged rooms in a communal flat at number 3, Vodopyany per. (which became part of Turgenevskaya pl. in 1972) were the home of Mayakovsky, and Osip and Lili Brik. The flat, number 43, was on the first floor, above a bakery, in what was by now a rather ramshackle building. Lili's room doubled as the sitting room. It was small, with three 'old Moscow windows', and contained a grand piano, on which there was a telephone, and her bed behind a screen. In Osip's room there was a studio couch upholstered in velvet, an old desk and lots of books. Mayakovsky slept in his studio flat near by at LUBYANSKY PROEZD, 3/6 (see p. 50), but spent the rest of his time here.

The flat was always filled with people. The eccentric genius Khlebnikov stayed here for a while in 1921. He arrived in fragile health, having taken a month to travel from Pyatigorsk, and turned up in the middle of winter without an overcoat, according to Mayakovsky. Other people who visited the flat on a regular basis included the various Formalists, Futurists and Constructivists who contributed to the avant-garde journal *Lef*, whose first issue appeared in 1923, under the editorship of Mayakovsky.

Tverskaya Pl., 2/6

On the southern corner of Tverskaya pl. (where the Aragvi Restaurant is now based) is the site of the former Dresden Hotel, which opened in 1840, and was one of the most popular hotels in Moscow, particularly with writers. Although he was not particularly fond of hotels, preferring both at home and abroad to stay with friends, Turgenev often stayed here when visiting Moscow. Ostrovsky also put up here for a while shortly before he died in 1886, and Chekhov did so in October 1900, while his play *The Three Sisters* was being rehearsed at the Moscow Arts Theatre. He stayed again in the hotel in May 1901 when he came to Moscow secretly in order to marry Olga Knipper. The hotel was taken over by the Bolsheviks in 1917.

Tverskaya Ul.

This street was named after Gorky in honour of the writer's return to Russia in 1931, but has now reverted to its pre-revolutionary name. The Master in Bulgakov's *The Master and Margarita* meets Margarita for the first time on this street, and falls in love with her immediately. 'You know the Tverskaya don't you? There must have been a thousand people on it but I swear to you that she saw no one but me.'

Tverskaya Ul., 6

The Poets' Café, opposite the Central Telegraph Office, was the most popular haunt of writers in the years immediately after the Revolution. Based in the premises of the former Café Domino,

Tverskaya ul. (the former Gorky Street) at the turn of the century

it was situated in a cellar like the Stray Dog in St Petersburg, but shared none of that venue's bohemian elegance or sophistication. Divided into two rooms (one for the public and the other for poets), the café was decorated with an empty birdcage and a pair of Kamensky's old black trousers. Its clientele sat at wooden chairs and miniature tables, arranged on a sawdust-strewn floor. The tables were covered with a glass top, lined with orange paper on which poets placed their latest verse for everyone to read. Mayakovsky appeared here several times to earn money. 'We tell the public to go to hell. We share out the money at midnight. That's all. Futurism is in great favour,' he reported in a letter to Lili and Osip Brik in St Petersburg. Evidently being rude to one's audience was also in favour at that time. When Esenin appeared here one night he also told his listeners he had come not to read poetry but to tell them, in the coarsest way imaginable, to go to hell. According to the novelist Ilya Ehrenburg, no one ever talked about poetry here, but everyone possible came to read their verse here. There were a 'billion' poets in Moscow in 1921, according to Tsvetaeva, and a 'new trend' appeared every day. As well as Tsvetaeva, Bryusov, Bely and Pasternak all came to the café during its heyday.

Tverskaya Ul., 7

The site of the Central Telegraph Office at number 7 was occupied in the nineteenth century by a pension for children of the gentry who were preparing for entry to Moscow University. Its only equivalent in Russia was the lycée at Tsarskoe Selo, attended by Alexander Pushkin. Famous writers who studied here include Lermontov, Zhukovsky and Griboedov. Lermontov wrote six of his most famous poems including 'Demon' while studying here. The pupils studied twenty-nine subjects, of which literature played a large part. Every week pupils would gather to discuss the latest publications. Forbidden works by Pushkin and Ryleev were passed around and read. The spirit of the Decembrists permeated the school, and Tsar Nicholas I, worrying about the pupils' liberal attitudes, paid an unexpected visit, appearing in the corridor among a crowd of noisy students; the young Lermontov was aware for the first time of the 'sergeant-major on the throne'. From then on the school was turned into an ordinary gymnasium.

Tverskaya Ul., 8

The prominent author and journalist Ilya Ehrenburg lived at this address from 1947 to 1967 (the year of his death), during which time he completed his best-known novel *The Thaw* (1954).

Tverskaya Ul., 12

A hotel named the Shevaldyshev used to stand here in the nineteenth century. It was where Afanasy Fet stayed on his first visit to Moscow as a fourteen-year-old boy in 1834, and his

and threw away 'tens of thousands of roubles for a light breakfast as if it were a mere copeck'.

Pegasus' Stable survived until 1924, rather longer than the infamous Futurists' Café, at TVERSKAYA, UL., 18 (see p. 130), which was founded by David Burlyuk and Vasily Kamensky in the autumn of 1917, and survived until the following spring.

Tverskaya Ul., 14

— *Nikolay Ostrovsky Museum (the N. A. Ostrovsky Humanitarian Centre 'Overcoming')* The building in which the Soviet novelist Nikolay Ostrovsky (no relation to the dramatist) spent the last years of his life has a distinguished literary pedigree. Built in 1790 by Kazakov, it was one of the few houses in Moscow to survive the 1812 fire, and originally sported a classical portico with six central columns on its façade. In the 1820s it became the home of Princess Zinaida Volkonskaya, whose famous literary salon was frequented by the leading writers of the day, including Pushkin, Baratynsky, Delvig and Odoevsky. In 1898 the house became the property of Russia's most famous grocer, Eliseev, and the interior of the elegant foodstore he opened here has been preserved on the ground floor. The other half of the building was also temporarily occupied at the turn of the century by members of the Moscow Arts Theatre troupe, while their building at KAMERGERSKY PER., 3 (see p. 38), was being finished. It was here that Gorky read his play *The Depths* for the first time.

After the Revolution, the upper part of the building was turned into flats. The three-room flat which Ostrovsky lived in with his wife from 1935 to 1936 opened as a museum in 1940. Ostrovsky had written his best-known work, *How the Steel Was Tempered*, considered to be a masterpiece of Socialist Realism, and reprinted 600 times, between 1932 and 1934. By the time he moved here, he was already blind and bedridden, but continued to write until his death. The austerely furnished bedroom where he was confined by this point, and the dining room, have been preserved as they were during the author's lifetime. The latter room includes part of Ostrovsky's library, and features a portrait of Lenin on the wall. André Gide was among Ostrovsky's many visitors here. The third room in the museum has been divided into two. The first part contains an exhibition about Ostrovsky's life and literary activities. On display are some of his belongings, including his traditional Russian peasant shirt and guitar, as well as photographs, autographs and letters. The other part of the room honours invalids and war veterans who, like Ostrovsky, have overcome severe physical handicaps to pursue successful careers in a number of different spheres. The museum now directs most of its energies to the promotion of such accomplishments, and has renamed itself the N. A. Ostrovsky Humanitarian Centre 'Overcoming' (Preodoleniye).

Tverskaya Ul., 15

In Tsarist times, the Hotel Madrid and Louvre stood on the corner of Tverskaya ul. and Vosnesensky per. This was where Alexander Blok stayed when he came up from St Petersburg in 1916 to read his play *The Rose and the Cross* to Stanislavsky and the company of the Moscow Arts Theatre, who were interested in staging it.

Tverskaya Ul., 18

The Futurists' Café, on the corner of Nastasinsky per., was founded by David Burlyuk and Vasily Kamensky in the autumn of 1917, and survived until the following spring. The walls were painted black and red, and decorated with lines from Mayakovsky's and Khlebnikov's poetry. Mayakovsky's line 'I like watching children die', for example, was intended to shock.

Tverskaya Ul., 21

Now the Museum of the Revolution, this Classical mansion mentioned in *Eugene Onegin*, *Anna Karenina* and *War and Peace* housed the exclusive English Club between 1831 and 1917.

Tverskaya Ul., 25

Many high-ranking official Soviet writers have been given accommodation in this block, including Alexander Fadeev, who lived here from 1946 to 1956.

Tverskoi Bulv., 25

Alexander Herzen, one of the greatest liberal thinkers of his time, was born at this house in 1812, the son of a Russian nobleman named Yakovlev and his common-law German wife. Shortly after Herzen's birth his parents had to flee the house when Napoleon entered Moscow in November 1812.

In the 1920s the building, known as the Herzen House, was set up as a centre for writers and journalists and Osip Mandelstam was given a room here in 1922. The building had different wings which varied in their grandeur. In her first book of memoirs, *Hope against Hope*, Nadezhda Mandelstam talks about the 'aristocratic' wing – a wing which was not given to her or her husband. Osip Mandelstam called it a 'vile mansion' with its view of 'Twelve lighted Judas' windows'. In her second book of memoirs, *Hope Abandoned*, Nadezhda writes how she had never seen her husband so 'preoccupied, sombre and withdrawn'. This was a time when Mandelstam was finding it increasingly difficult to get his work published. They returned here in 1931 and were given far more squalid rooms than before, and they were closely watched by two other inmates of the building. Mandelstam's name as a writer disappeared from the early 1930s right up until the late 1950s. Another writer who lived here was Boris

Pasternak, who was allotted a two-room undecorated flat on the first floor of the side wing (flat 7) in 1932.

In Bulgakov's *The Master and Margarita* the Herzen House is one of the possible prototypes for the literary club Massolit, known in the novel simply as 'Griboedov': 'The old two-storied cream building was situated on the boulevard ring, in the depths of a sickly garden, set off from the sidewalk of the ring by wrought-iron railings.'

The building now houses the Gorky Literary Institute, founded in 1933 by Maxim Gorky as a school for would-be writers, and a statue of Gorky by the sculptor Milberg, erected in 1959, stands outside the house.

Vasilievskaya Ul., 2, Korp. 6, Kv. 59

Varlam Shalamov, author of *Kolyma Tales* and veteran of the concentration camps, lived in a room in a communal flat on the third floor of this building after the house he had lived in previously on Khoroshevskoe Shosse was destroyed in 1972. In 1978, when it became clear that he was unable to look after himself, he was put in a nursing home on Ul. Vilisa Latsisa, 9, in the Tushino area of Moscow, from which he never went out. In 1982, the authorities, nervous about the number of visitors he received, removed him from here and placed him in a home for the mentally ill on Abramtsevsksaya ul., 32, in Medvedkovo, in the northern part of the city. Shalamov died from pneumonia three days afterwards, having been carried out poorly dressed in the cold.

Volkhonka Ul.

Boris Pasternak's family moved to a seven-room flat on this street in 1911, before they emigrated to Berlin. Pasternak and his wife returned here to live in 1923. The family flat had then been divided up to provide communal accommodation, leaving the

Pasternaks with a single room. The building where they lived no longer remains. The flat may well be the one described in his poem 'Waves':

> *I want to be home in the flat*
> *whose space floods me with sadness.*
> *I'll enter, take off my coat, assume*
> *a self in the light from the street.*
> *I'll pass through plaster and lath,*
> *pass through partitions like light,*
> *as image leads to image,*
> *as theme suggests theme.*
> *The task is lifelong, growing*
> *with every day: let us call it*
> *the sedentary life; even so*
> *I feel a pang of regret.*
> *The heart unlocks itself again.*
> *I will hear you, Moscow*
> *crawling, smoking, growing, building,*
> *will hear and put it into words*

Volkhonka Ul., 14/1

Until the middle of the nineteenth century, this imposing collection of buildings was the Golitsyn family's Moscow estate. In 1877, Alexander Ostrovsky, with his second wife and five children, moved into a spacious flat in the wing, which was later turned into the Knyazhy Dvor Hotel. Here they were less cramped than in their previous house at BOLSHOI NIKOLOVO-ROBINSKY PER., 3–9 (see p. 27), and much closer to the centre of town, in particular the Maly Theatre, where Ostrovsky's plays were performed. Among the many visitors received here were Tolstoy, Rimsky-Korsakov and Tchaikovsky. By this time, Ostrovsky had become the leading playwright of his day (he wrote forty-seven plays, twenty-nine of which deal with Moscow life), and in 1886 he was put in charge of the repertoires of the Imperial Theatres in Moscow. He died before taking up residence in the government apartment allotted to him, however, and his last days in Moscow, before leaving for his country estate, were spent in the Hotel Dresden on Tverskaya, where he stayed while making preparations for his family to move.

Volokalamskoe Shosse, 47

This pseudo-Gothic building, with its mass of towers, steep roofs and narrow windows, is one of the possible models for Stravinsky's clinic in Bulgakov's *The Master and Margarita*. The former home of a sugar manufacturer, it became a pre-revolutionary psychiatric hospital, which was nationalized in 1918. Bulgakov was a friend of one of the doctors, E. K. Krasnushkin, who worked there.

Vorobyevye Gory

The Sparrow Hills (in Soviet times known as the Lenin Hills), with their magnificent view over the city, are where, in their youth, Alexander Herzen and his friend N. P. Ogaryov swore an oath to fight for social justice: 'The sun illuminated all of Moscow, and all of Moscow looked on us ... we gave each other our hands and remained together all our lives.' The spot where they took their oath has been marked out.

The closing scenes of Bulgakov's *The Master and Margarita* take place here. Having wreaked havoc all over the city, Woland and his followers leave Moscow from here.

Vorovskogo Ul. (*See* POVARSKAYA UL., p. 96)

Vozdvizhenka, Ul., 16

Formerly the mansion of the wealthy factory owner A. Morozov, after the Revolution this curious Spanish-inspired building (built in 1898) housed the headquarters of the Moscow branch of Proletkult – the Proletarian Culture Organization. Esenin was one of the poets who gave a reading at the Literary Studio set up for young working-class writers, and he also took up residence here for a while with the proletarian poet Mikhail Gerasimov, head of the literary section of Proletkult, who had made himself a home in Morozov's spacious bathroom. The building was later turned into the House of Friendship.

Voznesensky Per., 6

Known in pre-revolutionary times as Bolshoi Chernyshevsky per., this was once one of the most aristocratic regions in Moscow. The eighteenth-century poet Alexander Sumarokov was born in his grandfather's house at this address and spent his childhood here. And it was here that the poet Evgeny Baratynsky lived in the 1820s. An elegant one-storey building painted yellow and white with ornate carvings on its stuccoed exterior, and surrounded by a garden full of trees, it was significantly remodelled before Baratynsky moved in.

When he resigned from the army in 1825, Baratynsky had decided to move permanently to Moscow to be near his ailing mother. His family had moved to Moscow from their estate at Mara in Tambov province back in 1808, but had returned there after the death of Baratynsky's father two years later. Baratynsky had spent little time in the city in the intervening period, and was not excited to be back. He felt very isolated in Moscow, where he did not belong to the literary community and was alienated by the Slavophile and Westernizer dispute which was beginning to divide intellectual life. Although he now had more time to devote to his writing (his first poetry collection was published in 1827), he missed his St Petersburg friends. Writing to his friend Nikolay Putyata in 1826, he complained:

> I am bored in Moscow. New acquaintances are unbearable
> to me. My heart demands friendship, not civilities, and a
> well-bred putting on of airs inspires a heavy feeling in me.
> I look on the people around me with cold irony. I return
> greetings with greetings, and suffer. Often I think of tried
> friends, of the earlier comrades of my life – all are far away!
> And when shall we meet? Moscow is a new exile for me.

Having lived for a while in a flat at Bolshoi Kharitonevsky per.,
3, and then at Stoleshnikov per., 14 (neither of these buildings
still stands), he finally took up residence here, following his
marriage to Anastasia Engelhardt in June 1826, in the house of
his father-in-law. The house had been bought by the Engelhardts
in 1810.

Baratynsky was still in his twenties, but had already lost any
desire to go to parties and balls and lead an active social life. For
the most part he and his wife settled into a life of uneventful
domesticity after their marriage; a friend of the couple reported
that they got up every morning at seven without fail, lunched at
midday and retired at nine. Baratynsky longed for the comrade-
ship of friends like Nikolay Putyata: 'I live quietly, peaceably,
content with my family life, but I admit that Moscow is not to
my liking. Imagine, I have not one comrade, not one person to
whom I might say: Do you remember? – with whom I could
open up. And that is hard. I wait for you as I wait for the rain in
May. Here the atmosphere is dry, and unbelievably dusty.' The
death of Baratynsky's close friend the poet Anton Delvig in 1831
was a great loss to him, as it was to Pushkin, who had visited the
Baratynsky home on several occasions, and had read his *Tales of
Belkin* there in 1830. During the 1830s, Baratynsky began to
spend several months at a time on his family estate at Mara,
where he concerned himself with farming and so had less time
to write, and then in 1836 he retired with his wife to MURANOVO
(see p. 156) outside Moscow, the family estate of his recently
deceased father-in-law General Engelhardt.

The house later belonged to the brother of the poet and philosopher Nikolay Stankevich, whose literary evenings were sometimes attended by Tolstoy when he was in Moscow.

Yelokhovskaya Ul. (*See* SPARTAKOVSKAYA UL., p. 114)

Yuliusa Fuchika, Ul., 11, Kv. 3

When the poet Khlebnikov first moved to Moscow in 1910, he lived here in a small room 'with one window, no sun, and a bed near the floor like a turtle on its iron legs'. His manuscripts were kept under this bed in a pillowcase. Khlebnikov quickly became a leader of the Russian Cubo-Futurists after his poetry was first published in 1908, and he spent most of his evenings at this time with the artist David Burlyuk who lived in rooms in the Romanov building on the corner of Malaya Bronnaya ul. and Tverskoi bulv.

Zhitnaya Ul.

The future playwright Alexander Ostrovsky lived at two addresses on this street in the 1830s. His father, a business lawyer and official with a prosperous private practice, bought two houses and lived in the smaller of the two until 1836, then moved to the other, the dilapidated two-storey wooden building which is now situated behind number 10 on this street. In 1835 Ostrovsky became a pupil at the 1st Moscow High School (Volkhonka ul., 16), which was one of the best educational establishments in the city, and it was from here that he entered (at his father's insistence) the law faculty of Moscow University in 1840, the year that his family moved once again.

Zubovsky Bulv., 25

Vyacheslav Ivanov lived here from 1913 to 1918. His daughter later remembered the view from their apartment on the upper floors as being magnificent, since it was not impeded by any other high buildings: 'a wide and open panorama of the whole city was spread out before us'. Ivanov continued to be actively involved in Russian literary life at this time. While he was here he published his third book of essays and his fourth book of poems, and met with other Moscow-based poets, including Balmont and Tsvetaeva. When the pipes began to burst in the winter of 1918, the Ivanovs were allocated three rooms in a communal apartment on Bolshoi Afanasievsky per., off the Arbat, where they stayed until 1920.

MOSCOW
REGION

Abramtsevo

About fifty miles north-east of Moscow lies the picturesque estate of Abramtsevo. Sold in 1870 to the railway magnate Savva Mamontov, it is best known today for the artists' colony he founded here, which attracted painters such as Repin, Vasnctsov, Vrubel, Polenov, Surikov, Serov and Levitan. The estate enjoys a literary as well as an artistic past. The eighteenth-century wooden house and grounds were acquired in 1843 by the Slavophile writer Sergey Aksakov. The peaceful and rural Abramtsevo was a fitting spot for the great chronicler of the Russian countryside, even though most of his writing relates to his childhood home in Orenburg province. At Abramtsevo Aksakov indulged in his favourite country pursuits such as fishing (in the nearby Vora river) and mushrooming. In the evenings his drawing room filled with family and friends. The prominent Slavophiles Khomyakov and Kireevsky came to stay here, as did the famous actor Mikhail Shchepkin. The authors Tyutchev and Turgenev also made visits here, but perhaps the Aksakovs' most notable house guest was Gogol, who came to stay here several times in the last few years of his life.

Gogol had made friends with the Aksakovs when he first went to Moscow in 1832 and came to stay here for the first time in 1849, settling in a large, airy room on the mezzanine floor of the graceful house built in typical Classical style. His window overlooked the front courtyard and oak grove. When Gogol came back to the house on subsequent occasions (he made three visits in 1851), he stayed in the same room, which has been restored to look as it did in his day.

Gogol enjoyed going on walks and on mushroom-picking expeditions during his stays at Abramtsevo, and he liked to spend his evenings reading Merzlyakov's translations of the classics (Homer was a particular favourite). He was also hard at work on the second volume of *Dead Souls*, and one night surprised his hosts by reading to them in the red drawing room extracts from some of the draft chapters which they had no idea he had already written. Gogol was so delighted with the letter he received from Aksakov after he had returned to Moscow, which contained fulsome praise for the new work, that he immediately ordered a carriage and came straight back to stay for a week.

The interior of the house reflects the differing but also very Russian style of both its owners, combining the simple taste of the writer with the more elaborate wooden decorations produced by Mamontov's circle.

Closed Mondays, Tuesdays and the last Thursday of the month

Arkhangelskoe

Built in 1780 by a French architect for Prince N. A. Golitsyn, Arkhangelskoe is one of the most impressive palaces on the Moscow outskirts, and is situated about seventeen miles west of the Kremlin. Many writers came to stay here in the early nineteenth century, by which time the estate belonged to Prince Yusupov, one of the richest men in Russia.

Yusupov's aim was to create a place 'for joy, and not for profit', and he employed more architects to work on the house after he bought it, turning it into the long ochre-yellow stuccoed building that we see today. Among his literary guests were Pushkin and Vyazemsky, both of whom are portrayed in an 1830 watercolour by de Courteil (in the Pushkin Museum in Moscow), which depicts one of Yusupov's soirées. An alleyway in the park here was later named after Pushkin, who dedicated the poem 'To a Grandee' to Prince Yusupov, and a statue to the writer was erected here in 1899. Alexander Herzen was also a guest at Arkhangelskoe, and has left a description of the colourful figure of Yusupov and his house in his memoir *My Past and Thoughts*:

> Old Yusupov was a sceptic and bon vivant; he had been the friend of Voltaire and Beaumarchais, of Diderot and Casti; and his artistic taste was beyond question. You may convince yourself of this by a single visit to his palace outside Moscow and a glance at his pictures, if his heir has not sold them yet by auction. At eighty this luminary was sitting in splendour, surrounded by beauty in marble and colour, and also in flesh and blood. Pushkin, who dedicated a noble epistle to him, used to converse with Yusupov in his country-house; and Gonzaga, to whom Yusupov dedicated his theatre, used to paint there.

Closed Mondays and Tuesdays

Boblovo

About sixty miles to the north-west of Moscow, east of Klin, lies Boblovo, the former summer estate of the great scientist Dmitry Mendeleev (born in 1834). The chief literary association is with the poet Alexander Blok, whose family spent their summers at the neighbouring estate of Shakhmatovo (see TARAKANOVO, p. 167), not far away to the south-east. Both families moved in the academic circles of St Petersburg, where they returned each autumn (the botanist Andrey Beketov, the poet's maternal grandfather, was from 1876 until 1883 the Rector of St Petersburg University). Blok came over often to Boblovo to take part in the amateur dramatics organized in the nearby barn, and over time he grew increasingly attracted to Mendeleev's daughter Lyubov, who played Ophelia to his Hamlet. Blok would ride over on his horse to visit Lyubov, whom he married, after a protracted courtship, in 1903.

Closed Mondays and Tuesdays

Bolshevo

— *Tsvetaeva Museum* It was in this small suburban town to the north-east of Moscow, near Shchelkovo, that Marina Tsvetaeva lived from 19 June to 11 November when she returned from emigration in 1939 with her son Georgy. Her husband Sergey, an NKVD agent, had returned to Moscow from Paris two years earlier, following a bungled mission. The one-storey wooden dacha with shutters where he settled upon his return to Moscow was a safe house run by the NKVD for Soviet agents forced to flee from the West, and it was where Tsvetaeva joined him on her return. Their daughter Ariadna, who had returned to Russia from Paris in 1937 a few months ahead of Sergey, also lived with them here. Several families lived in the house after Tsvetaeva left. In 1992, on the centenary of her birth, a three-room museum dedicated to the poet was opened in the house, after the previous occupants died. The museum's staff have also produced five Tsvetaeva-related publications so far.

This was not a happy time for Tsvetaeva. In Paris her son had continually wanted to go to Russia but hated it as soon as he arrived, and within a few months both Sergey and Ariadna were arrested here. Conditions became both psychologically and physically impossible (the dacha had no heating, and winter was approaching), and when her appeals to the Union of Writers for help fell on deaf ears, on 10 November Tsvetaeva took Georgy to stay temporarily with her sister-in-law Lilia Efron in Moscow (Merzlyakovsky per.) until other accommodation could be found. Tsvetaeva's position was extremely difficult. She could not earn any kind of living from her poetry, because it was not Socialist Realist in orientation, which meant she was forced to survive on the meagre earnings from the translation work she obtained through Pasternak.

Although many changes have been made to the house since Tsvetaeva lived in it, some of its furniture (government-issue) has been preserved. Tsvetaeva and her family shared the house with another family, the Klepinins, acquaintances from Paris days, and occupied two small rooms. Their decor has been restored as far as is possible. The museum's first room contains several Tsvetaeva autographs, donated by well-wishers, also a bracelet which belonged to her, and the notebook she had in her pocket when she hanged herself in Elabuga. In the room Tsvetaeva worked in, to the left, are a number of original items, including the oak dresser which previously stood in the communal sitting room in the house and a few items of clothing belonging to Tsvetaeva's son and husband.

Address: Ul. Tsvetaevoi, 15. The street on which the dacha is located, first called Ul. Novy Byt, then Ul. Sverdlova, is now named after Tsvetaeva. Bolshevo is a forty-five-minute journey on the suburban railway line from the Yaroslavsky Station in Moscow (Ul. Tsvetaevoi runs parallel with the railway line, and is about fifteen minutes' walk from the station, in the direction of the next station on the line)

Closed Mondays, Thursdays, Fridays, Saturdays

Chernaya Gryaz

Meaning literally 'black mud', this village contains the surviving building of a posthouse often visited by Pushkin, the first on the Moscow–St Petersburg road (it is near the railway station Skhodnya). The posthouse is also described in Radishchev's *A Journey from Petersburg to Moscow.*

Dedovo

During his childhood, Andrey Bely spent many summers with his family at the former estate of his friend Sergey Solovyov's grandmother, A. Kovalenskaya, who happened to be Alexander Blok's great-aunt. Dedovo was about thirty miles from Shakhmatovo, where Blok and his family used to spend their summers, his mother and sister slept upstairs (his father lived near by with his brother Ivan, but came here every day). An exhibition room on the upper floor of the house features contemporary photographs, manuscripts, first editions and other interesting memorabilia.

After the death of his brother Nikolay in 1889, Chekhov became depressed, and the following year left this house in order to travel to the island of Sakhalin, in the far eastern part of Siberia, to conduct a census of the penal colonies there. Upon his return the family moved to MALAYA DMITROVKA UL., 29 (see p. 58).

Closed Mondays and the last day of the month

Sechenovsky Per., 5

In 1919, Mayakovsky, Lili and Osip Brik lived in an apartment at this address (on the former Poluektov per.) together with the artist David Shterenberg and his wife. It was the first time that Mayakovsky officially lived with the Briks, and he mentions the room they all shared with their dog in his poem 'Good':

> *Twelve*
> > *square yards of living space,*
> *Four of us*
> > *in the room –*
> *Lilya,*
> > *Osya,*
> > > *I,*
> *And the dog*
> > > *Shchenik*

Both Mayakovsky and Lili Brik worked at the Russian Telegraph Agency during this time, making propaganda posters, but life was hardly luxurious. Keeping body and soul together during the Civil War posed many challenges, particularly during the winter months, as Lili Brik has described:

and in 1898 Blok came to visit. Bely's family also spent some summers at a dacha at Demyanovo, the estate of Vladimir Taneev (brother of the composer Sergey Taneev), which was just outside Klin, about fifteen miles from Shakhmatovo.

Dunino

— *Prishvin Museum* A few miles south-east of Zvenigorod, on the banks of the Moscow river, is the village of Dunino, where the Soviet prose writer Mikhail Prishvin lived from 1946 to 1953, the year before he died. The wooden house where the writer lived opened as a museum in 1980, and has five rooms. It is surrounded by an old garden tended by his relatives, and by woods. The decor and furnishings of the house have been kept completely as they were when Prishvin was alive.

Regarded by many as the heir to Aksakov in view of the important theme of nature in his writings, Prishvin originally came from a wealthy merchant family from the north of Russia, but settled in the Moscow area in the latter part of his life. Prishvin bought the house, which was built in the late nineteenth century, because of the slightly Finnish aspect of its veranda and the carved deer on the window frames, which reminded him of northern Russia, the setting of his early work. Dunino also reminded him of his mother's estate, Krushchovka, near the town of Lipetsk, which was burned down in 1917. Prishvin found it too painful ever to return, but cherished the few items he kept in his possession, which can be seen here, including a Chinese plate from the family dinner service, a coffee pot and his mother's rug. Also on display here are some 400 books from the author's library, some of his own photographs (this was a late hobby), and the special bed for his beloved hunting dogs: Dzhal, an English setter, who is buried here, and a spaniel called Nora.

Closed Mondays and Tuesdays

Golitsyno

The village of Golitsyno, some twenty-five miles west of Moscow, on the road leading west towards Mozhaisk, was in tsarist times the property of the aristocratic Golitsyn family, whose house, Bolshie Vyazyomy, situated a mile away, is now a museum. During the summer of 1849, Gogol went there with his friend the critic Stepan Shevyryov, an editor of the conservative journal *Moskvityanin* (the Muscovite), who had a dacha on the estate that year.

Golitsyno was where Marina Tsvetaeva moved from Bolshevo with her son at the end of 1939, the year she returned to Russia from emigration. The Union of Writers had a retreat (Dom Otdykha) here for its members, which had been the home of the theatre entrepreneur Korsh in pre-revolutionary times. In the context of Soviet literary life at that time, Tsvetaeva was not such an exalted figure, and was not allowed to live with the other dozen or so writers there. She was permitted to take her meals in the main building of the writers' home, but had to live in the village, where she and her son were given one room in a winter dacha (Kommunalny pr., 24), which was lit by kerosene lamps, and had no running water (this had to be fetched from the well). Tsvetaeva lived here for five months, during which time she worked on translations in order to earn enough money to live on. It was a meagre existence (contemporaries remember her looking thin and exhausted), and when she was asked to pay double for her room in the dacha, she was forced to leave and go back to Moscow in search of cheaper accommodation.

Other writers who spent time here in the 1930s include Gaidar, Kuprin and the critic Dmitry Mirsky.

Istra

About thirty miles west of Moscow is the former town of Voskresensk, which in Soviet times was renamed Istra. The New Jerusalem Monastery, built by the Patriarch Tikhon in the seventeenth century, is based on the topography of the Holy Land. During his childhood, Lermontov used to visit the monastery with his grandmother from their nearby estate at Serednikovo. These visits later inspired poems such as 'Confession' and 'Mtsyri'.

Another writer who used to spend time in this area, but rather later in the century, is Chekhov. His brother Ivan had taken a job as a school teacher in Voskresensk in 1880, and over the next few years the impecunious Chekhov family would come and stay here in his spacious apartment in the school building for their summer holidays. In the summer of 1884 Chekhov graduated from medical school, and got some practical experience as a doctor in the local hospital. Like the rest of his family, his favourite leisure occupations here were hunting for mushrooms and fishing.

In 1885, after Ivan lost his job, the family took a dacha at nearby Babkino for the summer, which was a few miles away, with a view of the monastery. Chekhov and his brothers enjoyed themselves so much that the family returned the following two summers. Their return was also due to the fact that they had become great friends with their landlords, the Kiselyov family, who lived in the main house on the estate. It was here that Chekhov got to know the artist Levitan, who was to become a close friend. Chekhov apparently joined in the parties and musical evenings, but also continued to work on his writing during his summers. Some of his best early stories were conceived at Babkino, including 'The Daughter of Albion', 'The Witch' and 'Volodya'.

Kuchino

Approximately nine miles east of Moscow on the suburban railway line, south of the Nizhny Novgorod road, is the village of Kuchino, where Andrey Bely moved from Moscow in 1925 with Klavdiya Vassilieva, who would become his second wife. The couple took two rooms in a dacha belonging to friends on the former estate of the affluent Ryabushinsky family (now Zheleznodorozhnaya ul., 40), which was divided up after the Revolution. They had suffered persecution in Moscow for being anthroposophists, and the dacha at Kuchino offered them a haven of tranquillity for the six years that they lived here.

Kuntsevo

In tsarist times, the village of Kuntsevo, which now lies on the outer ring road of Moscow, just off the main road to Mozhaisk, was an attractive place where many people spent the summer.

Karamzin, Gogol, Tolstoy, Dostoevsky, Turgenev and Nekrasov all came here on occasion. Kuntsevo is mentioned in Turgenev's novel *On the Eve*, and in the last part of Tolstoy's early work, the trilogy *Childhood, Boyhood, Youth*, when the narrator is taken by his friend Dmitry to stay at his family's summer home there:

> A little to the right, behind the trees and shrubs, we could already see the parti-coloured roofs of the cottages round the country house, some of which reflected the lustrous rays of the sun while others assumed the melancholy character of the other half of the heavens. To the left, lower down, a pond lay deep-blue and still, surrounded by pale-green willows which were darkly mirrored on its opaque and seemingly convex surface. Half-way up the hill beyond the pond stretched a black fallow field, and a straight line of bright green which ran across it disappeared in the distance, losing itself in the threatening leaden horizon.

Kuntsevo continued to be a haunt of writers in the twentieth century (it was also well known because Stalin had a dacha here). In 1913, the twenty-year-old Mayakovsky and his mother and sister rented the top floor of a two-storey wooden dacha here, with a wide, open veranda (2-aya Moskovskaya ul., 5). Mayakovsky had a room with a balcony looking out into the garden (the house still stands but has since been remodelled). His poem 'Vladimir Mayakovsky' was written here. At the time, Mayakovsky was just beginning to make a name for himself as a writer. His first published poetry had appeared the year before in the Futurist anthology *A Slap in the Face of Public Taste*, followed in 1913 by his first collection, *Me*. It was during the summer of 1913 that he wrote his verse-drama *Vladimir Mayakovsky: A Tragedy*, which was a sensation when performed later that year in St Petersburg together with the Futurist opera *Victory over the Sun*.

Another writer who spent time in Kuntsevo is Eduard Bagritsky, who lived here from 1926 to 1931 (Ul. Bagritskogo, 4). Nadezhda Mandelstam, who died in December 1980, lies buried in the Starokuntsevsky Cemetery here, after her wish to be buried near her brother in the Vagankov Cemetery was turned down by the KGB.

Marfino

The name Marfino comes from the estate built in the middle of the eighteenth century for Prince B. Golitsyn on the northern outskirts of Moscow near Ostankino. Special Prison No. 16, housed in the building of a former seminary here, was where Solzhenitsyn was held in 1946, having been arrested the previous year for criticizing Stalin in letters he had written from the front. He spent the next four years working at the prison research institute here, where he was assigned work as a mathematician. Marfino was later fictionalized as the Mavrino *sharashka* (the colloquial term for prison institutes for scientific research) in his novel *The First Circle*.

Melikhovo

— *Chekhov Museum* Approximately fifty miles from the centre of Moscow lies the delightful former estate of Anton Chekhov, who lived here from 1892 to 1899 with his parents, sister and younger brother, plus two dachshunds, Bromide Isaevich and Quinine Markovna. The dachshunds (patronymics courtesy of Chekhov) were the gift of one of Chekhov's first editors, Nikolay Leikin, and replaced the mongooses he had brought back from the Far East. These animals were now resident in Moscow Zoo. The estate passed from one owner to another after Chekhov sold it, and had fallen into complete disrepair again by the beginning of the 1930s. The painstaking work which was begun in 1940 to restore it culminated in the opening of the estate as a national museum in January 1960, the 100th anniversary of Chekhov's birth.

Increasing success as a writer made it possible for the thirty-two-year-old Chekhov to purchase this modest wooden brown and white one-storey house with veranda and adjoining grounds in 1892 for 13,000 roubles, without even seeing the property. It was the first house he had ever purchased, and becoming a landowner – albeit on a small scale – represented the fulfilment of a dream for a man from a former serf family who had all his life lived in rented accommodation.

The house and grounds were in a bad state of disrepair when the Chekhovs moved in, and the family immediately started engaging carpenters and decorators, and planting trees and flowers. The gardens and orchards (including, of course, a cherry orchard) can still be seen today. Apart from a keen interest in fishing, Chekhov's other favourite occupation here was tending the many varieties of trees and flowers he had planted, and he

*Chekhov at home in
Melikhovo in 1897*

was soon proudly describing in great detail to his correspondents
what he had planted, the kind of pond he had made, and the fish
he had put in it. At the same time, he was quite defensive about
his new home with affluent friends like Suvorin. Anticipating
that he would expect something much grander, Chekhov tried
to prepare for Suvorin's visit in 1892 by stressing its small scale:
'You won't like Melikhovo, at least not at first. Everything is in
miniature here: the avenue of limes is small, the pond is the size
of an aquarium, the garden and park are small, the trees are
small, but after a while, when you look round again, the feeling
of smallness disappears.'

Soon after moving in, Chekhov wrote to a friend about how
much he was enjoying being 'lord of the manor': 'There's lot of
room, it's warm, and the doorbell is not in continual operation.'
Despite not living in the centre of Moscow, however, Chekhov
was soon inundated with guests, which made it difficult for him
to work sometimes. It was to gain some peace and quiet that a

little two-room wooden cottage designed by Fyodor Shekhtel (a bed upstairs, a desk downstairs) was built in the middle of the garden in 1894, and it was here that Chekhov wrote his play *The Seagull*. Despite the constant throng of visitors, these were very productive years for Chekhov; he wrote over forty major works here, including the stories 'The Grasshopper', 'Ward Six', 'The Black Monk', 'Anna on the Neck', 'Peasants' and 'The Man in a Case'. Many aspects of Melikhovo life found their reflection in these stories, and also in *The Seagull*.

The main house consists of eight rooms: five bedrooms, plus dining room, sitting room and Chekhov's study (the kitchen is situated in an outhouse). Chekhov always liked to sit at the end of the dining-room table, near the door, so that he could slip away unnoticed and go and work in his study. After the drawing room, his study was the largest room in the house. Careful research has meant that much of the character of the house has been preserved – the same pictures hang on the walls of Chekhov's green study, and the photograph of Tchaikovsky still sits on his desk. The legendary piety of Chekhov's father can be felt in his tiny bedroom with its large icon, and the jollity of evenings spent around the piano or at the dinner table can be well imagined in the homely sitting room with its comfortable chairs, and the tastefully decorated dining room.

Chekhov contributed actively to local life while he was living at Melikhovo, by building three village schools in the vicinity, a fire station, and a surgery in nearby Kryukovo (now a museum with the writer's medical instruments on display), where he offered free medical care, particularly during the cholera epidemic of 1892. Later he took part in the census of the local Melikhovo population. He also brought in a priest from the nearby monastery to take services in the tiny wooden church (built in 1757) on the edge of the village, where his father enjoyed leading the choir. Neglected during Soviet times, the church has been restored in recent years and can be visited.

Although Melikhovo became his main base in the 1890s, and provided him with the stability necessary to concentrate on his writing, Chekhov continued to travel frequently during these years – to Yalta, St Petersburg, Nizhny Novgorod, Taganrog, the Caucasus, Yasnaya Polyana (to visit Tolstoy) and Western Europe. But it was to Moscow that he travelled most often, always taking room number 5 in the Grand Hotel Moscow (the Bolshaya Moskovskaya), which used to stand in Voskresenskaya Square (now Pl. Vosstaniya). It was during one of these trips that Chekhov suffered his first major haemorrhage in 1897, after which he was forced to make a drastic change to his style of living, leading in 1899 to him selling the house at Melikhovo and moving to the more temperate climate of the Crimea, where he built a house in Yalta.

Closed Mondays

Chekhov

— *Post Office Museum* The annexe of the Chekhov Museum is housed in the old post office at the railway station in the former village of Lopasnya, which opened in January 1896, after much lobbying and fund-raising on Chekhov's part. He made sure he bought all his stamps there in order to keep it going once it had opened, and sent hundreds of letters through it. The post office has been restored to its turn-of-the-century condition, with period furniture and equipment.

Address: Ul. Chekhova, 4

Kryukovo

— *Dr Chekhov's Surgery* The simple one-room surgery in the nearby village of Kryukovo, where Chekhov used to treat patients in 1892 and 1893 during the cholera epidemic (he saw over 500 patients in one month), has been restored, and now houses a small museum, featuring medical instruments of that time.

Talezh

One of the schools which Chekhov helped to set up still stands in this village. It was built in 1896.

Meshcherskoe

Otradnoe, the estate of Tolstoy's disciple Vladimir Chertkov, lies approximately thirty miles south of Moscow, to the east of the main road to Tula. Tolstoy came here in June 1910, the year that he died. It was his last visit to the Moscow area.

Molodenovo

In June 1930, feeling he needed to show political commitment, Isaak Babel became secretary of the village soviet here. The village is situated approximately twenty miles west of Moscow, just off the road to Zvenigorod, and has traditionally been a place where horses have been bred. Babel lived here on and off for the next few years, and tried to remain inconspicuous. His accommodation here was a former cowshed which he rented from a local farmer, who at one point offered to sell a cow in order to lend the impecunious writer some money. It stood on the top of a small hill overlooking a tributary of the Moscow river. Babel had just one big room, which was sparsely furnished with a table, stools and two narrow beds, and whose windows looked out on to the vegetable patch. There was a stud farm in the village where Babel took his visitors, for whom a horse would be waiting upon their arrival at the nearby station of Zhavoronki (on the surburban railway line from the Belorussky Station). Not far away, at Gorky-10, was Maxim Gorky's dacha – a much grander white house with columns, which he and his guests would pass on their walks.

Mozhaisk

Boris Pilnyak was born in Mozhaisk, and spent his youth in various towns in Moscow province, and in the middle-Volga area settled by German colonists. The provincial towns of rural Russia feature consistently as backdrops in his work.

Muranovo

— *Tyutchev Museum* The former estate of Muranovo is situated about thirty miles to the north-east of Moscow just off the main road to Sergiev Posad (Zagorsk), and about three miles from the station of Ashukino, on the suburban railway line from the Yaroslavsky Station in Moscow. Muranovo is connected with two writers, Evgeny Baratynsky and Fyodor Tyutchev, and most strongly associated with the latter, although the poet never lived here and supposedly visited the estate only once at the end of his life. Most of his possessions and papers are kept here, however, and Muranovo has thus become the main Tyutchev museum in Russia and something of a centre for Tyutchev study. It was founded in 1920 and has sixteen rooms. Its unspoilt state has made it one of the best-loved of literary museums in Russia.

The house was acquired by the Engelhardt family in the late eighteenth century. In 1826 their daughter, Anastasia Lvovna, married Baratynsky, and in 1836 the couple retired here, having lived previously in Moscow (on Bolshoi Chernyshevsky per.; see VOZNESENSKY PER., 6, p. 135). Baratynsky had tired of literary life in Moscow and his main occupation now became the running of the estate. Soon after moving here, he designed an entirely new main house to accommodate his family as well as the family of his friend Nikolay Putyata, who had also married an Engelhardt daughter, and this was built between 1841 and 1842, according to his plans. Baratynsky has left a poetic memory of Muranovo in his collection *Twilight*, which was published in

1842. (In his poem 'There Is a Beloved Land', for example, he describes Muranovo as a 'happy house'.) Baratynsky was not to appreciate the new house for long, dying two years later in Naples. Putyata committed himself to preserving Baratynsky's memory, however, which started off the house's tradition as something of a literary archive. The house at Muranovo also has an association with Nikolay Gogol, who came to stay here in 1849 on his way back to Moscow from nearby Abramtsevo, where he had been a guest of his friend Sergey Aksakov, whom he brought to meet Putyata, another of his good friends. The room where Gogol stayed hereafter became the 'Gogol room', and on display upstairs in the house is the couch the writer slept on during his visit.

The Tyutchev connection with Muranovo began in 1869 when Putyata's only daughter, Olga Nikolaevna, married Tyutchev's younger son, Ivan. Ivan Tyutchev ran the estate and spent much of his life here, building a wing for his mother's summer visits. When his father died, many of the poet's possessions were brought to Muranovo, and even more after the death of his mother. Ivan became the major guardian of his father's possessions. The Aksakov connection with Muranovo also began in earnest when Sergey Aksakov's son, the prominent Slavophile Ivan Aksakov, married Tyutchev's elder daughter, and became his father-in-law's first biographer. When he died, many of his belongings were transferred here too.

Muranovo was to remain in the possession of the Tyutchev family and was to survive the Bolshevik Revolution unscathed. This may possibly be because Tyutchev was one of Lenin's favourite poets. The house was officially named a museum by government decree and opened in 1920. The Tyutchev family maintained their guardianship of the property until 1980. The museum's collection has portraits and photographs of Tyutchev, autographed manuscripts of his poems, books from his library, personal belongings, furnishings such as the desk from his St

Interior at Muranovo, the Tyutchev family home

Petersburg flat, and his family archive, as well as the collections relating to Baratynsky and Aksakov. The result, thanks to the family's instinct for collection and preservation, is a very clear picture of the history of a house and its inhabitants throughout most of the nineteenth century.

Naro-Fominsk

Stanislavsky spent the summer of 1903 on the former Yakunchikov estate just outside Naro-Fominsk, about thirty miles southwest of Moscow. The company of the Moscow Arts Theatre used to rehearse here, and Chekhov came to stay with Stanislavsky during the summer.

Ostafievo

To the south of Moscow, just north of the town of Podolsk on the road which leads towards Tula and about two miles away from the station Shcherbinka on the local railway, is the large estate which belonged to the aristocratic family of Prince Pyotr Vyazemsky, the distinguished critic, poet and translator. Ostafievo is the estate in the Moscow region most closely associated with Russian literature, and has often been referred to as a kind of Parnassus for that reason. Not only was Pushkin a regular visitor here, but also Küchelbecker, Zhukovsky, Baratynsky, Batyushkov and the Polish poet Mickiewicz. The famous historian Nikolay Karamzin, who married Vyazemsky's sister, lived here for twelve years at the beginning of the nineteenth century, while he was working on his *History of the Russian State*. Many decades later, Gogol came to visit Vyazemsky with his friend Pogodin.

The two-storey estate house with its Corinthian porticoes has been well preserved, having been used in Soviet times as a sanatorium. Part of the old park has also survived, and now contains statues and monuments to the writers who have a connection with the estate. The bas-relief of Karamzin is situated on the lawn in front of the semi-circular window of the study where he used to work.

Closed Mondays, Tuesdays and the last Friday of the month

Peredelkino

The many houses spread out among the woods of Peredelkino, situated twelve miles south-west of Moscow, were built as country accommodation for the writers of Moscow by the Union of Writers – the all-powerful body created by Stalin in the 1930s. With its many Tyrolean-style houses and pine woods, Peredelkino in some respects looks rather more like an alpine resort than a Russian village. Before the writers' colony was built, the land was part of an estate belonging to Dmitri Samarin, Pasternak's friend from his university days. It is said that Samarin was the prototype for Yuri, the hero of *Dr Zhivago*. The houses are arranged along a grid pattern, on lanes named after famous Russian writers.

Most famous Soviet writers have spent time in Peredelkino at various points in their lives, particularly high-ranking 'official' writers, who were invariably allotted the largest dachas. Precisely because it meant he would have to toe the line politically, it was with some reluctance that Isaak Babel took a Union of Writers dacha here in 1938. It was not yet finished when he and his wife moved in, and was completely devoid of furniture. Babel got as far as commissioning a table and chairs from a local carpenter, and putting up some dovecotes in the garden, but no further, as he was arrested the following year. His manuscripts were confiscated, and he was shot two years later by his interrogators at the Lubyanka.

One lane in Peredelkino was always referred to, half in jest, as 'Classics Avenue', in view of the distinguished writers who lived on it. Nikolay Zabolotsky came to live here for a while after the war, and the poet's son talks about it in his biography of his father:

> Along it in the evenings would walk 'classic' writers, and on both sides lay their well-built dachas, with their flourishing families, their maids and their gate-keepers. It all exuded the half-forgotten feeling of well-being from times of peace. It was with obvious pleasure that Z entered into restrained conversations with these well-known writers, behaving politely with them, but somewhat at a distance, avoiding questions about his own past and present.

— *Chukovsky Museum* One of the well-known writers who lived on 'Classics Avenue' was the venerable Korney Chukovsky, who spent much time here in this spacious two-storey house at the end of his lifetime. The house opened as a museum in 1996. Its decor has been preserved as it was during the author's lifetime. Alexander Solzhenitsyn sought refuge here in 1965, living in a ground-floor room of the dacha. While staying with

Chukovsky, who was then in his eighties, Solzhenitsyn learned that the KGB had raided his literary archive:

> I strolled for hours through the dark cloisters of the pine trees in Chukovsky's grounds with a heart empty of hope, vainly trying to comprehend my situation, and more importantly, to discover some higher sense in the disaster that had befallen me ... I had come to grief and I did not understand. I seethed. I rebelled ... I had long ago come to understand the meaning of my arrest, my deathly illness, and many personal misfortunes, but this disaster I could make no sense of. It rendered meaningless everything that had gone before.

It remained his hide-out, a place where he could come and go as he pleased, until his expulsion from Russia in 1974. An old photograph of his room depicts a pitchfork standing at the end of his bed, which he kept to ward off the enemy if they came for him.

Address: Ul. Serafimovicha, 3

— *Pasternak Museum* Peredelkino is most closely associated with Boris Pasternak, whose house opened as a museum in 1990, on the centenary of the writer's birth. He died here in 1960, and is buried in the church's sprawling graveyard. Pasternak and his wife Zinaida Nikolaevna were given accommodation here in 1936. They first moved into a 'large two-storey, badly constructed house, built only three years ago but already collapsing', and then moved to the present building, which was 'half the size', but 'beside the fields, in the sun', and therefore 'better for the vegetable plot'. Pasternak's mistress, Olga Ivinskaya, also lived in Peredelkino and Pasternak spent much of his time with her during his last years. Meanwhile, his wife, who knew of the affair, ran the 'big' house. Boris Pilnyak was their neighbour until his arrest in 1937, and then Konstantin Fedin.

The brown wooden dacha is fifteen minutes' walk from the

*Boris Pasternak at home in
Peredelkino in 1958, the day
he received the Nobel Prize
for Literature*

station. The house has been preserved as it was during Pasternak's life. It is decorated with Pasternak's father's pictures, and, given the absence of books, hardly seems like the home of a writer. Pasternak liked to work in uncluttered spaces, however, and upstairs visitors can see the room where he would stand at his desk writing his *Peredelkino Cycle* of poems and *Dr Zhivago*, completed in 1954. The novel was to bring him international fame but persecution at home. He was awarded the Nobel Prize in 1958, but the two years up to his death here in 1960 were bleak ones. The writer was kept constantly under surveillance by the authorities, by a sinister black limousine outside his dacha, and inside it by a listening device which he would apparently bow to and greet in the morning.

Many writers came to visit Pasternak here. Early on, in the summer of 1937, his friends Osip and Nadezhda Mandelstam came out from Moscow to see him, but Pasternak and his wife refused to let them into the house, out of fear of political repercussions. Nadezhda Mandelstam later remembered Paster-

nak accompanying them back to the station, where they spent a long time talking on the platform, missing train after train.
Address: Ul. Pavlenko, 3
Closed Mondays, Wednesdays, Fridays

Perkhushkovo

Herzen used to come and stay at his uncle A. Yakovlev's house, which still stands here, to the west of Moscow, before Golitsyno, on the road leading to Mozhaisk. It was to this point that Gogol was accompanied by his friends in 1840 before setting off on his trip to Europe.

Pokrovskoe

Herzen used to spend his summers at the former estate of Pokrovskoe-Zasekino, situated to the west of Moscow on the road to Zvenigorod from Golitsyno, and he returned here in 1843–4, following his exile to Novgorod. The wooden estate house still stands, and is mentioned in Herzen's memoir *My Past and Thoughts*.

Pushkino

Now a suburban town approximately fifteen miles north-east of Moscow on the railway line to Sergiev Posad, Muranovo and Abramtsevo (which follows the main road to Yaroslavl), Push-kino was once a picturesque village situated in a rural setting. Its chief literary association is with Mayakovsky, who spent many summers here in the early 1920s with his constant companions Lili and Osip Brik. They took a dacha on the edge of the village surrounded by fields, which has been preserved but moved to another location. Mayakovsky was, like most Russians, a keen mushroom picker, which was just as well given the food short-ages of those years. Lili Brik remembered that mushrooms were their staple diet one year: 'as appetizers, cold slices of marinated mushrooms, then mushroom soup, sometimes with pirozhki made of rye flour with mushroom fillings, and finally the main course, boiled mushrooms'.

Summers here were spent watching the sunset (in a poem Mayakovsky wrote here, he invites the sun to come and have tea with him), and playing with their dog Shchen (Pup), whom they found here, and who accompanied them back to Moscow at the end of the summer. Mayakovsky came back here in 1927 and 1928, and was visited by Shklovsky and Rodchenko.

Rozhdestvenka

Just north of Serpukhov, on the main road to Tula, lie the house and park of the former estate of Count Sollogub, Telyatievo.

Rozhdestvo

Rozhdestvo is a small village to the south-west of Moscow in the Naro-Fominsk district, near Obninsk. In 1965 Solzhenitsyn acquired a plot of land here on which stood a small wooden summer house, with a corrugated-iron roof. This was where he completed *August 1914* and *The Gulag Archipelago*.

> This was the first patch of ground I had ever been able to call my own. I had a hundred yards of stream to myself, and an extraordinary feeling of intimacy with the natural world about me. Almost every year the little house was partly under water for a while, but I always hurried there as soon as the floods began to recede, although the floorboards would still be wet and a tongue of water from the gully crept up to my porch in the evenings ... Day by day the water falls, and now you can take your fork and clear the banks of the rubbish and drift-wood cast up by the river. Or simply sit thoughtlessly sunning yourself on the old work-bench or the oak seat. There are alders growing on my patch, and nearby there is a birch wood, and every

impressions of his first glimpse of the big city after provincial Orel are recorded in one of his short stories: 'I feasted my eyes on the infinite panorama of the white town and on the bright stars of gold cupolas, scattered across the horizon'. But, after arriving at the Shevaldyshev, Fet was surprised how similar Moscow was to his home town: 'I found it strange to see almost the same streets as in a provincial town. The same sentry boxes and policemen, the same lampposts and pavements. The road was as mercilessly bumpy ...'

Fet later came back to the hotel when visiting Moscow from his estate at Stepanovka. He met Tyutchev at the hotel in 1864, and in 1867 met Tolstoy, who was in the midst of writing *War and Peace*.

Tverskaya Ul., 13

In 1919, the café Pegasus' Stable, with decor by the avant-garde artist Georgy Yakulov, was founded here on the corner of Maly Gnezdikovsky per. by Esenin. Until the New Economic Policy era brought an end to the austere conditions of wartime communism, it was a centre of the city's bohemian life, and a kind of headquarters for Esenin and his fellow Imaginists, whose portraits hung on the walls. The café attracted a wide-ranging clientele from Moscow's creative elite of the time, including Bryusov, Meyerhold and a whole host of poets, novelists, composers, theatre directors and painters, who would sit here at the closely packed tables (autographed poems were placed under the glass tops) until the small hours, arguing about art and listening to poetry readings.

The café was not popular with the more politically engaged Muscovites, however, who characterized it as 'a stable of bourgeois spoilt children' frequented by people who did nothing useful for society (such as 'shrill and stupid young ladies, whose tiny hands are kissed in the old style by their poet admirers')

The house of Lermontov's grandmother in Serednikovo where the poet spent his early childhood holidays

spring the weather signs are there to be read: if the alders come into leaf before the birches it will be a wet summer; if the birches are earlier than the alders, a dry one.

Serednikovo

Serednikovo, the former estate of the Stolypins, the family of Lermontov's grandmother, lies approximately twenty-three miles to the north-west of Moscow (the nearest station is Firsanovka, on the suburban line from the Leningrad Station). Now the Mtsyri Sanatorium, it was where Lermontov spent his holidays while studying in Moscow in the years 1829, 1830 and 1831. The nearest village is Ligachovo, populated in Lermontov's day by cabinet-makers.

The main house is an elegant, two-storey, white Classical building, thought to be designed by the eighteenth-century architect I. E. Starov. It has three colonnaded wings around a central courtyard and is surmounted by a small cupola. Wide tree-lined steps lead down to a small lake. A bust of Lermontov, erected outside the house in 1900, depicts him not as the teenage boy that he was at the time of his visits, but as a young mustachioed guards officer.

In 1830, at the age of sixteen, Lermontov became infatuated with Ekaterina Sushkova, who was staying with her aunt at a nearby estate at Bolshakovo. More sophisticated than Lermontov, she treated his passion lightly, and the memory of his unrequited love was to haunt him for many years and informs much of his poetry. Among the poems written at Serednikovo during this time are 'Night', 'Desire' and 'Cemetery', which describes the village cemetery.

Sergiev Posad

In 1830 Lermontov was brought by his grandmother to see the Trinity Cathedral in Sergiev Posad (known as Zagorsk in Soviet times). They were accompanied by Ekaterina Sushkova, an early object of Lermontov's infatuations. During the visit, according to Sushkova's version of events, they witnessed a youth throwing a stone on to a beggar's plate instead of bread. Other accounts maintain it was Sushkova herself who threw the stone, but this small incident in any case made a deep impression on the sixteen-year-old Lermontov, and he was to describe it in his poem 'The Beggar'.

Serpukhov

Count Vladimir Sollogub was born here in 1813 in a house which still stands today. The main house of the family estate at Telyatievo is located to the north of the town. A room in the town museum also commemorates Chekhov, who used to make frequent trips here from his nearby estate at MELIKHOVO (see p. 151).

Spas Ugol

— *Saltykov-Shchedrin Museum* The writer–satirist Mikhail Saltykov-Shchedrin was born in the village of Spas Ugol in 1826, twenty miles to the north east of the town of Taldom in the northernmost part of Moscow province. The manor house was burned down in 1919, but the family cemetery, the village Church of the Transfiguration of the Saviour and the park remain. An exhibition about the writer's childhood is housed in the church.

Address: Ul. Saltykova-Shchedrina, 41

Tarakanovo

— *Blok Museum* Thirty miles to the north-west of Moscow lies the village of Tarakanovo, some ten miles from the nearest town of Solnechnogorsk, which is situated to the south-west. It was in the environs of this village that Shakhmatovo, the much cherished estate of Alexander Blok and his family, used to stand. Blok was first brought here as a six-month-old baby, and he returned almost every year thereafter to spend the summer months. A great deal of his poetry was written here. The estate – a modest one-storey wooden house which came with a small annexe, stable, barn and grounds – had been purchased by Blok's maternal grandfather in 1874. From the nearest railway station at Solnechnogorsk it was necessary to travel the last ten miles along a very bumpy, albeit scenic, track to get to the house. On the other side of the River Lutosnya, at the top of a wooded hill, was Boblovo, the estate of Dmitry Mendeleev, the famous chemist, whose daughter Blok married in 1903 in the eighteenth-century village church in Tarakanovo.

It was perhaps only in Shakhmatovo that Blok found true peace of mind; when he was seventeen he declared that this was the place where he most wanted to live. Among the friends who sometimes came to stay here were Andrey Bely, who visited in 1904 and fell (disastrously) in love with Lyubov. In 1910 Blok lived here from May to October, supervising the construction of an additional floor to the house, where he made himself a study. In view of the fact that the house was burned down in 1921 during the Civil War, it is ironic that Blok referred to the house in 1910 as 'Valhalla'.

The old railway station building at Podsolnechnaya still stands as it was in Blok's day, and the permanent exhibition which opened at the museum of the local school in 1994 (Krasnaya ul., 24) contains items from the estate.

Address: Ul. Naberezhnaya, 11
Closed Mondays

Tyoply Stan

The estate which belonged to the Tyutchev family is situated to the south of Moscow, just beyond the main ring road of the city. It is where the poet spent his early childhood. All that remains of the estate now are the park and its ponds.

Vasilievskoe

To the south-west of Moscow on the road to Mozhaisk was the estate where Alexander Herzen spent his summers as a child, remembered fondly by him in his memoirs *My Past and Thoughts*:

> I have seen few more charming spots than this estate of Vasilievskoe. On one side, where the ground slopes, there is a large village with a church and an old manor-house; on the other side, where there is a hill and a smaller village, was a new house built by my father. From our windows there was a view for many miles: the endless cornfields spread like lakes, ruffled by the breeze; manor-houses and villages with white churches were visible here and there;

forests of varying hues made a semicircular frame for the picture ... I had a tenderness for the old manor-house too, perhaps because it gave me my first taste of the country; I had a passion for the long shady avenue which led up to it, and the neglected garden. The house was falling down, and a slender shapely birch-tree was growing out of a crack in the hall floor ...

Voskresensk

Three miles out of Voskresensk (not to be confused with the town which later became ISTRA, see p. 148) on the Ryazan railway used to lie Spasskoe, the former grand estate of Gogol's friend Alexandra Smirnova-Rosset, whom he visited in June 1851, the year before he died.

The main house, situated on a hill, was built by Rastrelli, and was flanked by two annexes linked by trees and paths lined with flower beds. To the right lay a formal 'French' garden with summer houses and fruit trees, while to the left was an 'English' park with streams, grottoes and bridges. The terrace at the front of the house, dotted with marble statues, led to the lawn and the Moscow river, where one could bathe. Gogol resided in two rooms in one of the wings overlooking the garden, where he would work standing at a small desk. He would get up, according to the reminiscences of his hostess, at five in the morning, go for a walk in the garden until eight, when he would take coffee, then work until ten or eleven. Afternoons were spent taking drives or going for walks in the pine groves with Alexandra Ivanovna, who remembers that Gogol was also fond of bathing in the river, and liked to watch the cattle being driven home. At the time, Gogol was still working on the second volume of *Dead Souls*, and read to his hostess from its first chapter during his visit.

Yaropolets

Yaropolets is situated on the road to Rzhev, some ten miles north of the town of Volokalamsk, which lies to the north-west of Moscow. One of the two estates in this village, Yaropolets Goncharovykh, was inherited by Pushkin's mother-in-law in 1823. The fine Classical mansion is surrounded on the southern edge of the park by a red-brick stuccoed wall. Pushkin visited his mother-in-law here in August 1833, while on his way to Orenburg to look for materials on Pugachov, and he was delighted to find an old library in the house containing some important books that he was allowed to borrow. His mother-in-law treated him with unusual warmth on this occasion, and in a letter to his wife he wrote that his detour to Yaropolets 'was not in vain'. The next-door estate, Yaropolets Chernyshevskykh, had belonged to a relative of Pushkin's, Zakhar Chernyshev, in the 1760s, and had a grand park with many extravagant features such as a Chinese and Turkish house, as well as orangeries with exotic fruit trees. A. N. Muravyov described the house as 'a silvery swan, spreading out its wide wings, rising magnificently from the dense, green lime trees over the lake'.

Zagorsk (*See* SERGIEV POSAD, p. 166)

Zakharovo

— *Pushkin Museum* South-west of Moscow, near Golitsyno, used to lie the former estate of Pushkin's maternal grandmother, M. A. Hannibal. Pushkin came here for the first time in 1805, when he was six years old, and returned each year to spend his summers until 1811. The modest country house, with outbuildings, a garden and birch woods, used to stand on a small hill overlooking a lake and is remembered affectionately by Pushkin in his poem 'To Yudin'. Only a part of the park and the lake now remain.

Pushkin used to go to church at the nearby village of Vyazyomy, a couple of miles away. The Church of the Transfiguration, which still stands today, was built at the end of the sixteenth century when the land belonged to Boris Godunov. Pushkin's younger brother Nikolay, who died when the writer was eight, is buried in the graveyard. The church was part of the estate of Bolshie Vyazyomy, which belonged in Pushkin's time to Prince Boris Golitsyn (son of the Princess Golitsyn who became the prototype for the old countess in Pushkin's 'Queen of Spades'). The large Classical house with its two outbuildings, as well as some of the old lime trees which stood in the surrounding park, still stand, and are now part of the Pushkin Museum founded here.

Closed Mondays and Tuesdays

Zhukovka

The small village of Zhukovka in the western suburbs of Moscow was where Solzhenitsyn sought refuge in 1969, staying in the newly built wing of a dacha belonging to the musician Mstislav Rostropovich, whose next-door neighbours were Sakharov and Shostakovich. In her autobiography Rostropovich's wife Galina Vishnevskaya remembers their guest as he worked on *August 1914*:

> He lived only to write. He would get up at dawn, work until evening, and go to bed at nine or ten. He maintained that schedule for those four years, and lives by it still ... And in a corner of our garden, under the trees, an old man built him a table with birch legs and a bench so that he could work outside when it wasn't raining. Solzhenitsyn worked there from early spring until the cold spells set in. The window of my bedroom looked out on that same corner of the garden, and when I woke up in the morning,

the first thing I would see was Solzhenitsyn pacing off the kilometres like a tiger – walking alongside the fence, back and forth, back and forth. Then he would go to the table quickly and write. After that, he would go back to pacing again for hours. The bonfire he kept going beside his house almost never died out; he stoked it constantly with all the rough drafts and other papers he didn't need. I had never seen such tiny, exquisite handwriting as his, and when I told him that he laughed. 'It's a habit I acquired in camp: to put as much as possible on tiny scraps of paper. They're easier to hide.'

Zvenigorod

In 1884, just after graduating from Moscow University as a doctor, Chekhov was offered a job with the district council here in this small town west of Moscow. Although he decided not to take the job, in July of that year he did agree to replace one of the town's resident doctors for two weeks and spent his time here tending to the local population, carrying out post-mortems and minor operations. The ramshackle little house where he lived, not far from the fourteenth-century cathedral and museum, bears a plaque, and the hundred-year-old lime tree under which he liked to work is now protected.

St Petersburg

Admiralteisky Pr., 12

This former nobles' mansion, which looks out over Senate Square, still has the two marble lions in front of it described in Pushkin's poem 'The Bronze Horseman'. This is where the clerk Evgeny takes refuge from the flood:

> On Peter's square where, built but lately,
> A mansion stood, most rich and stately,
> Beside whose entrance lions two
> Rose lifelike, huge, their paws uplifted,
> Yevgeny who had somehow drifted
> To this fine neighbourhood and who
> Was hatless, with his face the hue
> Of death, immobile sat and quiet
> Astride a marble beast . . .

Akademika Pavlova, Ul., 13

When Nikolay Leikin, editor of the humorous Petersburg journal *Oskolki* (Fragments), brought his most successful author Anton Chekhov to Petersburg in 1886, he put him here in a dacha on the northern side of the city on Aptekarsky Island (so called because of the apothecary garden founded by Peter the Great, which later became the Botanic Gardens). This was the twenty-six-year-old Chekhov's first visit to St Petersburg. He had been writing, under his pseudonym of Antosha Chekhonte, for Leikin's publication for the past three years, and writing to order had been a good training. He was now developing into a serious writer, however, and though he remained on good terms with Leikin he now began to seek outlets which gave more creative freedom. In 1886 he published his first story in a serious daily newspaper, *Novoe vremya* (New Time). Chekhov never liked St Petersburg very much, and his visits to the capital in the future were to be rare.

Alexandra Nevskogo, Pl.

The Classical archway here leads into the Alexander Nevsky Lavra, a monastery founded in the time of Peter the Great. 'Lavra' (laura) is a title bestowed upon a monastery of the highest order, and before the Revolution there were only four in Russia. The graveyards have traditionally been the burial place of prominent figures, from the eighteenth century to the present day, and among the famous musicians, artists and sculptors buried in the Tikhvin Cemetery here are numerous Russian writers who lived in the city. They include Karamzin, Zhukovsky, Krylov and Dostoevsky, whose grave lies to the right of the entrance to the monastery. Dostoevsky's headstone is engraved with the quotation from St John xii:24 which appears at the beginning of *The Brothers Karamazov*: 'Verily, verily, I say unto you, Except a corn of wheat fall unto the ground and die, it abideth alone: but if it die, it bringeth forth much fruit.' The grave is decorated with Dostoevsky's bust. Dostoevsky's funeral, a memorial service of solemn vespers, was held in the Church of the Holy Spirit on 30 January 1881. Anna Dostoevsky recalls the formality of the occasion in her memoirs and, most poignantly, how she was not recognized as Dostoevsky's widow at the door of the church and was nearly sent away.

The Lazarus Cemetery which lies opposite the Tikhvin Cemetery contains the graves of satirist Denis Fonvizin (mentioned in Pushkin's *Eugene Onegin* as 'A friend of freedom') and Pushkin's wife Natalya Goncharova. The founder of Moscow University, Mikhail Lomonosov, is also buried here (the length of the engraving on his headstone – in both Latin and Russian – serves perhaps as proof of the great respect in which he was held during his lifetime).

Alexandrinsky Sad

The gardens outside the Admiralty buildings, known in Soviet times as the Gorky Gardens, contain a group of statues. Among the writers represented are Mikhail Lermontov, Nikolay Gogol and the poet Vasily Zhukovsky.

Angliiskaya Nab.

It is on the Angliiskaya nab., which became known as Nab. Krasnogo Flota in Soviet times, that the government bureaucrat Appollon Appollonovich Ableukhov and his son Nikolay, the central characters in Bely's Symbolist novel *Petersburg*, live in an imposing yellow house. In pre-revolutionary times this was an affluent and fashionable area of the city, in contrast to the Vasilievsky Island opposite (which also features in the novel), a rather less salubrious area, traditionally inhabited by people of lower class. At a later point in the novel, the house of the Ableukhovs appears to be situated on Gagarinskaya nab., before returning finally back here to the English Embankment. This is no authorial flaw, but a deliberate decision on Bely's part to confuse the reader, and emphasize what he, in true Symbolist tradition, believed to be the illusory nature of reality.

Angliiskaya Nab., 4

This magnificent Classical building was the house belonging to Count Laval. It was at a ball held here in February 1840 that Lermontov quarrelled with the son of the French Ambassador, Ernest de Barantes, who challenged him to a duel. Versions differ as to the cause of their quarrel. Some say they fought over Maria Shcherbatova, others claim it was over Teresa von Bach-erach, while there is a third body of opinion convinced the duel was fought over Lermontov's poem about the death of Pushkin, 'The Death of a Poet'. This duel, fought on the outskirts of St

Petersburg – without casualties – foreshadowed a later duel, fought near Pyatigorsk in the Caucasus, in which Lermontov was killed at the age of twenty-seven.

Angliiskaya Nab., 32

In tsarist times, this long two-storey Classical building constructed in the eighteenth century by Quarenghi housed the Ministry of Foreign Affairs, and it was where Griboedov worked from 1815 to 1818.

Bolshaya Konyushennaya Ul., 13

The flat that Turgenev rented in Weber's House from 1858 to 1860 on this street (known in Soviet times as Ul. Zhelyabova) looked out on to the courtyard. It was here that he finished working on his novel *A Nest of the Gentry*, and on its completion it was read aloud in the flat by the writer Annenkov at a reading that lasted two days. Turgenev was unable to give the reading himself as he had lost his voice due to acute laryngitis. Among the literary figures who attended the reading were Nekrasov and Goncharov. Turgenev also wrote his acclaimed novella *First Love* at this address.

Bolshaya Konyushennaya Ul., 14

Turgenev took furnished rooms in this house, situated on the corner of the Nevsky pr., on a trip to Russia in 1877. Now living permanently in Paris, his visits to Russia were becoming less frequent, and were usually made to attend to business matters. Two floors were added to the building in 1910.

Bolshaya Morskaya Ul., 14

This was the playwright Griboedov's last St Petersburg address, where he had a modestly furnished flat on the third floor for

May and June of 1828 before departing again to Persia as Russian minister. He was killed in Tehran the following year during the hostilities following the peace negotiations between Russia and Persia.

Bolshaya Morskaya Ul., 25, Kv. 21

Alexander Herzen, after whom the street was named in Soviet times, lived at this address (on the corner of Gorokhovaya ul.) in 1840–1. This was Herzen's first St Petersburg residence after six years of exile in Perm and Vyatka for participation in revolutionary circles as a student in Moscow. One of Herzen's relations wrote of his living accommodation as follows: 'he is spending 2,500 roubles, 100 for water and almost the same amount to have firewood brought up to the third floor. The rooms are tall and partitioned just as in the best Moscow houses.' Herzen did not stay here long, however. In 1842 a letter he wrote to his father criticizing the St Petersburg police was intercepted and he was exiled to Novgorod.

Bolshaya Morskaya Ul., 45

In the late 1920s, a small room on the third floor of the former mansion of the aristocratic Meshchersky family was home to the 'peasant poet' Nikolay Klyuev, who had grown up in the far north of Russia. Klyuev was in his early forties, and considered by this time an 'older' poet by the young upstarts in the Oberiu group (see FONTANKI NAB. REKI, 21, p. 202) who occasionally visited him here. Apparently, when one of its members, Nikolay Zabolotsky, entered Klyuev's lodgings for the first time, he was 'astonished to see that the room was artfully decorated like a peasant house with plank walls, oaken benches, decorated boxes, an icon-corner, oil lamps and peasant utensils'. This was, after all, an apartment in the middle of the city. Zabolotsky was just as bemused to encounter his 'bearded host, in a hempen shirt, looking like Father Christmas', and did not take to being kissed heartily and immediately addressed, in Klyuev's northern accent, as Mikolka (the peasant version of his name). Klyuev moved to GRANATNY PER. (see page 38) in Moscow in 1931, as pressure mounted on him from the authorities to conform to the new ideological strictures.

Bolshaya Morskaya Ul., 47

— *Nabokov Museum* This splendid three-storey building, on one of the city's most prestigious and elegant streets, was once the town house of the distinguished Nabokov family. As a plaque beneath the first-floor oriel reveals, it was here that the future author and lepidopterist Vladimir Nabokov was born, in 1899, and where he spent his childhood. The house was taken over by the Red Guard after the Revolution in 1917, and the Nabokov family emigrated from Russia two years later, never to return. The first and second floors are now occupied by the offices of a local newspaper and other organizations, but in 1993 a tiny one-room museum was established in the former pantry on the ground floor by the Nabokov Foundation, and visitors may see the rest of what remains of the house's original decor upon request. With the exception of a few details such as the wood-panelled former library, the chandelier at the top of the staircase and the stained-glass windows, few traces of the mansion's sumptuous interior have been preserved, but the house was fortunately never turned into communal flats, and part of its original layout and design still survives. The museum describes the history of the house, and is dedicated to the memory of a major Russian writer never recognized by the Soviet literary establishment. A small section of the author's extensive butterfly collection (donated to the museum by Harvard University) may also be viewed here upon request.

The aristocratic Nabokov (who never in his life went to

Moscow, which he considered provincial) describes his privileged and precocious childhood in his remarkable memoir *Speak,
Memory*, with occasional glimpses of the house where the family
spent their winters, before departing each summer to their
country estate at Vyra, in the village of ROZHDESTVENO (see
p. 323), south of the city. The house, which Nabokov describes
as 'an Italianate construction of Finnish granite', dates back to
the eighteenth century. From its original one-storey state in the
1730s, the house was gradually enlarged and remodelled in
accordance with the fashions of the times, passing through a
succession of owners as it did so. Until the 1870s, the façade was
purely Classical, and included four central columns and a
portico. By the time the house was bought by Nabokov's parents
in 1898, it looked quite different, however, and had acquired
another floor. A third floor was added in 1901 to make room for
the growing family and their retinue. It was with the addition of
this floor that the building acquired its Art Nouveau façade: an
ornate floral frieze runs along the top of the house, and some
delicate ironwork graces the central part of its roof. The Nabokov house was the first Art Nouveau building on this street, and
was handsomely appointed. There was room for three cars in its
spacious garage (only ten houses in St Petersburg had garages as
large as this); it was equipped with both electricity and telephone,
and boasted seven bathrooms.

The main room on the ground floor of the Nabokov house,
to the right of the front door, was the well-preserved wood-
panelled dining room, which visitors pass through to get to the
museum, on the left. At the other end of the dining room, facing
the street, was the small green drawing room with its persistent
Christmas smell of fir, hot wax and tangerines. The walls of this
room, it is interesting to note, are still painted green. Next came
the library, which once housed 10,000 volumes (it was here that
Nabokov's father would fence in the mornings), and a committee
room where he would hold meetings. The young Nabokov

would know when a meeting was about to take place when he came home from school and found the doorman sharpening pencils in his cubbyhole under the marble staircase which leads from the front door. The staircase used to lead to a red-carpeted landing above, 'where an armless Greek woman of marble presided over a malachite bowl for visiting cards'. The latter is no longer there, of course, but the chandelier and the beautiful stained-glass window have survived and are extremely evocative.

Nabokov was born in his mother's dressing room on the first floor of the house, which he describes in *Speak, Memory* as a magic kingdom he would visit with delight:

> My mother did everything to encourage the general sensitiveness I had to visual stimulation ... Sometimes, in our St Petersburg house, from a secret compartment in the wall of her dressing room (and my birth room) she would produce a mass of jewelry for my bedtime amusement. I was very small then, and those flashing tiaras and chokers and rings seemed to me hardly inferior in mystery and enchantment to the illumination in the city during imperial fêtes, when, in the padded stillness of a frosty night, giant monograms, crowns, and other armorial designs, made of colored electric bulbs – sapphire, emerald, ruby – glowed with a kind of charmed constraint above snow-lined cornices on housefronts along residential streets.

Astonishingly, the secret compartment is still intact, and can be inspected. Doors graced with the initial of Nabokov's mother lead to her bedroom. It was from the oriel in this room, with its intricately carved fireplace (the only wooden fireplace to be built in the Art Nouveau style in St Petersburg), that the young Nabokov would watch what was going on down on the street below, 'lips pressed against the thin fabric that veiled the windowpane'. In 1917, at the beginning of the Revolution, it was from here that he saw his 'first dead man'. Also on the first floor used to be his father's study. Nabokov's father, 'jurist, publicist and statesman', became a respected figure in the first Russian Duma (Parliament) in 1906, and was a man with varied interests, reflected in his study's decor, which included 'the *objets d'art* of crystal or veined stone, fashionable in those days; the glinting family photographs; the huge, mellowly illumined Perugino; the small, honey-bright Dutch oils; and, right over the desk, the rose-and-haze portrait of my mother by Bakst'. Nowadays all that remains is the beautiful stove.

The second floor was where the five Nabokov children had their bedrooms, together with that of their nanny:

> In 1908 ... I still shared a nursery with my brother. The bathroom assigned to Mademoiselle was at the end of a Z-shaped corridor some twenty heartbeats' distance from my bed, and between dreading her premature return from the bathroom to her lighted bedroom next to our nursery and envying my brother's regular little wheeze behind the japanned screen separating us, I could never really put my additional time to profit by deftly getting to sleep while a chink in the dark still bespoke a speck of myself in nothingness. At length they would come, those inexorable steps, plodding along the passage, and causing some fragile glass object, which had been secretly sharing my vigil, to vibrate in dismay on its shelf.

By 1911, when Nabokov began to attend the Tenishev School at MOKHOVAYA UL., 33 (see p. 260), he had his own bedroom, where he would be woken at eight in the morning. At this time, according to Nabokov, the outside world was 'still cowled in a brown hyperborean gloom':

> The electric light in the bedroom had a sullen, harsh, jaundiced tinge that made my eyes smart. Leaning my singing ear on my hand and propping my elbow on the pillow, I would force myself to prepare ten pages of unfinished homework. On my bed table, next to a stocky

lamp with two bronze lion heads, stood a small unconventional clock: an upright container of crystal within which black-numbered, ivory-white, pagelike lamels flipped from right to left, each stopping for a minute the way commercial stills did on the old cinema screen...

Closed Mondays

Bolshaya Morskaya Ul., 61

Mikhail Lomonosov owned a stone house on the Moika between 1750 and 1765. This stood between Ul. Bolshaya Morskaya, 61, and Ul. Soyuza Svyazi, 16/18. Here he liked to entertain his friends from Arkhangelsk at a large wooden table on his wide porch. When it was hot he worked in his summer house in the garden, from where he would run down to his cellar to fetch ice-cold beer. There was a workshop in the garden where he made his famous mosaic of *The Battle of Poltava*. He died at this address in 1765.

Bolshaya Moskovskaya Ul., 6, Kv. 4

Chernyshevsky and his wife moved here in 1861, and it was where he was arrested by the tsarist secret police the following year. The flat the couple rented was on the ground floor, with windows looking out both on to the street and on to the yard at the back. Chernyshevsky in preceding years had become more and more involved with social problems; he attacked the terms of the emancipation of the serfs in 1861 and encouraged student disturbances. The journal *Sovremennik* (the Contemporary), to which Chernyshevsky was a leading contributor, led the campaign against what it felt were half-hearted reforms which did not go far enough, and started organizing protests. As a result the tsarist police shut the journal down for eight months in 1862 and arrested Chernyshevsky in July of that year, having bribed one of his servants to send over the contents of his wastepaper basket. Chernyshevsky was imprisoned in the Peter and Paul Fortress, and later exiled to Siberia.

Bolshaya Podyacheskaya, Ul., 12

Turgenev lived at this address from the mid-1840s. During this time he fell in love with the Spanish singer Pauline Viardot, who had appeared for the first time on the Russian stage in October 1843 as Rosina in *The Barber of Seville*. The reason for Turgenev's subsequent journey to Berlin and then to Paris in 1847 was to see Viardot. Although it has not been established whether their relationship was ever anything more than friendship, Turgenev was to spend most of the rest of his life living with her and her husband in an unusual *ménage à trois*.

Bolshaya Raznochinnaya Ul., 4, Kv. 1

Mikhail Zoshchenko was born at this address on the Petrograd Side on 9 August 1895 into a family of impoverished nobility. In a short piece written about his father's funeral, Zoshchenko creates a tiny vignette of his childhood: 'The coffin is carried by artists – father's friends. In front on a small cushion, they carry the medal which father received for his picture "Suvorov's Departure". This picture hangs at the Suvorov museum. It is made out of mosaic. In the left corner of the picture is a small green fir tree. Its lower branch was done by me. It came out crooked, but father was happy with it.'

Bolshaya Zelenina Ul., 17, Kv. 3

Mikhail Zoshchenko lived on this street on the Petrograd Side in 1908, four years after his family had moved to St Petersburg from Poltava in the Ukraine. After pursuing many different careers he decided to become a writer and was to live on this street again with his wife at number 9, kv. 83, in the 1920s.

Bolshoi Nevki, Nab., 20

Alexander Pushkin rented a wooden dacha between May and September 1836 on this small island, known as Kamenny Ostrov or Stone Island. The dacha no longer remains, but would have stood on the banks of the river, where houses 18–20 now stand.

Bolshoi Pr.

Dostoevsky chose this street, 'the endless —oi Prospekt' on the Petrograd Side, as the place of Svidrigailov's suicide in *Crime and Punishment*. Svidrigailov spends his last night in the Arianopol Hotel at the end of the street and shoots himself on the corner of Syezhinskaya ul. in front of the firetower.

'A couple of steps' from Bolshoi pr. was the 'very ramshackle long low wooden house' where the inebriated Ivan Ilyich Pralinsky in Dostoevsky's 'A Nasty Story' goes uninvited to a wedding party and causes a scene of great embarrassment. Before he even enters the party, he commits a *faux pas*:

> He walked boldly through the open gate, disdainfully pushing away with his foot the hoarse shaggy little dog that launched itself with a wheezy bark under his feet, more for form's sake than because it meant business. Planks laid on the snow led to the little enclosed porch projecting like a sentry box into the yard, and he went up the three rickety wooden steps into the tiny entrance passage. Here, although a tallow candle-end or a twist of wick floating in a saucer was burning somewhere in the corner, it did not prevent Ivan Ilyich from putting his left foot, galosh and all, into a dish of galantine which had been put out in the cold to set.

Bolshoi Pr., 37

In 1891 Alexander Blok started to attend the Vvedensky Gymnasium, which was located here on the Petrograd Side where he lived. Founded in 1781, it was one of the city's oldest educational institutions, and the only secondary school in that part of town. It was during his time as a pupil here that Blok started to write poetry. Supposedly he made his first visit to a brothel in a building opposite during this time. Mikhail Zoshchenko, who suffered from despression from an early age, attempted to take his life while studying her between 1903 and 1913.

Botkinskaya Ul., 9

When the poet Akhmatova moved from Tsarskoe Selo to St Petersburg in 1917, she first lived here, with her childhood friend Valeria Sreznevskaya, who had married a professor of the Military–Medical Academy. She moved out a year later, when she married the Assyriologist Vladimir Shileiko. In 1919 they went to live with him in the 'Marble Palace' at MILLIONNAYA UL., 5 (see p. 252).

Brinko Per. (See TAIROV PER. P. 296)

Chaikovskogo Ul., 7, Kv. 12

By 1920, Akhmatova was living in a state of utter poverty with her second husband Vladimir Hileiko, and had also become very ill. In order to help her leave what had become a very destructive relationship, her friend Arthur Lourie found Akhmatove a job working in the library of the Agronomy Institute, and a first-floor apartment at this addres (on the former Sergievskaya ul.). While she was living at this address, Akhmatova was at the height of her fame, but a vibrant literary life could not entirely compensate for the hardship of continuing poverty and hunger, and the deaths in these years of her brother, her great contemporary Alexander Blok, her friend from Paris days, the artist Modigliani, and her first husband Nikolay Gumilyov, who was shot by the Cheka (an earlier incarnations of the KGB). In the autumn of 1921, Akhmatova moved from this address and went to live with Arthur Lourie and

Olga Sudeikina at FONTANKI, NAB. REKI, 18 (see p. 200).

Chaikovskogo Ul., 20

Mikhail Lermontov stayed here with his grandmother after his period of exile in the Caucasus in 1838. The twenty-four-year-old poet was now famous in the capital as the author of the celebrated poem 'The Death of a Poet', which essentially blamed the government for Pushkin's untimely death. The poem had circulated in samizdat (leading the critic Belinsky to declare that 'Pushkin has died not without an heir') before Lermontov was arrested and exiled. Now that he was back, however, he was treated as something of a celebrity, and received constant invitations to society gatherings. During the two years he spent in St Petersburg (1838–40), he worked on *A Hero of Our Time*, the novel for which he is best known.

Chekhova, Ul., 6

It was here, on the former Ertelev per., that the important conservative pre-revolutionary newspaper *Novoe vremya* (New Time) had its editorial offices and printing house from the mid-1880s. The street was renamed after Chekhov in Soviet times in honour of the writer's close association with the newspaper's editor Alexey Suvorin. By publishing his stories from 1886 onwards, Suvorin played an important role in supporting his work. *Novoe vremya* was the first major newspaper to publish Chekhov's fiction, the writing of which he had hitherto not taken at all seriously. Suvorin built himself a four-storey house in the neo-Russian style here in 1889, but moved in only in 1893. Chekhov usually stayed with Suvorin during his visits to Petersburg, and was given his own set of rooms at the top of the building, which became known as 'Chekhov's apartment'.

Chekhova, Ul., 7

When Tolstoy came to St Petersburg in March 1878, he stayed with his mother-in-law Lyubov Aleandrovna Bers, who had a flat in this three-storey house. He had just finished *Anna Karenina*, and had come to St Petersburg to research materials about the Decembrists, whom he was still interested in writing about. This was the first time he had visited the city for seventeen years. During his stay he visited the Peter and Paul Fortress, where the Decembrists had been imprisoned in 1825, and, among other things, attended a lecture by the philosopher Vladimir Solovyov, where he narrowly missed meeting Dostoevsky, which both writers later regretted. He also spent time with the critic Vladimir Stasov, and met with Ivan Kramskoy, who had painted his first portrait in 1873.

When Tolstoy came back to St Petersburg in January 1880 for a short visit, he stayed here again, but by this time had undergone his religious crisis, and his visit was marred by a rancorous disagreement with his cousin Alexandra Alexandrovna Tolstoya, a lady-in-waiting at court. She was shocked by Tolstoy's abandonment of his Russian Orthodox beliefs.

Chernaya Rechka

Chernaya Rechka (Black River) is the name both of the nearby metro station and of the area surrounding it on the Petrograd Side. It was on its banks in 1837 that Pushkin fought his famous duel with D'Anthès, who was allegedly having an affair with his wife. Pushkin knew the area well, as in the summers of 1833 and 1835 he had rented a dacha on the river bank. On the day of the duel, Pushkin arrived with his second, Danzas, just before dusk. They had travelled from the Nevsky pr. in a sleigh, past the Dvortsovaya nab. (Palace embankment), where Pushkin failed to see his wife among the passers-by, past the Peter and Paul Fortress and up Kamenoostrovsky pr., where they turned left at Chernaya Rechka. The two seconds went to choose a spot for the duel. To avoid the strong wind and onlookers they selected an area by a small wood, behind the Commandant's dacha. They trod down a patch in the snow and marked out with coats two barriers at each end. Pushkin and D'Anthès then walked away from each other towards the barriers. Before he reached his barrier, D'Anthès turned and fired at Pushkin, hitting him in the stomach. 'I am wounded,' shouted Pushkin, falling into the deep snow. Danzas gave him another pistol, as the muzzle of his first had filled with snow. He fired at D'Anthès, who fell. Pushkin cheered, convinced he had killed him, but in fact he had only wounded his arm. Pushkin's wound was fatal, and he died two days later. D'Anthès went on to make a distinguished career in France. A red granite obelisk marks the spot of the duel, and a statue of Pushkin by the sculptor Anikushin can be found inside the Chernaya Rechka metro station.

Pushkin was not the only Russian writer to fight a duel here. In 1840 Lermontov fought in a duel near Chernaya Rechka with the son of the French Ambassador, de Barantes. He escaped alive, only to be killed in another duel one year later in Pyatigorsk in the Caucasus (where, ironically, he had been exiled for fighting in the duel with Barantes).

Probably the last duel to be fought here was between Voloshin and Gumilyov in 1909. Voloshin had challenged Gumilyov during a meeting at the Mariinsky Theatre at TEATRAL-NAYA PL., 1 (see p. 300), and had insisted on replicating the Pushkin–D'Anthès duel exactly, right down to the antique pistols. Both missed, however.

Dekabristov, Ul., 5

When Tolstoy returned to St Petersburg in January 1856, after travelling to Orel to visit his dying brother Dmitry, he took a flat here on the former Ofitserskaya ul. It was during his five months in the capital in 1856 that he started to feel uncomfortable among the new literary acquaintances he had made the previous year, as the famous photograph of writers associated with *Sovremennik* (the Contemporary) taken that year shows. His passion for telling the truth, coupled with an individualism that encouraged contradiction almost for the sake of it, and an inbuilt aristocratic snobbery, produced in him inevitable feelings of disillusionment with the St Petersburg literary milieu, who in turn were alienated by his arrogance.

Apart from provoking his fellow writers and visiting brothels, Tolstoy also spent time in St Petersburg mingling with its high society, to which he belonged by birth, and the brilliance of his descriptions of the life of the *haut monde* in *War and Peace* and *Anna Karenina* owes much to his having attended so many court functions during this time. Yet Tolstoy felt an outsider in this environment too, and his instinctive enjoyment of its opulence and splendour was tempered by a growing intellectual contempt for its inauthenticity, a sentiment which also finds its way into his great novels. After a few months in Russia's most cosmopolitan metropolis, Tolstoy was ready to go back to Yasnaya Polyana. Apart from the two months he spent at the end of 1856, when he rented a flat on what is now PLEKHAN-OVA UL., at number 43 (see p. 280), he was to make only a handful of return visits to St Petersburg over the course of his lifetime.

Dekabristov, Ul., 17

Osip Mandelstam, who was born in Warsaw in 1891, spent his childhood in St Petersburg. The family first lived in Pavlovsk, before moving to this address in 1899. His parents favoured the cultural milieu of St Petersburg, and wanted to educate their children in this city. The family often moved flats, but, as Mandelstam recalls in *The Noise of Time*, the same familiar objects would always travel with them:

> The little red bookcase with the green curtain and the armchair with the motto 'Slow but Sure' often moved from

apartment to apartment. They stood on Maximilian Lane – where, at the end of the arrow-straight Voznesensky Prospekt, one could see the galloping statue of Nicholas – and above Eylers's Flower Shop on Ofitserskaya Street not far from A Life for the Tsar, and on Zagorodny Prospekt.

Dekabristov, Ul., 28

Turgenev was held under arrest here in April 1852 for writing a positive article about Gogol after the latter's death. The actual building no longer remains. He also wrote one of his most famous short stories, 'Mumu', at this address before being exiled to his country estate Spasskoe Lutovinovo for one and a half years. The street is mentioned in Turgenev's last novel *Virgin Soil* (1877), the first chapters of which take place in St Petersburg. The character Nezhdanov lives in this street in a poky, dark little house, which very much resembles the abodes of many of Dostoevsky's characters.

Dekabristov, Ul., 39

It was here that the Nemetti Operetta Theatre used to stand in the nineteenth century. In 1906, the building was taken over by the famous actress Vera Komissarzhevskaya, who two years earlier had founded her own theatre company at Italianskaya ul., 19, at the back of the nineteenth-century department store Passage. The newly reorganized company, under the directorship of the radical stage director Vsevolod Meyerhold (who had all the velvet seats ripped out in favour of hard wooden chairs), opened in November 1906. Its third production was the world première of *The Puppet Show Booth*, the first play of the Symbolist Alexander Blok, an habitué of the theatre (and its actresses). The stylized *commedia dell'arte* nature of the play continued with an informal masquerade at the apartment of one of the actresses, where the ladies donned brightly coloured paper costumes and masks, very much in keeping with the atmosphere of the times, when life and art were seen as being indivisible.

Two very different premières took place here in December 1913, by which time the building housed the Luna Park Theatre. The two performances were of the first Futurist theatrical works, the two-act drama *Vladimir Mayakovsky: A Tragedy*, written and produced and acted by Mayakovsky himelf, wearing his signature yellow shirt, and the opera *Victory over the Sun*, with a libretto by Kruchonykh, music by Matiushin and Cubist sets and costumes by Malevich. The enterprise had been given the early-twentieth-century equivalent of hype in the capital's newspapers, and played to packed houses. Even to the jaded St Petersburg audiences, these performances represented something shockingly new, and created a sensation.

Dekabristov, Ul., 45

This house, which has remained unchanged in its appearance, was where Nikolay Chernyshevsky lived in 1850–1. He also lived here for a few months in 1853.

Dekabristov, Ul., 57, Kv. 21, 23

— *Blok Museum* This was the poet Alexander Blok's last address. It is where, in 1918, he composed his poetic masterpiece 'The Twelve', set on the streets of the city, and where in 1921 he died. The building now houses a museum dedicated to his memory.

Blok and his wife moved here in July 1912, when they rented a spacious flat on the third floor of this unpretentious corner building at the end of the street, with a fine view of the River Pryazhka and the edges of the city. This was a quiet part of town, but Blok had no great desire to live nearer to the centre. He felt much more at home here in the outskirts, which he believed were much more Russian in character than the

The dining room of Alexander Blok's apartment

Westernized façades of the original city. Blok's main reason for moving here was to be near his mother, who had returned to live in the city with her husband, now promoted to the rank of general, and had a few months previously taken a flat up the street at number 40.

The Bloks arranged their living accommodation here in a similar way to previous flats they had lived in. Blok's study was near to the front door and was separated from Lyubov's room by the sitting room and dining room. The furniture was largely the same as it had been in their former flat on Malaya Monetnaya ul., with the exception of the large couch that Blok had brought from his father's apartment in Warsaw. Blok decorated his west-facing study simply, in dark greens, placed his grandmother's desk in front of the window, and hung a few small photographs and reproductions on the wall. Heating was supplied by a traditional stove, the firewood for which Blok fetched himself after the Revolution. In the harsh conditions of the Civil War, this meant hacking at old barges on the Pryazhka, and even chopping up family furniture. Although Blok preferred to keep to himself at home, he did receive many visitors here, including

Stanislavsky, Mayakovsky and the young Sergey Esenin, who came straight over to see him upon arrival from Moscow in 1915, once he had found out his address (see MALAYA POSAD-SKAYA UL., 14, p. 244). After the Revolution, despite his fame and stature, it became increasingly hard for Blok and his wife to justify their having so much living space. Finally, in February 1920, Blok and Lyubov Dmitrievna moved down to flat 23 on the first floor, where they now lived with his mother, recently widowed (she and her late husband had moved to this building in 1918). In August 1921, at ten in the morning, he died.

The museum was opened here in 1980, on the 100th anniversary of the poet's birth, and incorporates both his former residences in this building. In the third-floor flat, his study, dining room, sitting room and bedroom have been restored, while on the first floor, where he died, there is a memorial room featuring a plaster-of-Paris death mask and an exhibition of manuscripts, photographs and first editions.

Closed Wednesdays and the last Tuesday of every month

Dekabristov, Pl. *(See SENATSKAYA PL., p. 288)*

Dvortsovaya Nab., 26

The opulent surroundings of the former palace of Grand Duke Vladimir Alexandrovich (an uncle of Nicholas II) were in 1918 co-opted by the theatre department of the People's Commissariat of Education, presided over by Anatoly Lunacharsky, and this was where Alexander Blok was employed until the beginning of 1919.

The building is now occupied by the House of Scholars, which was created by KUBU, an acronym for the Commission to Improve Scholars' Living Conditions, which moved into the building on 12 January 1920. Maxim Gorky was on this commission and a bust of his head stands in the hall. Unlike other houses such as the House of Writers and the House of Arts, the Scholars' House exists to this day.

Dvortsovaya Pl.

The huge curved Main Staff buildings at number 10, formerly government offices, were where Griboedov was kept in detention for four months in 1826. He had been arrested for suspected involvement with the Decembrist Rising which had taken place the previous year. In 1837 the twenty-three-year-old Mikhail Lermontov was placed under arrest here for having written 'On the Death of a Poet', an angry response to the untimely death of Alexander Pushkin. He was kept in solitary confinement but managed to write poetry with a matchstick dipped in soot on the paper wrapped around his ration of bread. He spent five days here before he was exiled to the Caucasus.

The Ministry of Finance was housed on Palace Square in the left wing of the Main Staff building. One of its employees was Goncharov, who had started his career as a civil servant in provincial Simbirsk, but had decided to transfer to the more exciting capital in 1835. He found the work here just as tedious, and it offered him little time to pursue his work as a writer. Despite complaining of the St Petersburg climate and its 'leaden skies', he was to spend the next thirty years there working as a civil servant. With the exception of a government-sponsored trip to Japan, recorded in *The Frigate Pallada* (1855-7), his life was uneventful, and thus bears more than a passing resemblance to that of his hero in his great masterpiece, the novel *Oblomov* (1859).

Opposite the government buildings, dominating the square, is the Winter Palace. The scene of so many earth-shattering events in Russia's history, it has also been immortalized in its literature. The famous building makes an inevitable appearance in Bely's novel *Petersburg*, for example. In the nineteenth

century, the Winter Palace used to be painted dark red, a colour
Bely uses symbolically:

> An enormous crimson sun raced above the Neva, and the
> buildings of Petersburg seemed to be melting away, turning
> into the lightest of smoky amethyst lace. The windowpanes
> sent off cutting flame-gold reflections, and from the tall
> spires flashed rubies. And indentations and projections
> stretched away into the burning conflagration: caryatids,
> cornices of brick balconies.
>
> The rust red Palace bled . . .

In 1916, the year that Bely's novel was first published, Nabokov
used to skip school in order to hold secret trysts with his first
girlfriend Tamara, whom he had met that summer in the country.
As well as walking in parks, visiting museums and visiting the
two cinemas on Nevsky pr., the couple would go on moonlit
walks through the city, which would sometimes take them to
Palace Square:

> Solitary street lamps were metamorphosed into sea crea-
> tures with prismatic spines by the icy moisture on our
> eyelashes. As we crossed the vast squares, various architec-
> tural phantoms arose with silent suddenness right before
> us. We felt a cold thrill, generally associated not with height
> but with depth – and with an abyss opening at one's feet –
> when great, monolithic pillars of polished granite . . .
> zoomed above us to support the mysterious rotundities of
> St Isaac's cathedral. We stopped on the brink, as it were, of
> these perilous massifs of stone and metal, and with linked
> hands, in Lilliputian awe, craned our heads to watch new
> colossal visions rise in our way – the ten glossy-gray
> atlantes of a palace portico, or a giant vase of porphyry
> near the iron gate of a garden, or that enormous column
> with a black angel on its summit that obsessed, rather than
> adorned, the moon-flooded Palace Square, and went up
> and up, trying in vain to reach the sub-base of Pushkin's
> 'Exegi monumentum'.

Dzerzhinskogo Ul. (*See* GOROKHOVAYA UL., p. 212)

Fontanki, Nab. Reki

The Fontanka runs straight through the heart of St Petersburg, surrounded by rather grand buildings at its eastern end, and distinctly shabbier edifices in the western part of the city, where it flows out into the Neva. In the mid-nineteenth century, the area north of the Fontanka and to the west of the Kryukov canal used to be known as the Kolomna district. It makes an extended appearance in Gogol's 1842 story 'The Portrait':

> Everything there is quite unlike any other part of St Petersburg. There we are no longer in a capital city, and not even in the provinces. Indeed, as you walk through the streets of Kolomna, you seem to feel all the desires and passions of youth leaving you. There the future never seems to bother to look in; there everything is quiet, silent, dead; there everything is suggestive of retirement from active life, everything is in strange and striking contrast to the movement and noise of a capital city. The people who live there are for the most part retired Civil Servants, widows, poor people, people who at one time or another have had some acquaintance with the Supreme Court and who have therefore sentenced themselves to life imprisonment in that district ... Life in Kolomna is terribly dull; you rarely come across a carriage in its streets, except perhaps one carrying the actors to and from the theatre, which alone breaks the universal silence by its clatter and din. Here almost everyone goes on foot, and a cab very often crawls along at a snail's pace without a fare, but with a bundle of hay for its bearded nag ...

And it is typically the Kolomna area of the Fontanka (rather than its more opulent area in the eastern part of the city) which appears in Dostoevsky's novel *Poor Folk*:

And what a quantity of boats there would be on the canal. It made one wonder how they could all find room there. On every bridge were old women selling damp gingerbread or withered apples, and every woman looked as damp and dirty as her wares. In short, the Fontanka is a saddening spot for a walk, for there is wet granite under one's feet, and tall, dingy buildings on either side of one, and wet mist below and wet mist above.

Fontanki, Nab. Reki, 2

This was where Akhmatova lived in 1924. (Before the Revolution the building had housed the Imperial laundry.) By this time Akhmatova had begun to be attacked for the lack of ideological commitment in her verse, and was finding it increasingly difficult to find work or publish her poetry. It was only in 1926 that, through the intervention of Sologub, she was granted a meagre pension by Lunacharsky, the head of Soviet culture at the time.

Fontanki, Nab. Reki, 6

Ivan Turgenev was invited to a literary evening held here by his tutor Pyotr Pletnyov in 1837, at 'the big house on the Fontanka by the Obukhov Bridge'. As he entered, he briefly met a man who was leaving. 'I only managed to catch a glimpse of his white teeth and lively, quick eyes. How sad I was when I later found out that this person was Pushkin ... At that time Pushkin was for me, and for all my contemporaries, something of a demi-God. We really worshipped him.' Turgenev was only to meet Pushkin twice in his life, both times in St Petersburg. He was among the visitors who came to see the dead poet lying in his coffin. Turgenev took a lock of the poet's hair which he kept in a locket worn around his neck.

Fontanki, Nab. Reki, 14

When Tolstoy made his last visit to St Petersburg in February 1897, at the age of sixty-nine, he and his wife Sofya stayed with his friends the Olsufievs at this address. He had come to visit his two disciples Biryukov and Chertkov, who were just about to be sent into exile for publicizing the plight of the Dukhobors, a religious sect persecuted by the government due to their refusal to serve in the army. Tolstoy fought a vigorous campaign on their behalf, by donating his royalties to their cause, by publishing a letter in the London *Times*, and by signing the pamphlet that Biryukov and Chertkov began to distribute in January 1897 (which caused their immediate arrest). When 4,000 Dukhobors were allowed to emigrate to Canada in 1898, Tolstoy paid a large part of their expenses. During his week-long stay in St Petersburg on this occasion, when he also met with Stasov, Repin and other friends, Tolstoy was pursued by the secret police, who followed his every move, even down to noting his visit to the barber's ('had his hair and beard cut'). Dressed in his peasant garb, Tolstoy must have cut a strange figure on the streets of St Petersburg (the servant of one of his friends wondered who this *muzhik* was who had come to see her employer so late one night), but he was by now a public figure, recognized on the street, and at several points during his visit attracted crowds of people curious to see this great writer in the flesh, and express their admiration.

Fontanki, Nab. Reki, 18

This was the grand abode of the eighteenth-century poet Gavrila Derzhavin, who was regarded as the greatest poet of his day and who is renowned for first recognizing Pushkin's talent. The house, which Derzhavin acquired in 1791 and lived in each winter until his death in 1816, was typical of a town house built in the country-house style, with large gardens behind its river façade (apparently laid out by his wife). In Derzhavin's day the house was two-storeyed. His study had a huge Venetian window which looked out on to a courtyard.

The poet Akhmatova lived in a small room with a bed and table here from the autumn of 1921 to February 1923, with her friends Olga Sudeikina and the composer Arthur Lourie, who emigrated to Germany in 1922. Akhmatova was at that time the most popular living writer in Petrograd, and people who visited her were surprised by the discrepancy between her fame and the modesty of her living arrangements. 'Small rooms, a corridor through the kitchen,' wrote Korney Chukovsky; 'Who would have said this is that same Anna Akhmatova who, alone in Russian literature, has replaced Gorky, Lev Tolstoy and Leonid Andreev ... about whom dozens of articles and books have been written.'

Fontanki, Nab. Reki, 20

At number 20 is a three-storey yellow house with Classical columns built at the end of the eighteenth century. Two similar buildings are on either side of it. Alexander Pushkin came here in 1817 to attend the meeting of the literary society Arzamas. Arzamas was one of 400 similar groups in existence then and only met for a few years, but among its members were some of the finest writers and poets of the time. Political as well as literary in intent, there was also a certain lightheartedness about the society's meetings. Minutes were written in mock-heroic hexameters, and each member had a nickname, Pushkin's being 'The Cricket'. Arzamas is the name of the town neighbouring the estate of historian Karamzin, who also attended the meetings.

Arzamas met in the top-floor flat, which was rented by the brothers Alexander and Nikolay Turgenev; a plaque on the building also says that Decembrist meetings took place here between 1819 and 1824. It has a striking view across the river on to the Mikhailovsky Castle (Engineer's Castle). At one meeting someone suggested to Pushkin that he write a poem about the castle, which then lay empty and desolate. According to a witness, Pushkin 'suddenly jumped onto a big, long table which stood in front of the window, stretched out on it, seized his pen and paper and with a laugh, began to write'. The result was the famous poem 'Liberty', a portrait of Tsar Paul I and his murder in the Mikhailovsky Castle on 11 March 1801.

Fontanki, Nab. Reki, 21

From 1926 to 1929 the former Shuvalov Mansion accommodated the House of the Press (Dom Pechati), and in 1928 it was where the members of the Oberiu (Association for Real Art), a group of avant-garde Leningrad writers led by Daniil Kharms and Alexander Vvedensky, made their debut with a performance called *Three Left* [that is, avant-garde] *Hours*. At the beginning, Kharms was brought in on top of a large wardrobe carried by two members of the group who were inside it. His face heavily powdered, and wearing a long jacket decorated with a red triangle and a gold hat, he then proceeded to extract a watch from his waistcoat and announced that Nikolay Kropachev was at that exact moment reading his poems on the corner of Nevsky pr. and Sadovaya ul. Similar spectacles of an equally absurd nature followed, culminating in the performance by the group of Kharms' dramatic masterpiece *Elizaveta Bam*.

Fontanki, Nab. Reki, 25

Not far from where the Anichkov Bridge crosses the Fontanka is a house known in Pushkin's day as the Muravyov House. It was named after Ekaterina Fyodorovna Muravyova, mother of Nikita and Alexander Muravyov, both famous Decembrists (as recorded in the plaque on the wall outside). Muravyova was renowned for her hospitality, and often as many as seventy people (most of whom were relations) would sit down to dinner (Russians enjoy the pun on the word muraveinik which appropriately means ant-hill).

The highly influential writer and historian Nikolay Karamzin was a family friend who often stayed here, and he moved into a flat on the top floor in 1818. He is renowned for his twelve-volume *History of the Russian State*, to which he devoted the last twenty-three years of his life. When he moved in, the first volume had just come out. As Pushkin later recollected, 'The appearance of this book ... caused much noise and made a strong impression; 3,000 copies were sold in one month ... an unprecedented occurrence in our country. Everyone, even society women, rushed to read the history of their country ... It was a new discovery for them. Ancient Russia, it seemed, had been discovered by Karamzin as America by Columbus.'

Fontanki, Nab. Reki, 26

Karamzin moved into a wing of this building fronted with columns and bas-reliefs in 1823. He died here in 1826.

Fontanki, Nab. Reki, 34

— *Akhmatova Museum* From 1926 to February 1952, the third-floor flat, number 44, overlooking the garden, was the home of Anna Akhmatova. It is now the location of the main Akhmatova Museum in Russia, which opened in June 1989, marking the centenary of her birth.

Until the Revolution, this spacious eighteenth-century palace was the St Petersburg residence of the Sheremetev family, who had originally been given the land by Peter I in 1712. After its last owner Count Sergey Sheremetev handed it over to the state, the estate was attached to the nearby Russian Museum by

Anatoly Lunacharsky, and turned into communal flats. Akhmatova came to live here when the art historian Nikolay Punin (who was later her third husband, 1923–38), was allocated a flat in the garden wing of the main house on the third floor. She and Punin lived in his study, while his first wife and daughter, with whom they ate their meals, resided in the other room of the flat. During the construction of a fourth floor to the building in 1954, the staircases were rebuilt, and the front door to the flat is now on the opposite side to where it used to be.

The years that Akhmatova spent in the 'House on the Fontanka', or the 'Fountain House', as she called the palace, were for the most part bleak ones. Despite the renown she had acquired with her first collections of verse, after the Revolution her intimate and personal poetry was condemned as bourgeois and unacceptable to the new regime. Branded an 'internal émigrée', she was unable to publish any poetry between 1925 and 1940 (a brave attempt was made to publish a two-volume collection of her verse in 1925, but it remained at the galley stage). In this inhospitable climate Akhmatova devoted herself to studying and writing about Pushkin and to translation. It was here in 1945 that she received Sir Isaiah Berlin, then a diplomat with the British Embassy in Moscow. The indiscretion of Randolph Churchill, who came to find Berlin at Akhmatova's apartment, regrettably brought the visit to the attention of the authorities. Surveillance of Akhmatova's activities was increased, and in September 1946 the poet was branded an enemy of the people by Andrey Zhdanov, Secretary of the Communist Party Central Committee, and expelled, together with Mikhail Zoshchenko, from the Union of Writers. Copies of the volume of her poetry which had just been published in Moscow were destroyed. The situation eased during the 'Thaw' years under Khrushchev, but it was not until many years after her death that the possibility of creating a museum to honour the memory of this great Russian writer could be broached.

The museum consists of six rooms, which have been arranged to document different stages in Akhmatova's life. The first explores her life until 1920, and contains exhibits relating to her childhood in Tsarskoe Selo, her travels in Europe with her first husband Gumilyov, the summers they spent at his family's country estate, her first publications, and her early adulthood in Petersburg, where she became queen of the bohemian literary circles who congregated at the Stray Dog cabaret at MIKHAILOV-SKAYA PL., 5 (see p. 249). With the aid of manuscripts of her poems, rare editions, posters, photographs and portraits of Akhmatova and her contemporaries, as well as some of the poet's personal belongings, the museum's other rooms trace her life from then on. The second room is devoted to Akhmatova's life in the revolutionary years. The third room, Punin's former study, is where Akhmatova lived until 1938, and contains pieces of original furniture, such as a red sofa and Punin's desk, bookcase and table. The original white ceramic stove still stands in the far corner of the room. The fourth room in the museum follows Akhmatova's life during the 1930s, while the fifth room is where she lived from 1938 to 1941.

It was in 1938 that Akhmatova decided to end her marriage with Punin, and she took up residence in the room that had hitherto been inhabited by his first wife (with whom she now changed places). It was in this small room with one window, sparsely furnished and unkempt, that Akhmatova had to eke out her existence at the height of the purges. Not only was Punin arrested at the apartment in 1935 and 1949, but many of her closest friends, including Osip Mandelstam, also fell victim to Stalin's terror at this time. In 1938 her son Lev Gumilyov was arrested for the third time, and the experience of standing outside the prison every day for seventeen months waiting for news about him forms the central inspiration for her poetic master-piece 'Requiem'. Like all her other poems written at this time, this work (published for the first time in Russia only in 1987) was committed to memory and the paper on which it was composed immediately burned. Lydia Chukovskaya, in whose journals we find a vivid and harrowing record of Akhmatova's life at this time, was one of the few friends entrusted with participating in this process, which she described as a beautiful and sorrowful ritual. The room has now been restored to look as it did when Akhmatova was living here. As well as books from her library, the few other personal possessions she had at the time are on display, including her writing desk, an icon, a mirror and a candlestick. A chair stands next to the shabby chaise-longue along the right-hand wall. Above the small table opposite, next to the white stove, hangs a copy of one of Modigliani's famous portraits of the poet.

The 'House on the Fontanka', like other Petersburg landmarks, appears in many of Akhmatova's poems. Chief among them is her famous 'Poem without a Hero', which was begun here in 1940, and is the subject of the final room in the museum. Other items of interest in this room include Shostakovich's copy of Akhmatova's 1958 collection, together with her inscription, and Mandelstam's NKVD file.

A poem of 1952 recorded her departure from the house:

> *I don't have any special claims*
> *On this illustrious house,*
> *But it happens that almost my whole life*
> *I have lived under the celebrated roof*
> *Of the Fountain Palace... As a pauper*
> *I arrived and as a pauper I will leave...*

Closed Mondays and the last Wednesday of every month

Fontanki, Nab. Reki, 38

Turgenev rented a small but comfortable flat on the first floor of this house overlooking the Fontanka in 1854, and stayed here for two years. Despite the addition of two further storeys, its external appearance has changed little over the years. While at this address, Turgenev worked on his novel *Rudin* and planned his next work, *A Nest of the Gentry*.

Turgenev's flat was where Tolstoy stayed for a few weeks on his second visit to the capital in November 1855, having just completed his tour of duty in the Crimean War in Sebastopol. Three years earlier, Tolstoy had published his first piece of fiction (*Childhood*) in Russia's leading literary journal *Sovremennik* (the Contemporary), whose offices were situated on the opposite side of the canal. Tolstoy's story had attracted a great deal of attention, and the publication in that same journal of his extraordinary Sebastopol stories in the second half of 1855 made such an impression that he had become quite a celebrity by the time he arrived in the capital.

During his stay Tolstoy made the acquaintance of the literary elite of his day, who were all eager to meet the young artillery officer with such astounding creative talents. Tolstoy initially formed a close friendship with Turgenev, whose writing he much admired, and who invited him to stay, but their relationship became tense. The urbane and sedate Turgenev found Tolstoy rather coarse, and did not share his enthusiasm for dissolute living, while Tolstoy thought Turgenev's political interests hypocritical; both resented each other's pretensions.

It was during this visit that Tolstoy first met the poet Afanasy Fet, with whom he was to become good friends. Fet came round for morning tea one day, and was startled to see a gleaming sabre in the corner of the entrance hall, which belonged, he learned from the trusty servant Zakhar, to Count Tolstoy. Fet and Turgenev then had to spend the next hour talking in whispers, as Tolstoy was still asleep on the couch in the drawing room next door, having been up carousing with the gypsies the night before. Turgenev explained that Tolstoy went out on the town every night, and that he had long since given up on him. A memorial plaque was put up on this house in 1962 which records that 'Tolstoy lived here' but fails even to mention the name of Turgenev.

Fontanki, Nab. Reki, 57

Turgenev worked in this building in the 1840s for the Ministry of Internal Affairs, a job in which he had little interest. However, he was able to observe high-ranking St Petersburg officials, who provided inspiration for many of the characters in the novels he began to write later, such as Panshin in *A Nest of the Gentry*.

Fontanki, Nab. Reki, 143

Until 1911 the poet Sergey Gorodetsky had a flat here, and it was where, that year, the first meeting of the Poets' Guild was held. The Poets' Guild was an organization set up to discuss the writing of poetry, and brought together several poets who later called themselves Acmeists, chief among whom were Gumilyov, Akhmatova and Mandelstam.

Fontanki, Nab. Reki, 149, Kv. 9

Until the Revolution, this was the home of the 'peasant poet' Nikolay Klyuev, whose sister lived here. Until he was called up for active service in the First World War, it was also temporarily home to Sergey Esenin, with whom Klyuev was (rather hopelessly) in love.

Fontanki, Nab. Reki, 164

This was the site of the former Blagorodny Pension, a boarding school for the nobility, and it is where Wilhelm Küchelbecker (a Russian poet born to German parents) began teaching in 1817, combining a civil service career with a job lecturing on Russian literature. Küchelbecker had recently graduated from the famous lycée at Tsarskoe Selo, where he had studied with his great friends Pushkin and Delvig. He had published his first poem in 1815, and took an active involvement in literary circles now that he was in St Petersburg. His outspoken political views brought him the unwelcome attentions of the government, however, and political expediency led him in 1820 to take a job with a high-ranking member of the Russian government travelling to Europe. A year later Küchelbecker was sent back after giving politically risqué lectures on Russian literature in Paris, but, after failing to obtain any kind of job upon his return, was persuaded by his friends to see the wisdom of spending some time away from the capital. In September 1821 he set off with General Ermolov for the Caucasus.

Fontanki, Nab. Reki, 185

A plaque decorates the front of this green five-storey building where Alexander Pushkin lived with his parents between 1817 and 1820 after he had graduated from the lycée at Tsarskoe Selo.

It is this part of the Fontanka which used to be known as Kolomna. It was a poor region, considered to be almost the back of beyond, and was populated by tradesmen as well as impover-ished nobility such as Pushkin's family. The house they lived in was known as Klokachev's House after the admiral from whom they rented it, and at that time it would have been three-storeyed, with a large basement and a very low first floor. There would have been a small garden inside the yard at the back.

The Pushkin family's two-storey flat was reasonably spa-cious and they of course kept servants, including Nikita Kozlov, who stayed with Pushkin to the grave, and Pushkin's beloved nanny Arina Rodionovna. Contemporaries have described the house's appearance as threadbare and untidy, however. If you stayed for a meal, plates had to be borrowed from the neigh-bours. Pushkin's mother was always rearranging the furniture in confusing and illogical ways. She also detested both beards and smoking – the men in the house could only sport sidewhiskers and Pushkin's father had to smoke in secret.

This was a time when the young poet was living a reasonably debauched society life – rather like that of his hero in *Eugene Onegin*. The friends of his generation, much influenced by the liberal ideas of the West, also met to air their political views, and Pushkin attended the nearby Green Lamp Society at TEATRAL-NAYA PL. (see p. 299). His small room combined the dwelling of both a society man and, with its strewn books and papers, the untidiness of a scholar. One of his most famous poems, 'The Little House in Kolomna', was inspired by this area.

Frantsuzskaya, Nab. (*See* KUTUZOVA, NAB., p. 225)

Furmanova, Ul., 16

The salon of Ekaterina Andreevna Karamzina, the widow of the famous historian Nikolay Karamzin, was often frequented by writers on the former Gagarinskaya ul. It was here that Gogol read his first chapters of *Dead Souls* and Lermontov recited his poem 'Demon'. The view through the window on to the Fontanka river inspired Lermontov's poem 'Heavenly Little Clouds'. Although Pushkin frequented the salon, he never met Lermontov, who was to meet the poet's widow, Natalya Goncharova, here in 1841.

Furshtadtskaya Ul., 20

Alexander Pushkin rented a flat here on the former Ul. Petra Lavrova between May and December 1832. The building has now been demolished, but it would have stood on a part of the space now occupied by house number 20.

Furshtadtskaya Ul., 62

Nikolay Leskov wrote some of his finest short stories at this address where he lived between 1866 and 1875. These include 'The Enchanted Wanderer', 'The Sealed Angel' and 'Peacock'. The building was then two-floored and looked straight out on to one of the orangeries of the Tauride Gardens. Leskov lived on the same street at number 50 between 1895 and 1897.

Gagarinskaya Ul. (*See* FURMANOVA, UL., above)

Galernaya Ul., 41, Kv. 4

This was the home of Alexander Blok and his wife Lyubov Dmitrievna from 1907 to 1910. Their flat was on the first floor, and was decorated as modestly as their previous abode at LAKHTINSKAYA UL., 3 (see. p. 226). Apart from the huge portrait of Lyubov's father Dmitry Mendeleev which hung in the sitting room, and the odd engraving, the walls were bare. There were books neatly arranged on bookshelves, but nothing on Blok's uncluttered desk in the study to suggest that this was the home of a great writer. The Bloks had previously lived on the Petrograd Side, and it is probable that Blok wanted to move to the centre of town to be nearer the actress Volokhova, with whom he was in love. Understandably his wife resented his meetings with Volokhova and moved out for the first half of 1908.

Galernaya Ul., 53

Known as Krasnaya ul. in Soviet times, this is where the thirty-two-year-old Alexander Pushkin and his young wife, the sixteen-year-old Natalya Nikolaevna Goncharova, lived in 1831–2. The house, considered 'modest' by Pushkin, belonged to the widow Briskorn, who in 1829 had built on to the back of a building that looked on to the Angliiskaya nab. She divided the building into flats to let 'for 25,000 roubles a year'. The four-floored building, Pushkin's only St Petersburg flat which has not changed structurally since the day it was built, has two entrances with an arched gateway in the middle. Pushkin and his wife lived on the third floor, which has two balconies.

This was their first family flat and during the next six years they were to move six times. They came here from Tsarskoe Selo, where they had spent the summer, after their marriage in Moscow. Pushkin wrote how 'Women appear to commend my choice but in my absence they pity my wife: the poor thing! She is so young, so innocent and he is so frivolous, so immoral.'

Gertsena, Ul. (*See* BOLSHAYA MORSKAYA UL., p. 178)

Glukhoi Per. (*See* PIROGOVA PER., p. 279)

Gogolya, Ul. (*See* MALAYA MORSKAYA, UL., p. 240)

Gorokhovaya Ul.

As one of St Petersburg's main thoroughfares, Gorokhovaya ul., known in Soviet times as Dzerzhinskogo ul., features frequently in fiction set in the city. The denouement of Dostoevsky's *The Idiot*, for example, takes place in Rogozhin's house 'on Gorokhovaya ul. not far from Sadovaya ul.'. The gloomy, sinister appearance of the house is described fully in the book, but we are not told exactly which one it is. 'Your house,' says the prince, 'has the appearance of the whole of your family and the whole of your Rogozhin way of life ... It's so dark here, you dwell in darkness.' Inside the house is a copy of Dostoevsky's favourite picture, Holbein's *Dead Christ*. The character of Stavrogin in Dostoevsky's *The Devils* commits his crime on the street, and the richer end of the street, nearest to the Admiralty building, is described in *Poor Folk* by Makar Devushkin: 'what sumptuous shops and stores it contains! Everything sparkles and glitters, and the windows are full of nothing but bright colours and materials and hats of different shapes. One might think that they were decked merely for display; but no, people buy these things and give them to their wives!' Goncharov's novel *Oblomov* opens on Gorokhovaya ul.: 'Ilya Ilyich Oblomov was lying in bed one morning in his flat in Gorokhovaya Street in one of those large houses which have as many inhabitants as a country town.' Oblomov is a highly indolent character, and this is reflected in the appearance of his room:

> Dust-covered cobwebs were festooned round the pictures on the walls; instead of reflecting the objects in the room, the mirrors were more like tablets which might be used for writing memoranda on in the dust. The rugs were covered in stains. A towel had been left on the sofa; almost every morning a dirty plate, with a salt cellar and a bare bone from the previous night's supper, could be seen on the table, which was strewn with crumbs. If it had not been for this plate and a freshly smoked pipe by the bed, or the owner of the flat himself lying in it, one might have thought that no one lived there – everything was so dusty and faded and void of all living traces of human habitation. It is true there were two or three open books and a newspaper on the book-stands, an inkwell with pens on the bureau; but the open pages had turned yellow and were covered with dust – it was clear that they had been left like that for a long, long time; the newspaper bore last year's date, and if one were to dip a pen in the inkwell, a startled fly was as likely as not to come buzzing out of it.

Another literary character who lived on this street is Vera Pavlovna in Chernyshevsky's revolutionary novel *What Is To Be Done?* The novel was written while its author was under arrest in the Peter and Paul Fortress in 1862. The novel fictionalizes young revolutionaries and concerns the emancipation of women, as seen through Vera Pavlovna, who escapes her stifling background to become an independent free-thinker, dedicated to the feminist cause:

> The education of Vera Pavlovna was very ordinary, and there was nothing peculiar in her life until she made the acquaintance of Lopukhov, the medical student ... Vera Pavlovna grew up in a fine house on Gorokhovaya Street, between Sadovaya Street and the Semenovsky Bridge.
>
> This house is now duly labelled with a number, but in 1852, when numbers were not in use to designate the houses of any given street, it bore this inscription: House of Ivan Zakharovich Storeshnikov, present Councillor of State.

Gorokhovaya Ul., 44

It was in a house on this site (now demolished) belonging to a merchant of the third guild called Galibin that the nineteen-year-old Nikolay Gogol took a room for a couple of weeks with his school friend and travelling companion Alexander Danilevsky and servant Yakim in December 1828. They had just arrived in St Petersburg from their Ukrainian home town of Nezhin in the Poltava region, and Gogol hoped to find his fame and fortune in the capital. The romantic Gogol had idealized the capital city of Russia in his imagination to the point where it had become the symbol of all his hopes and dreams. But, when he finally arrived in Petersburg one cold winter's evening by sleigh, his dreams and illusions began to crumble: he immediately caught a cold, and quickly discovered, as soon as he had to start paying for things, that the city was hardly the paradise on earth he had thought it to be, and certainly not as beautiful as he had anticipated.

Grafsky Per., 5

This building used to be the home of the patron of the Russian avant-garde, Levky Zheverzheev, whose Friday-night salons attracted Futurist poets such as Mayakovsky, Khlebnikov and Kruchonykh, as well as the artists Malevich, Tatlin and Filonov. Zheverzheev played a significant role in the avant-garde by financing the important Union of Youth organization, whose activities culminated in the production of the Futurist master-pieces *Vladimir Mayakovsky: A Tragedy* and *Victory over the Sun* in 1913 at the Luna Park Theatre at DEKABRISTOV ul., 39 (see p. 192).

Griboedova, Kanal

Unlike many of the straight waterways in the city, the Griboedov canal twists and turns and was once called the 'Krivushchy' or 'twisting river'. Catherine the Great turned it into a canal with granite embankments and it then became nicknamed the 'Katkina Kanavka' or Catherine's gutter or sewer. It flows through the very heart of the slum area where most of the action in *Crime and Punishment* takes place.

Griboedova, Kanal, 36, Kv. 47

When the eighteen-year-old Chernyshevsky first arrived in St Petersburg from his native Saratov in 1846, to go to university, he rented a room here, in a house which belonged to Prince Vyazemsky. The excitement of the eighteen-year-old's first impressions of the capital city is reflected in his letters to his family in Saratov:

> A house where a thousand, or one and a half thousand people live is not a rarity. Such is Prince Vyazemsky's house...
> Come and see St Isaac's Cathedral when it is finished,

and admire it! Its bell is higher than Ivan the Great's [in Moscow] by three sazhens ... people seem so small against the huge buildings.

Chernyshevsky's penniless circumstances soon forced him into an itinerant way of life which involved frequent moves. For a while he lived at Bolshaya Konyushennaya ul., 15, then at Ul. Dekabristov, 45. His favourite occupation was reading Russian and European journals and newspapers in the various cafés along Nevsky pr., including Café Wolff (Nevsky, 18), Café Dominic (Nevsky, 24) and Café Ivanov (Nevsky, 27).

Griboedova, Kanal, 69/18

A flat on the top floor of this building on the corner of Stolyarny per. (known as Ul. Przhevalskogo before 1917) was where Gogol settled with two friends from home when he arrived back in St Petersburg after his abortive six-week trip to Germany in 1829. Once the tallest building in St Petersburg, and the first to have four floors (restrictions had been placed on the height of buildings in Peter the Great's time), it belonged to a rich merchant and money-lender called Zverkov, and features in Gogol's story 'Diary of a Madman', where it is described as teeming with cooks and civil servants, living on top of one another like dogs. The building has since undergone alteration.

After his attempts to become an actor had met with no success, Gogol obtained the first in a succession of clerical jobs in government departments, where he acquired some first-hand experience of the stultifying life of civil servants and bureaucrats, which he later portrayed so masterfully in his St Petersburg short stories. Meanwhile, the publication in 1830 of his first short story (which later became part of his collection *Evenings on a Farm near Dikanka*) began to bring him recognition as a writer.

Griboedova, Kanal, 73

It is most commonly thought that in *Crime and Punishment* Sonya Marmeladov's lodgings are at number 73. Number 63 also closely fits the description given in the book, particularly its yard and staircase. Svidrigailov rents a room in the same building, from where he eavesdrops two key conversations between Sonya and Raskolnikov.

Griboedova, Kanal, 74

This is the site of Nikolay Gogol's second St Petersburg address. Gogol and his friend Danilevsky spent the first few months of 1829 living in two small rooms in a three-storey house that formerly stood here just by the Kokushkin Bridge, next to Voznesenskaya Church. They probably moved to this location because of its proximity to the Guards School, which Danilevsky planned to join. According to the letter Gogol sent to his mother shortly after moving here, their landlord (an apothecary named Trut) charged them the exorbitant sum of eighty roubles a month, just for the 'bare walls', firewood, water and the right to use his kitchen. Gogol also complained that living in such poverty meant he could not go to the theatre, which he considered to be his greatest pleasure in life.

Griboedova, Kanal, 104

From the exact descriptions in *Crime and Punishment* we can deduce that Alyona Ivanovna, the old woman whom Raskolnikov murders, lived at number 104:

> he approached an enormous tenement building that overlooked the Canal on one side, and — Street on the other. This building consisted entirely of tiny apartments and was inhabited by all kinds of jobbers and people trying to make a living: tailors, locksmiths, cooks, Germans of various

descriptions, prostitutes, petty clerks and the like. People kept darting out of both entrances and through both courtyards ... The staircase was dark and narrow ...

Griboedova, Kanal, 104/25

A flat in a two-storey house belonging to a vinegar manufacturer on the former Ekaterinsky canal here was where the playwright Griboedov lived from 1816 until 1818. Griboedov had first come to the capital in 1815, while on leave from his regiment. The war with France was now over, and during his stay he decided to resign his commission and settle in Petersburg, where he had friends and could pursue his literary and theatrical interests. For the next three years he earned his living as a civil servant in the Ministry of Foreign Affairs. At the same time, he began to write plays, but his promising career as a comic dramatist was seriously hampered when he was ordered to go to Persia as secretary of the Russian foreign mission in 1818, as a punishment for having been involved in the scandalous 'duel for four'. Griboedov was originally a second in a duel that was to be fought over the legendary ballerina Istomina (fêted in Pushkin's *Eugene Onegin*), but an argument with the opponent's second led to a second challenge. Griboedov finally faced his opponent a year later in Tiflis, and was annoyed, having been shot in the arm, to miss him.

Grivtsova Per. (*See* KONNY PER., p. 222)

Isaakievskaya Pl.

St Isaac's Cathedral is described by Dostoevsky in *The Insulted and Injured* and *Crime and Punishment*. In the former, the dome of the cathedral is described as 'dark and huge ... unclearly delineated against the gloomy colouring of the sky'. In *Crime and Punishment* its appearance is quite the opposite, when viewed by Raskolnikov from the Nikolsky Bridge (known as the Most Lieutenant Schmidta in Soviet times) near Vasilievsky Island: 'The dome of the cathedral, which is in no other spot so clearly delineated as when viewed from here on the bridge ... was fairly gleaming, and through the pure air it was possible to discern clearly each one of its adornments.'

Isaakievskaya Pl., 6

Lermontov attended the School for Cavalier Officers here in 1832. He had intended to complete the education he had received at Moscow University at St Petersburg University, but decided not to attend as it meant taking exams and starting the course from the very beginning. He wanted to embark on a literary career, but instead found himself following the career of 'a warrior'. After classes he would find an empty room, trying to make his way there unnoticed by his classmates, and write until late at night. During this time he wrote his famous long poem 'Demon' and worked on a novel about the Pugachov Uprising, later to be called *Vadim*.

Isaakievskaya Pl., 7

This was the poet Küchelbecker's last St Petersburg address. He moved here in 1825, to share lodgings with his friend Alexander Odoevsky (Griboedov moved here in 1824), since the naval barracks he had been staying in with his brother Mikhail (at Pr. Rimskogo-Korsakogo, 22) had proved very damp.

Küchelbecker's chequered career had taken him to many places since he had last been in the capital in 1821. Having been sacked from his government job in the Caucasus for fighting a duel, he had first lived with his sister in Smolensk province, and had then moved to Moscow for a few years. Küchelbecker now engaged in journalism to earn a living, but also became involved with the Decembrists. In December 1825, he took part in the famous uprising. After being intercepted by the tsarist police, he was imprisoned in the Peter and Paul Fortress, and eventually exiled to Siberia.

Iskusstv, Pl. (*See* MIKHAILOVSKAYA PL., p. 249)

Izmailovsky Pr.

Dostoevsky married Anna Grigorievna Snitkina in the blue-domed Cathedral of the Holy Trinity on this street on 15 February 1867. He had met her four months before when she came to his house to be interviewed as his stenographer.

Kamenny Ostrov (Stone Island) (*See* BOLSHOI NEVKI, NAB., p. 186)

Karavannaya Ul., 14

Turgenev stayed here in 1867, on the first floor of a three-storey house (now five-storey) belonging to the critic Vasily Botkin. Turgenev now spent most of his time living abroad, but came to Russia on several long visits during the last decade of his life. He had just finished his novel *Smoke*, and read it here aloud, in the presence of Pavel Annenkov and Vladimir Sollogub. In the novel he portrays what he saw as the falseness and emptiness of the St Petersburg beau monde.

Karpovki, Nab. Reki, 19, Kv. 4

Evgeny Zamyatin lived at this address after the Revolution, from 1918 to 1922. Here he wrote the short story 'The Cave', a powerful evocation of the starving capital in which he was living, where the protagonist, Martin Martinych, has to debase himself by stealing firewood from his neighbour to keep his flat warm on his wife's nameday. In the end, the only alternative to their predicament is suicide. They are the cavemen of the story living in the Ice Age:

> At night among the cliffs where ages ago stood Petersburg, a grey-trunked mammoth was roaming. And muffled up in hides and coats and blankets and rags, the cave dwellers were constantly retreating from cave to cave. On the feast of the Intercession of the Holy Virgin Martin Martinych and Masha shut up the study; three weeks later they moved out of the dining room and entrenched themselves in the bedroom. They could retreat no further: there they must withstand the siege or die.

Kavalergardskaya Ul., 4, Kv. 3

When the Arctic Institute took over the apartment in the House on the Fontanka in 1952, Akhmatova was given a room in a five-room communal flat on the second floor here, on a street known in Soviet times as Ul. Krasnoi Konnitsy. Before the Revolution, the building (which overlooks the hospital where Mussorgsky died) had housed an inn and stables for cab drivers. Akhmatova continued her spartan existence in her new flat, surrounded by books rather than furniture. When her son Lev was finally released from prison in 1956, he came first to live with her here. In 1961, Akhmatova began to spend most of her time at a dacha in KOMAROVO (see p. 315), and a flat at LENINA UL., 34 (see p. 227), became her new Leningrad base.

Kaznacheiskaya Ul.

Dostoevsky lived in three different houses on this street, which was called Malaya Meshchanskaya ul. before the Revolution. In 1861–3, before his first trip to Europe, he lived in Astafiev's House at number 1, by the Griboedov canal on the second floor. In April 1864 he lived in Evreinov's House at number 9. A fourth floor has been built on since then. Between August 1864

*The house where
Dostoevsky completed*
Crime and Punishment

and January 1867 he lived at number 7 in Alonkin's House (second floor, flat 13). Here he worked on the journal *Epokha* (Epoch), *Notes from the Underground*, *The Gambler* and the final chapters of *Crime and Punishment*. He met his future wife, Anna Grigorievna, while living at this address. She first appeared at the house in October 1866 to work for him as his stenographer. He needed help to meet sharp deadlines for *The Gambler* and *Crime and Punishment* and managed to dictate the last instalment of the latter, some 115 pages, completing the novel, some of which had already appeared in instalments, in four weeks. In her memoirs Anna Dostoevsky remembers coming here for the first time: 'The house was big with many tiny flats, lived in by merchants and tradesmen. It immediately reminded me of the house in *Crime and Punishment* where the hero of the novel, Raskolnikov, lived.'

Khalturina, Ul. (*See* MILLIONNAYA UL., p. 251)

Konny Per.

Running off Sennaya pl. is Konny per. (known in Soviet times as Per. Grivtsova), a small side-street where Raskolnikov overhears Elizaveta Ivanovna's conversation. This conversation vitally and decisively influences his murder plot.

Konyushennaya Pl., 1

The name Konyushennaya means 'stable', and in the middle of the court stable buildings in this square stands a small working church with a dome and columns on its façade called Tserkov Nerukotvornikh. This is where Alexander Pushkin's funeral took place on 1 February 1837. The authorities were afraid that the sheer number of people who were mourning Pushkin would have political implications and fooled the populace into thinking the funeral was to take place in the much larger St Isaac's Cathedral. Pushkin's body was brought to this church in secret. This did not prevent a large gathering of people standing in the spacious square who, according to a witness, resembled 'a thick carpet of human heads'. Many people came to say their last farewell to the poet, who lay in an open coffin, although university students and professors had been given strict orders to be present at their lectures. The crowd was evidently not a peaceful one, as a witness remembered: 'all the flaps of Pushkin's frock coat were torn to shreds, and he was left lying in little more than his jacket; his sidewhiskers and the hair on his head were carefully cut out by lady admirers.' In his memoirs, *The Diary of a Russian Censor*, Alexander Nikitenko writes how the crowd came to the coffin: 'in secret, like robbers, they had to steal their way to it'.

Krasnaya Ul. (*See* GALERNAYA UL., p. 211)

Krasnoarmeiskaya Ul.

The streets which run between Lermontovsky pr. and Moskovsky pr. share the same name, but are numbered from 1 to 13. Originally named after the divisions in the Tsar's Izmailovsky Regiment, following the Revolution the streets were renamed

Krasnoarmeiskie, meaning 'Red Army'. Dostoevsky lived on the 3rd Krasnoarmeiskaya ul., then known as 'the third division of the Izmailovsky Regiment', from March 1860 to September 1861. He lived in a part of what is now house number 5, on the corner of Ul. Yegorova in Palibin's House. This has now been reconstructed. He had just returned to St Petersburg after an absence of ten years, during which time he had served a prison sentence in Omsk, then a period of exile in Semipalatinsk. Under the more relaxed regime of the new Tsar, however, he was able to publish the journal *Vremya* (Time) with his brother. Both *Notes from the House of the Dead* and *The Insulted and Injured* were published in the January and April issues.

From September 1871 to 1873 Dostoevsky lived on 2nd Krasnoarmeiskaya ul., house 11 in General Meves' House. The annexe where he lived has not survived. During this time he wrote and published *The Possessed*.

This is an area which continued to be associated with Russian writers. The Union of Writers housed many of its members here in Soviet times.

Krasnogo Flota, Nab. (*See* ANGLIISKAYA NAB., p. 177)

Kronverksky Pr., 23, Kv. 10, 9

This Art Nouveau building of 1911, on the Petrograd Side, was where Gorky lived from 1914 until 1921, first on the fifth floor in flat 10, then later in flat 9, which was larger. He had been out of the country from 1906 to 1913, due to his involvement with the Bolshevik Party, but resumed his political activities when he returned. As well as working on his memoirs at this time, Gorky founded a journal, *Letopis* (Chronicle), in 1915. In Soviet times the street was later named Pr. Maksima Gorkogo in honour of its former resident.

Kutuzova, Nab., 32

Alexander Pushkin lived near the Prachechny Bridge here from 1834 to 1836, when the street was known as the Frantsuzskaya nab. He first occupied a flat on the second floor, and then moved to cheaper accommodation on the third. In 1836 Pushkin founded the journal *Sovremennik* (the Contemporary), which he edited from his study. It was to become Russia's leading literary journal for the next twenty years. In 1836 he left this flat for new accommodation on the Moika, his last St Petersburg residence.

Kuybysheva, Ul.

The prose writer Olga Forsh lived on this street (known as Bolshaya Dvoryanskaya ul. in tsarist times) on the Petrograd Side between 1954 and 1961, the year of her death. She was then eighty-eight, and had published her last novel in the early 1950s.

Kuznechny Per., 5

— *Dostoevsky Museum* Near the yellow Vladimirskaya Church is the flat where Dostoevsky spent the last three years of his life; it is now open as a museum. He and his wife decided to move here in 1878 to escape the memory of their last flat, where their son Alexey had died. The building is very typical of Dostoevsky's preferred residence: he liked corner houses, and particularly liked to live in view of a church. He had lived in another flat in this building in 1836.

The flat has seven rooms, each arranged to reflect its appearance when the writer lived here with his wife, Anna Grigorievna, and their two children, Lyubov and Fyodor, and contains some of their personal belongings. Anna Grigorievna, to whom Dostoevsky had been married for eleven years, had put much order into his life, working as his stenographer, arranging his finances and helping to cure his addiction to gambling. The flat reflects a stable period in Dostoevsky's life, when he lived as a solid family man, and was enjoying much success as a writer.

The desk in the study is where Dostoevsky completed his last work, *The Brothers Karamazov*. He finished the epilogue in November 1880 and delivered it to his publisher Katkov with a letter saying, 'I have the intention of living and writing for another twenty years.' In December the novel was published in volume form. In January 1881, Dostoevsky suffered a throat haemorrhage. The news of the writer's illness spread throughout St Petersburg, and the flat was filled with many visitors. On the morning of the 28th, Dostoevsky asked his wife to read to him from the Bible, the same Bible that had been given to him in 1850 by the Decembrist wives when, as a convict, he had passed through Tobolsk on his way to Omsk.

After two more haemorrhages, Dostoevsky died. The room in which he died has a clock in it whose hands point to the exact hour and minute of his death, 8.38pm. He died at the age of sixty, leaving his young widow aged thirty-five.

Closed on Mondays and the last Wednesday of each month

Lakhtinskaya, Ul., 3, Kv. 44

To this very ordinary three-room flat overlooking the courtyard on the fourth floor of this large new building on the Petrograd Side the poet Alexander Blok moved with his wife Lyubov Mendeleeva in 1906. After three years living with Blok's mother and stepfather they were setting up home for the first time on their own.

Blok was at the height of his fame at this time. The 1906 production of his play *The Puppet Show Booth* had been directed by Meyerhold, his second book of verse had come out in 1907, and his legendary good looks had won him female admirers all over Russia whose numbers were probably only increased by rumours of his turbulent personal life. It was in his study here that he sat for the famous portrait by Konstantin Somov in 1907. The Bloks did not live here for long. By the end of 1907, they had moved to the centre of town, to GALERNAYA UL., 41 (see p. 211).

Lakhtinskaya, Ul., 8

In the early 1900s, the minor Symbolist writer Georgy Chulkov had a flat here. Chulkov was born in Moscow, and had studied medicine there. He had come to St Petersburg after a period of exile in Siberia and Nizhny Novgorod due to subversive political activities. He published a book of verse in 1904, helped edit the Symbolist journals *Novy put'* (the New Way) and *Voprosy zhizni* (Questions of Life), then became involved in the outlandish doctrine of Mystical Anarchism, a strange utopian fusion of artistic and political ideas which went absolutely nowhere.

Lenina, Ul., 34, Kv. 23

This was Anna Akhmatova's last Leningrad address. She moved here to the Petrograd Side in 1961, when she began to divide her time between her dacha in KOMAROVO (see p. 315) and the city.

Lermontovsky Pr., 2

Osip Mandelstam describes the Jewish quarter of St Petersburg and its synagogue in his autobiographical series of sketches *The Noise of Time*; it was an area which begins 'just behind the Mariinsky Theatre, where the ticket scalpers freeze':

> The synagogue with its conical caps and onion domes loses itself like some elegant exotic fig tree amongst the shabby buildings. Velveteen berets with pompoms, attendants and choristers on the point of physical exhaustion, clusters of seven-branched candelabra, tall velvet headdresses. The

Jewish ship, with its sonorous alto choirs and the astonishing voices of its children, lays on all sail, split as it is by some ancient storm into male and female halves. Having blundered into the women's balcony, I edged along stealthily as a thief, hiding behind rafters.

Lermontovsky Pr., 8

While serving in his regiment outside St Petersburg at Tsarskoe Selo in 1834, Lermontov often came to St Petersburg to stay with his great-uncle, N. V. Arseniev, in his two-storey mansion house. The building now has six floors.

Lermontovsky Pr., 54

A statue of Mikhail Lermontov stands in front of the former School of the Ensign of the Guards and Cavalry Officers, where the poet studied in 1832.

Letny Sad (*See* SUMMER GARDEN p. 295)

Ligovsky Pr., 65

Dostoevsky's father found his sixteen-year-old son lodgings at this address in 1837–9, when he became a pupil at the School for Engineers. This is Dostoevsky's first known St Petersburg address, and he was to live in this city, with the exception of his years of exile and imprisonment, for the rest of his life, changing flats some twenty times. He returned to house number 5 on the same street thirty-five years later in 1873–4, to be nearer the offices of the journal *Grazhdanin* (Citizen) which he edited between 1871 and 1874.

Liniya, 1-aya, 8

The fabulist Ivan Krylov spent the last three years of his life at this address on Vasilievsky Island. He retired here from his flat in the buildings of the St Petersburg Public Library, where he had worked for twenty-nine years. During his life he wrote many short fables, and his reputation as the Russian Aesop survives. He died here in 1844.

Liniya, 8-aya, 20

From the 1890s until 1907, this was the Vasilievsky Island address of the Symbolist writer Fyodor Sologub, who had a flat at the Andreevsky Municipal School, where he worked.

Unlike many of his contemporaries among the Symbolists, Sologub's origins were extremely humble. The son of a tailor and former serf who died when he was four years old, he had been brought up by his penniless mother in the house where she was employed as a servant. Educated as a teacher, Sologub had spent a bleak decade at secondary school in the Russian provinces before moving back to St Petersburg in 1892, when he got a job as teacher of mathematics here. It was while he was living at this address that he established his reputation, having begun to write when he was twelve years old. Upon his return to St Petersburg in 1892, he began to mix with modernist writers associated with the journal *Severny vestnik* (the Northern Messenger), which published his first poem. In 1907, he published his best-known work, the novel *The Petty Demon*, which drew on his experiences of Russian provincial life. Politically, Sologub leaned towards the left, and was forced to resign his position as a school administrator that year, following the publication of some revolutionary verse, and this also meant giving up his school flat. Fortunately, the success of *The Petty Demon* now enabled him to give up teaching and devote his energies to literature.

Liniya, 8-aya, 31

This flat, now bearing a memorial plaque, was where Osip and Nadezhda Mandelstam stayed at the end of 1930 after a year spent in Armenia. The flat belonged to Mandelstam's brother Evgeny Emilevich, and Mandelstam hoped to find his own accommodation in the city soon. But he was now a blacklisted writer and wholly out of favour with the St Petersburg Writers Organization, which refused him living accommodation. He felt rejected by the city where he had grown up and which he considered to be his home. Two famous poems of that time, 'Leningrad' (which mentions this flat) and 'Help Me, O Lord, to Get through This Night', record his feelings about the city, how 'Living in St Petersburg is like sleeping in a coffin.' The Mandelstams left St Petersburg for Moscow in 1931.

Liniya, 10-aya, 3/30

In the spring of 1831, through his new literary connections, the twenty-two-year-old Gogol was able to leave the office job he loathed so much to take a teaching job here at the Patriotic Institute, an educational establishment for girls from noble families. He came here twice a week for the next two years. At this point, Gogol was just at the beginning of his literary career, and his appointment at the Patriotic Institute gave him time to work on his stories of Ukrainian life, whose publication later that year would make him famous. It was in 1831 that he was finally introduced to Pushkin, a meeting that he had been longing for ever since his arrival in St Petersburg. Pushkin was to play an important role in Gogol's development as a writer.

Liniya, 10-aya, 5, Kv. 1

This building on the corner of Bolshoi pr. was where the writer Fyodor Sologub was living when his wife, the playwright

Anastasia Chebotarevskaya, committed suicide in 1921. Despite initially being in favour of the Revolution, and later becoming chairman of the Leningrad Union of Writers, Sologub's life as a writer in Russia was to become increasingly difficult. From 1923, he was unable to publish his work. He died in 1927.

Liniya, 11-aya, 48, Kv. 18

The eccentric poet Velimir Khlebnikov found a room here in September 1909. 'My room gets a lot of light and is very comfortable. I get my tea in a tiny little samovar,' he reported in a letter to his parents. The previous year, at the age of twenty-three, Khlebnikov had entered St Petersburg University as a science student, but was now switching to history and philology, in order to be able to concentrate on Russian literature, which was what he was really interested in. He was still finding it hard to make ends meet, and changed addresses several times during this period. In December 1909 he moved to nearby Donskaya ul., 11, kv. 10 (entrance on Maly pr.), and then in February 1910 he moved to the outskirts of the city, to Volkovsky pr., to work as a tutor.

Liniya, 17-aya

The character of the double-agent Lippanchenko in Bely's novel *Petersburg* (1916) lives in a large grey house decorated with yellow wallpaper on this street.

Liteiny Pr.

In Dostoevsky's novel *The Idiot*, the character of General Yepanchin lives near Liteiny pr., not far from the Church of the Transfiguration. It was a street where wealthy people lived, as Ptitsyn, another character in the novel, at one point makes clear: 'I shall never be a Rothschild, and I don't want to be ... but I shall certainly have a house on Liteiny Prospekt and perhaps even two, and that will be as far as I'll go ... but beyond four houses nature will not go, and this is all Ptitsyn can hope to achieve.'

Liteiny Pr., 21

While Andrey Bely was living in Petrograd in 1920, he devoted his energies (until illness forced him to return to Moscow) to founding and participating in a new but short-lived centre of oral culture called the Free Philosophical Academy (Volfila), which was based here.

Liteiny Pr., 24, Kv. 27, 28

The so-called Muruzi House which stands on the corner of Liteiny pr. and Ul. Pestelya has a famous literary pedigree. Among the writers who have lived in flats here are Nikolay Leskov, Dmitry Merezhkovsky and his wife Zinaida Gippius, and, most recently, Joseph Brodsky.

The house bears the name of its first owner, Prince Muruzov. It was built on the site of a wooden house, which was supposedly the Liteiny pr. accommodation of General Yepanchin in Dostoevsky's *The Idiot*. Wooden accommodation was no longer considered appropriate on this smart street, however, and Muruzov built the house of his dreams on its site in 1874 (architect A. K. Serebryakov). The Muruzi House was famous first of all for the extravagance of its architecture, its Moorish façade and luxurious interiors, but then later because of its inhabitants. In 1879 the short-story writer and novelist Nikolay Leskov took a modest three-roomed apartment on the fourth floor. Then, at the turn of the century, Dmitry Merezhkovsky and his wife, the poet and writer Zinaida Gippius, leading figures in the Russian Symbolist movement, moved in. They lived here for almost a quarter of a century, first renting a four-roomed flat on the fifth floor (flat 27), and later moving to a humbler apartment on the second floor before emigrating in 1919.

Merezhkovsky and Gippius were renowned for the religious-philosophical meetings which they founded in 1901, in an attempt to bridge the gap between the church and the godless intelligentsia. They were better known in the gossip columns of the St Petersburg press, however, as the decadent aesthetes whose weekly soirées were attended by the city's literary elite. Indeed, Zinaida Gippius' desire to bring a degree of pagan sensuality to religious experience earned her the sobriquet of the 'decadent madonna'. Red-haired and green-eyed, the sylph-like Gippius was certainly striking; dressed always in white with a cross round her neck and rings on her fingers, she traded ruthlessly on her image, lorgnette in one hand, cigarette in the other.

Until the beginning of Ivanov's 'Wednesdays' at his home at TAVRICHESKAYA UL., 38 (see p. 296), in 1905, the Merezhkovskys' salon was the most fashionable meeting place for writers associated with the Symbolist movement, and was frequented by the leading modernist poets of the time. It was with the Merezhkovskys that the Moscow-based Symbolist writer Andrey Bely stayed when he came to visit St Petersburg for the first time in January 1905. Bely's arrival chanced to coincide with the 1905 Revolution, and he found his St Petersburg friends in a state of great agitation. Bely made several subsequent visits to St Petersburg over the course of the next year, during which he attended Ivanov's 'Wednesdays' and other literary gatherings, and also became emotionally involved with Alexander Blok's wife Lyubov Mendeleeva.

In 1918, the Muruzi House once again became a meeting place for poets and writers when Gorky's publishing house World Literature (see MOKHOVAYA UL., 36, p. 262) opened three departments here. Gumilyov was put in charge of producing translations of classics in world poetry, Chukovsky and Eikhen-baum assumed responsibility for literary criticism and Zamyatin and Shklovsky became editors of prose works.

The building and its many flats were later divided into communal apartments, but the literary history of the house did not end here. Flat number 28 was the childhood home of the poet Joseph Brodsky, who grew up here with his parents in a communal flat shared with three other families. Life in the 'room and a half' they occupied in this flat (where his parents remained until their deaths in the 1980s) was memorably recreated by the poet in his collection of essays *Less Than One*:

> Oddly, the furniture we had matched the exterior and the interior of the building. It was as busy with curves, and as monumental as the stucco moulding on the facade or the panels and pilasters protruding from the walls inside, skeined with plaster garlands of some geometrical fruits. Both the outside and inner decor were of a light-brown, cocoa-cum-milk shade. Our two huge, cathedral-like chests of drawers, however, were of black varnished oak; yet they belonged to the same period, the turn of the century, as did the building itself. This was what perhaps favourably disposed the neighbours toward us from the outset, albeit unwittingly. And this was why, perhaps, after barely a year in that building, we felt we had lived there forever. The sensation that the chests had found their home, or the other way around, somehow made us realize that we, too, were settled, that we were not to move again.
>
> Those ten-foot-high, two-storey chests (you'd have to take off the corniced top from the elephant-footed bottom when moving) housed nearly everything our family had amassed in the course of our existence. The role played elsewhere by the attic or basement, in our case was performed by the chests. My father's various cameras, developing and printing paraphernalia, prints themselves, dishes, china, linen, tablecloths, shoe boxes with his shoes now too small for him yet still too large for me, tools,

batteries, his old Navy tunics, binoculars, family albums, yellowed illustrated supplements, my mother's hats and scarves, some silver Solingen razor blades, defunct flash-lights, his military decorations, her motley kimonos, their mutual correspondence, lorgnettes, fans, other memorabilia – all that was stored in the cavernous depths of these chests, yielding, when you'd open one of their doors, a bouquet of mothballs, old leather, and dust.

At the age of fifteen, Brodsky left school and began work at an agricultural machinery plant. Over the next seven years he was to have several different jobs, including working in a morgue and assisting on geological expeditions. During this time he also continued his education under his own tutelage, however, and began to realize his true vocation as a poet; Akhmatova immediately recognized him as such at their first meeting in 1962.

Liteiny Pr., 33

This was the first and only official residence of Sergey Esenin, a writer who otherwise stayed with friends or lived in hotels. Esenin lived here from 1917 to 1918 with his second wife Zinaida Raikh (later the wife of Vsevolod Meyerhold), whom he had married in August 1917, three months after meeting her. Their two-room flat on the second floor looked out on to the courtyard. Although never politically active, Esenin embraced the Revolution, and in 1918 he signed up after demobilization led to fears of German invasion. This was a very productive time for him as a writer. Blok, Bely and Zamyatin were among the writers with whom he shared ideas during this period. The Sergey Esenin Club in Petersburg intends one day to turn this flat into an Esenin Museum, but there is little prospect of it being opened in the near future. Prose writer Konstantin Fedin lived in this building from 1922 to 1937.

Liteiny Pr., 36

— *Nekrasov Museum* The Memorial Museum of the Russian lyric poet Nikolay Alekseevich Nekrasov was founded in 1946. As one of the leading figures of the Realist School in Russian poetry, Nekrasov drew particular attention to the plight of the Russian peasant. He lived here in the 1840s.

As well as being a poet, Nekrasov is also remembered for the important role he played as co-owner and chief editor of Russia's leading nineteenth-century literary journal, *Sovremennik* (the Contemporary), founded by Pushkin in 1836. Nekrasov bought the journal and became its editor in 1846. The editorial offices were housed in this building and were frequented by contributors such as Turgenev, Tolstoy, Goncharov and Chernyshevsky. Many of these writers' great works were first published in instalments in the journal. It had a progressive outlook and addressed such political questions of the 1860s as women's emancipation and the emancipation of the serfs. After twenty years of Nekrasov's editorship, it was suspended by the Tsar, who deemed its content too radical. Nekrasov went on to acquire another progressive leading journal, *Otechestvennye zapiski* (National Annals) in 1867.

The spacious flat is laid out both as a home and as an editorial office. It contains many of the poet's personal belongings, his books and many portraits. Visitors are reminded of Nekrasov's love of hunting by the stuffed bears and wildfowl on display here. There are also rooms dedicated to *Sovremennik*'s co-owner Ivan Panaev, whose flat was joined to Nekrasov's. This arrangement suited Nekrasov, as he was besotted with Panaev's wife, Avdotya, as Panaev himself was. Panaeva was an important Russian woman writer in her own right, whose fiction addressed topical issues such as the emancipation of women in Russia. She left a valuable record of the literary life of the 1840s and 1850s in her memoirs (1889–90).

Closed Tuesdays and the last Friday of the month

Liteiny Pr., 52

Goncharov rented a flat in this classically façaded building in 1837. During this time he was fully employed in government service, but managed to write in the evenings, and sometimes all night long. He described the room where he wrote his first novel, *A Common Story*, as a 'modest official's room'. After living here for fifteen years, he accepted a job as secretary to an admiral commanding an expedition to Japan. This meant leaving his otherwise sedentary existence in Russia to go on what was to be an exceptional adventure, which he recorded in his book *The Frigate Pallada*, written on his return two years later.

Liteiny Pr., 60, Kv. 4

Mikhail Saltykov-Shchedrin spent the last thirteen years of his life at this address. Already famous for the dozens of satirical sketches he wrote about Russian life, and for his novels *History of a Town* and *The Golovlyovs*, Saltykov had spent much of his life working for the government, the target of much of his satire. Ironically, one of his arch enemies, the notorious Pobedonostsev, a government official in charge of the Holy Synod, lived right next door.

Saltykov had also played a leading role in the journal *Otechestvennye zapiski* (National Annals). When Nekrasov died in 1878, Saltykov became its chief editor and spent hours at his desk in this flat correcting proofs as well as writing his own volumes of satire. It was at his desk that he died, pen in hand, in 1889.

Makarova, Nab., 4

— *Institute of Russian Literature* At number 4 is the Institute of Russian Literature (IRLI), also known as Pushkinsky Dom (Pushkin House). Situated in the former customs house, the institute was opened in 1905 and is an archive, research centre and museum of Russian literature. There are also rooms open to the public on the second floor dedicated to various writers and containing photographs, portraits, manuscripts and first editions. The exhibitions in these rooms continually change, but all come from the main collection.

Closed Saturdays and Sundays

Maksima Gorkogo, Pr. (*See* KRONVERKSKY PR., p. 224)

Maksimiliansky Per. (*See* PIROGOVA PER., p. 279)

Malaya Konyushennaya Ul., 4/2, Kv. 119

— *Zoshchenko Museum* It is apt that the flat of a writer whose bestselling, humorous, satirical sketches about the cramped conditions of Soviet housing should be so small. This was Mikhail Zoshchenko's last flat, where he lived between 1954 and 1958. The flat was part of a writers' co-operative which occupied two floors built on to the original nineteenth-century building in the 1930s. The building's address in Soviet times was Kanal Griboedova, 9. Other writers who lived here include Evgeny Shvarts, the critics Eikhenbaum and Tomashevsky, and the poet Nikolay Zabolotsky, who moved with his family into a co-operative extension to the building in 1934. This was the first self-contained flat the thirty-one-year-old had ever lived in. He was arrested here in 1938 and later sentenced to five years in a hard-labour camp in Komsmolsk-on-Amur, in the far eastern part of Siberia.

The museum occupies two small rooms. The first displays a literary 'exhibition', a collection of artefacts, photographs and the author's own possessions as well as various editions of his work. A poster from that time reads, 'When you enter the bathroom, wash carefully with hot water and soap paying particular attention to fibrous parts, as that is where lice particularly like to hide.' Before becoming a writer Zoshchenko held a number of different

Mikhail Zoshchenko at home

jobs: 'I was a militiaman, accountant, shoemaker, a poultry raising instructor, a frontier guard telephonist, an agent of the Criminal Investigation department, a secretary of the law-court, a clerk.' The display aims to show the various stages of Zoshchenko's life, from his childhood to the First World War (during which he was gassed, causing permanent damage to his health), and to his first literary successes. The astonishing popularity these brought him was suddenly reversed after the publication of *Before Sunrise* in 1943, however, when his work was forbidden for being too pessimistic and devoid of ideological content. Melancholic by nature, he wrote *Before Sunrise* partly as an exercise in self-analysis. The next room is Zoshchenko's spartan bedroom, containing a bed, bookshelf and typewriter. After his death his widow Vera Vladimirovna stayed on in the flat, and it then passed to their son Valery Mikhailovich. After his death, it remained empty until the opening of the museum in August 1992. The result is an authenticity lacking in many of the reconstructed literary museums.

Closed Tuesdays

Malaya Meshchanskaya Ul. (*See* KAZNACHEISKAYA UL., p. 221)

Malaya Monetnaya Ul., 9, Kv. 2

In 1910, Blok and his wife moved back to the Petrograd Side of Petersburg into a bright and airy four-room flat here on the fifth floor of a new building with windows looking out on to Kamenoostrovsky pr. They paid fifty-five roubles a month, which was at least half Blok's literary earnings, but an inheritance from his father enabled the couple to live comfortably for many years without seeking regular income. During the time that Blok lived here, he worked on his great poem 'Retribution' and his play *The Rose and the Cross*.

Married life had not become any easier for Blok and his wife in the intervening years, and the question of separation arose more than once. The couple remained together, however, and moved in 1912 to be nearer Blok's mother on Ofitserskaya street (now DEKABRISTOV UL., see p. 190).

Malaya Morskaya, Ul.

In his memoir *Speak, Memory*, Nabokov recollects many aspects of his St Petersburg childhood. One of those memories is of going for spring rides in the family carriage past the Fabergé shop, which used to be located on this street (known in Soviet times as Ul. Gogolya):

> How utterly foreign to the troubles of the night were those
> exciting St Petersburg mornings when the fierce and tender,
> damp and dazzling arctic spring bundled away broken ice

down the sea-bright Neva! It made the roofs shine. It painted the slush in the streets a rich purplish-blue shade which I have never seen anywhere since ... On those glorious days on allait se promener en équipage ... In the open landau I am joined by the valley of a lap rug to the occupants of the more interesting back seat, majestic Mademoiselle, and triumphant, tear-bedabbled Sergey, with whom I have just had a row at home ... We drift past the show windows of Fabergé whose mineral monstrosities, jeweled troykas poised on marble ostrich eggs, and the like, highly appreciated by the imperial family, were emblems of grotesque garishness to ours. Church bells are ringing, the first Brimstone flies up over the Palace Arch, in another month we shall return to the country ...

Malaya Morskaya, Ul., 10

This eighteenth-century Baroque-style building is known as the Queen of Spades House. The unnamed Countess — of Pushkin's famous short story 'The Queen of Spades' is thought to be based on the old woman who lived here, Princess N. P. Golitsyn. In the story she guards an astonishing gambling secret involving three cards. Princess Golitsyn, who lived to the age of ninety-seven, outliving Pushkin, was once a society beauty, renowned for her intelligence and cunning. In Pushkin's day her nickname was 'Princess Moustache'. The American Ambassador to Russia at the time later recalled that he had never met a woman with such a beard.

Malaya Morskaya, Ul., 13

Ivan Turgenev received many guests in flat 9 of Gillerm's House, which he rented between 1851 and 1854. The building, which is on the corner of Gorokhovaya ul., is much altered.

Malaya Morskaya, Ul., 17

This was Nikolay Gogol's last Petersburg address, and it was where he wrote some of his most famous works. He moved to this eighteenth-century building, which belonged to a court musician, in 1833, taking a modest two-room flat looking out on to the courtyard at the back, on the second floor. For the previous two years Gogol had been earning his living by teaching at the Patriotic Institute (on LINIYA, 10-AYA, 3/30, see p. 230), but in September 1834, began a new job as an adjunct professor of world history at St Petersburg University, which lasted all of four months (see UNIVERSITETSKAYA NAB., p. 302). It was in creative fiction that Gogol felt much more at home. His Ukrainian tales had catapulted their author into the literary limelight in 1831, and while living at this address Gogol wrote his short stories 'The Nose', 'The Portrait', 'Diary of a Madman' and 'Nevsky Prospect' and his dramatic masterpiece *The Government Inspector*, which was first performed on 19 April 1836 in the presence of Tsar Nicholas I. Despite its success, Gogol felt the nature of his satire had been drastically misunderstood, and such were his feelings of persecution that he decided to leave St Petersburg for good. On 6 June 1836, he departed for Rome, thereafter returning to the Russian capital only for short visits, the last of which took place in 1848.

Malaya Morskaya, Ul., 24

The former Hotel Angleterre, whose buildings now form part of the Astoria, one of Petersburg's best-appointed hotels, is best known in literary history as the place where the poet Esenin hanged himself in 1925, an event the plaque on the wall commemorates. Esenin had first stayed here with his third wife, the dancer Isadora Duncan (whom he had met in 1921), but was already married to his fourth wife by the time he returned to

Petrograd in 1923, to visit Nikolay Klyuev, and by this time had acquired a notorious reputation for his unstable behaviour. Esenin finally decided to move back to Leningrad from Moscow in December 1925, and took the same room on the second floor of the Astoria that he had stayed in with Isadora in 1922. Despite his avowals that he was going to start a new life and give up drinking, within five days Esenin had ended his life with a piece of rope from one of the suitcases given to him by Isadora, leaving a suicide poem written in his own blood. Recent speculation has suggested that Esenin was in fact murdered, although any official investigation would now probably be hampered by the extensive renovations to the hotel which have made the room where Esenin hanged himself unrecognizable.

Malaya Morskaya, Ul., 39

Now part of the Hotel Astoria, this was once the site of the Hotel Napoleon, and it was where the twenty-one-year-old Lev Tolstoy stayed on his first visit to St Petersburg in 1849, having left his estate at Yasnaya Polyana due to boredom. Ever seeking a noble purpose in life, Tolstoy decided here that he was going to devote himself to serving his country, and began taking the necessary law examinations for the civil service. In reality, however, he was much more interested in pursuing more hedonistic goals. Within a few months he had decided that a career in the Horse Guards would be more suitable for him, but had spent so much money gambling (one of the family estates had to be sold to pay off his debts) that this idea soon palled as well, and by the time he returned to Yasnaya Polyana, with a German pianist in tow, he was thinking about becoming a composer, an idea which, needless to say, was also short-lived.

Malaya Posadskaya, Ul., 14, Kv. 8

A flat on the fourth floor of this building on the Petrograd Side became in 1911 the home of Sergey Gorodetsky. Among the many writers who spent time here was the 'peasant poet' from Ryazan, Sergey Esenin, who came to Petrograd for the first time in May 1915 to further his career as a poet, and stayed with Gorodetsky for most of his visit. The nineteen-year-old poet had published several poems by now, but wanted to bring out a book, which he had not so far been able to do in Moscow, where he had been living for the past three years. Immediately upon arrival from Moscow, therefore, he went to the first bookshop he came across to find out the address of Alexander Blok, Russia's most famous living poet (DEKABRISTOV UL., 57, see p. 193) so that he might go and make his acquaintance. Blok was home the second time that Esenin called, and he was impressed by the young man's verses. Esenin went away with introductory letters to Gorodetsky and another peasant writer, having eaten a plate of fried eggs and a complete loaf of bread. Within days he was frequenting the capital's literary salons, and such fashionable establishments as the Stray Dog (MIKHAILOVSKAYA PL., 5, see p. 249). By the time he returned to Moscow at the end of the following month, the angelic-looking poet had become a celebrity.

Maly Pr., 19, Kv. 20

Velimir Khlebnikov, later to become a central figure in the Cubo-Futurist avant-garde, lodged here temporarily in the autumn of 1908, having enrolled as a third-year student in natural sciences at St Petersburg University (he had begun his studies at the university in Kazan, where his family were living at that time). Like most students, Khlebnikov was not well off: 'I pay 10 roubles for a single room, I eat at the dining hall for 10–50 kopecks – the food is always terrible,' he wrote to his parents; 'I could eat at the landlady's for 11 roubles, but that's for when times get better.' For reasons that are not clear, he was thrown out of this accommodation in November 1908, and moved in temporarily with family friends before renting another room on Gulyarnaya ul., 2, kv. 2. It was in 1908 that Khlebnikov published his first poetry in a weekly journal based in St Petersburg edited by Vasily Kamensky, who was also to become involved with the Cubo-Futurist movement a few years later.

Marata Ul., 14

This is the house where Alexander Radishchev, best known as the author of *Journey from Petersburg to Moscow*, settled in 1775. It was in this house that he unofficially printed the *Journey* on his own printing press. In 1790 the book came to the attention of Catherine II, who, disturbed by its negative political message, found evidence within it of a masonic plot to oust her from the throne. Radishchev was imprisoned, given a mock execution and then exiled for ten years to Siberia.

When Radishchev came to live here the street was known as Gryaznaya (Dirty) ul. It was a street which consisted mainly of gardens and orchards and contained few houses. The house belonged to the family of Radishchev's wife, the Rubanovskys. Living conditions became cramped following the birth of Radishchev's first child and then the return of his wife's two sisters, who had completed their education at the Smolny Institute. Although the Rubanovsky family had their own house on Millionnaya ul. they preferred to live together.

Radishchev decided to expand his living quarters, and luckily there was room to do this in his spacious courtyard. He built a stone house for his own family and a wooden house for his sisters-in-law. The result was a huge property, looking out over two streets. The appearance of the building has now considerably altered.

Mayakovskogo, Ul., 11

It was in the third-floor flat of V. Posse, editor of the Marxist journal *Zhizn* (Life), on the former Nadezhdinskaya ul. that Maxim Gorky stayed when he first came to the city in 1899. By this time Gorky was already an established writer, and he gave his first public reading here. During his visit he met the great painter Ilya Repin and sat for his portrait. Although he did not particularly like St Petersburg, which seemed to him to be inhabited by devious people, he came back for a second visit in 1901, and stayed with Posse again. It was at this time that Gorky became involved with the Znanie (Knowledge) publishing house, which had been set up in 1898 with the object of perpetuating the Russian Realist tradition (at a time when Modernism was in the ascendant) by bringing out popular works for mass readership. Gorky also at this time took part in political protests against the government policy of expelling left-wing students, and as a result came under suspicion himself. From 1901 to 1903 he was prohibited from living in St Petersburg.

Mayakovskogo, Ul., 11, Kv. 8

The eccentric experimental writer Daniil Kharms (pseudonym of Daniil Yuvachev) moved here with his parents at the end of 1925, when he was ten years old. Apart from a short period during the Civil War and another when he was exiled to Kursk for a few months, this was his home for the rest of his life. Kharms was a true Petersburg native, and liked to walk about the city on foot, bowing with reverence to ancient lampposts. 'I love walking by the Neva, the Field of Mars, through the Summer Garden, across the Troitsky bridge ...' he wrote in 1933; 'I love to walk by myself. I love to be amongst delicate people.' In his quasi-English costume (which included the obligatory plus-fours and pipe), he must have cut a strange figure.

In 1924 Kharms became a student at the Leningrad Elektro-tekhnikum, but never graduated. A year later he put in an application to join the Leningrad Union of Poets (founded in 1920) with two notebooks filled with verse. After acquiring his pseudonym ('Kharms' was one of thirty names he considered), he started giving readings, collaborating with other eccentric-minded writers, and working on the publication of children's journals. The late 1920s were an inauspicious time for practical jokes, let alone avant-garde art of any kind, however. Kharms was arrested in 1931 for distracting the Soviet people from the tasks of industrial construction, and exiled for a brief period to Kursk. Thereafter it was difficult to earn a living through writing and Kharms and his wife often had nothing to eat. In 1941 he was arrested again (he was taken away by the secret police half-dressed and in his slippers), and declared insane. He died a few months later in a psychiatric prison hospital.

The decoration of Kharms' living quarters was as eccentric as his behaviour. At one point his bedroom was decorated with poems and aphorisms (such as 'we are not pies') from ceiling to floor, which were later replaced with a list of people he 'particularly respected', including Bach, Gogol, Glinka and Knut Hamsun. Other things on the walls included a silver watch on a chain ('this watch has particular superlogical significance' read the label attached to it), a portrait of Kharms, a lithograph of a mustachioed colonel from the times of Nicholas I and a painting in the style of Malevich. The furniture included a beloved harmonium, on which Kharms would play Bach and Mozart, and a selection of books on the supernatural.

The building was badly damaged during the war, and Kharms' flat was destroyed.

Mayakovskogo, Ul., 33

Turgenev stayed at his brother's house in 1842. Both the flat and its situation pleased him a great deal: 'My brother has given me a wonderful room with a stove and three Voltaire armchairs, and so many cushions ... We live in a secluded street – there is no noise at any time of day ... In the morning I drink glorious tea from large English tea cups ...' After studying in Moscow and Berlin (where he was much influenced by Western liberal thinking), he returned to Russia, and in 1842 completed his final examinations at St Petersburg University, graduating as a Master of Philosophy. His literary career began shortly afterwards.

Mayakovskogo, Ul., 52

Turgenev was sixteen years old when he came to stay with his brother here in a 'new stone house'. This was Turgenev's first St Petersburg address, and he lived here from 1834 to 1838, while studying at the university.

The house the Turgenevs lived in was later demolished, and replaced by the building which currently stands here. One of its inhabitants was Mayakovsky, who settled here in 1915 and stayed until December 1917. Mayakovsky had just fallen madly in love with Lili Brik (who immediately became the heroine and muse of his poetry), and he moved here to be near her. The large sunny room with two windows he rented in the fourth-floor flat of a stenographer was just round the corner from the Briks' apartment at ZHUKOVSKOGO UL., 7/9 (see p. 309), which is where he spent most of his time.

Mayorova, Pr. (See VOZNESENSKY PR., p. 306)

Mikhailovskaya Pl.

In Soviet times this square was called Pl. Iskusstv or Square of the Arts because of the many cultural institutions which line it – the Russian Museum, the Maly Theatre of Opera and Ballet and the Philharmonic Hall. The square is dominated by the Russian Museum, originally the Mikhailovsky Palace, designed by architect Carlo Rossi. Rossi constructed several identical buildings in the square at the same date to give it a stylistic harmony. Thus houses 3 and 4, both lived in by the Karamzin family, face each other across the square. In the middle of the square stands the famous statue of Alexander Pushkin with an arm outstretched, designed by the St Petersburg sculptor Mikhail Anikushin who wanted 'joy' and 'light' to radiate from the statue. It was unveiled in 1957.

Mikhailovskaya Pl., 3

In the first half of the nineteenth century, an apartment in this house was the St Petersburg residence of Mikhail Vielgorsky, whose salon was at the centre of musical life in the city in aristocratic circles. Many writers came to these soirées, including Vasily Zhukovsky, who translated into Russian the text of Haydn's oratorio *The Seasons*. Zhukovsky was also a frequent visitor to the apartment on the next floor up, where members of the Karamzin family lived. Apparently theirs was the only salon in St Petersburg where people did not play cards, and spoke Russian rather than French. Pushkin, Vyazemsky and Pletnyov were also frequent visitors here in the 1830s.

Mikhailovskaya Pl., 5

From the end of 1911 to 1915, the cellar of this building was the home of the semi-private café–cabaret the Stray Dog, and one of the smartest night-spots in town. Run by the actor Boris Pronin

The emblem of the Stray Dog Café,
designed by M. V. Dobuzhinsky

(who became known as the 'Hund-Direktor'), the Stray Dog quickly became the centre of avant-garde artistic and literary life in the capital, attracting writers of all persuasions, as well as actors, dancers, artists, musicians and even the odd affluent member of that distinctly lesser species, the General Public, who paid handsomely for the privilege. The Stray Dog was never as elitist as Vyacheslav Ivanov's soirées had been, not least because it was situated in a basement rather than at the top of a tower.

Entertainment at the Stray Dog (which ranged from serious lectures to musical improvisations) was usually spontaneous, lasted until the early hours of the next morning, and was provided by whomever happened to have called in that night. Among the writers who appeared here were Futurists such as Mayakovsky, who did their best to be as shocking as possible and live up to their reputation. Mayakovsky had come to St Petersburg for the first time in early 1912, and returned later in the year to take part in a dispute about contemporary poetry with his friend the artist David Burlyuk, another of the first Russian Futurists. The Stray Dog was also frequented by the more sophisticated and urbane Acmeists as well, however, who were typified by its most famous habituée, the elegant and beautiful Anna Akhmatova, universally regarded as this establishment's *grande dame*.

Mikhailovskaya Ul., 1–7

The Grand Hotel Europe, built in 1875, is probably beyond the budget of most writers now, but that has not always been the case. Ivan Turgenev stayed here in the spring of 1879, just after it was built. When Gorky returned to Russia in 1928, he came to St Petersburg and stayed in room 8 of this hotel. From 1924 onwards, Mayakovsky always stayed at the Evropeiskaya on his visits to Leningrad, and would stay either in room 25 or in room 26, both of which were more spacious than his Moscow living quarters. In January 1926 he gave a poetry reading to a capacity audience at the Philharmonia across the street.

Millionnaya Ul., 1

As the name suggests, this was a street where the wealthiest people in St Petersburg lived (in Soviet times it was named after Khalturin, who in 1880 had planted a bomb in the Winter Palace). In the late eighteenth century Ivan Krylov lived in this building, which overlooks the Field of Mars, and he set up his own printing house here. An earlier attempt at publishing a satirical journal had been short-lived, and Krylov was to run into the same difficulties with his new journal, *Krylov s Tovarishchimi* (Krylov and Friends). Catherine II ordered its closure six years later.

Krylov, Russia's greatest writer of fables, mixed in the same circles as Alexander Pushkin, and a picture by Chernetsov entitled *Parade on the Field of Mars* depicts them standing in a group with Zhukovsky and Gnedich.

Millionnaya Ul., 5

Anna Akhmatova moved to the so-called Marble Palace here in 1919 with her second husband Vladimir Shileiko, who was assigned two rooms in the former servants' wing looking out over the Field of Mars. The opulent eighteenth-century palace with its façade of pink marble and granite, designed by Rinaldi in the Classical style, was originally built by Catherine the Great for her lover Grigory Orlov, and had been the residence of Grand Duke Konstantin Romanov before the Revolution. Akhmatova and Shileiko might have had a wonderful view, but their life here was extremely hard, as it was for most people in the years immediately after the Revolution. An abundance of books and the beauty of their surroundings could not make up for the lack of heat, kitchenware and basic foodstuffs. Akhmatova later described this time to her friend Lydia Chukovskaya as 'three years of hunger', when even matches were in such short supply that she had to go out into the street each morning to get a light from someone. The couple's problems were exacerbated by the fact that neither was in the least bit domesticated; they survived on the money Shileiko received for his translation work for World Literature (the publishing house set up by Gorky which enabled many writers to eke out a living at this time), but even that source eventually dried up, leaving them both in a parlous state.

Millionnaya Ul., 32, 34

In the 1820s, when he was at the beginning of his literary career, Pushkin often attended soirées on Millionnaya ul. at houses 32 and 34, which stand side by side. At number 32 lived the famous actress Semyonova, and at number 34 Avdotya Golitsyna, known as 'Princesse Nocturne'. She was once told by a fortune-teller that she would die at night and, afraid of death, she decided to turn her nights into days. Her night-time salons were frequented by many St Petersburg literati and were watched suspiciously by the police.

Millionnaya Ul., 35

In 1827 Vasily Zhukovsky moved to an apartment in the two-storey Classical building which used to stand here (it was replaced by the New Hermitage in the 1840s). The building was part of the Winter Palace, and the apartment was allotted to Zhukovsky in his capacity as tutor to Alexander II. Zhukovsky had one extremely large room here, which served as his study and library, and it was where he received his guests and held literary salons. A painting by Mikhailov and Mokritsov (pupils of Venetsianov) has preserved one such soirée held here, and shows Pushkin, Gogol, Krylov, Odoevsky and Vielgorsky among the guests. Zhukovsky lived here until 1840, when he was finally able to retire from his duties at court, and go abroad.

Mira Pl. (See SENNAYA PL., p. 289)

Moiki, Nab. Reki

It is a building somewhere on the Moika canal which is inhabited by Sofya Petrovna Likhutina, a central character in Bely's Symbolist novel Petersburg (1916). Her small apartment, decorated in Japanese style with countless landscapes depicting Mt Fujiyama, cannot be positively identified, as it displays features of several buildings in this area. As with the house of the Ableukhovs in the novel, Bely is anxious to undermine any illusion the reader might have that Likhutina's apartment actually exists in reality. The Moika canal is one of many topographical references in the novel, and is mentioned frequently: 'A shaft of light flew by: a black court carriage flew by.

Past window recesses it bore blood-red lamps that seemed drenched in blood. They played and shimmered on the black waters of the Moika. The spectral outline of a footman's tricorne and the outline of the wings of his greatcoat flew, with the light, out of the fog and into the fog...'

Moiki, Nab. Reki, 12

— *Pushkin Museum* The former Volkonsky House is the largest and most visited literary museum in St Petersburg. It was Alexander Pushkin's last residence, and was where he died in 1837 after he was wounded in a duel.

The building – a three-floored house with two arched gateways leading into a courtyard with outbuildings and stables – is now restored to its appearance in Pushkin's day. Constructed in 1727, it was rebuilt in the 1740s for Elizabeth I's government minister, Baron Cherkasov, and was bought by the Volkonsky family in 1806. After Sergey Volkonsky's involvement in the Decembrist Rising, which led to his exile to Siberia, followed by his devoted wife, the family was left in debt, and in the 1830s they decided to rent out flats within their house. The Pushkins were family friends and rented the eleven-roomed flat from autumn 1836 to September 1838. After Pushkin's death the flat changed hands many times and it is believed that it was occupied by one of the departments of police as well as a society of masons. A memorial plaque was put up in 1880, but the building did not become a museum until 1925.

Pushkin, his wife, their four children and his wife's two sisters lived in the flat, served by some fifteen staff. During this time, Pushkin edited his journal *Sovremennik* (the Contemporary), finished *The Captain's Daughter* and worked on a history of Peter the Great. But his personal life was much disturbed. Not only was he under constant suspicion from Tsar Nicholas I, but he was ever watchful of his wife, Natalya Goncharova, supposedly the most beautiful woman in St Petersburg. She was attracting the attention of a French cavalry officer called D'Anthès, an attachment which was noted not just by Pushkin. He decided to forbid D'Anthès from paying any more visits to the house. The insulted D'Anthès insisted that he was visiting the house only to pay court to one of the sisters – not to Pushkin's wife. Pushkin then insisted upon and arranged their marriage. The irony was that by this action Pushkin only brought D'Anthès and his wife closer together. Pushkin started to receive anonymous letters congratulating him on being a cuckold. Two months later, Pushkin challenged D'Anthès to a duel, and was fatally wounded (see CHERNAYA RECHKA, p. 189). After Pushkin was brought home, he lay dying for two days. During this time he received crowds of visitors who came to pay their last respects. People taking carriages on the streets had no need to give the address of their destination, the two words 'To Pushkin' being sufficient to bring them to his door. He died on 29 January 1837 at 2.45pm.

The popularity of the museum reflects the poet's almost godlike status in Russia and it is a shrine to the poet. Appropriately the emphasis is on his death. The entrance is facing the main staircase where Pushkin's friend Zhukovsky kept a notice-board, informing visitors of Pushkin's state of health during the days after the duel. The dining room was the furthest room to which visitors were admitted. Pushkin spent the final hours of his life in his study and the clock shows the exact time of his death. There are some of the poet's possessions on display – from a decanter and wine glass to scissors, walking sticks, pipe and inkwell. Of particular interest is the display in the nursery which indulges the fascination of the duel to the hilt – we can see the waistcoat complete with bullet hole Pushkin wore in the duel, a candle from the church funeral and one of the gloves

*The three-storey house with two arched gateways on the River Moika,
where Pushkin had his last apartment.*

worn by his friend Vyazemsky – the other was placed in the
poet's coffin. After Pushkin's funeral Zhukovsky left a plan of
the layout of the apartment, a document which has proved
invaluable for its reconstruction.

Closed on Tuesdays and the last Friday of the month

Moiki, Nab. Reki, 24

In 1909 this building housed the editorial office of *Apollon*
(Apollo), which quickly became Russia's leading modernist
journal, and was the brainchild of Nikolay Gumilyov and the art
critic Sergey Makovsky. The journal was founded at a time when
the Symbolist movement was disintegrating, and espoused the
aesthetic ideas of Acmeism, the literary movement which arose
to replace it, headed by Gumilyov, Akhmatova and Mandelstam,
whose poetry was first published here in 1910.

Moiki, Nab. Reki, 40

This was the location of the former Hotel Demouth, which is where the dramatist Griboedov first settled in June 1824. He had come to St Petersburg to try and get his play *Woe from Wit* published while on extended leave from his duties as diplomatic secretary to General Ermolov, commander of the Russian army in the Caucasus. Griboedov also stayed here from March to May of 1828, when he came to deliver to Nicholas I the Turkmenchai peace treaty he had helped negotiate with Persia. During this time, Griboedov began planning a trip abroad with his friends Zhukovsky, Pushkin, Krylov and Vyazemsky, and attended a reading of Pushkin's unpublished play *Boris Godunov*.

Pushkin lived here later on in the 1820s, and Gogol boldly attempted to pay a call on his idol soon after his arrival in St Petersburg in 1829. Such was the shyness of the twenty-year-old Gogol, however (his first literary success would not come until several years later), that he had to go and down a glass of liqueur at a nearby hostelry in order to summon up the courage to knock on the door. When he finally did so, he was bitterly disappointed to learn that Pushkin was asleep, having stayed up all night playing cards.

Another famous Russian writer who stayed here was Turgenev, who took a room in the hotel during his visits to Russia from abroad in the 1870s. The building has been much altered since that time.

Moiki, Nab. Reki, 59

On 19 December 1919, on the initiative of Maxim Gorky, a literary centre and hostel for writers called the House of the Arts was opened on the corner of the Moika river and the Nevsky pr. in the former home of one of the richest St Petersburg merchants,

Eliseev. Blok read his essay 'The Collapse of Humanism' on the day of its opening.

At the time, St Petersburg, then called Petrograd, was devastated by the Civil War. Writers and intellectuals were not spared the desperate privations of its inhabitants, such as shortages of food and firewood. Despite this, a very active literary life continued in St Petersburg which many attribute entirely to the creation of organizations such as the House of Arts.

Among the many writers who lived in this building (known as DISK, an acronym for Dom Isskustv) at one time or another were Osip Mandelstam, Evgeny Zamyatin, Viktor Shklovsky, Vladislav Khodasevich, Mikhail Zoshchenko and Andrey Bely. The house was described in many memoirs, by Korney Chukovsky and others, and also in fiction. An example of the latter is Olga Forsh's roman-à-clef, the appropriately titled *The Mad Ship*, in which she writes about many of the inhabitants under fictitious names. The building also features in Evgeny Zamyatin's story 'Mask' and in a sketch entitled 'House of the Arts' in Mikhail Zoshchenko's *Before Sunrise*.

Mandelstam describes his accommodation as 'heavenly luxury', despite the fact that he lived in one of the less sumptuous wings. Many literary events such as lectures and public readings were organized in the building and the House of Arts published its own magazine, of which Evgeny Zamyatin was the editor. But the creative atmosphere of the house was to be short-lived – it closed suddenly at the end of 1922. Today the building houses a cinema.

Moiki, Nab. Reki, 78

The twenty-four-year-old Mikhail Lermontov often attended the salons of Alexandra Osipovna Smirnova here in 1838. The heroine of his poem 'Shtoss' is modelled on her. Smirnova's salons were among the most celebrated in St Petersburg, and were attended by all the famous literati of the time.

Moiki, Nab. Reki, 84

In 1832 the eighteen-year-old Mikhail Lermontov stayed here in Count Lansky's House, a building that no longer exists, but which would have occupied part of the site of the present number 84. He lived here with his grandmother, Mme Arsenieva, who took charge of his upbringing after his mother's death. They came to St Petersburg from Moscow to complete Lermontov's education in the capital and Lermontov attended the nearby School for Cavalier Guards on St Isaac's square. Lermontov's first impressions of the city were not positive ones. He found it foggy and depressing, and the people unsympathetic. He stayed in this flat until he had completed his schooling in 1834.

Mokhovaya Ul., 3

Goncharov spent the last thirty years of his life at this address. He chose the flat because it was grander than his previous one and, he felt, more suited to his new status as literary censor under the new Tsar, Alexander II. In 1859 his novel *Oblomov* was published, bringing him immediate fame. Although it is said that Goncharov lived a lonely life at this address, he did nevertheless receive visitors, among them Turgenev, Nekrasov and Saltykov-Shchedrin.

The three-roomed flat on the first floor looked out on to a courtyard. One of its main features was a large sofa which had once belonged to Nekrasov; a friend visiting the flat observed its likeness to the one on which the indolent Oblomov spends most of his days in Goncharov's novel. According to memories of contemporaries, the flat was bleak and gloomy, hardly ever letting in the sun. Goncharov, who enjoyed going on long walks around the city, found the climate oppressive, and whenever possible would escape to European resorts in search of the sun.

He died here in September 1891 and it is said that crowds gathered on the street. Goncharov was buried at the Alexander Nevsky Monastery, but in August 1956 his remains were transferred to a new spot at the Volkov Cemetery at Rasstanny per.

Mokhovaya Ul., 26

In the latter part of the nineteenth century this was the home of the influential cultural critic Vladimir Stasov, who wrote on a wide variety of topics, particularly Russian art and music, which he defended to the hilt. He occupied a senior post at the nearby Public Library from 1872 to 1906, the year he died. Tolstoy came to visit him here during his visit to St Petersburg in 1878.

Mokhovaya Ul., 33

In pre-revolutionary times, this was the location of the famed Tenishev School, a modern, forward-thinking institution attended by the sons of the liberal intelligentsia. Osip Mandelstam became a pupil here in 1900, but was not enamoured of the emphasis on the sciences in the school curriculum:

> Our corridors were not corridors but riding halls with tall ceilings and parqueted floors, the atmosphere of which, crossed by slanting columns of dust-laden sunlight, generally smelled of gas from the physics laboratories. The practical demonstrations consisted of cruel and needless vivisections, the expulsion of all the air from a glass bell in order to observe a poor mouse die of suffocation on its back, the torturing of frogs, the scientific boiling of water, with a description of this process, and the melting of little glass rods on the gas burners.

The Tenishev School was where Vladimir Nabokov became a pupil in 1911, at the age of twelve, having hitherto received his education from private tutors. One of the family's two chauffeurs would drive him here each morning from Bolshaya Morskaya ul.:

> Upon reaching Nevski Avenue, one followed it for a long stretch, during which it was a pleasure to overtake with no effort some cloaked guardsman in his light sleigh drawn by a pair of black stallions snorting and speeding along under the bright blue netting that prevented lumps of hard snow from flying into the passenger's face. A street on the left side with a lovely name – Karavannaya (the Street of Caravans) – took one past an unforgettable toyshop. Next came the Cinizelli Circus (famous for its wrestling tournaments). Finally, after crossing an ice-bound canal one drove up to the gates of Tenishev School...

An individualist from an early age, Nabokov did not endear himself to his teachers by refusing to join societies or to participate fully in school games. Nor were they enthusiastic about his turning up at school each morning in a chauffeur-driven car and his free use of English and French expressions in his essays, which seemed to them to be pretentious. In 1916, one of his teachers, the poet and Gogol critic Vladimir Gippius, cousin of the more famous Zinaida (and a great influence on the young Mandelstam), read aloud from the volume of adolescent love poetry the young Nabokov had just published, to the great amusement of his classmates. The ensuing embarrassment proved instrumental in hardening the author to hostile reviews in the future.

The amphitheatre-shaped auditorium at the school was often rented out for meetings, and many leading poets gave readings here in the pre-revolutionary years. In October 1915, the 'peasants poets' Klyuev and Esenin gave a poetry reading wearing rustic shirts and large crosses round their necks in an attempt to accentuate their Slavonic origins.

Mokhovaya Ul., 36

From August 1919, this building housed the editorial offices of Vsemirnaya Literatura (World Literature), the publishing house founded by Gorky after the Revolution, which was intended to make the classics of world literature available to the proletarian masses. It was a hopelessly idealistic scheme, but nevertheless provided a modicum of financial support to the many hungry writers drafted in to help with translation and editorial work during the harsh years of the Civil War.

Many of the contributors to the World Literature project were also given accommodation in the building. Evgeny Zamyatin lived here between 1922 and 1928. Zamyatin wrote the introductions to works by H. G. Wells and Jack London. In his 'Soviet Heretic' he describes the enterprise: 'As though recalling once again its role as a window on Europe, Petersburg flung this window wide open, and European works, in the excellent translations provided by Vsemirnaya Literatura, poured out in editions of many thousands to all ends of Russia.' He also describes the offices where they worked:

> Petersburg – swept out, emptied; boarded-up stores; houses pulled down bit by bit for firewood; brick skeletons of stoves ... we gathered in one of the small backrooms of World Literature. A dining table, a lamp under a green shade; faces in the shadow. To the left of the door, a warm tile stove bench, and on it and around it Blok, Gumilyov, Chukovsky ... it is difficult to repair plumbing or build a house, but it is very easy to build the Tower of Babel. And we were building the Tower of Babel: we planned to publish a Pantheon of Russian Literature – from Fonvizin to our days. One hundred volumes!

These ambitions were never achieved, partly because of paper shortages after the Civil War but also because of Gorky's emigration.

Moskovsky Pr.

The inn on the former Zabalkansky pr. where Raskolnikov makes his confession of murder to Zamyotov in *Crime and Punishment* stands at the beginning of Moskovsky pr. In a seedy part of town, the inn is named ironically as the Palais de Crystal, after a smarter establishment which opened on Voznesensky pr. in 1862.

Moskovsky Pr., 19

This was the home in the late 1890s of the Mendeleev family, and Alexander Blok became a frequent visitor here in 1898. Earlier that summer he had become involved with Lyubov Mendeleeva, daughter of the famous scientist, while holidaying at his dacha (the Mendeleev estate, BOBLOVO (see p. 143), was near to Shakhmatovo, where he spent his summers). On his return to the city in the autumn, Blok entered St Petersburg University, and started visiting Lyubov Dmitrievna at her family home here, which from 1897 was a flat in the Chamber of Weights and Measures on the former Zabalkansky pr., where her father was director. Blok eventually married Lyubov Mendeleeva in 1903.

Moskovsky Pr., 96

— *Voskresensky Novodevichy Convent* The grey pseudo-Russian building of the New Convent of the Virgin was built in 1845. Both Tyutchev and Nekrasov lie buried in the cemetery.

Nekrasova Ul.

The streets of St Petersburg, particularly those in the immediate vicinity of Daniil Kharms' flat on Ul. Mayakovskogo, feature in many of his writings, including his tiny story 'Sonnet', written in the 1930s, one of the so-called 'Happenings' from his Blue Notebook (Znamenskaya ul. is now Ul. Vosstaniya, and Bassei-naya ul. is now Ul. Nekrasova):

> An amazing thing happened to me: I suddenly forgot which came first, 7 or 8.
>
> I went round to my neighbours and asked them what they thought.
>
> Imagine their and my surprise when they suddenly discovered that they too could not remember the right numerical order. They remembered 1, 2, 3, 4, 5 and 6, but had forgotten what came next.
>
> We all went over to the grocer's on the corner of Znamenskaya and Basseinaya streets and asked the cashier about our problem. The cashier smiled sadly, took a tiny hammer out of her mouth and said, twitching her nose, 'In my opinion, seven follows eight whenever eight follows seven.'
>
> We thanked the cashier and left the shop happily. But when we thought about what the cashier had said, we grew despondent again, because her words seemed to be completely devoid of any meaning.
>
> Whatever were we to do? We went to the Summer Garden and started counting the trees in it. But when we had counted as far as six, we stopped and started quarrelling: some of us thought 7 came next and others thought it was 8.
>
> We would have gone on arguing for a long time, but, as it happened, a child fell off a bench just at that point and broke both his jaws. That distracted us from our quarrel.
>
> And then we went back to our respective homes.

Nekrasova Ul., 11

Established here in 1918, the Writers' House provided many helpful facilities for writers and journalists in an impoverished city suffering from paper shortage and lack of heating. These included a library, a dining room serving meals at reduced prices for up to 500 people, and warm rooms in which to work. Less selective than its rival, the House of Arts on the River Moika (see MOIKI, NAB. REKI, 59, p. 257), it was traditionally associated (and therefore criticized) with the older pre-revolutionary literary generation. However, its cultural activities did not exclude younger writers such as Akhmatova and Zamyatin, who served at one time on the governing board, and Blok, Bely and Zamyatin were among those who took part in readings. Like the House of Arts, the Writers' House closed in 1922. By this time living conditions in St Petersburg had improved and there was a less urgent need to protect writers.

Nevsky Pr.

The central street of the city, the Nevsky is almost three miles long. Most nineteenth-century travellers entering the city would approach it from the end of the Alexander Nevsky Lavra Monastery. Up to the intersection with the Fontanka river, the houses were plain and homely. But after this point the avenue expanded and became grander. When Nikolay Chernyshevsky first stayed in St Petersburg in 1846 as an eighteen-year-old student, he was amazed by the number of bookshops on the street, most of which were laid out between the beginning of the street at the Admiralty and the Anichkov Bridge: 'In general, the best bookshops are to be found in private houses, rather than in Gostinny Dvor. In Gostinny Dvor, the best bookshop is Isakov's (marvellous French books) and Sveshnikov's.'

The city's main thoroughfare was immortalized in Gogol's eponymous story of 1834:

> There is nothing finer than Nevsky Avenue, not in St Petersburg, at any rate; for in St Petersburg it is everything. And indeed, is there anything more gay, more brilliant, more resplendent than this beautiful street of our capital? I am sure that not one of her anaemic inhabitants, not one of

her innumerable Civil Servants, would exchange Nevsky Avenue for all the treasures in the world. Not only the young man of twenty-five, the young gallant with the beautiful moustache and the immaculate morning coat, but the man with white hair sprouting on his chin and a head as smooth as a billiard ball, yes, even he is enthralled with Nevsky Avenue. And the ladies ... Oh, for the ladies Nevsky Avenue is a thing of even greater delight? But is there anyone who does not feel thrilled and delighted with it?

Gogol's ambivalence about St Petersburg is reflected at the end of the story, however, which ends with his narrator expressing rather different feelings about the main street of St Petersburg: 'Oh, do not trust that Nevsky Avenue! I always wrap myself up more closely in my cloak when I walk along it and do my best not to look at the things I pass. For all is deceit, all is a dream, all is not what it seems...'

Dostoevsky, the other great chronicler of St Petersburg, rarely described the Nevsky pr. in his work, his characters frequenting much humbler areas. The narrator of *Notes from the Underground* does not feel at home here:

Sometimes on holidays between three and four o'clock I used to hang around the Nevsky Prospekt, strolling along the sunny side. That is to say, I did not really stroll but rather experienced countless torments, disparagements, and outbursts of spleen; but to be honest there was something about it that I needed. I darted about like a rabbit, in the most unattractive way, amidst the passers-by, continually making way for generals, or horseguards officers or hussars, or fine ladies; at these moments I would feel a convulsive pain in my heart and a burning sensation in my back at the mere thought of the misery of my outfit...

Although he never lived here, Andrey Bely became Gogol's and Dostoevsky's true heir in the way that he describes the city's streets in his novel *Petersburg* (1916): 'A Petersburg street in autumn is piercing; it both chills you to the marrow and tickles. As soon as you leave it and go indoors, the street flows in your veins like a fever ... Petersburg streets possess one indubitable quality: they transform passersby into shadows...'

Nevsky Pr., 15

The hero of Pushkin's *Eugene Onegin* frequents Talon's Restaurant, once housed in this building. In another part of the building was the Club of the Nobility, where in 1839 Turgenev and Lermontov attended a New Year's Eve masquerade. Turgenev remembers how the Tsar's daughters, Mariya and Olga, wearing masks and blue and pink dominoes, 'incessantly pestered him, linked hands with him; one mask replaced another, and he practically never left his place and silently listened to their chirpings, by turns fixing them with his gloomy eyes'.

Nevsky Pr., 18

This building houses both a second-hand bookshop and a literary café. In the 1830s this was the Wolff et Beranger Café, a fashionable spot frequented by young society as well as the secret police who watched their movements. On 27 January 1837, the fatal day of his duel with D'Anthès, Alexander Pushkin awaited his second (his schoolfriend Danzas) here. Before meeting him, Danzas went to Kurakin's firearms shop at Nevsky, 12, to fetch the pistols. The two then set off in a sleigh together at about 4pm towards the Troitsky Bridge over the River Neva. A few days later, Lermontov's poetic tribute to Pushkin 'The Death of a Poet' was circulated in the café. The poem was considered too overtly critical of the government, which it accused of being involved in Pushkin's murder, and Lermontov was exiled to the Caucasus.

In the 1840s there was a reading and smoking room in the café as well as the exotic Café Chinois. Fyodor Dostoevsky, as yet unknown as a writer, would come here to read the newspapers and new journals.

Nevsky Pr., 20

The journal *Otechestvennye zapiski* (National Annals) was based at this address in 1839. One of the leading journals of its time, *Otechestvennye zapiski* was popular among Westerners rather than Slavophiles. It published the poems of Lermontov, Nekrasov and Turgenev. The journal suffered in 1846 when it lost some of its best writers such as Belinsky to the rival *Sovremennik* (the Contemporary), but was taken over by Nekrasov in 1787, who became its editor-in-chief. Under the editorship of Nekravsov and Saltykov-Shchedrin, the journal became one of the leading publications of the Russian Populists in the 1870s.

Nevsky Pr., 42

The writer Daniil Kharms (real name Danill Yuvachev), who was born at Glinskay ul., 1, on 17 December 1905, went to school here. Later to become one of Russia's leading Absurdist writers, Kharms demonstrated eccentric tendencies from an early age. While he was a pupil at the Peterschule, the main German school in St Petersburg, housed in a Baroque eighteenth-century building next to the Lutheran church (it remained a school in Soviet times) and known for its iron discipline, Kharms would sometimes behave in unpredictable ways. A contemporary remembers him bringing a french horn to school one day, for example, and surreptitiously trying to play it during class. His school friends and neighbours were equally bemused by the long conversations he held in their presence with an invented 'Mütterchen' who lived under the staircase.

Nevsky Pr., 30

Now the St Petersburg Maly Concert Hall, this used to be the house of a man named Engelhardt, a friend of Pushkin. Engelhardt put on lavish masquerade parties here, some of which were attended by the Tsar and other members of the Imperial family. Lermontov found in these parties direct inspiration for his drama *Masquerade*, a satirical and critical portrait of St Petersburg high society. The play did not pass the censors and was never staged in the poet's lifetime.

Nevsky Pr., 38

Until 1899, Suvorin's bookshop had its premises here, on the corner of Nevsky Pr. and Mikhailovskaya ul. When the Hall of the Nobility was rebuilt and enlarged, the bookshop, one of the largest in the city, moved up to Nevsky Pr., 40., next to the Armenian church.

Nevsky Pr., 42

To the right of the small blue and white Armenian church, which is set back from the street, is house number 42, where the poet Fyodor Tyutchev spent the last eighteen years of his life, from 1854 to 1872. Originally designed by Y. Veldten, the house forms part of an ensemble with the church and number 40 next door. The building of number 42 has undergone several changes in its appearance.

As well as an Armenian church, many churches stood in this area of the Nevsky – Lutheran, Catholic, Dutch and Russian Orthodox. In his *Travels across Russia* Alexandre Dumas named the Nevsky pr. the 'street of religious tolerance'. The building of the church ensemble was funded by a rich Armenian named Ivan Lazarus, whose family had settled in Russia in the eighteenth century. He had to ask special permission from Catherine the Great to build a church for the city's Armenian community, and consequently named it St Catherine.

The Tyutchev family were friends of the Lazarus family, and it was no coincidence that the Tyutchev family house in Moscow on Armyansky per., where the poet grew up, also stood next door to an Armenian church built by Veldten from Lazarus family funds. In St Petersburg they rented from Lazarus the large fourteen-roomed apartment on the fourth floor here. In a letter to his wife Tyutchev described the seventy-eight-step climb to the flat. But what astonished him in particular was the flat's generous size; it could fit his large family quite comfortably, however much they spread themselves out in it. The flat looked out on the Nevsky pr. 'Instead of Mont Blanc,' Tyutchev wrote to his daughter, who was convalescing in France, 'I can see Gostinny Dvor, wet from the rain.'

During his St Petersburg period, Tyutchev mixed with many writers from the literary circle surrounding the journal *Sovremennik* (the Contemporary), to which he contributed. Turgenev was a visitor here, and wrote the introduction to a volume of Tyutchev's poetry. To support his wife and family Tyutchev worked at the Ministry of Foreign Affairs and was president of the Committee of Foreign Censorship. Tyutchev died at Tsarskoe Selo, where he spent his last summers. He is buried in St Petersburg at the Novo-devichy Monastery, where Nekrasov is also buried.

Nevsky Pr., 47

This branch of Palkin's restaurant, resurrected in recent times, was one of the most famous in the city, and was frequented by Dostoevsky (who lived nearby) and other literary celebrities. It opened in 1875, and featured a marble staircase, a winter garden with tropical plants, a pool stuffed with small sturgeon, a concert hall and numerous private dining rooms, all richly furnished. When Chekhov was taken to dine here amongst the aspidistras in the ornate main dining room in 1885, during his first visit to St Petersburg, he declared he had never been anywhere so smart.

Nevsky Pr., 51

In 1855, on his return from an exciting round-the-world voyage as secretary to Admiral Putyatin, Goncharov resumed his sedentary life in St Petersburg, working for the government service. He described his flat here as 'wretched' and its staircase 'revolting', but managed to invite guests to come and inspect the Chinese and Japanese objects that he had collected on his travels. On his promotion to literary censor a year later, he decided that he ought to live in a 'more presentable manner' and moved to a flat at MOKHO-

VAYA UL., 3 (see p. 259). While living at this address he started work on his travel notes, which later became the book *The Frigate Pallada*, and worked on his major novel *Oblomov*.

Nevsky Pr., 57

From 1920 to 1923, this building housed the offices of the private publishing house Alkonost, conceived in some respects as the descendant of the pre-revolutionary firm of Sirin. Having initially begun its activities in a second-hand bookshop in 1919 (Kolokolnaya ul., 1), Alkonost became the sole publisher of Blok's poetry and prose (it issued a famous edition of his poem 'The Twelve' with illustrations by Annenkov), and also published writings by Bely, Remizov and Ivanov.

Nevsky Pr., 64

From 1822 until 1827, this was the residence of the pety Vasily Zhukovsky, who received many literary figures here, including Batyushkov, Karamzin and Vyazemsky.

Nevsky Pr., 64

From October 1850 to April 1851, Turgenev (by this time largely resident in Europe) lived here in Lopatin's House, on the corner of Nevsky pr. and the Fontanka river. Here he worked on the short play *The Provincial Lady*, which he saw performed in Moscow in January 1851. One of Lopatin's previous tenants was the critic Visarion Belinsky. The great Russian critic had lived in a variety of places since arriving in St Petersburg from Moscow in 1839. He had already moved six times when he took up residence here in 1842, and was to move a further three times before his death in 1848. The four years he lived in the Lopatin House here, however, were the longest period of time he spent in any one place. Turgenev greatly admired Belinsky and often came to visit him here. He is buried near to Belinsky in the Volkov Cementary at RASSTANNY PER., 30 (see p. 282), as he requested.

Nevsky Pr., 84

From 1815 to 1817, this was the first St Petersburg residence of the poet Vasily Zhukovsky, whose literary talents led him to be invited to the capital from Moscow to become reader to the Empress Maria Fyodorovna, mother of Alexander I. His career at court continued in 1825, when he was appointed tutor to the future Alexander II.

Nevsky Pr., 86

When Isaak Babel first came to St Petersburg in 1915, he rented a flat in a cellar on Pushkinskaya ul. for a while, which he apparently shared with a drunken waiter. He had been born and grew up in Jewish Odessa, but moved to the capital at the age of twenty-one to pursue a career as a writer. In this he achieved a degree of success, as Gorky published his first stories in his journal *Letopis* (Chronicle) in 1916. This journal had been founded by Gorky the previous year, following his return from exile in 1913. Its editorial offices were located at Bolshaya Monetnaya ul., 18. At the time of the Revolution, Babel served for a short time in the army, but returned to Petrograd due to illness. It was probably at this time that he lived here on Nevsky. Viktor Shklovsky, who used to visit him during these hungry years, remembers there always being a samovar and 'sometimes bread' in his room.

Nikolaevsky Most

The Nikolaevsky Bridge links the Angliiskaya nab. to Vasilievsky Island, areas of the city which figure prominently in Bely's *Petersburg*: 'From far, far away, as though farther off than they should have been, the islands sank and cowered in fright; and the buildings cowered; it seemed that the waters would sink and that at that instant the depths, the greenish murk would surge over them. And over this greenish murk the Nikolaevsky Bridge thundered and trembled in the fog.'

Ostrovskogo Pl.

In tsarist times, the square was known as Aleksandrinskaya pl., after the theatre which dominates it, but was renamed in honour of the nineteenth-century playwright after the Revolution. The Alexandrinsky Theatre, which in Soviet times was named after Pushkin, is housed in a yellow Classical building, constructed in 1832. In tsarist times it was Russia's most important showcase for drama, and was a government-run institution which came under the umbrella of the Imperial Theatres administration.

Among the classics of Russian drama which had their premières here are Gogol's *The Government Inspector*, first performed in 1836, and Chekhov's *The Seagull*, first performed in 1896. For both authors, the experience of seeing their works performed on this stage was deeply traumatic, and both fled the city soon afterwards (in Chekhov's case the night after the première). Neither felt their intentions had been understood.

Numerous Russian writers came to see plays performed here throughout the nineteenth century. Mikhail Lermontov often visited this theatre as a young officer and in his unfinished novel *Princess Ligovskaya* he describes the theatre. Lermontov always hoped that his play *Masquerade* would be staged here, but it never passed the censors during his lifetime (the play was staged in full only in 1917). In his student years Turgenev had attended the first-night performance of Gogol's *The Government Inspector*, and his own plays *The Provincial Lady* and *A Month in the Country* were staged at the theatre in 1851 and 1872 respectively. The actress Maria Savina played the part of Vera in a revival of *A Month in the Country* in 1879 and overwhelmed Turgenev by her performance.

Perhaps the strangest Russian work ever to be performed

here was a farcical comedy about a pug dog called *Fantasia* written in 1850 by Count Alexey Tolstoy and his cousins Alexey and Vladimir Zhemchuzhnikov. An irreverent parody of contemporary vaudeville, it shocked its first-night audience when it was produced in January 1851 in the presence of Nicholas I and was promptly banned from further performances. Before walking out, the humourless Tsar was apparently particularly offended by the 'small interlude' in the middle of the comedy featuring the pug dog running across the stage, followed, to the accompaniment of a tune from *The Barber of Seville*, by a bulldog 'sniffing its traces'.

Ostrovskogo Pl., 1

The Russian National Library (known in Soviet times as the Saltykov-Shchedrin Library) was founded in 1795, for the preservation of foreign works. It was opened for public use in 1814, and is now Russia's second-largest library. The great Russian fabulist, Ivan Krylov, spent twenty-nine years of his life working here, as well as writing the many volumes of fables for which he is renowned. The critic Vladimir Stasov was another well-known employee with literary connections.

Ostrovskogo Pl., 7

As the plaque outside commemorates, it was in this building, on 21 November 1895, that Bunin gave his first public reading.

Panteleimonovskaya Ul., 4, Kv. 6

It was to a damp flat on the third floor at this address on the former Ul. Pestelya that the poet Alexander Blok's family moved in 1883, upon vacating the Rector's House at St Petersburg University. They remained here until 1885. Until Blok's mother married again in 1889, the family moved several times, first to a spacious flat in building 18/29 on the corner of Sotsialisticheskaya ul. (formerly Ivanovskaya ul.) and Ul. Dostoevskogo in the winter of 1885. Even with a grand piano and large numbers of tropical plants from the university greenhouse, the flat seemed spacious, but proved too expensive, and the family moved again to Bolshaya Moskovskaya ul., 9 (opposite Svechny per.), in 1886.

Panteleimonovskaya Ul., 5

Pushkin rented a flat in Olivio's House, opposite the church, in 1833–4. Although delighted with its proximity to the Summer Garden, he quarrelled with the owner, Olivio, as he was continually locked out when he returned home late at night – the gates were locked by the doorman at 10pm. In a letter to his wife in June 1834, Pushkin relates the argument he had with his landlord, saying that he had written Olivio a letter telling him he wanted to change flats 'to which the idiot has still not replied'. More floors have been built on, but the three-floored dwelling of Pushkin's day is just discernible.

Pestelya, Ul. (*See* PANTELEIMONOVSKAYA UL., p. 274)

Peter and Paul Fortress (*See* PETROPAVLOVSKAYA KREPOST, p. 277)

Petra Lavrova, Ul. (*See* FURSHTADTSKAYA UL., p. 210)

Petrogradskaya Nab., 44, Kv. 2, 7, 13

The nine-year-old Alexander Blok moved to this address on the former Nab. Bolshoi Nevki on the Petrograd Side in St Petersburg's most industrial suburb in 1889, when his mother married Franz Kublitsky-Piottukh, a lieutenant in the Grenadier Guards. It was in a succession of first- and second-floor barracks flats here (they changed each time his stepfather was promoted) that

Blok was to spend the next sixteen years. After the Rector's House and the large, airy flats in the centre of town Blok and his mother had lived in previously, moving to this austere-looking military building was quite a shock. Neither was very happy to have officers and their families as neighbours. The building, which had a further floor added in the 1930s, now houses a student hostel for the Medical Institute.

Blok continued to live here while he was a student at St Petersburg University, where he studied first law (chosen because it seemed easiest), then languages. He also spent the first three years of his marriage living here with his wife Lyubov Mendeleeva under the same roof as his mother and stepfather. The flat was then divided into three parts – one section for Blok and his wife, another for his mother and stepfather, and the third for dining and receiving guests. Blok and Lyubov Dmitrievna were allotted two rooms – a study and bedroom. The large desk with many drawers, which Blok worked at throughout his life, and which can be seen in the Blok Museum at DEKABRISTOV, UL., 57 (see p. 193) was part of the furniture here, as was his grandfather's armchair, where Andrey Bely remembered him sitting with his wooden cigarette holder when he came to visit in 1905.

By this time Blok had begun to acquire recognition as a poet of mystical inclination; his first book of poetry, the ethereal *Verses about the Beautiful Lady*, had appeared in 1904, and was championed by Symbolist writers who recognized him as one of their own. Chief among them were the Merezhkovskys, whose *jours-fixes* he had begun to frequent (see LITEINY PR., 24, p. 232). The tensions which arose as a result of the peculiar nature of the Bloks' marriage were soon inevitably exacerbated by the attentions of Andrey Bely, who fell madly in love with Lyubov Dmitrievna and started making frequent visits from Moscow to plead with her here, sometimes accompanying himself on the Bloks' piano as he did so. Relations were further strained by hostility which arose between Lyubov Dmitrievna and Blok's doting mother. In 1906, having finally graduated from university, and broken off with Bely, the couple moved into their own apartment.

Petropavlovskaya Krepost

Originally built as a fortress by Peter the Great in 1703 to stave off enemy attack, the Peter and Paul Fortress soon became a prison, and the Bastille of tsarist Russia.

Alexander Radishchev, author of the subversive *Journey from St Petersburg to Moscow*, published in the time of Catherine the Great, was imprisoned here for three months in 1790. Following a mock execution, he was then exiled to Siberia for ten years. Around half a century later Dostoevsky was imprisoned here for his role in the Petrashevsky conspiracy before and after the last-minute reprieve from his death sentence on Semyonovskaya pl. (now Pionerskaya pl.). He was housed in a cell in the Trubetskoy Bastion in the Secret House (demolished in 1884), which had been built in the so-called Alekseevsky Ravelin. The Secret House was where many nineteenth-century revolutionaries, including the Decembrists, were imprisoned. Dostoevsky was held in rooms 7 and 9 from 23 April to 24 December 1849 until his exile to Siberia. During this time he wrote the short story 'A Small Hero'. Some of the cells in the Trubetskoy Bastion have been reconstructed and in 1924 it was opened as a museum.

Chernyshevsky wrote his famous novel *What Is to Be Done?* while imprisoned here in 1862–3 for 678 days. It is said that he was arrested and brought here by the same Colonel Rakeev who in 1837 had overseen the secret journey of Pushkin's coffin from St Petersburg to his country estate at Mikhailovskoe. From prison Chernyshevsky wrote to his wife: 'our lives will belong to history; hundreds of years will pass, and our names will still

Joseph Brodsky on the roof of the Peter and Paul Fortress in 1967

be dear to people; and they will remember us with gratitude'. In 1864 he was led to the scaffold, as Dostoevsky had been fifteen years earlier, only to receive a reprieve. He was sentenced instead to seven years' hard labour, followed by twelve years of exile in Siberia. He never returned to St Petersburg, dying finally in Saratov in 1889.

Pionerskaya Pl.

Semyonovskaya square, once the parade ground of the Semyonovsky Regiment, no longer exists, but it once occupied the territory between the Vitebsk Station and Marata ul. The Theatre of Young Spectators now stands on a large part of the former square. As well as a parade ground it was also a place of execution. The twenty-eight-year-old Dostoevsky was sentenced to death here on 22 December 1849 for his involvement with the subversive Petrashevsky Circle. The execution turned out to be a mock one, and just as the offenders were about to be hanged the Tsar issued a last-minute reprieve. Dostoevsky was haunted by the experience throughout his life, and the episode is invoked several times by Prince Myshkin in *The Idiot*:

> The chief and the worst pain is perhaps not inflicted by wounds, but by your certain knowledge that in an hour, in ten minutes, in half a minute, now, this moment your world will fly out of your body, and that you will be a human being no longer, and that that's certain, the main thing is that it is certain ... here you have been sentenced to death and the whole terrible agony lies in the fact that you will certainly not escape, and there is no agony greater than that ... Why this cruel, hideous, unnecessary, and useless mockery? Possibly there are men who have sentences of death read out to them and have been given time to go through this torture, and have then been told, You can go now, you've been reprieved. Such men could perhaps tell us. It was of agony like this and of such horror that Christ spoke ...

Pirogova Per.

In Dostoevsky's *The Insulted and Injured*, Ivan Petrovich, the narrator of the tale, lives on this street, the former Maksimilian-sky per. and it is where Nelly's grandfather dies. In *Crime and Punishment*, it is thought, the entrance to the yard where Raskolnikov hid the stolen goods was from Pirogova per. (*See also* VOZNESENSKY PR., p. 306)

Plekhanova Ul., 39

In April 1829, Gogol moved out of the rooms on the Griboedov canal he had shared with his friend Danilevsky, and came to live here, on the former Bolshaya Meshchanskaya ul., as a tenant of a famous coach-builder of the time called Johann-Albert Jochim (who is mentioned by Khlestakov in Gogol's play *The Government Inspector*).

This area of St Petersburg was the centre of the capital's coach-building industry, and the German wheel- and coach-builders in St Petersburg tended either to live on Meshchanskaya or nearby Liteiny pr. The slightly gloomy aspect of this building with its three balconies and iron railings gave rise to legends among tenants that there were ghosts. Despite sharing an abode which housed two tailors, a dress shop, a cobbler, a tobacconist, a mender of broken china, a baker, a storage facility for winter clothing and a midwife, Gogol was certainly very lonely here; this was the first time that he had ever lived by himself, and the eight months that he spent in his rooms on the top floor beneath the roof were unhappy ones. His literary ambitions led him to the pseudonymous publication (at his own, or rather his mother's, expense) of *Hanz Kuechelgarten*, a poem he had written before coming to St Petersburg, but the enterprise ended in disaster. Derision by a handful of critics impelled Gogol to buy up all the copies and burn them. He then decided to flee abroad, telling his mother he was going to Lübeck to meet secretly with a woman he was tragically involved with. He gave his worried mother even more cause for alarm when he later explained that he was in Germany because he had to be treated for an illness he had contracted. None of this, of course, was true.

Plekhanova Ul., 43, Kv. 22

Tolstoy rented a flat here on the corner of Voznesensky pr. for two months at the end of 1856. The building has since been slightly altered.

Pokrovskaya Pl. (*See* TURGENEVA, PL., p. 302)

Povarskoy Per., 13

Ivan Turgenev rented a flat on the fourth floor of Tulubev's House from December 1853 to November 1854 after his period of exile on his country estate at Spasskoe Lutovinovo. The original building remains. The same flat was lived in by Nekrasov in 1845, and by Chernyshevsky in 1855. When he returned to St Petersburg in 1853 with his wife, having taught for two years in his native Saratov, Chernyshevsky again spent little time in one place. But it was in this modest apartment that he lived the longest in St Petersburg – from 1855 to 1860. He now became a leading critic with *Sovremennik* (the Contemporary), the famous journal founded by Pushkin, and the radical views he expressed in his own writings, such as *The Aesthetic Relations of Art to Reality*, which was his master's dissertation (1855), soon won him notoriety.

Przhevalskogo, Ul. (*See* STOLYARNY PER., p. 293)

Pushkarskaya Ul., 22

Mikhail Zoshchenko lived in a ground-floor flat in this building on the Petrograd Side in 1922. He had to move upstairs at one point because the house was flooded, and describes the 'water on the stairs' in his series of autobiographical sketches, *Before Sunrise*. He found it hard to work here, and was particularly disturbed by a neighbour's baby crying, so he moved into the more comfortable House of the Arts on Nevsky pr. for peace and warmth.

Pushkinskaya Ul., 10

The Symbolist publishing house Sirin (the bird of joy in Slavonic mythology), founded in October 1912, was based here. It was a venture into which a significant amount of energy was invested by Alexander Blok, who was responsible for bringing about the publication of Bely's novel *Petersburg*, in instalments in the publishing house's almanac between 1913 and 1914, and then in book form in 1916.

Pushkinskaya Ul., 20

A street near to the Moscow Station is where the Hotel Palais-Royal was situated earlier this century, and it was where Mayakovsky stayed in 1913, on an early visit to St Petersburg. The hotel, whose previous guests had included Chekhov and Chaliapin, had a reputation as a kind of bohemian refuge for artistic types. It was built in the 1880s, and was already rather run down by the time Mayakovsky took a room there.

It was during his 1913 visit that Mayakovsky, then twenty years old, gave the first public reading of his poetry, and appeared with other Russian Futurists at several locations, including the Stray Dog, at MIKHAILOVSKAYA PL., 5 (see p. 249), the Tenishev School, at MOKHOVAYA UL., 33 (see p. 260), and at the former Troitsky Theatre, on Ul. Rubinshteina, 18. In December 1913, he was producer and chief protagonist in the first performance of his two-act play *Vladimir Mayakovsky: A Tragedy* at the Luna Park Theatre on the former Ofitserskaya street (DEKABRISTOV UL., 39, see p. 192).

Mayakovsky also took a room here in July 1915 on the day he officially met the great love of his life, Lili Brik. He had come down from Chukovsky's dacha at Kuokkala (then in Finland) to see Elsa, Lili's sister, but fell so madly in love with Lili that he decided he had to remain in Petrograd on the very day he met her, leaving all his belongings behind at Kuokkala, and his clothes at the laundry. Mayakovsky stayed here until November, when he rented a room on Nadezhdinskaya ul. (now MAYAKOVSKOGO UL., p. 246), round the corner from the Briks, on ZHUKOVSKOGO UL. (see p. 309).

Rasstanny Per., 30

Turgenev's body was brought to the Volkov Cemetery here from Paris in September 1883. In accordance with his wishes, he was buried close to the grave of his friend Vissarion Belinsky. Other writers buried in the north-western 'Literatorskie Mostki' section of the cemetery include Radishchev, Saltykov-Shchedrin, Andreev, Blok, Kuprin and Leskov. In a 'posthumous request' Leskov had written the following: 'I ask that no kind of memorial is placed on my grave, other than an ordinary, simple wooden cross. If this cross disintegrates, and there be found a person who wishes to replace it with a new one, let him do this and accept my gratitude for his remembrance. Yet if there is no such well-wisher, that means that the time has passed for anyone to remember my grave.'

Razezzhaya Ul., 31

It was in this building that Fyodor Sologub and his wife Anastasia Chebotarevskaya took a flat in approximately 1910. The couple held noisy soirées here on Thursday nights, rivalling the famous 'Wednesdays' in Ivanov's tower (which ended with his departure to Moscow in 1912), at which masquerades, debates and dances would take place, attended by writers such as Leonid Andreev, Alexey Tolstoy, Anna Akhmatova and Mikhail Kuzmin, as well as actresses and the odd newspaper reporter. Blok was repeatedly invited, but grew to dislike large gatherings.

Rimskogo-Korsakogo, Pr., 3

Dostoevsky and his wife took two furnished rooms at number 3 on the former Ekateringofsky pr. between June and September 1871, just after their return from abroad, and it was here that their son, Fyodor, was born. In *Crime and Punishment* Marmeladov's accident takes place at the crossroads of this street and Voznesensky pr. He is run down by a grand and elegant barouche as he is crossing the road.

Rimskogo-Korsakogo, Pr., 43

The poet Zhukovsky took an apartment here in 1818 with his friend Pleshcheev. The literary soirées they held on Saturdays attracted the leading writers of the time, including Krylov, Pushkin, Küchelbecker and Vyazemsky.

Ruzovskaya Ul.

It was in a house owned by coffee merchant Ezhevsky somewhere along this street that the young poet Evgeny Baratynsky lived in 1818–19, latterly with his fellow poet and friend Anton Delvig. At the time, Baratynsky was serving as a private in the Life Guard Chasseurs. A contemporary recalls that the two poets lived a spartan life here, with barely a stick of furniture between them, and a servant, Nikita, who was permanently drunk and prone to considering whatever money he found in Delvig's pockets his own. This did not happen very frequently, however. On some occasions, the pair had run up so many debts that they were forced to live on an exclusive diet of jam furnished by an indulgent and trusting grocer near by. Their penniless but carefree existence came to an end, however, in 1820 when Baratynsky was promoted to under-officer and sent to Finland for five years with the Neslotsky Foot Regiment. Baratynsky had no wish to go to Finland, but his expulsion from the elite Corps de Pages military school in 1816, owing to his involvement in a theft, had denied him the privilege of entering military service as a guardsman. Joining the army as a regular soldier and winning promotion offered him the only possibility of obtaining a pardon and the chance of retiring honourably, which he was able to do in 1825, when, thanks to the intervention of well-placed friends, he was promoted to officer.

Sadovaya Ul.

Sadovaya street, which runs through the centre of the city, is one of its main thoroughfares and inevitably makes the odd appearance in fiction set in St Petersburg. The Yusupov Gardens, which stretch from the Yusupov Palace on the Fontanka to Sadovaya, are where Raskolnikov wanders at one point in *Crime and Punishment*, and Sadovaya street is mentioned in the story 'The Old Woman', written in 1939 by the experimental writer Daniil Kharms. The story, one of Kharms' masterpieces, has strong thematic associations with other classics of Russian literature set in St Petersburg, particularly *Crime and Punishment* and 'The Queen of Spades', and is set in the area of the city the author himself lived in. This is how it begins:

> There is an old woman in the yard holding a clock in her hands. As I walk past the old woman, I stop and ask her:
> 'What's the time?'
> 'Have a look,' the old woman says to me.
> I look and see that there are no hands on the clock.
> 'There aren't any hands,' I say.
> The old woman looks at the face and tells me:
> 'It it now a quarter to three.'
> 'Ah, I see. Thanks a lot,' I say and head off.
> The old woman shouts out something to me as I'm going away, but I carry on walking without looking round. I go out on to the street and walk along the sunny side; the spring sun is always pleasant. I am on foot, squinting and smoking a pipe. At the corner of Sadovaya street, I run into Sakerdon Mikhailovich. We say hello, then stop and talk for a long while. I get bored of standing in the street so I invite Sakerdon Mikhailovich for a drink in a bar. We drink some vodka, and eat some hard-boiled eggs and sprats, then we say goodbye and I go on alone . . .

Sadovaya Ul., 2

Overlooking the Mikhailovsky Gardens is the former Mikhailovsky Zamok, the Engineer's Castle, built by Paul I. He was murdered here on the night of 11 March 1801, about forty days after he had moved in. The castle lay empty for some time, but in 1823 became the Military Engineering Academy. This is where Dostoevsky studied, between 1837 and 1843. It was an unsuitable training for someone who wanted to become a writer, and Dostoevsky much regretted his father's decision to send him here.

Sadovaya Ul., 3

Lermontov was held under arrest here following a duel with the son of the French Ambassador in 1841. During this time he wrote the poem 'The Neighbour', based on one of the daughters of an official who worked in the building. The critic Vissarion Belinsky came to visit him here.

Sadovaya Ul., 20

The fabulist Krylov lived in a flat on the second floor of this building. It was part of the Public Library, where he worked. Krylov was a well-known storyteller who translated La Fontaine's fables into Russian in 1805 and then went on to write his own, which became extremely popular in Russia. Through a gallery of characters, often animals, he would portray the social evils of his day. This did not prevent him from pursuing a career working at the library between 1812 and 1841 for twenty-nine years of his life. He lived above a bookshop in a flat consisting of three rooms. Above him lived his friend Lobanov, who discovered and preserved many of Krylov's fables after he found them in his attic many years later.

Sadovaya Ul., 61

A plaque marks the front of the building where Lermontov rented a flat in 1836. Here he wrote his unfinished novel about St Petersburg, *Princess Ligovskaya*, and the poem 'On the Death of a Poet'. This long poem, prompted by Pushkin's death, was not only a response to the untimely death of a great poet, but a direct criticism of the events which had led to the duel in which Pushkin was fatally wounded. Copies of the poem, which quickly spread through St Petersburg, angered the censors and Lermontov was exiled to the Caucasus. Lermontov's fame spread as quickly as his poem: 'The pistol shot which killed Pushkin, aroused Lermontov's spirit,' wrote Alexander Herzen, and Vladimir Sollogub commented that 'Pushkin's death has heralded the appearance of a new poet in Russia.' Turgenev remembers meeting Lermontov at this time, noting his tragic appearance: 'inwardly he was probably desperately sad. He was suffocating in the tight sphere where fate had flung him.'

Saperny Per., 10

In 1903 this building housed the editorial office of the journal *Novy put* (the New Way), edited by Dmitry Merezhkovsky and his wife Zinaida Gippius. The journal principally disseminated the ideas of the Religious–Philosophical Society they had founded in 1901, but also provided a platform for the writings of the Russian Symbolists, including Blok and Ivanov, whose mystical aesthetic views were at that point fundamentally similar. Difficulties with the censor forced the journal to close in 1904, to be replaced by *Voprosy zhizni* (Questions of Life).

Semyonovskaya Pl. (*See* PIONERSKAYA PL., p. 278)

Senatskaya Pl.

In Soviet times this square, part of the city's imposing administrative centre, used to be called Pl. Dekabristov (Decembrists Square). It was here in 1825 that Nicholas I's bodyguard fired on some 3,000 soldiers and spectators, many of whom were innocently forced into action by revolutionary-minded young officers who had come to protest Nicholas I's nomination as Tsar. Many of Alexander Pushkin's contemporaries took part in the uprising and Pushkin himself would definitely have been among them had he not been in exile in Mikhailovskoe.

The statue of Peter the Great on a rearing horse which is situated here was completed in 1782 by the French sculptor Etienne Falconet. For many Russian writers, it has seemed an eloquent symbol of Russia itself. In 1833, it was the central inspiration for Pushkin's great poem 'The Bronze Horseman', which raises many questions about the ambiguous legacy of the city and its founder, by presenting the terrifying might of the autocracy as witnessed by the man on the street. A humble clerk named Evgeny, whose sweetheart has perished, seeks shelter from the rising flood from the overflowing Neva in 1824 by sitting astride a marble lion which decorates the porch of one of the mansions on the square (the house with its lions still stands at Admiralteisky pr., 12). From here he can see the huge and, to him, terrifying statue, which later comes to life and chases him through the city. Bely's great novel *Petersburg* (1916) resumes the meditation on Russia's destiny initiated by Pushkin, and also focuses on Falconet's statue as a symbol of the nation's divided soul:

> A shadow concealed the enormous face of the Horseman. A palm cut into the moonlit air.
> From that fecund time when the metallic Horseman had galloped hither, when he had flung his steed upon the Finnish granite, Russia was divided in two. Divided in two

Falconet's statue of Peter the Great, immortalized by Pushkin in his poem, 'The Bronze Horseman'

as well were the destinies of the fatherland. Suffering and weeping, Russia was divided in two, until the final hour.

Russia, you are like a steed! Your two front hooves have leaped far off into the darkness, into the void, while your two rear hooves are firmly implanted in the granite soil.

Sennaya Pl.

Sennaya pl. (the Haymarket) is most famous for its connections with Dostoevsky, and particularly with *Crime and Punishment*. In the nineteenth century, the square stood in the heart of the slum area, the area most frequented by Dostoevsky's characters. The square was then occupied by a prosperous market, selling not only hay, but other goods such as flowers, salt and horses. The metro station, built in the 1960s, stands on the site of a church named Spas na Sennoi (Church of the Saviour). In *Crime and Punishment* Raskolnikov often walks through this square: 'Raskolnikov preferred these haunts, along with all the neighbouring lanes and alleyways, to any other part of town, whenever he went out walking with no purpose. Here his rags drew no snooty attention, and it was possible for him to go about looking any way he chose without scandalizing anyone.' Just as he is drawn here before he commits the murder, so it is here that he returns at the end of the novel to make his confession: 'He knelt in the middle of the square, bowed down to the earth and kissed that dirty earth, with pleasure and happiness. He got up and bowed down a second time.' When out walking across the square one day, Dostoevsky was sold a silver cross by a drunken soldier, an event which he later fictionalized in *The Idiot*:

> I saw a cross on a filthy blue ribbon which he had evidently just taken off, but it was really made of tin, as one could see at a glance, a very big, octagonal cross of a regular Byzantine pattern. I took out a twenty copeck piece and gave it to him and at once put the cross round my neck ... I walked away thinking 'I mustn't be too quick to condemn a man who has sold his Christ.'

In the centre of the square stands a small Classical building, which is the guardhouse where Dostoevsky was held under arrest for two nights on 21 and 22 March 1874 for failure to observe the laws of censorship (he had printed the Tsar's name in the journal *Grazhdanin*). According to the memoirs of Anna Dostoevsky, he much enjoyed the seclusion, managing to re-read one of his favourite works, Hugo's *Les Misérables*.

Nikolay Nekrasov, whose poetry expressed great sympathy for the plight of the peasant, witnessed a scene on the Haymarket which prompted his poem, 'Last Night'. It tells of a young peasant girl being flogged, and shuddering underneath the heavy knout: 'And yet she gave no cry, the only sound / Was the whip cracking through the twilight air / And I spoke to my Muse and bade her look: "There is your sister – there!" '

Serpukhovskaya Ul., 10

Before their marriage in 1903, Alexander Blok and Lyubov Mendeleeva met secretly for a while in a room near the Mendeleev home which they rented here.

Shirokaya Ul., 19, Kv. 4

This address on the Petrograd Side is where the writer Sologub moved to in 1907, the year of the publication of his novel *The Petty Demon*. In 1908, Sologub married the playwright Anastasia Chebotarevskaya, after which the couple moved many times in St Petersburg before later settling at RAZEZZHAYA UL., 31 (see p. 283).

Soyuza Pechatnikov, Ul., 5

From August to November 1824 Alexander Griboedov lived here on the ground floor of the historian Mikhail Pogodin's house on the former Torgovaya ul. After almost drowning here in the famous flood of 1824, he moved in with his friend Alexander Odoevsky, who had a flat at ISAAKIEVSKAYA PL., 7 (see p. 219). He stayed there until July 1825, when he returned to the Caucasus.

Stachek Pr., 67, Korp. 4

— *Akhmatova Museum: 'The Silver Age'* The first Akhmatova Museum to be founded in Russia is located in the south-western part of the city, a short walk north from the metro station Avtovo. The entrance to the museum is actually from nearby Kronshtadstkaya ul., which runs parallel with Pr. Stachek. The building itself otherwise has no connection with Akhmatova or with the main Akhmatova Museum on the Fontanka (see FONTANKI, NAB. REKI, 34, p. 203).

The museum was established in 1974 by its current director, Valentina Bilichenko, then a young Akhmatova enthusiast, who had conceived the idea of exhibiting her personal collection of Akhmatova memorabilia long before the 1946 ban on the poet was lifted. Careful negotiations with the local authorities led to space being allotted first of all in a local school, but the political climate of the time demanded a great deal of tenacity on the director's part to ensure the museum's survival. In 1980, however, when Akhmatova's memory once again began to be revered officially, the museum was given the premises it occupies now (it was not until the centenary of Akhmatova's birth in 1989 that the official memorial rooms were opened in the famous 'House on the Fontanka'). The museum runs a vigorous programme of Akhmatova-related concerts, readings and talks, which, together with the six rooms which make up the permanent exhibition now called 'Anna Akhmatova: The Silver Age', have come under the aegis of the municipal authorities since 1992.

On display here is the collection of Akhmatova memorabilia belonging to the museum's director, which has been significantly added to over the years, and includes autographed books and portraits. Everything on show is well documented, but there are no English translations. The rooms are arranged chronologically, beginning with the Tsarskoe Selo period of Akhmatova's life. The first room has dark-blue walls, and features plaster copies of Classical statues and autumn foliage in an attempt to evoke the grand and verdant atmosphere of the tsars' summer retreat. The second room is devoted to Slepnyovo, the estate of the Gumilyov family in the Tver region (see GRADNITSY, p. 408), where Akhmatova spent her summers with her first husband. The third room is devoted to Nikolay Gumilyov, and to Lev Gumilyov, Akhmatova's son. The other rooms in the museum document Akhmatova's life in St Petersburg, and explore the background of her great work, 'The Poem without a Hero'.

Closed Saturdays and Sundays

Stolyarny Per.

Known in Soviet times as Ul. Przhevalskogo, this is the street where Raskolnikov is thought to have lived in Dostoevsky's *Crime and Punishment*. Although Dostoevsky gives only the street's initial in the novel, it is possible to deduce that this was the one intended, as he was careful to give precise and topographically accurate descriptions of the area. He almost invariably placed his characters in the poor areas of the city, particularly those that lay around Sennaya pl. He himself also lived in these areas, and was constantly changing flats.

When we read that Raskolnikov lived on S— per. and set off towards K— Bridge, he clearly has in mind Stolyarny Per. and the nearby Kokushin Bridge. Many of Raskolnikov's walks can be traced accurately on a map, using the street initials and the other directions and descriptions that Dostoevsky provides.

Entry into the houses on Stolyarny per. is hardly ever gained through front doors; it tends to be through yards. Inside, the houses were divided into many small blocks of flats rented out by a landlord. They were known as *dokhodny* or lodging houses and used to cover large areas of the city. The houses were known after the name of their landlord, often a rich merchant – such as 'Schiller's House' or 'Schiel's tenements'. Each block had its own yardkeeper. Inside, the yard was and is still known as a *dvor kolodtsov*. *Kolodets* means 'well', and the name conjures up the dark and narrow depths of those poky courtyards from which the sky can be glimpsed only by craning one's neck. All the windows of the houses, rather than looking out on to a view, face on to each other, adding to the claustrophobic atmosphere.

Dostoevsky firmly believed that living conditions affected character. He describes Raskolnikov's restricted living quarters at great length:

He surveyed his little room with detestation. It was a tiny little cell, about six paces long, and it presented a most pitiful aspect with its grimy, yellow wallpaper that was everywhere coming off the walls; it was so low-ceilinged that to a person of even slightly above-average height it felt claustrophobic, as though one might bang one's head against the plaster at any moment.

Later on Raskolnikov tells Sonya that 'low ceilings and cramped rooms cramp the soul and the mind'. The nearby streets were similarly claustrophobic, 'like rooms without ventilators', without the open vistas that characterized those in the grander areas of town. To take the idea of claustrophobia further, the novel is set 'during a spell of exceptionally hot weather' when the streets stank even more than usual.

Two flats on Stolyarny per. could well have been Raskolnikov's. The first, and the one most favoured as the correct address, lies at the corner of Stolyarny per. and Grazhdansky pr. (formerly Srednaya Meshchanskaya ul.). Its street address is Grazhdansky pr., 19/5. Inside the building there is a mansard at the very top. From it you can count the famous 'thirteen steps' which Raskolnikov would descend 'cautiously, inaudibly, like a cat'. A corner house such as this was convenient for Dostoevsky, as his major protagonist could approach it from various directions.

The second house which has a claim to have been Raskolnikov's, mainly because of its former yardkeeper's room, is number 9, Stolyarny per. Perhaps what Dostoevsky was most interested in, when choosing a dwelling for his hero, was the manner of a house, rather than its exact grid reference, and he probably combined the details of a few nearby houses. Despite his attention to topographical detail, he probably also did not want to pin down an exact address for Raskolnikov. But the public, favouring house number 19, has written on the walls of its staircase, and a tour of Dostoevsky's St Petersburg from the

Dostoevsky Museum will take you here, the guide knowing in advance the changing code number on the main entrance, which the residents of the house prefer to keep permanently locked.

Summer Garden

The Summer Garden (Letny Sad), laid out in the time of Peter the Great, is one of the finest parks in the city, full of Classical statues and shaded by lime trees. Alexander Pushkin loved to walk here when he was living in the nearby Panteleimonovskaya ul. and, in a letter to his wife, wrote that the Summer Garden was his 'kitchen garden': 'I go there in my dressing gown and slippers when I wake up. After lunch I sleep there, read and write. I am at home there.' In *Eugene Onegin*, Eugene is taken for walks here by his governess as a child.

Dostoevsky's Prince Myshkin in *The Idiot* sits in contemplation in the gardens, before he is overcome by his customary epileptic condition: 'A strange and most terrible demon has most certainly taken possession of him and refused to leave him any more. That demon had whispered to him in the Summer Garden, as he sat lost in thought under a lime tree.'

Another scene from Russian literature that takes place here is in Goncharov's novel *Oblomov*. In one of Oblomov's unsatisfactory attempts to court Olga, he hopes to find her there with her aunt or with her friend, as he feels that extra company will ease his embarrassment, but is terrified when he sees that 'a veiled woman' is approaching him alone.

Osip Mandelstam remembers the formality of the Summer Garden of his childhood in his autobiographical *The Noise of Time*:

> The entrances to the Summer Garden – both the one near the river, where the railing and the chapel are located, and the one across from the Engineers' Palace – were guarded

by cavalry sergeant majors bedecked with medals. They determined whether a person was suitably dressed. Men in Russian boots they drove away, nor would they admit persons in caps or in the attire of the lower middle classes.

As well as the many Grecian statues decorating the garden, there is a large statue of the early-nineteenth-century Russian fabulist Ivan Krylov, erected in 1855. The base of the statue is decorated with bas-reliefs of animals from his fables, including 'The Fox and the Grapes' and 'The Crow and the Fox'.

Tairov Per.

This is the former Brinko per. down which Raskolnikov walks many times in Dostoevsky's *Crime and Punishment*: 'It made a bend, and led from the square to Sadovaya Street.' A street with such a pronounced bend in it is unusual for St Petersburg and means that it offers no view out when one stands at the end of it. Raskolnikov walks down this claustrophobic passage as a form of self-punishment 'so as to feel even sicker'.

At number 4 on this street was the house of Zhernakov's printing press. This published an early translation of Balzac's *Eugénie Grandet* by Dostoevsky.

Tavricheskaya Ul., 7, Kv. 23

The eccentric writer Alexey Remizov lived and worked here from 1911 to 1913 in rooms decorated with silver and gold paper, and tiny monkeys and imps he had made, which he hung on the walls.

Tavricheskaya Ul., 38

The top-floor flat of the rotunda at the corner of Tavricheskaya and Tverskaya streets was from 1905 until 1912 the home of the leading Symbolist writer Vyacheslav Ivanov, an important figure of Russia's 'Silver Age'. It has been described in detail by Ivanov's daughter Lydia:

> The form of the house was peculiar: its corner was built in the shape of a tower. Half of this tower had external walls with large windows, and the other half was part of the inner section of the apartments. A cupola rose over the tower roof, and one could cautiously climb up there to enjoy the marvellous view of the city, the Neva, and its environs. I would often betake myself there, and now and then even Vyacheslav and his guests would too. In the apartments below us the tower formed a large round hall (on the first floor was the Znamensky Dancing School, on the second a public reading room). In our apartment the tower hall was divided into three small rooms with a tiny dark foyer. In each room there was a very big window with a view of the sea of treetops in the Tavrichesky Garden. Father's room was the central one in the tower. Our apartment on the fifth floor was a modest one. All the rooms except the tower had small mansard windows.

Ivanov had spent the previous nineteen years in Europe, first as a student of Theodor Mommsen at the University of Berlin (where he wrote a dissertation in Latin on the Roman tax system), then as an independent scholar, pursuing his interest in the ancient Greek religion of Dionysus, which was to inform all areas of his life. Although he had grown up in Moscow, it was in St Petersburg that he set up residence when he returned to Russia in 1905 at the age of thirty-nine, with his second wife Lydia Dmitrievna Zinovieva-Hannibal. Ivanov published his first collection of verse in 1903, and he quickly assumed a role as a leading poet and theoretician of the Russian Symbolist movement upon his return to Russia.

Known as the 'Tower' in view of the building's shape, Ivanov's flat was home to a number of stray poets during the seven years that he lived here, but was most renowned among St Petersburg bohemian circles for the weekly soirées held there, which attracted the city's artistic and intellectual elite. These influential *jours-fixes*, the so-called 'Ivanov Wednesdays', were inspired by Plato's symposia, and drew a diverse assortment of writers, artists, musicians, intellectuals, politicians and theatrical figures, who came to stay up all night talking about art. On one occasion in 1905 there were so many visitors that the police came to search the flat, mistaking the atmosphere of Dionysian mysticism for revolutionary fervour. As well as the brilliant conversation which Ivanov was able to stimulate, poets were often exhorted to read their verse. On one white summer night Alexander Blok climbed out on to the roof to read his poem 'The Stranger', accompanied by the song of nightingales from the Tavrichcsky Gardens below.

Ivanov and Lydia Dmitrievna's marriage was an unconventional one. In 1906, the poet Sergey Gorodetsky and the artist Margarita Sabashnikova were invited to become part of their relationship, as a way of putting into practice their mystical ideas about Eros which were consonant with the Symbolists' desire to turn life into art. Three years after the tragic death of Lydia Dmitrievna from scarlet fever in 1907, Ivanov married Vera, her daughter from her first marriage, and the Wednesday gatherings, which had stopped after Lydia's death, were resumed. The couple left St Petersburg finally in 1912 to take up residence in Moscow.

Tavrichesky Gardens

'A Man Is Teased by Sleep' (written in the 1930s) is one of the many so-called 'Happenings' from the *Blue Notebook* of the Absurdist writer Daniil Kharms set near his home in central St Petersburg, in an area in which the author liked to stroll:

> Markov took off his boots and lay down on his bed with a sigh. He wanted to go to sleep, but as soon as he closed his eyes, the desire to sleep instantly deserted him. Markov

opened his eyes and stretched out his hand for a book. But sleepiness again overcame him so he lay down and closed his eyes again without even picking the book up. But just as soon as Markov had closed his eyes, sleep once more eluded him and he became so wide awake that he could solve algebra in his head with all the usual equations, as well as two unknown ones.

Markov agonised for a long time about what he should do: should he go to sleep or stay awake? Finally, he worked himself into a state of self-loathing, so he put on his coat and hat, took up his cane and went outside. A light breeze calmed him down, his spirits lifted, and he decided he wanted to go back home to his room.

He felt an agreeable tiredness in his limbs as soon as he entered his room, and it made him want to go to sleep. But as soon as he had lain down on the bed and closed his eyes, his desire to sleep immediately evaporated.

Markov jumped up in a fury from the bed and stormed off without his hat and coat in the direction of the Tavrichesky Gardens.

Teatralnaya Pl.

This spacious square contains two very important Russian cultural institutions, the green and white Mariinsky (formerly Kirov) Theatre of Opera and Ballet and, opposite, the Rimsky-Korsakov Conservatory. The square was initially called Carousel square, reflecting its traditional role as a place of public entertainment.

At the beginning of the eighteenth century there was a theatre where the Conservatory now stands at number 3 known as the Bolshoi Kamenny Theatre (Big Stone Theatre). Later known simply as the Bolshoi, it was then the leading theatre of St Petersburg and supposedly the largest in Europe. Pushkin was a keen theatre-goer and on 27 November 1836 attended the première here of Glinka's opera *Ivan Susanin* (also known as *A*

Life for the Tsar). The Russian theatre was enjoying much success at this time and Pushkin writes lovingly of it in the first chapters of *Eugene Onegin*. The building was declared unsafe in 1889 and was replaced in 1896 by the current buildings of the Conservatory.

After the opera Pushkin headed off to the Zelyonaya Lampa or Green Lamp Society, which met at number 8, Teatralnaya pl. The society met some twenty times over the course of a year and consisted of young bon viveurs whose interests were chiefly literary, although politics, theatre and history were discussed. The members, who included Pushkin's friend the poet Delvig, sat at a round table by the light of a green lamp, green being supposedly the colour of hope. The host, Nikita Vsevolozhsky, according to the poet Fyodor Glinka, 'wore a golden soul under his golden kaftan'. Members took an obligatory oath to join and wore red Phrygian caps and rings whose emblem was a green lamp. Their meetings were overseen by a Kalmyk servant who took offence if he heard bad language. Pushkin called Vsevolozhsky 'the best of my momentary friends from my momentary youth' and has described the meetings in his verse. The granite-faced building where the Green Lamp Society meetings took place now has six floors (three formerly) and bears a plaque commemorating the literary association.

Teatralnaya Pl., 1

The Mariinsky, which became Russia's premier theatre for the performance of opera and ballet in the late nineteenth century, and has been patronized by countless Russian writers throughout its history, was the scene of a bizarre event in 1909 involving two poets who should have been posing for a portrait, but ended up challenging each other to a duel.

The studio of the artist Alexander Golovin, located under the rafters of the theatre directly above the stage (where he painted set designs), was designated the meeting place for all the poets and writers associated with the journal *Apollon* (Apollo), who had come to pose for a portrait commissioned by the journal's vain and ambitious editor Sergey Makovsky. Besides Makovsky himself, the group included Blok, Ivanov, Annensky, Kuzmin, Alexey Tolstoy, Gumilyov and Voloshin. The painting never materialized, however, as Gumilyov challenged Voloshin to a duel.

The notorious Cherubina de Gabriac affair, over which the two fought, concerned a poet invented by Voloshin and Elizaveta Dmitrieva, a woman Gumilyov had previously been involved with and who was now Voloshin's lover. Verse had just appeared under the fictitious name in *Apollon*, as an intended spoof on the Symbolists (writers who took themselves very seriously), but the joke backfired when personal insults started flying. Voloshin accepted Gumilyov's challenge but insisted the duel be fought at the same spot where Pushkin had fought his duel with D'Anthès in 1837, using pistols from that same era. The fiasco, keenly followed in the gossip press, ended with both duellists rather lamely missing each other.

Tuchkov Per., 17, Kv. 29

This was Anna Akhmatova's St Petersburg address from 1912 to 1917. Her husband Gumilyov took a room here while he was attending courses at St Petersburg University, and Akhmatova spent part of her winters here, and part of them in Tsarskoe Selo, looking after their young son, Lev. It was during this time that she began to discover the truth about her husband's infidelities, but she remained married to Gumilyov until 1918, due to her mother-in-law's devotion to her grandson. Akhmatova's second collection of verse, *Rosary*, containing many allusions to St Petersburg and Tsarskoe Selo, was published in 1914, while she was living here.

Turgeneva, Pl.

In the nineteenth century a small wooden house belonging to M. V. Petrashevsky stood in the middle of this square (formerly Pokrovskaya pl.). This is where the Petrashevsky Circle met on Fridays in the 1840s to discuss social problems. Dostoevsky frequented some of these Friday-night meetings from 1847 onwards, and on the night of 15 April 1849 read out Belinsky's banned letter in which the critic attacked Gogol for supposedly abandoning his political beliefs. Among the listeners was an informer from the tsarist secret police. A week after the reading, Dostoevsky and other members of the Petrashevsky Circle were arrested and sent to the Peter and Paul Fortress.

Universitetskaya Nab.

One of the oldest buildings in St Petersburg, the red building of the twelve colleges that stand on Vasilievsky Island was built in Peter the Great's time. The long building runs down a large part of Mendeleevskaya liniya. Other old university buildings are on the other side of Vasilievsky Island, Nab. Makarova.

Turgenev was first a student at Moscow University before coming to St Petersburg in 1834 to continue his studies. He studied in the philosophy faculty, where one of his tutors was Pyotr Pletnyov, who had taken an active part in the literary circle surrounding Alexander Pushkin. Another of Turgenev's lecturers was Nikolay Gogol, but, as Turgenev later admitted, neither he nor his fellow students realized at the time that their lecturer was the famous author of *Evenings at a Village near Dikanka*. Turgenev left the university in 1837 to complete his education abroad. Gogol had begun his new job as an adjunct professor of world history at the university in the autumn of 1834. This was a rather miraculous appointment in view of Gogol's lack of knowledge of the subject and complete absence of any kind of university degree. After a brilliant start (Pushkin and Zhukovsky came to hear him), Gogol's inspiration rapidly began to fail him, and he left the post after only four months. Merezhkovsky, Blok and Khlebnikov are three of the many Russian writers who have studied at the university since Gogol's and Turgenev's day.

Universitetskaya Nab., 3

— *Lomonosov Museum* Inside the building of the Kunstkamera is a small museum dedicated to Mikhail Lomonosov, and a plaque which decorates the outside of the building elucidates the writer's association with it: 'In this building – the cradle of Russian Science – Lomonosov worked from 1741 to 1765.' As well as being one of Russia's most important scientists, Lomonosov also wrote poetry and created a new Russian lexicon. Many of his odes praise the new city founded by Peter the Great.

Universitetskaya Nab., 9

The eighteenth-century Rector's House of St Petersburg University on Vasilievsky Island was where the poet Alexander Blok was born in 1880. Blok's grandfather, the liberal-minded botanist Andrey Beketov, had become rector of the university in 1876, and his daughter Alexandra had returned to live here in 1880, following a very short-lived marriage to a talented but difficult young law lecturer who remained in Warsaw where he had an appointment. Their son was born in a room on the first floor of the house, and he spent the first three years of his life here, where he developed a fondness for visiting his grandfather's study to look at his botanical textbooks and watch the traffic along the Neva. These idyllic circumstances changed, however, in 1883, when repressive measures taken against university students in the wake of the assassination of Alexander II forced Professor Beketov to hand in his resignation, thus obliging him to vacate the Rector's House. Blok became a student at the university in 1898.

Volkov Cemetery (*See* RASSTANNY PER., 30, p. 282)

Vladimirsky Pr., 11

Dostoevsky lived at number 11 in a corner house which also stood on Grafsky per. (Ul. Mariy Ulyanovi) from 1842 to 1846. During this time he finished his first novel *Poor Folk*. One of the rooms of his flat was let to a German doctor whom he was later to meet up with in exile in Siberia. The room was re-let to a man named Dmitry Grigorovich in the winter of 1844/5. It was Grigorovich who took the manuscript of *Poor Folk* to the editor and writer Nikolay Nekrasov. Moved to tears by Grigorovich's reading of the script, Nekrasov went back to the house with him at four in the morning to acquaint himself with the sleeping Dostoevsky: 'So what if he's asleep! This is much more import-ant than sleep!' They found Dostoevsky awake after one of his nocturnal walks during the St Petersburg white nights when darkness never falls. The next morning, Nekrasov took the manuscript to show his friend Belinsky, extolling it. 'A new Gogol has been born to us!' 'Your Gogols grow like mushrooms' was Belinsky's retort. However, on reading the script, he was as convinced as Nekrasov of Dostoevsky's genius.

Vosstaniya Ul., 20, Kv. 29

This was the first flat (it was formerly the editorial office of the Marxist journal *Zhizn* (Life)) that Gorky rented on his own, following his return to St Petersburg in 1903, when he was no longer under police surveillance. He resumed his work for the Znanie publishing association, and also his political activity. In January 1905 he was arrested for taking part in the 1905 Revolution, and was jailed in the Peter and Paul Fortress. That summer he joined the Bolshevik Party and in December went abroad, where he stayed until a general amnesty allowed him to return to Russia in 1913.

Vosstaniya Ul., 36

It was here that the secret trial of Joseph Brodsky took place in 1964, following which he was exiled to the far north of Russia, to an arctic village in the Arkhangelsk region. There he spent eighteen months doing manual work at a collective farm, until international pressure brought an early release.

As his stature as a poet increased, Brodsky had begun to attract the attentions of the Soviet authorities, who were irritated by his unwillingness to conform and his unconcealed interest in publishing his work, whether at home or (when that proved impossible) abroad. Brodsky had first been denounced by a Leningrad newspaper in 1963 for writing 'pornographic' and 'anti-Soviet' poetry. In February 1964 he was arrested and forced to undergo 'psychological testing' at a psychiatric prison, which was followed by the now famous trial where he was charged with 'parasitism'.

Brodsky was able to return to Leningrad at the end of 1965, and the city remained his chief place of residence until June 1972, when he was forced to leave the Soviet Union, becoming the first major figure to leave the country in what was to become the 'third wave' of emigration. The poems that appeared in the Moscow journal *Novy mir* (New World) in December 1987 at the height of perestroika constituted his first Russian publication since that time, an event he regarded as the restoration of stolen goods to their rightful owner, and certainly no cause for celebration. Reluctant to court the kind of publicity surrounding Solzhenitsyn's return to Russia, Brodsky made no attempt to go back to his native city.

Voznesensky Most

This bridge crossing the Griboedov canal was a favourite spot for suicides. In *Crime and Punishment*, Raskolnikov, who is himself considering suicide from the bridge, watches a woman's failed attempt to end her life. The woman, who is standing right next to him, flings herself over the bridge and into the dirty water. She floats to a spot from where she is rescued by a policeman.

Voznesensky Pr.

Known as Pr. Mayorova in Soviet times, this is the street where Raskolnikov hides the goods he has stolen from the old woman in *Crime and Punishment*, as Dostoevsky's wife, Anna Grigorievna, has confirmed:

> During the first weeks of our married life, out for a walk with me one day, Fyodor Mikhailovich led me into a courtyard of a certain building and showed me the stone block beneath which his Raskolnikov had hidden the goods he stole from the old woman. The courtyard is situated on Voznesensky Prospect, the second along from Maksimilianov Lane; on its site an enormous building has now been constructed, which at present houses the offices of a German newspaper. When I asked him: 'Why did you come into this deserted courtyard?' Fyodor Mikhailovich replied: 'For the purpose that passers-by usually go to secluded spots.'

Maksimilianov Lane is now called Pirogova per., and it is thought that the entrance to the courtyard was from this street.

Voznesensky Pr., 8

Dostoevsky lived here in 1847–9 on the corner of Malaya Morskaya ul. This was at the time of his involvement with the

Petrashevsky Circle, which led to his arrest on the night of 23 April 1849. While he lived in this house he wrote the short stories 'The Landlady' and 'White Nights'. Dostoevsky lived again on Voznesensky pr. for a few months in 1867 at number 29. This was the year of his marriage to Anna Grigorievna Snitkina.

Voznesensky pr. is often mentioned as V— pr. in *Crime and Punishment* and it is one of the main routes Raskolnikov follows on his many walks. On the corner of Voznesensky pr. and Glukhoi pr. (now Per. Pirogova) is the yard where Raskolnikov buries the old woman's possessions he has stolen. The street features in other works by Dostoevsky. In his story 'A Weak Heart', Vasya buys Lizochka a hat 'in the Manon Lescaut style' in a fashionable corner shop on the street, and there is also a cake shop on the street described at length in *The Injured and Insulted.*

Voznesensky Pr., 36

A monument to the nose of Major Kovalyov, hero of Gogol's famous story 'The Nose' (1835–6), was recently unveiled here, as a spoof on the many serious literary landmarks in the city. It takes the form, appropriately enough, of a large nose sticking out of the building. It was on Voznesensky pr. that Major Kovalyov's barber lived in the story, and it is Ivan Yakovlevich who finds his client's nose in his bread one morning at breakfast. Dressed in the gold-embroidered uniform of a State Councillor, the nose is pursued into the Kazan Cathedral by Major Kovalyov (who lives on Sadovaya street) and is later sighted walking on Nevsky pr. and in the Tavrichesky Gardens.

Yusupovsky Sad (*See* SADOVAYA UL., p. 285)

Major Kovalyov's nose from Gogol's story The Nose

Zagorodny Pr., 1

The poet Anton Delvig, a close friend and former schoolmate of Pushkin, and a leading figure in Petersburg literary life in the 1820s, moved with his wife to a flat in this building, opposite the Vladimirskaya Church, on the corner of Shcherbakov per., in 1829. The Delvigs had spent the first year of their marriage (which took place in 1825) living in an apartment on the top floor of a three-storey house belonging to the court surgeon Ebeling at Millionnaya ul., 26. They had then moved to an apartment in the former Kuvshinnikov House, which stood on this street, approximately where number 9 stands today, near the Five Corners.

The phlegmatic and bespectacled poet (he maintained he had been forbidden to wear spectacles while at the Lycee, and was sorely disappointed to discover, when he was finally free to do so, that women were not as beautiful as they had previously appeared to him in his myopic state) was known for his easygoing manner; he was so relaxed that he could relate with aplomb and even amusement that one of his servants never posted any of his letters. Upon leaving the Lycee, Delvig followed the usual route and became a civil servant, working in the Imperial Public Library from 1821 under the famed writer of Russian fables Krylov, but directing his real energies to furthering the literary interests he had been encouraged to develop at the Lycee. In 1824 appeared the first issue of what was to become an extremely successful and important almanac, *Northern Flowers*, edited by Delvig. It was the nucleus for a group of the most talented writers of the time, who all became regular visitors to the noted salons at the Delvigs' home, together with numerous young men attracted to Delvig's wife. The Delvigs received guests on Wednesdays and Sundays, and among the writers who frequented their salons were Pushkin and Zhukovsky, the Polish poet Mickiewicz and, from 1830 onwards, the writer Nikolay Gogol. As well as being Delvig's home, this apartment also became the editorial office of the journal *Literaturnaya gazeta* (the Literary Gazette). Delvig had set up this journal with Vyazemsky in 1830, and it appeared every five days. In the harsh climate of censorship and repression ushered in by Nicholas I, it was destined not to survive for long, however. Delvig was soon summoned to the offices of Benkendorff, head of the notorious Third Department, the tsarist secret police, and threatened with exile to Siberia for the heinous crime of printing some inoffensive verse by a French poet. The incident wounded Delvig deeply, and, according to some contemporaries, contributed to his untimely death soon thereafter in January 1831.

Zhelyabova, Ul. (*See* BOLSHAYA KONYUSHENNAYA UL., p. 178)

Zhukovskogo, Ul., 7/9, Kv. 42

A three-room flat on the top floor of this six-storey apartment building became one of the more notable literary landmarks in

St Petersburg in 1915, when Mayakovsky read his most famous poem 'A Cloud in Trousers' to Osip and Lili Brik. It was an event which changed all of their lives, and marked the beginning of one of the most famous love affairs in literary history. Mayakovsky fell passionately in love with Lili on that day, and immediately moved to Petrograd to be near her, taking a room the same evening in the Hotel Palais-Royal at PUSHKINSKAYA UL., 20 (see p. 282), rather than go back to Chukovsky's dacha, which was out of town on the Bay of Finland. Later that year he rented a room round the corner from the Briks' flat on the former Nadezhdinskaya ul. (now MAYAKOVSKOGO UL., p. 246), and, in 1918, moved in with them. This was a development that all three found perfectly natural, since Lili's relations with Osip were by this time purely platonic. This unconventional living arrangement continued until Mayakovsky's death in 1930, by which time he and Lili had also long since ceased to be lovers themselves.

Lili immediately became the heroine of all Mayakovsky's poetry, and she sometimes found his intensity rather overpowering. In 1916, he wrote a long poem called 'Don Juan', which at first he did not tell her about. 'Volodya recited it to me unexpectedly as we were walking along the street, the whole thing, by heart,' she later recalled; 'I got angry because it was about love again – as if I wasn't fed up with it! Volodya tore the manuscript from his pocket, shredded it into tiny pieces and let the wind blow it away along Zhukovsky street.'

The Briks' flat, on the former Malaya Italyanskaya ul. (the street was renamed in 1902 to mark the fiftieth anniversary of the poet Zhukovsky's death), had rooms with windows looking out on to the yard at the back. After Mayakovsky had entered the Briks' lives, it soon became a kind of literary salon for the Futurists, and was constantly full of visitors. It was therefore with some relief that in 1917 the Briks were able to move to a flat that was twice as big on the floor below. Mayakovsky brought all his Futurist friends here, including Burlyuk, Khleb-nikov and Kamensky (who decorated the walls with drawings and poems). The flat was also visited by a more diverse crowd of writers which included Kuzmin, Pasternak and Gorky. Meanwhile, Osip Brik, who published 'A Cloud in Trousers' at his own expense, had developed a serious interest in contemporary poetry. In 1917 he became a leading member of the OPOYAZ group (the Society for the Study of Poetic Language), founded that year. The critics Viktor Shklovsky and Roman Jakobson, as well as other academics, now also became regular visitors here. When the Briks left for Moscow in 1919, their flat was taken over by Shklovsky, and it was through Jakobson that Mayakovsky found an apartment in Moscow.

Zhukovskogo Ul., 18

Until the late 1880s this address served as the main office of the newspaper *Novoe vremya*, and also the main residence of its editor Alexey Suvorin. Chekhov met Suvorin for the first time in December 1885, and from 1888 onwards usually stayed with his family here during his visits to Petersburg.

Zhukovskogo Ul., 21

The former Malaya Italyanskaya ul. used to be the heart of the city's newspaper publishing industry. In pre-revolutionary times, this building housed he editorial offices of the major national newspaper *Rech* (Speech).

Zhukovskogo Ul., 21

Evgeny Zamyatin lived here from 1928 to 1931, before he emigrated to Paris, where he was to spend the last three years of his life. Having been recognized as one of the leading figures in Russian literature immediately after the Revolution, during the 1920s he was attacked by communist critics for his supposedly 'pernicious' ideology and totally ostracized by the literary world in 1929. Zamyatin is best know outside Russia as the author of *We*, a precursor of Orwell's *1984*. After Zamyatin's death 300 letters between him and his wife were found at this address.

LENINGRAD
REGION

Kobrino

— *Puhkin Museum* A small museum in the village of Kobrino to the south of St Petersburg, is dedicated to Pushkin's nanny, Arina Rodionovna, to whom he was devoted. Founded in 1974, the museum is located in the house which belonged to her son, E. Tropkov. The interior of the one small room is arranged to reflect the decor of a traditional peasant izba (hut).

Komarovo

From 1961 to 1966, the year of her death, Anna Akhmatova spent much of her time at a green wooden dachia here (on Ul. Osipenko, 5), which belonged to the Union of Writers. The dacha consisted of a study and a bedroom, and was so small that she used to refer to it as her 'booth'. Many visitors eager to make the acquaintance of Russia's greatest living poet came to see her here. And it was here that she first met Joseph Brodsky in 1962, when Evgeny Rein, another young poet in what Akhmatova used to call her 'magic choir', brought him up from Leningrad to meet her. Akhmatova's grave in in the cemetery on Ozyornaya ul.

Pavlovsk

The small town of Pavlovsk, situated approximately sixteen miles south of St Petersburg, is best know for the palace built here by Catherine the Great for her son Paul I. It is also a holiday town, where many people own dachas. As the character Lebedev says in Dostoevsky's *The Idiot*, 'You see, sir, the reason why everyone goes to Pavlovsk is because it's so very nice there – high up, green, cheap, fashionable, and musical.'

It was 'musical' because fashionable concerts that took place in a building at Pavlovsk Railway Stations. Osip Mandelstam remembers these concerts in his autobiographical essays *The Noise of Time*:

In the middle of he Nineties all Petersburg streamed into Pavlovsk as into some Elysium. Locomotive whistles and railroad bells mingled with the patriotic cacophony of the 1812 overture, and a peculiar smell filled the huge station where Tchaikovsky and Rubinstein reigned . . . As it turned out, we became 'winter people' in Pavlovsk, that is, we lived the year round in our dacha in that old ladies' town, that Russian demi-Versailles, the city of court lackeys, widows on high officials, red-headed policemen, consumptive pedagogues.

Many scenes from Dostoevsky's *The Idiot* take place in Pavlovsk. The Yepanchin family have a 'luxurious country house' in Pavlovsk in the Sadovaya region. Not far from here is Lebodev's dacha, where 'the idiot', Prince Myshkin, comes to stay. On Matrosskoi ul. (formerly Krasnoarmeiskaya ul.) lives Nastasya Filippovna and it was on a bench in an alley of the 'dark park' surrounding the palace that Aglaya sits with Prince Myshkin. The scandalous whip scene takes place at the musical square on Pavlovsk Station, and the church at Sadovaya ul., 17 (formerly Ul. Rovolyussi), was where Nastasya Filippovna was due to get married.

Priyutino

Priyutino is an enchanting place which has been beautifully restored and refurnished in the past thirty years. Its owners were famous for their hospitality to writers and musicians. It was the summer house of Alexei Nikolaevich Olenin (1765-1843) and his wife Elizabeth. Olenin was an archeologist, writer and patron of the arts. He was the first Director of the Imperial Library in St. Petersburg and the Head of the Imperial Academy of Fine Arts. He was responsible for commissioning the Alexander Column.

The atmosphere at Priyutino was comfortably informal, the hosts only requesting that guests be punctual for meals. The conversation tended to be about art, architecture, books, history and music. Glinka and Griboedov played the piano at various gatherings and Krylov, who was a frequent guest, was an enthusiastic player of charades. Pushkin, who believed himself to be in love with the Olenin's youngest daughter Anna, dedicated various poems to her. The pleasant park around the house contains a lake surrounded by trees, as well as the grave of the Olenin's eldest son, Nikolai, killed at Borodino. The estate was sold in 1838, after the death of Olenin's wife.

Tsarskoe Selo

In 1937 Tsarskoe Selo was renamed Pushkin, in honour of Alexander Pushkin, who studied at the lycée here from 1811 to 1817. The town has now gone back to its old name Tsarskoe Selo, meaning Tsar's Village. Situated approximately fifteen miles south of St Petersburg, it has grown since Pushkin's time into a sprawling town with many wooden dachas built around its outskirts, but is still a very popular summer resort, whose position supposedly matches the height of the top of St Isaac's Cathedral in St Petersburg. Its main attraction for visitors is the magnificent turquoise and gold Catherine Palace, the creation of successive rulers and architects, chiefly the fun-loving Elizabeth I and her extravagant Italian architect Bartolomeo Rastrelli, but both the palace and several buildings in the town have literary associations. Indeed, because of its links with Pushkin and the so-called Golden Age of Russian poetry, which he initiated here, Tsarskoe Selo has traditionally been seen by writers as the 'town of the muse'.

Numerous Russian writers have spent times in Tsarskoe Selo, including Anna Akhmatova, grew up here, as well as the poets Annensky and Komarovsky, whom Akhmatova regaded as her teachers. Sergey Esenin ws stationed here during the First World War, and Daniil Kharms completed his education here in the early 1920s at a school where his aunt was headmistress.

Osip and Nadezhda Mandelstam lived at various addresses (though which ones is not known) in Tsarskoe Selo in the years 1925–8 after the Revolution had quite changed the meaning of the 'Tsar's Village'. They first stayed at a boarding house with their friends Anna Akhmatova and Nikolay Punin. In 1926 they were to return, but as Nadezhda was suffering from tuberculosis she went to recover in the warm south, while Mandelstam came on alone and rented various properties, including a room in the wing of the large palace, an apartment in the lycée building and a flat in the Chinese Village. In a letter to Nadezhda, he describes a flat that he has found, which he sets down on paper in the form of a plan:

> Here's the floor plan:
>
> | large room | bedroom | dining room | bathroom | kitchen |
> | no stove | stove | stove | stove | stove |
>
> ... the new apartment is warm and dry ... The walls are clean and white ... We live across from the Kikinaya bell tower ... It rings every morning at nine am, but on the orthodox holidays at six am.

Nadezhda Mandelstam, who returned to Tsarskoe Selo with her husband in the winter of 1927/8, struck up a lifelong friendship with Anna Akhmatova as they both lay ill at their boarding house: 'My real friendship with Anna Akhmatova began on the veranda of the boarding house as we lay there swaddled in fur coats breathing the salubrious air of Tsarskoe Selo. It really must have had healing properties given that we both survived.'

Chinese Village

In the grounds of the Alexander Park is a small village built in the 1780s in the then fashionable Chinese style, by the Scots architect Charles Cameron. At the centre is a large rotunda where balls were held in the nineteenth century. Lermontov, who was stationed at Tsarskoe Selo in the Life Guard Hussars between 1834 and 1838, met the historian Karamzin here, and Karamzin was to introduce him to the town's literary society. On another occasion, Lermontov was put under arrest for attending a ball here incorrectly dressed (instead of wearing the uniform of his Guards regiment, he appeared in a coat with an embroidered collar, with the cuffs of a dress-coat).

The grounds of the main palace are the setting for a scene in Pushkin's story 'The Captain's Daughter' where the heroine, unknowingly, meets the Empress Catherine the Great.

Komsomolskaya Ul. (*See* SADOVAYA UL., p. 320)

Oktyabrsky Bulv.

It was in a dark-green wooden house which formerly stood at this site on the corner of Shirokaya ul. and Bezymyanny per. (which in Soviet times became Oktyabrsky bulv.) that the poet Anna Akhmatova spent most of her childhood years after her family left Odessa, where she was born in 1891. The house belonged to a merchant's wife called Elizaveta Shukhardina, and was shared with another family. Originally it had been a tavern, and during Akhmatova's childhood housed a dairy down in the basement. The family left the house in 1905 when Akhmatova's parents separated, and the future poet was sent to school in Kiev. Tsarskoe Selo changed unrecognizably after the Revolution, but Akhmatova found when she returned that this street where she once lived still smelt of oak trees, and the crows still cawed in the same way, and the statues still looked the same in the park.

Pushkinskaya Ul., 2

— *Pushkin Museum* A few minutes' walk from the lycée is a small Pushkin museum. This is the dacha where Pushkin and his young wife Natalya Goncharova spent their first summer together after their marriage in Moscow in 1831. It is a wooden house with a mezzanine built in 1827, which became a museum in 1958. Above the dining room and bedrooms on the first floor is Pushkin's study in the mezzanine. Orderly in appearance, it hardly matches the descriptions of great untidiness witnessed by many of Pushkin's contemporaries. During the few months that he was here Pushkin completed 'The Story of the Tsar Sultan' and 'Onegin's Letter to Tatyana' for the sixth chapter of *Eugene Onegin*.

Closed Mondays, Tuesdays and the last Friday of the month

Revolyutsii, Ul., 63

Anna Akhmatova married a fellow poet, Nikolay Gumilyov, in 1910, and when the young couple returned from their honeymoon in Paris they settled for the next few years with Gumilyov's parents here, on the former Malaya ul. After Paris, Tsarskoe Selo seemed very parochial, and Akhmatova and Gumilyov increasingly spent their time in St Petersburg, where they had become part of the literary scene, or at the Gumilyov estate at Slepnyovo. The green, two-storey house with a fenced-in garden which once stood here had been purchased by Gumilyov's mother. Gumilyov's room was decorated in yellow, and contained exotica and artefacts brought back from his travels in Africa; Akhmatova's room was painted blue, and was rather more spartan. Akhmatova returned here in the 1920s, and was devastated to encounter the debris and ruins of a town which in pre-revolutionary times had been known for its spotlessness, and had used to look like Versailles.

Sadovaya Ul., 2

— *Pushkin Museum* The building of the lycée (on the former Komsomolskaya ul.) which is now preserved as a museum is connected above all with Alexander Pushkin, who studied here between 1811 and 1817, and the poets who later made up the so-called Pushkin 'pleiad'. Another writer who studied here later in the century was Mikhail Saltykov-Shchedrin.

The lycée was created by the liberal Tsar Alexander I to attract boys from noble backgrounds who would later rise to high positions in government. Its intake, however, consisted mainly of boys from families of the lesser nobility, such as

The building of the lycée in Tsarskoe Selo where Pushkin was once a pupil

Alexander Pushkin, the high aristocracy preferring to educate their offspring at home, with private tutors.

Despite the rule that the uniformed boys, who sported tricorn hats, were not allowed home during their six-year course, the school's regime and curriculum, especially if compared to a boarding school in England at the time, were liberal. There was no corporal punishment, many hours were devoted to leisure and the pupils could wander freely round the park, visiting the houses of the tutors, even meeting members of the opposite sex. Alexander Pushkin wrote over 130 poems while he was here, most famously his 'Reminiscences of Tsarskoe Selo'. It was at the lycée that his talent was noticed by the aged poet Derzhavin, a famous episode in Russian literary history. Pushkin recited his 'Reminiscences' at a public examination, standing some two yards from the seventy-year-old poet, who up until then had been nearly asleep: 'I do not remember how I finished my recitation. I do not remember whither I fled. Derzhavin was delighted; he demanded I come, he desired to embrace me ... there was a search for me but I was not discovered.'

Pushkin made lasting friendships at the lycée with Baron Delvig, his closest friend, and the two Decembrists, Ivan Pushchin and Wilhelm Küchelbecker. Delvig (who also studied at the lycée from 1811 to 1817) was something of a teller of tall tales, able to convince his classmates that he had participated alongside his father in the 1807 campaign, even though he had been only nine years old at the time.

The lycée building is joined by an arch to the main Catherine Palace. It is a four-storey wing, built by the architect V. P. Stasov in 1811, and was made into a museum in 1949. Visitors can inspect the classrooms, music rooms and physics laboratory and, upstairs, a long dormitory divided into small rooms where Pushkin slept (in number 14).

Closed on Tuesdays

Sadovaya Ul., 12

This is the house where Karamzin stayed on his arrival from Moscow in 1816. He led a secluded existence here, as he was working on his *History of the Russian State*. But he was often visited by the young Mikhail Lermontov, who between 1834 and 1838 served at Tsarskoe Selo in the Life Guard Hussars.

Repino

In the early 1900s, the former Finnish village of Kuokkala became the home of the writer and critic Korney Chukovsky (the pen-name of Nikolay Korneichukov). Chukovsky was by this time an established literary figure, having lived for the previous eight years in St Petersburg, where he wrote for the Symbolist journal *Vesy* (the Scales).

Born illegitimately, Chukovsky had been brought up in Odessa by his mother. It was because of the deep shame he felt over this that he later changed his name. An autodidact who left school early, he began his writing career as a journalist with an

Odessa newspaper, which sent him to London as a correspondent in 1903–4, after which he settled in St Petersburg. Among Chukovsky's neighbours here were many writers and artists, including Repin, Kuprin and Andreev, with whom he became friends. Mayakovsky and other writers made frequent visits while Chukovsky was living here. The house unfortunately burned down in 1986.

Rozhdestveno

The Historical–Literary and Memorial Museum of V. V. Nabokov used to be situated here in the gracious wooden house of Nabokov's uncle, perched on a bluff high above the road, overlooking the Oredezh river. Unfortunately, however, all that remains now of the house, which was an orphanage for a while after the Revolution, are badly charred stoves and burned timbers, following a tragic fire in 1995. Work has begun to reconstruct the house, but it is hampered by a lack of funds. The house was one of three estates in the area which belonged to the family of Nabokov's mother, and which the writer describes in his autobiographical memoir *Speak, Memory* as 'three linked rings in a ten-mile chain running west–east across the Luga highway', about thirty miles south of St Petersburg. The houses at Vyra and Batovo were destroyed much earlier.

It was at Vyra that the family of Vladimir Nabokov spent their summers, in a large house of simple design with carved wooden decorations on the exterior. The Nabokov family led an idyllic life here, attended by fifty permanent servants (whose quarters the writer's mother never even set foot in). The walnut-panelled dining room was situated on the ground floor, as was the drawing room, dreamily evoked by Nabokov many years later: 'the gleaming white mouldings of the furniture, the embroidered roses of its upholstery. The white piano. The oval

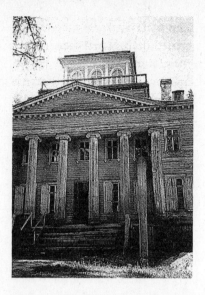

Rozhdestveno, one of the Nabokov family homes, before it was destroyed by fire in 1995

mirror ... The chandelier pendants. These emit a delicate tinkling (things are being moved in the upstairs room where Mademoiselle will dwell).' Somewhat ironically, the house's central staircase had been built of iron by Nabokov's great-grandfather because he was afraid of fires, and when the house later burned down, it was all that remained. The house was surrounded by a tennis court and beautiful gardens, and an 'English' park separated the estate from the hayfields. According to Nabokov this was 'an extensive and elaborate affair with labyrinthine paths, Turgenevian benches, and imported oaks among the endemic firs and birches. The struggle that had gone on since my grandfather's time to keep the park from reverting to the wild state always fell short of complete success ...'

The house became a school after the Revolution, then was taken over by the Nazis in 1942, when they turned it into a staff headquarters of the German army, who burned it to the ground when they left two years later. After the bricks from the foundations had been taken by villagers to make chimneys, nothing remained of the once opulent estate except its trees and a fragment of the former orangery.

Sestroretsk

Mikhail Zoshchenko bought a dacha here at Polevaya ul., 14a, in 1939. He is buried nearby. Daniil Kharms loved to walk by the sea here and at Olgino and Lakhta, the villages just outside Petersburg on the suburban railway line which follows the north shore of the Gulf of Finland. These same towns appear in his story 'The Old Woman' (1939), which ends with the narrator taking a suitcase containing the corpse of the old woman he finds dead in his apartment by train to Lisy Nos (another village on the line) in order to get rid of it.

Zelenogorsk

Zelenogorsk, situated some forty miles north of St Petersburg on the Karelian Isthmus, was and still is a popular resort for the inhabitants of St Petersburg. Leonid Andreev, a writer who enjoyed great popularity in his lifetime for his stories and plays, such as 'The Seven That Were Hanged' and 'The Red Laugh', bought a plot of land here in 1908 and built a large wooden house, Vammelsuu, where he could devote time to sailing, painting, entertaining and photography as well as live closer to nature. He lived here with his second wife for just over ten years until his death in 1919 aged forty-eight. Sadly, the house no longer exists.

Andreev has now been reinstated as a major Russian writer and his works began to be republished in the 1950s. Born in tsarist Russia in 1871, his early work showed great sympathy for the revolutionary cause, but later on in life he became violently anti-Bolshevik. The mood of the turbulent time in which he lived, as the old order collapsed, giving way to Revolution and the First World War, is reflected in his writing. But his private life at Vammelsuu is best represented by an astonishingly beautiful collection of his own colour photographs, discovered in 1978 and first published in 1989. These appear to reflect a harmonious and idyllic lifestyle, but they also contain a Chekhovian sense of doom, perhaps due in part to the subject's manner of gazing at the camera without a trace of a smile.

Andreev's personality was larger than life, and this was reflected in the scope of his house. He chose as his architect Andrey Ol, a student from Eliel Saarinen's studio in Helsinki. In his memoirs, Korney Chukovsky writes,

> This lack of moderation was his chief characteristic. He was drawn to everything colossal. The fireplace in his study was the size of a gateway, while the study itself was like a square. His house in Vammelsuu towered over all the other houses: every beam weighed over a ton, the foundations were cyclopic blocks of granite. Shortly before the war, I remember him showing me the plan of a huge building. 'What's this building?' I asked. 'It's not a building, it's a desk,' Andreev replied. It turned out that he had commissioned the design for a multi-storeyed desk from an architect: an ordinary desk was too restricted and small for him.

He decorated the walls of his spacious study with his own enlarged drawings of Goya's etchings.

Built entirely of wood, the house was not strong enough to withstand the harsh coastal climate and barely lasted Andreev's lifetime. It is interesting that a writer who was born in the depths of provincial Russia should, in the tradition of Peter the Great, choose to make his home by the sea.

Vyra

— *Postmaster's Cottage Museum* About an hour's drive south of St Petersburg is the small village of Vyra. In 1972 a museum opened in the small house that was once the postmaster's cottage.

The nineteenth-century traveller would stop at such post stations, which lined the main routes, to change horses, eat or drink and sometimes spend the night. The museum's chief literary association is with Pushkin, who passed through this station many times on his way to MIKHAILOVSKOE (see p. 379), as it is on the main Belarus–Kiev road. It would be his third stop after leaving St Petersburg. There is a milestone by the house which says 'From St Petersburg – 69, to Pskov – 239'. The building of the former post office has also been preserved here.

The museum, as well as being dedicated to the traveller, is named after the hero of Pushkin's short story 'The Postmaster'. In the story the old postmaster loses his daughter Dunya to a rich hussar who passes through to change horses. The old man never recovers from the loss and drinks himself to death. There are three rooms in the main part of this small museum: the main room where travellers would rest, 'Dunya's room', and a room for the coachmen, who would not sleep during stop-overs here. On display are maps showing Pushkin's travels throughout Russia, the scores of coachmen's songs, and the texts of verses Pushkin wrote on his travels. The sleigh carrying Pushkin's body from St Petersburg to the Svyatogorsk Monastery would have passed through here.

Closed Mondays and Tuesdays

EUROPEAN
RUSSIA

Arkhangelsk Region

Lomonosovo

— *Lomonosov Museum* The great Russian scholar, scientist and man of letters Mikhail Lomonosov was born in 1711 at Kurostrov (now Lomonosovo) near the town of Kholmogory, by the White Sea. Lomonosov, born of peasant stock, went on to have an extremely distinguished career. Many Russian institutions have been named after him, and he is the founder of Moscow University. He is probably more famous as a scientist, but his literary output was considerable. As well as writing poetry and celebratory odes to accompany state occasions, extolling the virtues of Imperial Russia, he wrote major scholarly works on rhetoric (1748) and on Russian grammar (1757). He was an admirer of Peter the Great, who is the eponymous hero of an unfinished epic poem.

The one-storey wooden building, built in 1868, which houses the Lomonosov Museum was once a school. It lies near the estate where Lomonosov was born, which no longer exists. The museum was opened in 1941 and takes up seven rooms. It is devoted to the many aspects of Lomonosov's career.

The first two rooms are devoted to the history of the northern part of Russia, and of the local area, which is made up of islands created by the many tributaries of the River Dvina. The region was famous for its breed of cattle, which supplied milk to the Tsar's table. A map orientates the visitor and a model has been made to show how the tiny village – then called Mishaninsky – must have looked when Lomonosov was born. The museum is especially proud of the metal font from the old Kurostrov wooden church (it burned down in 1718) in which, it is claimed, Lomonosov was christened.

The third room is devoted to Lomonosov's 'scientific path': his education in Moscow at the Slavo-Graeco-Latin Academy

(1730) and the St Petersburg Academy of Sciences (1735), and his sojourn in Germany (1736–41), where he studied physics, chemistry and metallurgy. The fourth room charts his achievements as a scholar, and his professorship at the St Petersburg Academy of Sciences. Various installations recreate his scientific laboratory.

Lomonosov said of his combined interests, 'Science is my exercise, poetry is my pleasure', and the fifth room, 'Poet and Enlightener', explores his achievements in literature and poetry, displaying copies of his literary works. The sixth and seventh rooms of the exhibition are dedicated to Lomonosov's achievements as a whole.

Closed Fridays

Norinskaya

Joseph Brodsky was exiled to this village east of the town of Konosha, in the southern part of Arkhangelsk region, to do manual labour on a collective farm in March 1964, following his infamous trial, but had his five-year sentence reduced after Jean-Paul Sartre appealed to the Soviet government. Brodsky returned to Leningrad in November 1965.

Nosovaya

In 1667, for refusing to follow the church reforms initiated by Patriarch Nikon, the Archpriest Avvakum, leader of the Old Believers, was exiled to Pustozersk, at the mouth of the Pechora river, in the northern part of the region. It was here, while he was sitting in the dungeons (the edict read: 'Imprison Avvakum in the earth, in a log frame, and give him bread and water'), that he began writing his autobiography, which was considered so heretical by the church authorities that it had to circulate in samizdat until 1861. He was burned at the stake in Pustozersk (approximately where the town of Nosovaya now lies) in 1682.

Astrakhan Region

Astrakhan

— *Chernyshevsky Museum* The radical journalist and novelist Nikolay Chernyshevsky was exiled to Astrakhan in 1883, following the completion of his sentence in Siberia. Before this he had spent seven years in a labour camp in the Irkutsk region, followed by twelve years of exile in the arctic village of Vilyuisk.

Chernyshevsky had been sent to Siberia in the 1860s for engaging in political agitation in St Petersburg. His criticisms of the terms of the emancipation of the serfs in 1861, in particular, had led him to become involved in organizing student and peasant protests. Chernyshevsky and his family changed their accommodation frequently during their six years of exile here, but there is now a small museum in the three rooms he lived in with his wife and son on the former Pochtovaya ul.
Address: Ul. Chernyshevskogo, 4

Bashkortastan Republic

Ufa

— *Aksakov Museum* The town of Ufa, once the principal town of Orenburg province, is the birthplace of Sergey Aksakov. The large wooden house belonged to his grandfather. There is also an Aksakov literary museum near by at Nadezhdino, in the Belebeevsky region. This is the estate where Aksakov lived as an adult between 1821 and 1826. Its fictional name in his *Chronicles* is Parashino.
Address: Ul. Blagoeva, 4

Bryansk Region

Krasny Rog

— *A. K. Tolstoy Museum* The estate of Krasny Rog, near the town of Pochepsk, was the country home of Prince A. K.

Tolstoy, the nineteenth-century poet, novelist and parodist (not to be confused with the Soviet A. N. Tolstoy). In 1967, a five-room museum dedicated to his memory opened here in the reconstructed main house of the former estate, which traces his life and works and contains some of Tolstoy's belongings from his estate.

Tolstoy spent his early childhood at Krasny Rog, before moving to St Petersburg, where he pursued a distinguished career as a diplomat and member of the Imperial Court. During his long years of service, Tolstoy came here to spend his summers, and it was in the summer of 1852 that he got together with his cousins, the three Zhemchuzhnikov brothers, and invented Kozma Prutkov, the fictitious writer and bureaucrat, and one of Russia's most humorous literary creations. Tolstoy shared with the Zhemchuzhnikovs a wicked sense of humour and a penchant for practical jokes, and Prutkov came into being after a succession of summers spent here concocting literary pranks. During the reactionary time of Nicholas I's final years as tsar, Prutkov provided his authors with a way of amusing themselves and others in an otherwise gloomy time. The sheer incongruity in their eyes of creating someone who was a self-righteous, pompous bureaucrat and loyal subject of Nicholas I *and* a poet meant that the personality of Kozma Prutkov was comic from the start, and the humour only increased when the fictitious author started producing pretentious but utterly banal poetry and prose. From 1854 onwards, works signed by Prutkov began to appear in *Sovremennik* (the Contemporary) and other monthly journals which published parodies and humorous verse, and were widely imitated. Much of Prutkov's writing is pure nonsense: his fables lack the customary moral at their conclusion, his children's alphabet begins nonsensically with 'Anton is leading the goat' as a mnemonic for the letter 'A', and his famous aphorisms, satires on hoary old proverbs, are preposterous in their complete obviousness and fatuity ('One cannot encompass the unencompassable', 'Be vigilant!', 'Many people are like sausages: the things used to stuff them they have inside themselves', 'Buy a picture first, then the frame!').

Tolstoy moved permanently to Krasny Rog in 1861, after he had resigned his position at court, and could now devote himself to literary pursuits. It was his favourite residence, and he enjoyed personally reading the proclamation of the emancipation of the serfs at the villages on his estate the year that he retired. Among the literary visitors who came during these years was Afanasy Fet, who was lured by Tolstoy's descriptions of the abundant grouse on his estate. After being picked up at Bryansk Railway Station by the Count's troika one summer's day in 1869, Fet was housed in a wing separate from the fine wooden estate house (designed by Rastrelli), so that he could get up early and go hunting. In the afternoons, Tolstoy read to Fet from the historical play about Boris Godunov that he was currently writing, and took him on walks.

Tolstoy died here in 1875, and is buried in the village cemetery.

Ovstug

— *Tyutchev Museum* The village of Ovstug, situated about twenty-two miles to the north-west of the town of Bryansk, is the birthplace of the poet Fyodor Tyutchev. The family estate is on the outskirts of the village and opened in 1985 as a museum.

Tyutchev was born on 23 November 1803 and educated both here and in Moscow until his seventeenth year, when he entered Moscow University. The house, with its impressive six-columned Classical façade, is magnificently situated above a sloping garden and parkland. It fell into disrepair after the poet's death and was completely destroyed during the Second World War. At the beginning of the 1980s it was rebuilt from scratch using old sketches and photographs. When the final architectural plans had been drawn up, the original ones were discovered in the family archive. The two ground plans differed by some thirty centimetres.

The five-roomed museum contains many letters, documents and photographs illustrating the life and works of Tyutchev. One of the rooms commemorates the school that Tyutchev's daughter Mariya built for the local peasant children. Although Tyutchev spent his early life at Ovstug, he never returned here to live permanently. His second wife Ernestina visited the estate more often, bringing their children to the country in the summer months. Although in one of his poems he recalls Ovstug with nostalgia, as a place that is 'radiant and serene', Tyutchev's attitude to the estate appears to have been ambivalent, and he clearly preferred town life. In a pilgrimage to Ovstug in 1846, after a twenty-two-year absence, he refers to it as 'native but undear'. However, Ovstug and its surrounding countryside seem to have informed much of his poetry about nature.

Chelyabinsk Region

Magnitogorsk

The industrial town of Magnitogorsk, deep in the Urals, was immortalized for ever in literature when its metal factory became the setting for Valentin Kataev's Socialist Realist classic of 1932, the novel *Time Forward!* The author spent time here talking with the factory's model Stakhanovite workers while researching for this novel, which celebrates the breaking of the world record for pouring concrete.

Ivanovo Region

Gumnishchi

It was in an old house surrounded by a shady garden which used to stand in a modest estate at the edge of this village, in the Shuya district, that the Symbolist poet Konstantin Balmont was born on 4 June 1867. The Balmonts were a noble family, originally from Sweden, but impoverished by the late nineteenth century. Balmont attended the local gymnasium in Shuya before entering the law faculty of Moscow University in 1886.

Novo-Talitsy

— *Tsvetaev Family Museum* It was in this village that Tsvetaeva's father was born, into a family of village priests. Ivan Tsvetaev was later to become a scholar and move to Moscow and found the Museum of Fine Arts, now known as the Pushkin Museum. The Tsvetaev family home, a one-storey wooden house with shutters and a mezzanine, still stands (as does the parish church of St Nicholas next to it), and its current owners have founded a museum about the Tsvetaev family here.

Kalmykia

Malye Derbety

In this village, fifty miles south-east of Tsaritsyn (known as Stalingrad in Soviet times), the poet Velimir Khlebnikov was born in 1885. His father was the Russian administrator of the Kalmyk Nomads, who were Mongolian Buddhists, and the family lived in the only house in the area, surrounded by the tents inhabited by the Kalmyks and their camels.

Kaluga Region

Bogimovo

The Chekhov family spent the summer of 1891 at a dacha in this village, near the town of Aleksin in neighbouring Tula province. They had first gone to Aleksin because Chekhov's younger brother had found a job there, but by chance met the owner of the estate of Babkino in nearby Bogimovo, from whom they rented the top floor of his huge two-storey stuccoed house, which came with a garden, a park, a mill and a pond. The

Chekhovs spent a delightful summer here in these spacious surroundings. Chekhov, who had just returned from his first trip to Europe, particularly enjoyed the fishing here, but got up at five each morning to work on his study *The Island of Sakhalin*, his assessment of the Siberian penal colony he had visited the previous year. The only concern during the summer was with one of the mongooses which he had brought back with him from his travels; it ran away, but was found a couple of weeks later. Chekhov did not entirely neglect fiction writing during the summer months; the story 'The House with the Mezzanine' was conceived and written here.

Radishchevo
— *Radishchev Museum* The village of Radishchevo (formerly Nemtsovo), north of Kaluga, is where the prose writer, poet and political thinker Alexander Radishchev was born in 1749. He spent the first seven years of his life here before going to Moscow, where he was to be educated.

The estate, first known as Verkhnee Ablyazovo, dates back to the early eighteenth century; it was founded by Radishchev's grandfather. He built himself a large stone manor house, a church and many outbuildings in the extensive grounds. Only the white Spas Preobrazheniya Church remains today, with its restored icons and frescoes dating from that time. In Radish-chev's childhood, the manor house was joined to the upper part of the church by a wooden corridor, supported by columns. This meant that the inhabitants of the house could enter the church privately, without having to worship with the peasants below.

Radishchev is best known for his politically provocative *Journey from St Petersburg to Moscow*, which was banned by Catherine the Great, and for which he was sentenced to ten years' exile in Siberia. Following his return from Siberia he was forced to continue his exile here under police surveillance from

1797 to 1801, when he was finally allowed to return to St Petersburg by the new Tsar Alexander I. He killed himself the following year, by drinking the sulphuric acid he used to clean his clothes.

The Radishchev Museum, which opened in 1945, is housed in a former school in the grounds of the former estate, and is devoted to the literary life and work of Radishchev.

Kozelsk

— *Dostoevsky Museum* Directly south-west of Moscow, just outside the town of Kozelsk, lies the famous monastery of Optina Pustyn, which has played an important part in Russia's religious life since it was founded in the fifteenth century. Despite its forced closure under Peter the Great, by the middle of the nineteenth century the monastery was firmly re-established, and had begun to attract people from all over the world who came to seek wisdom from its *startsy* (elders). Among the monastery's literary pilgrims were Gogol and Tolstoy – the latter came here several times towards the end of his life. Tolstoy's first visit took place in 1878, at the time of his spiritual crisis following *Anna Karenina*, when he came to seek an audience with Elder Amvrosy, who had become chief elder the previous decade. Apparently the elder found Tolstoy a particularly exhausting supplicant.

It was in 1878 that Dostoevsky and his wife came to see Elder Amvrosy, following the death of their child. The visit inspired many of the descriptions of the monastery in *The Brothers Karamazov*, and, in particular, the character of Elder Zosima. The wooden house where Dostoevsky stayed, behind the Church of St John the Baptist, is now a museum.
Address: Ul. Kuznechnaya, 2

Polotnyany Zavod

Meaning 'linen factory', Polotnyany Zavod is situated to the south of Moscow, north-west of Kaluga, and was the estate of the family of Pushkin's wife, the Goncharovs.

There were two factories here, one which made linen for ships' sails, and another which made paper. The factories were set up in the time of Peter the Great under a merchant from Kaluga. When he died, one of his partners in the firm, a former potter, who was a Goncharov, became its new owner. The factory grew and became famous throughout Russia and by the end of his life Afanasy Goncharov had become a member of the hereditary nobility. The estate passed on to his son, the uncle of Pushkin's wife. Natalya Goncharova spent her childhood here and came here later with her husband, although the estate had certainly seen more prosperous times by then.

The main house no longer exists, and the grounds suffered further in the Second World War when, according to Soviet accounts, all the old trees were chopped down by the German army for firewood.

Tarusa

— *Tsvetaeva Museum* Tsvetaeva's family used to spend their summers here, in a rented dacha twelve miles from the nearest railway station, and a mile from Tarusa itself, a town on the Oka river. The dacha, a small wooden house with a first-floor balcony (unfortunately pulled down in the 1960s to make room for a sanatorium), was called Pesochnaya and was described by Tsvetaeva in the essay she wrote about her father as 'an old gentry house of a vanished estate now turned into a "summer house"', which was 'entirely isolated, in the woods, on a high bank of the river Oka'. The family enjoyed the simple pleasures of walking and bathing here, and the beauty of the surroundings clearly made a deep impression on Tsvetaeva, as there are references to them from time to time in her writings, such as in her essay 'My Pushkin': 'where we live in Tarusa if you walk through the Pachevian willow ravine, the one mother named "Scotland", toward the Oka, suddenly there is a whole red island: pines! With noise, creaking, colour, smell; after the willows' wave shape, their one shape – a whole conflagration!' Tsvetaeva's mother died here in 1906, and a stone has been placed on the river bank at the spot where the poet wished herself to be buried. Her daughter Ariadna and half-sister Valeriya are buried here, but the rest of the Tsvetaev family, including the poet's mother, are buried at the Vagankov Cemetery in Moscow.

The Tsvetaeva Museum is located in the former house of the poet's grandfather. Other writers who spent time in Tarusa include Nikolay Zabolotsky, who passed his last years here, Alexander Solzhenitsyn, who came here for his honeymoon following his marriage to Natalya Reshetovskaya in 1940, and Konstantin Paustovsky, who edited an important almanac, *Pages from Tarusa* (1961). Published during Khrushchev's 'Thaw', it included work by young writers as well as materials by previously anathematized figures such as Tsvetaeva and Zabolotsky. Had Paustovsky tried to publish his almanac in Moscow, it would never have got past the censors, but he circumvented them by having it printed in Tarusa. The 75,000 print-run sold out in a matter of days.

Address: Ul. Rozy Lyuksemburg, 30

Kostroma Region

Shchelykovo
— *Ostrovsky Museum* This enchanting property set in the gently undulating countryside of the Upper Volga area was the beloved former estate of Russia's leading nineteenth-century playwright, Alexander Ostrovsky, and is now a five-room museum.

Ostrovsky died here in June 1886 at the age of sixty-three, shortly after taking up his new job as head of repertoire for Moscow theatres, a post he had long coveted. His father had originally bought the estate in 1848 (which is when Ostrovsky made his first visit there), and had died there in 1853. Ostrovsky and his brother had bought the estate from their stepmother in 1867 for 7,357 roubles and 50 copecks, and spent every summer in Shchelykovo from then on, travelling out from Moscow in May and returning each September. Ostrovsky's original plan was to abandon the theatre and become a farmer on the land attached to the estate, but tending the land required dedication, energy and money, and his enthusiasm for this aspect of the Russian landowner's life soon faded.

Until the railway had been built in 1871, Ostrovsky and his family would travel by boat to Kineshma from either Nizhny Novgorod or Yaroslavl, and there they would await horses sent from the estate, some fifteen miles away. The interior of the spacious grey two-storey wooden house, with its two verandas, looks just as it did during Ostrovsky's lifetime, with the original wallpaper, and much of the furniture still in place. Ostrovsky was a fine carpenter, and he not only made the large desk to be seen in his study, as well as numerous items of furniture in other rooms, but also the exquisitely carved wooden picture frames to be seen on the walls, which he worked on in the other house on the estate, at the end of the path lined by birch trees, where his brother usually stayed. Ostrovsky loved to fish in the River Kueksha, which runs through the estate.

Krasnodar Territory

Gelendzhik

— *Korolenko Museum* Visited by over 150,000 Soviet tourists in the 1970s, this museum is located in the Populist writer's two-storey summer house with wooden balcony and veranda, on the

Black Sea. Set in mountainous scenery, the house was landscaped when it was built in 1902 (to Korolenko's design) to fit into the natural environment. The museum consists of five rooms. The first recreates Korolenko's surroundings during the time that he lived here, including some of his family's personal belongings and original furniture and decor, while the other four contain an exhibition about Korolenko's life and works.
Address: Ul. Lenina, 23

Novorossiisk
— *Fyodor Gladkov Museum* This one-room museum commemorates Fyodor Gladkov, whose famous novel *Cement* (1925), about a communist who dedicates his life to the building of socialism, was inspired by his experiences living here from 1919 to 1921. It is housed in the attic of the Soviet Cement Industry Museum.
Address: Novorostsement Industrial Complex

Taman
— *Lermontov Museum* Taman is a small port on the Black Sea directly west of Krasnodar, which was visited by Lermontov in 1837, on his way to join General Veliaminov's military expedition at Anapa, and in 1840. It has been immortalized in his famous story 'Taman' in *A Hero of Our Time*. The story is very autobiographical, as the character Pechorin stops here for the same reasons as Lermontov had done. According to the account of one of Lermontov's fellow officers who stayed here the following year, the characters and the lodgings described in the story were drawn straight from life. Lermontov also drew a sketch of the hut where he stayed. Neither Lermontov nor his hero seems to have been particularly enamoured of the town. Pechorin finds it 'the foulest hole among all the sea-coast towns of Russia'. Despite his distaste for the place there is now a tiny museum (opened in 1976) inside the hut where

Lermontov stayed. It is situated at the top of a cliff looking out to sea. The museum's interior is based on the novel's description: 'There was no furniture apart from a table, a couple of benches and a huge chest by the stove. There wasn't a single icon on the wall – a bad sign.' There is also an exhibition in a nearby building, which describes Lermontov's two journeys to Taman. A statue of Lermontov by I. D. Brodsky was erected in 1964.

Address: Ul. Lermontova

Kursk Region

Kursk

Daniil Kharms was exiled here from July to November 1932 with his friend Vvedensky:

> We lived in two rooms. My friend had the smaller room and I took the one that was quite big, with three windows. My friend would not be home for days at a time, and would come back to his room just to sleep at night. I sat in my room almost all the time, and if I went out, it was just to the post office or to buy something for lunch. I also got pleuritis, and that kept me at home even more. I love being by myself. But after a month had gone by, I got bored of solitude...

Lipetsk Region

Elets

— *Bunin Museum* In the late nineteenth century, Elets was a small provincial town in the Orel province, and is best known now as the place where Ivan Bunin spent part of his early youth. Bunin entered the gymnasium here in 1881, at the age of eleven, having spent the last seven years living not far away at Butyrki, one of his family's small estates, which was sold in 1883.

The imposing building of the school where Bunin was a pupil still stands. Since Elets was too far to travel each day from Butyrki, Bunin stayed for a time with his cousin, then in 1883 rented accommodation in a house belonging to an official on the corner of the former Sharov per. and Rozhdestvenskaya ul. (now Ul. Gorkogo). In this one-storey wooden house where the future author rented a room, the first museum dedicated to the memory of Bunin in Russia was opened in 1989. Bunin's life in Elets is reflected in his fictionalized autobiography *The Life of Arseniev* (1952). He enjoyed wandering round the old town in his spare time, but was unhappy at school, and left early in 1886.

The present museum was created not only by its custodians, but also by students of the Elets Pedagogical Institute, and the enthusiastic members of various local clubs. On show is the room Bunin rented, now carefully restored with period furniture, and an exhibition of documents, photographs, portraits and personal artefacts belonging to the writer (including his pen, pince-nez, compass and suitcases) culled from a variety of different sources; some were found, for example, during excavation of the Bunin estate at Ozerki, while others were sent from Edinburgh by Militsa Green, entrusted with the writer's archive after his death.

Address: Ul. Pugacheva, 16

Lev Tolstoy

— *Tolstoy Museum* It was in the station master's house in the former village of Astapovo that Lev Tolstoy died of pneumonia at the age of eighty-two on 7 November 1910. The building immediately became a museum after his death. After the Revolution the village of Astapovo was named after Tolstoy.

Tolstoy had not wished to die here. Having left Yasnaya Polyana a week earlier, intending never to return, he was in fact on his way to see his niece at Novocherkassk, and had bought a ticket to Rostov-on-Don. However, as he was travelling through the Lipetsk region, about one hundred miles south of Tula, he fell ill, and had to leave the train at the obscure junction of Astapovo. The station master gave up his lodgings to the sick writer, and it was here that Tolstoy spent the last days of his life, surrounded by the world's press, a man with a movie camera, representatives of the Russian Orthodox church (who hoped they could persuade the excommunicated writer to return to the fold), officials from the tsarist government, various members of his family, and dozens of his followers.

Tolstoy's relations with his wife Sofya were so acrimonious by the time he left Yasnaya Polyana that she was almost the last to discover that her husband lay dying at Astapovo. His followers could do nothing to prevent her making the journey as soon as she did find out, and she even rented a private train for the purpose. But, once she had arrived, Tolstoy's chief disciple Vladimir Chertkov managed to prevent her gaining access to her husband until he was unconscious.

Before Tolstoy's body was taken back to Yasnaya Polyana, the artist Leonid Pasternak came to make sketches, accompanied by his son, the twenty-year-old Boris. The poet describes the scene at the station in his *Essay in Autobiography*:

> But what there was in the far corner of the room was not a mountain but a wrinkled little old man, one of the dozens of old men invented by Tolstoy and scattered through his books. The place bristled with fir saplings which stood round the bed, their outlines sharpened by the setting sun. Four slanting sheaves of light reached across the room and threw over the corner where the body lay the sign of the big shadow of the crosspiece of the window and the small, childish crosses of the shadows of the firs.
>
> That day the station at Astapovo had turned into the braying camp of the world press. Trade was brisk at the station restaurant. Waiters were run off their feet, hardly able to keep up with orders and galloping with plates of underdone beef steaks. Beer flowed like a river.

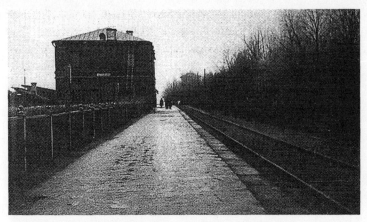

The railway station at Astapovo where Tolstoy died in 1910

The house is now a museum, consisting of eight rooms, and featuring an exhibition about the last year of Tolstoy's life. Visitors may inspect the bed that Tolstoy died in, his medicines and the few other personal items he had taken away with him, including a rug and umbrella.

Address: Privokzalnaya ul., 12
Closed Mondays and the last Friday in the month

Kropotovo

Kropotovo, a village near the town of Efremov, north of Elets, has associations with Mikhail Lermontov, whose father owned a small estate here. Following his mother's untimely death when he was three years old, Lermontov was brought up by his grandmother, but came to stay here with his father during his childhood.

Although their estate was fairly large (it covered several thousand acres and included 350 serfs) the family were considered to be impoverished, and any meagre profits that the estate brought in had to be divided between six children. Lermontov was very proud of his father's side of the family, as one of his early forebears was a Scottish bard named Thomas Learmonth (1220–97), also known as Thomas the Rhymer. The name of Thomas the Rhymer can be found in the works of Thomas Mallory, John Keats, Walter Scott and J. R. R. Tolkien.

The twelve-room wooden estate house was surrounded by outbuildings, orchards and an avenue of silver poplars. Unfortunately it was occupied by the German army in the Second World War and burned down in 1941.

Mordovian Republic

Pomaevo

Khlebnikov's family moved to this Mordovian village (which lies about sixty miles from Simbirsk) in 1895, when he was ten years old. It was here that he developed his interest in wildlife and began writing poetry. In 1897 Khlebnikov was sent to boarding school in Simbirsk, but he missed his family so much that they moved themselves to the city to be near him.

Saransk

The great critic and literary theorist Mikhail Bakhtin taught at the Mordovian Pedagogical Institute here in 1936, and he returned here in the 1940s, following the submission of his dissertation on Rabelais at Moscow University. He would return to Moscow only in 1969, where he spent the last six years of his life.

Nizhny Novgorod Region

Bolshoe Boldino

— *Pushkin Museum* Bolshoe Boldino, a village once famous for its bazaars, lies about 185 miles to the south-east of Nizhny Novgorod (formerly Gorky), set in a wide expanse of gentle landscape. In the village is the estate of Boldino, which for many centuries belonged to the family of Alexander Pushkin's father.

Here Pushkin wrote some of his most important works of the 1830s. His output here was considerable given that he only spent a total of five months here during his three visits of 1830, 1833 and 1834.

The estate fluctuated in size with each new Pushkin generation. In 1790 it was divided between Pushkin's father and his brother, whose much humbler residence no longer remains. Under Pushkin's father, an absentee landlord, Boldino fell into a state of neglect but its fortunes revived under the more attentive care of Alexander Pushkin's descendants. In 1911 it passed out of the hands of the Pushkin family and became state property. A museum was opened in 1949.

Pushkin spent three autumns here, a time of year he was particularly fond of: 'With every autumn I blossom afresh,' he wrote at Boldino in his poem 'Autumn'. His first visit in 1830 was made before his marriage to Natalya Goncharova when he was thirty years old. This business trip to attend to the transfer of part of the nearby village of Kistenevo into his name (a wedding present from his father) turned out to be a time devoted mainly to writing. He was forced to prolong his visit when a cholera epidemic, which had spread huge distances, prevented his return to Moscow. His mind, at first restless with worry about the present and future, calmed as he shut himself away and concentrated only on literary endeavours. This first trip came to be known as the 'Boldino autumn'.

During these two months he finally completed *Eugene Onegin*, which had taken seven years, four months and seventeen days to write, wrote *The Tales of Belkin*, the four dramatic sketches of *The Little Tragedies*, *A History of the Village of Goryukhino* and some thirty short poems, as well as the story in verse *Little House in Kolomna*.

Pushkin's second trip was in 1833, after he had travelled across Russia researching the Pugachov Rebellion. During October and the first half of November he completed *The*

History of Pugachov and wrote two of his most famous works, 'The Bronze Horseman' and the story 'The Queen of Spades'. His third trip in 1834 was far less fruitful than the first two – he wrote just one story, 'The Tale of the Golden Cockerel'.

Of all these works, the one that draws most immediately on the background of Boldino is *A History of the Village of Goryukhino*:

> The inhabitants of Goryukhino are for the most part of medium height and of strong and manly build; their eyes are grey and their hair is blond or red. The women are remarkable for their somewhat raised noses, their prominent cheek-bones and their fatness ... The men are well behaved, hard-working (especially on their own land), brave and of warlike disposition: many of them have fought single-handed with bears, and they have a reputation in the district for fist-fighting. In general they are all inclined to the sensual delights of drunkenness. In addition to domestic work the women share with their husbands a large part of their work; and they do not yield to them in courage, few of them having much fear of the village-elder. They make up a powerful public guard, keeping a tireless vigil in the courtyard of the big house, and they call themselves 'spearwomen'. The principal duty of these 'spearwomen' consists in beating a cast-iron plate with a stone, in this way intimidating anyone of evil design. They are as chaste as they are beautiful and reply dourly and expressively to the advances of men bold enough to make them.

Unlike Mikhailovskoe, Boldino was not damaged in the Second World War. But, whereas the former estate could be rebuilt as a museum from scratch so that it closely resembled its appearance in the poet's day, Boldino's appearance has changed considerably since the 1830s. The main house where Pushkin stayed on his first two visits would have looked simpler than it does now, as it has since been remodelled with veranda and columns. It is now a museum, as is the neighbouring estate office where Pushkin stayed on his third visit, although it then lay in a different spot. Next to the main house is a larch tree, supposedly planted by the poet.

Visitors can walk through the grounds, which contain old trees including a 200-year-old willow, a church built in the eighteenth century, ponds, two summer houses and various avenues lined with cherry, birch and lime trees, or travel further afield to the village of Kistenevo (five miles to the north-east of Boldino) or to Maloe Boldino (three miles to the south-west). This gives a feel of the size of the estate, but neither of these villages has a museum. Unlike at Mikhailovskoe, Pushkin's neighbours did not live on his doorstep and he had to travel some six to twelve miles to reach the estates of his friends at Apraksino and Chernovskoe.

Nizhny Novgorod
Nizhny Novgorod was renamed Gorky in the 1930s in honour of the writer and former inhabitant, who became the doyen of the official literary establishment, but the city, like the region, has now reverted to its original name. Other writers who have spent time in the city include Chekhov (who came here on several occasions in the early 1890s, mostly in connection with famine relief, in which he was heavily involved), Korolenko, and Chernyshevsky's successor, the radical critic Dobrolyubov, whose museum is at Ul. Lykova Damba, 2.

— *Museum of Gorky's Childhood* Maxim Gorky (actual name Alexey Peshkov) was born in another part of town at Ul. Kovalikhinskaya, 33, in March 1868, but grew up here, in the house of his grandparents, following the death of his father. The house has been open as a museum since 1938, and the rooms of Gorky's mother, grandparents and uncle have been restored, as has the kitchen. Various items belonging to the family are on display here, among furnishings typical of the time. The family was lower-middle-class, and sixteen people lived in this small one-storey wooden house with shutters. The fence beneath the front windows was installed to keep out prying neighbours, and the forbidding nail-studded fence which surrounds the yard was erected to ward off little boys. The house is evoked in Gorky's autobiographical work *Childhood*:

> We reached the end of the path. At the very top, leaning against the embankment on the right, and the very first house in the street, stood a squat, single-storeyed house painted dirty pink, with a roof hanging low over its bulging windows like a hat pulled down. From the street it looked very big, but inside its dim little rooms it was very cramped. Angry people rushed about in all directions like passengers about to disembark from a ship, ragged children swarmed all over the place like thieving sparrows, and the whole house was filled with a strange pungent smell.

Gorky spent an unhappy childhood in this house, which he remembers as being 'filled with the choking fog of hostility'. After he had had a few years of schooling, his mother died, and his grandfather threw him out on the street; he was eleven years old. There followed a variety of menial jobs before he ran away to work on a Volga steamer. In 1882, he worked for a time in the city here for an icon painter on Ul. Kostina.

Address: Pochtovy sezd, 21
Closed Wednesdays
— *Gorky Museum* Gorky lived with his wife and children on the first floor of this house on the former Martynovskaya ul. from 1902 to 1904. Their former flat opened as a museum in 1971 and contains eleven rooms. The three-storey wooden house was built in 1861, and had bright, airy rooms with tall ceilings. Gorky had begun writing in 1889, and it was at this time that he first met Vladimir Korolenko (who lived on Kanatnaya ul., 11), a Populist writer with an established reputation who gave the budding author much useful advice. He went on to publish his first story while working in the Caucasus in 1892, and had

acquired a solid reputation by the time he moved here, both on the literary scene and in the more political world of the revolutionary intelligentsia, of which he was a committed member. In 1902, he was elected to the Russian Academy and, when the government vetoed the election, Chekhov, with whom he had become friends in 1899, resigned in protest. Gorky had also by this time met and become friends with Tolstoy. While he was living here he wrote his famous play *The Lower Depths*, which was performed to great acclaim at the Moscow Arts Theatre in 1902. Guests here included Chaliapin, the pianist Goldenweiser and the writer Leonid Andreev. The museum features authentic furniture belonging to Gorky and his family, as well as books and other personal possessions. Rooms which have been restored include the writer's study, the drawing room, the dining room and the children's nursery.

Address: Ul. Semashko, 19
Closed Mondays and Thursdays

— *Gorky Literary Museum* The museum was founded in 1928, and contains eight rooms which trace the life and works of this city's famous former resident. The exhibits include, among other things, the piano that Beethoven's *Appassionata* sonata was played on for Gorky and Lenin in 1920, brought from Moscow, and a carpet given to Gorky by Lenin.

Address: Ul. Minina, 26
Closed Mondays and Tuesdays

Novgorod Region

Chudovo

— *Nekrasov Museum* The village of Chudovo is where Nikolay Nekrasov came to hunt and to write during the last seven years of his life. He knew the province well, as he had often hunted here with the Panaev brothers, who had an estate at Bainevo in the nearby Baldai region. Hunting brought him closer to the land and to the local people and fuelled one of the major themes of his poetry – the hardships of the Russian peasant.

Nekrasov had for some time been looking for a place of his own to stay in when he came to the province. At last he heard that a local landowner was selling his small estate. He went to look at it with Zinaida Nikolaevna, the last love of his life, and decided to buy it immediately. The sale went through very quickly.

The word 'estate' has an extremely broad meaning in Russia, ranging from a small abode with some land around it to a grand palace. This belonged to the former category. The house, which is now open as a museum, is two-floored, wooden and painted green. It stands on the River Kerest, where the river bends. It was surrounded by fifty acres of land which, with its forests and marshland, was extremely rich in wildfowl and game.

Nekrasov found he could write well here and in 1874 enjoyed a period of great creativity, writing some eleven lyrics which were later known as the 'Chudovo cycle'. He was already well known as a writer and as editor of the successful journal *Sovremennik* (the Contemporary), which was closed down by the censor in 1866. In 1867 Nekrasov bought another journal called *Otechestvennye zapiski* (National Annals); he was able to edit it from Chudovo. He would often hunt with one of its printers, V. M. Lazarevsky, who was able to inform him of the constant battles with the censor and other developments in St Petersburg.

The museum has four rooms arranged and decorated after surviving descriptions by Nekrasov's contemporaries. There is Nekrasov's study, which also turned into a room used by the woodsman, the 'woodland glade', which contains the poet's own kerosene lamp and powder flask for his gun, a guest's room containing Nekrasov's own mirror, Zinaida Nikolaevna's room and a drawing room. The last is furnished simply with photographs and pictures of his contemporaries as well as hunting memorabilia, very much in the style of a huntsman's lodge. His own possessions were looked after by the children and grand-children of one of Nekrasov's friends, the peasant hunter Mironov.

Nekrasov came here for the last time in 1876. He found hunting very difficult after the death of his favourite dog, who was shot accidentally by Zinaida Nikolaevna. The dog's grave is by the house bearing the inscription, 'Here Kado lies buried. A formidable hunter and irreplaceable friend of the house. Born 15 July 1868. Killed by accident while out hunting 2 May 1875.'

After Nekrasov's death the house was left to his wife and brother and was eventually bought by his sister; on her initiative a Nekrasov memorial school for peasant children was built. The school opened in 1892 but was closed fifteen years later due to lack of funds. Nekrasov's sister also gave the house to the Novgorod City Council together with money received from Nekrasov's work and proceeds from his journal, on the con-dition that they change nothing inside or outside the house.

After the Revolution both buildings were used as hospitals. There was much damage to the village in the Second World War but remarkably Nekrasov's house remained unscathed.

A plaque to Nekrasov was put up in 1946 together with a statue of the writer and his dog. The house was opened as a museum in 1983.

Address: Ul. Nekrasova
Closed Tuesdays and last day of the month

Krestsy

The Symbolist poet and novelist Fyodor Sologub was educated originally as a teacher, and in 1882 took his mother and sister with him to the town of Krestsy in Novgorod province where he would spend three miserable years employed at the local secondary school. In 1892, he was able to move back to St

Petersburg, when he got a job as teacher of mathematics, and in 1899 became a school inspector.

Staraya Russa

— *Dostoevsky Museum* In the nineteenth century Staraya Russa was a small spa town on the banks of Lake Ilmen, where Dostoevsky brought his family to spend the summer months as 'a place of physical and mental tranquillity'. Today it is one of the largest towns in the Novgorod region and is visited by holidaymakers who come to its sanatorium for the curative powers of its waters and mud. Staraya Russa's first settlers are mentioned in a Novgorodian twelfth-century manuscript. In the nineteenth century it was to become a prosperous trading town, initially for its rich supply of salt.

Dostoevsky first came here in 1872 and was to spend the last eight summers of his life in the town. He rented a room in and later bought the two-floored green wooden house which stands on the willowy banks of the River Pereritsa. It was the only property that he ever owned.

Now open as a museum, the six main rooms of the house have been recreated to approach their appearance when Dostoevsky still lived here, with contemporary furnishings and some of the writer's own possessions.

The hall displays travelling items such as two trunks, and Dostoevsky's own top hat and a single white glove. The drawing room has copies of his favourite works by Balzac, Shakespeare, Pushkin and Dickens on display as well as a complete edition of Dostoevsky's own works. The harmonium was played by his wife, Anna Grigorievna.

Dostoevsky's study is where he started to write *The Adolescent*, completed the short story 'Scales' and wrote most of *The Brothers Karamazov* with his wife working as his stenographer. It looks out over the river. On the walls are photographs of his favourite works of art – Titian's *Tribute Money*, Holbein's *Dead*

Christ and Raphael's *Sistine Madonna*. The dining-room table, laid with some of the family's own china, stands by the doorway leading into Anna Grigorievna's room, where a small bag that she stitched herself can be seen.

Dostoevsky led a quiet life here, working until the early hours of each morning. He liked to walk along the river banks, avoiding the holidaymakers who came to the resort. He drew on many of the places of the town in *The Brothers Karamazov*, not least his own house, where Fyodor Karamazov lives and dies:

> Fyodor Karamazov's house was some distance from the centre of the town, but it was not quite on its outskirts, either. It was rather old, but of a pleasant exterior: it was a one-storeyed house with an attic, painted grey and with a red iron roof. It was spacious and snug and there was no reason why it should not last for a long time yet. It had all sorts of box-rooms, hidden passages, and unexpected staircases. There were rats in it, but Karamazov was not altogether cross with them: 'Anyway,' he used to say, 'one does not feel so bored in the evenings when one is left alone.' And it was indeed his habit to send the servants away to the cottage for the night and shut himself up alone in the house. The cottage was in the yard. It was a large and solid building; Karamazov had his kitchen there, though there was a kitchen in the house; he disliked the smell of cooking, and the dishes were carried across the yard in winter and summer. The house was built for a large family, and there was room in it for five times as many people, masters and servants.

The hut in the garden was described as Smerdyakov's lodgings in the novel:

> A tumble-down, little wooden house of two rooms, divided by a passage . . . There was a tiled stove in the room and it was very hot. The walls were covered with blue paper, which was, it is true, in shreds and in the cracks under it

'The road of the Karamazov brothers', Staraya Russa

cockroaches swarmed in great numbers, so that there was a
continual rustling from them. The room was poorly furnished: two benches along the walls and two chairs by the
table. The table, though of plain wood, was covered with
a cloth with a pink pattern on it. There was a pot of
geraniums in each of the two little windows and a case
with icons in one corner of the room. On the table stood
a very dented little copper samovar and a tray with two
cups.

A map in the museum shows the places in the town mentioned
in the novel.

Other sites in the town believed to feature in the novel and
shown in a map in the museum include the house of Dostoevsky's friend Agrippina Menshova. This two-storeyed white
house on the opposite side of the river and closer to the town
centre than Dostoevsky's house is believed to be the model for
Grushenka's house in the novel. On the corner of the large main
square was the site of Plotnikov's shop, opposite it the *traktir* or
tavern where Ivan and Mitya meet and where the 'Grand
Inquisitor' chapter is set. Also on the square is the school which

Ilyusha is described as attending. The Ul. Karla Marksa leading from the square is believed to have been the street on which Katerina Ivanovna lived.

At Ul. Pushkina, 1a, a green wooden house stands on the site of the now destroyed Vladimirskaya Church – in front of which Ilyusha is described in the novel as being buried. Three hundred paces away on the corner of Ozernaya ul. and Dubrovina per. lies the famous 'Ilyusha's stone'.

After Dostoevsky's death, Anna Grigorievna continued to visit Staraya Russa. She created an unofficial Dostoevsky museum in his former study. The museum was not opened officially to visitors until 1981.

Address: Nab. Dostoevskogo, 42/2

Orenburg Region

Aksakovo

— *Aksakov Museum* Aksakovo is the childhood home of Sergey Aksakov, who grew up at the end of the eighteenth century on his family's country estate in a house built by his grandfather. He was also to spend the first five years of his married life here, during which time his son Konstantin, the famous Slavophile, was born.

No Russian writer before or after has so vividly described the natural beauty of the Orenburg oblast. Aksakov, whose first major novel was not written until he was in his sixties, had an astonishing gift of recall. His two classic novels, *A Family Chronicle* and *The Childhood Years of Bagrov the Grandson*, offer a very detailed, almost photographic record of life on a Russian estate from the middle of the eighteenth century, the *Chronicle* being described by Ivan Turgenev as 'an authentic document of an epoch'. *Chronicle* is in fact a thinly veiled family memoir, an account of how Aksakov's grandfather (known fictitiously as Bagrov) came to live on the estate (Bagrovo) and how he ran it. When Bagrov dies, the narrator Sergey takes up the story of his own life on the estate in *The Childhood Years*. As well as these two novels of reminiscences, Sergey Aksakov wrote *Notes on Fishing* and *Notes of a Hunter in the Orenburg Province* (1852), both equally detailed in their descriptions of contemporary practices.

The estate called Bagrovo in *Chronicle* is, of course, Aksakovo. *Chronicle* describes the grandfather's decision to move from his family estate in the Simbirsk province to the province of Orenburg. From hearsay Orenburg sounded like the promised land with 'the inexhaustible wealth of its vast plains of virgin soil and its incredible abundance of game, fish and all the fruits of the earth; also of its simple inhabitants'. The inhabitants were the 'kindly' Bashkirs, a Muslim race of Finnish–Tatar stock who lived in yurts or huts which in the winter had bladders fixed in the window frames instead of glass.

The move was something of an upheaval, not just because of the distance involved, but also because Aksakov's grandfather decided to take half his serfs with him from Simbirsk and there is a poignant description of these 'emigrants' being uprooted from their homeland and 'the church where they had been baptised and married and the graves of their fathers and forefathers'. Once they had made the move to Orenburg, a 'stately manor house' was built, huts for the peasants and, later, a white stone church.

The estate was inherited by Aksakov's father when, according to archive material, it consisted of nineteen buildings, 300 acres of land and 100 peasants. The peasants would work for their landlord for three days in the week, spending the rest of the time on their own plots. A mill in the village brought in between 700 and 1,000 roubles a year.

When Aksakov's father died, the estate was inherited by the writer's brother and it stayed in the family until 1907, when it became public property. Both the house and the church were then demolished. Now only a few of the estate buildings remain, such as the servants' room. In 1989 work began on rebuilding the manor house from its ruins. This is to house the Aksakov Museum, which is now temporarily based in a former school building in the grounds.

Closed Mondays

Samara

When Tolstoy fell ill in 1862, shortly before his marriage, his doctors advised him to come here to take the famous fermented mare's milk cure kumiss, drunk by the Molokans ('Milk drinkers'), an obscure religious sect whose adherents drank no alcohol. Samara, known in Soviet times as Kuibyshev, was an unspoilt area also inhabited by the nomadic Bashkirian tribes. Tolstoy liked not only the simplicity of these people's lives, but the beauty of the countryside, and in 1871 he bought a 67,000-acre estate near Buzuluk. He travelled from Yasnaya Polyana for a brief visit the following year and a lengthier one in 1873. This time he spent the entire summer at his new estate, where he ended up throwing his energies into famine-relief work, due to crop failure. He did the same during the great famines of 1891–2.

Tsvetaeva and her fiancé Sergey Efron travelled to Usen-Ivanovskoe in 1911, the year before they were married, to take the kumiss cure. They had met earlier that summer at Voloshin's dacha in Koktebel, in the Crimea. A small museum there commemorates their visit.

— *Gorky Museum* Gorky moved to Samara in 1895 to work on the local newspaper, and lived at first in a single room furnished only with a bed, table and chair. He then moved to this address, where there is now a small four-room museum. The ground-floor room he lived in, whose iron bed and scant furnishing reminded Gorky's contemporaries of a monk's cell, has been restored. The other room on the ground floor contains an exhibition about the impact Samara made on Gorky's work.

Upstairs, on the first floor, there is a two-room literary exhibition about Gorky and other writers who spent time here.

Address: Ul. Stenka Razina, 126

— **A. N. *Tolstoy Museum*** The novelist Alexey Nikolaevich Tolstoy was born in the village of Sosnovka outside Samara in 1883 into a family of the nobility. It is hardly surprising that he became a writer; through his father's family he was a distant relation of the more famous Tolstoy, while his mother was born a Turgenev. Tolstoy's mother left her husband and the family estate when Alexey was very young, and the wooden house where he grew up in Samara was opened as a museum in 1983, exactly one hundred years later. Tolstoy left for St Petersburg as a young man, and returned here only in 1936, nine years before his death, by which time he had published the first part of his historical novel, *Peter the First*, and had become a leading member of the official Soviet literary establishment. The contents of the Tolstoy house have been described by Lesley Chamberlain in her travel book *Volga, Volga*, which contains an account of her visit to the museum:

> The house was full of beautiful objects, of the kind seldom seen in present-day Russia ... The furniture here was mahogany, ebony and that Russian preference, Karelian birch, a pale, mottled timber like a cross between walnut and bamboo. There were French novels, parasols, Turgenev family porcelain, a Singer sewing machine and a Remington typewriter. On the desk in the stepfather's study stood a fine black abacus with the labelled face of Gutenberg...

Address: Ul. Frunze, 155

Orel Region

Orel

Orel (Eagle) is the capital town of the Orlov province. It grew up around its fortress, which was built in 1566. According to legend, when the trees around the mouth of the Oka and Orlik rivers were being cleared to build the town, an eagle was frightened away. Deciding that the eagle was 'the real owner of the land, the woodcutters named the town Orel.

The town is most famous in literary terms as the birthplace of Ivan Turgenev, and several buildings and institutions bear his name. The town has other literary connections as a surprising number of other, lesser-known writers were born or lived here. The main literary museum in the town is the Turgenev Museum and, until recently, the other writers were represented only by the Museum of Orel Writers. However, there are now separate museums dedicated to Bunin, Leskov and Andreev.

— *Turgenev Museum* Turgenev was born in Orel on 28 October 1818 in a wooden house at the corner of Georgiyevskaya and Borisoglebskaya ul., a small town estate which bordered on the estates of other Orel nobles. Like many of the wooden houses in the town, it burned down in the 1840s and no trace of it remains.

Turgenev lived in Orel until the age of three, when the family moved to his mother's nearby estate, Spasskoe Lutovinovo. Throughout his life it remained his local town, together with the smaller Mtsensk. He often visited Orel and took an interest in local affairs, particularly in the years before 1861 and the abolition of serfdom. He had friends in the town with whom he corresponded all his life. When away from Orel he said that to receive a letter from Orel or from Mtsensk was 'like manna'.

The building which houses the Turgenev Museum is at Ul. Turgeneva, 11, and is known as Galakhova's House. Olga Vasilievna Galakhova, a relative of Turgenev, was also his literary heiress; she inherited many of his belongings, including a library containing some 5,000 books, a collection built up over the years by Turgenev and his ancestors which included the library of Turgenev's friend Belinsky, bought by Turgenev on Belinsky's death. Galakhova also inherited the furniture from Spasskoe Lutovinovo, which was stored in this house, thus saving it from destruction when the estate burned down in 1839. Much of the furniture has now been returned to the restored house in Spasskoe Lutovinovo.

The museum has many pictures of Spasskoe Lutovinovo and the surrounding countryside and portraits of Turgenev and his friends, as well as documents such as his student notebooks and first editions of his works. Other personal exhibits include the gown he wore as Doctor of Civil Law at Oxford University, the desk and chair from his Paris study and his death mask, as well as a cast of his hand.

Turgenev wrote about Orel in many of his novels, but most directly in *A Nest of the Gentry*, which takes place in 'The town of O'. Set in the 1840s, the novel describes Turgenev's own group of noble intellectuals who, like him, were educated in the West, where they were much influenced by European liberalism. On returning to Russia, they found it hard to adapt to the life on their estates and began to question the feudal system of serf ownership which went against many of their acquired values. Orel provides the background to the novel, the town where many of the nobles lived, but which seemed, after the capitals of Europe, 'rather provincial', as Turgenev described it in a letter to Pauline Viardot.

An area of the town at the end of Oktyabrskaya ul. has come to be called Nest of the Gentry; it is on the banks of the river, which Bunin called 'Turgenev's bank'. Apparently Turgenev's nurse used to push her charge along a steep path by the river banks which resemble a cliff face. At the top of the bank is a statue of Turgenev and a pagoda. The area is associated with the doomed love between Liza Kalitina and Fyodor Lavretsky described in *A Nest of the Gentry*. Bunin, in his novel *The Life of Arseniev*, describes this area and its associations with Turgenev's work:

There is an estate nearby which was allegedly described in Turgenev's *Nest of the Gentry*. We walked towards the edge of the town, along an out-of-the-way street buried in verdure, to an old garden perched on the steep bank of the Orlik river, where a grey, long-deserted house stood. We lingered awhile, looking at it over a low fence, at the neglected garden, its tree branches strewn with tiny April leaves and tracing a fanciful pattern against the sunset sky ... Liza, Lavretsky, Lemm ... And suddenly I passionately yearned for love.

The house stands to this day, at the end of Oktyabrskaya ul.

— *Leskov Museum* At Oktyabrskaya ul., 9, is the two-storeyed wooden house where Nikolay Leskov spent his childhood. It opened as a museum in 1974. Leskov is best known for his short story 'Lady Macbeth of Mtsensk', the source of the libretto for Shostakovich's opera. Leskov was born near Orel at Gorokhovo, the son of a legal investigator. He lived in Orel as a boy, until the age of eight, when his father retired and the family moved to a small farm at Panino in the Kromsk region. At the age of ten he was sent to the Orel Gymnasium, where he stayed for six years, without completing the full course. His first job was as a clerk in the Orel criminal court. Here he witnessed the criminal underworld of the provinces which provided inspiration for his fiction and may well have influenced his portrayal of Katerina Izmailova in 'Lady Macbeth of Mtsensk':

In these parts one occasionally comes across individuals of such character that, no matter how many years may have passed since one's last encounter with them, one can never recall them without experiencing an inward tremor. An example of this type was Katerina Lvovna Izmailova, a merchant's wife who once enacted a drama so awesome that the members of our local gentry, taking their lead from someone's light-hearted remark, took to calling her 'Lady Macbeth of Mtsensk'.

Portrait of Nikolay Leskov in 1895

There are five rooms in the museum, which are arranged chronologically, and trace Leskov's life from his early childhood. The last room reproduces the decor of his study in St Petersburg, where he moved in the early 1860s. On display here is Leskov's desk, his wooden clocks, and the various pictures and icons which used to line the walls of his study (he found himself unable to work in a room with bare walls).

A statue of Leskov was unveiled in Orel in 1981 on the bank of the River Orlik, near Ul. Lenina.

Address: Ul. Oktyabrskaya, 9

— *Andreev Museum* Leonid Andreev proudly named himself 'A wild Orel-dweller', and his reputation as a successful womanizer suggests he lived up to his epithet. Andreev was born here in 1871, the son of a local government land-surveyor. The small terraced house with an orchard, where he spent his childhood and youth, is now open as a museum. Andreev's family lived a comfortable existence until the death of his father, after which they found it difficult to make ends meet. Andreev went to the Orel grammar school and soon discovered the adventure novels of Thomas Mayne Reid and James Fenimore Cooper, after which he tried unsuccessfully to run away to America. His first short story, entitled 'He, She and Vodka', was published in the local Orel newspaper, the *Orlovsky vestnik* (Orel Herald). Andreev found Orel 'waterless and dusty' and left for Moscow, where he graduated from the university in 1897. He was to enjoy great success and wealth as a writer and, having spent much of his childhood in poverty, was to live a life of extravagance. He passed the last years of his life in the house of his dreams, a wooden mansion which he built himself on the Gulf of Finland at Vammelsuu near St Petersburg.

Address: Vtoraya Pushkarskaya ul., 41

— *Museum of Orel Writers* The Museum of Orel Writers is next door to the Turgenev Museum, and has rooms dedicated to the following: Boris Zaitsev, Mikhail Prishvin, Aleksey Apukhtin, I. A. Novikov, Leonid Andreev and Afanasy Fet. The latter, a friend of both Tolstoy and Turgenev, grew up at his father's Orel estate, Novosyolki in the village of Kozyulkino, to the south-east of Mtsensk. He was not allowed to take on his father's name – Shenshin – until 1873 as his parents were not married when he was born. This deprived him of the privileges of a nobleman and caused him much grief. In 1860 he bought his own estate in the Orel province called Stepanovka, where he lived for seventeen years; he discusses the process of settling in there at great length in his memoirs: 'Finally our little house began to look as if it could be lived in. At the beginning of May it had a green roof with stucco ceilings and walls, and my only fear was that it would be damp; but even that inconvenience diminished as each day went past, thanks to keeping the heating at a higher temperature ...' The house with its parquet floors and grand piano was furnished simply, but unfortunately no longer remains. In 1877 Fet bought a larger estate, Vorobyovka

near Kursk, where he spent the rest of his life. He is buried at Kleimenova, north of Orel. Fet is buried with his wife in a hideous church built by his niece, Olga Vasilievna Galakhova née Shenshina (see p. 363) who was also a niece of Turgenev's mother. (She was also the maternal great-grandmother of my Nikita who knew her in Paris when he was 4–5 years old. What a pity he was too young to understand all her reminiscences about Turgenev, Fet and their writer friends.)
Address: Ul. Turgeneva, 13
— *Bunin Museum* Orel is a city with close connections with Ivan Bunin, who spent his childhood in the Elets area (see p. 344), some hundred miles away to the east, on the family estates of Butyrki and Ozerki. In 1889, at the age of nineteen, he moved here and got a job as assistant editor on the Orel newspaper, where he worked for two years. His first poem had been published two years earlier, and in Orel his writing career began in earnest. His paper, *Orlovsky vestnik*, published a whole series of poems, stories, reviews, and sketches by him, as well as his translation of Longfellow's 'Song of Hiawatha', culminating in the appearance in 1891 of his first poetry collection. During his time in Orel, Bunin became involved with Varvara Pashchenko, who also worked on the newspaper. Her parents opposed the match because he was so impecunious, and in 1892 they moved to Poltava, where his brother was living. Bunin later moved to Moscow, but led a largely nomadic life until his emigration after the Revolution. His life in Orel is reflected in his fictionalized autobiography *The Life of Arseniev*, published in Paris in 1952. Bunin often came back for summers here, and lived for much of 1916 and 1917 in the village of Glotovo-Vasilievskoye at the estate of his cousin in the province.

The Bunin Museum opened in 1991, in an old gentry house on Georgievsky per., a quiet, tree-lined street. It began life as a room in the Orel Literary Museum in 1957, four years after the author's death. Although Bunin was recognized as a Russian writer by his time, he was still not the kind of officially celebrated author of whom the authorities commissioned statues (this happened only in 1995), and the acquisition of materials for the

museum was a gradual process. Bunin's pre-revolutionary archive had initially been given to his brother, then to his nephew. An attempt was made to sell the contents of his Paris flat to the Soviet Ministry of Culture in 1961, but it was turned down. Friends took some personal items and pieces of furniture, while the bulk of his archive was given to Militsa Green, of Edinburgh University, who in 1988 donated it to the Soviet Cultural Foundation, which passed everything finally to the museum here. The museum now contains more than 5,000 exhibits, donated by many people and institutions in difference contries. Of particular interest is Bunin's Paris study, which has been faithfully recreated in one of its rooms, right down to the books on the shelves, the photographs and pictures on the mantelpiece (including a signed portrait by Tolstoy), and the icon, in the same corner, to the right of his desk, which is pushed against the fireplace. Visitors can hear a tape of Bunin reciting his poem 'Loneliness' to the accompaniment of music by Rachmaninov, who was a close friend. On display are examples from the museum's collection of 3,000 publications by or about Bunin, and an exhibition of documents, paintings and photographs about his life and works, as well as an assortment of oddities such as a Fabergé crystal yacht with a silver sail given to Bunin to celebrate twenty-five years of writing, a cork hat bought during his travels in Egypt, Syria and Ceylon in 1907, and a silver tray and salt cellar presented to the author in 1933 by the Russian population in Stockholm on the occasion of his being awarded the Nobel Prize for Literature.
Address: Per. Oktyabrskyl, 1

Spasskoe Lutovinovo

— *Turgenev Museum* In a letter to Émile Zola in 1874 Turgenev described where he lived:

> If you have an atlas, find the map of Russia and move your finger from Moscow in the direction of the Black Sea; on

your way – a little north of Orel – you will discover the town of Mtsensk. There it is! My village is ten kilometres away, bearing, as you will see, a name that is hard to pronounce. It's a very remote corner – quiet, green, and sad.

Later, in 1876, he described his house to Gustave Flaubert: 'Would you like me to describe my house?... It's wooden, very old, panelled, pale lilac in colour; there's a verandah, covered with ivy; the roof is iron and painted green...'

The land on which the estate was built was bequeathed to the Lutovinov family in the sixteenth century by Tsar Ivan the Terrible. Spasskoe Lutovinovo was laid out at the beginning of the nineteenth century by Turgenev's great-uncle, Ivan Lutovinov. The colonnaded house had two storeys and was flanked by two stone galleries which each ended in wooden annexes. In 1839 the main house was burnt down, leaving only the wooden wing with part of the attached curved stone building that we see today. When Turgenev came to live here as a three-year-old (before the fire) it had seemed to him to be as big as a whole town. The Turgenev family fortunes derived from his mother's side. Spasskoe Lutovinovo was a large estate with 5,000 serfs, whereas his father – a guardsman – owned only a small estate at Turgenevo in the Tula province with 200 serfs. The narrator of Turgenev's short novel *First Love* viewed a similar background without illusions: 'My father, then still a young and very handsome man, married my mother for her money.' Turgenev's mother, Varvara Petrovna, is said to have been a domestic despot; such a tyrannous woman is portrayed in Turgenev's 'Mumu', 'Punin and Baburin' and 'The Privy Officer'.

When Varvara Petrovna died, her wealth and land were inherited by Turgenev's elder brother, but the reduced estate of Spasskoe Lutovinovo came to Ivan himself, who was to run it in a far more relaxed manner than his mother. He never lived here on a permanent basis, spending much time abroad. In 1852 he was sent here as an internal exile from St Petersburg for the publication of a short piece in a Moscow newspaper about the recently deceased Gogol. His term of exile in fact lasted one and a half years.

Although he lived abroad for long periods, Turgenev always found he could work here with greater ease and, on subsequent visits, he was to produce in rapid succession three novels, *A Nest of the Gentry*, *Fathers and Sons* and *On the Eve*. The draft of *Rudin* was completed in seven weeks.

The place settings of these novels as well as many of their characters are taken straight from life. The 'town of O' in *A Nest of the Gentry* is nearby Orel. The short story 'Mumu' is set on a large estate taken from the Spasskoe Lutovinovo of Turgenev's childhood. Turgenev himself felt the short story 'Faust' to be most closely connected with Spasskoe. His *Hunter's Sketches*, written outside Russia in 1845–51, are set entirely in the country-side around the estate which he loved and knew so well as a hunter.

Some of the sketches have place-names as their titles, such as 'Bezhin Lug' (Bezhin Meadow) and 'Malinovaya Voda' (Raspberry Water), both real spots in the countryside surrounding the estate. The short story 'Khor and Kalinich', the first of the sketches, is based on two peasants from the estate. Turgenev's neighbour Fet later remembers staying in the eighty-year-old Khor's hut on a hunting expedition. The descriptions of provincial life on an estate on the eve of reform in both *Fathers and Sons* and *On the Eve* drew heavily on Turgenev's experience of Spasskoe, although the Kirsanov estate in *Fathers and Sons* appears to be based on the village of Peredovik (formerly Petrovskoe), half a mile north of Spasskoe Lutovinovo. This was the centre of the Lutovinov estate before Spasskoe was built.

Turgenev entertained many of his friends at Spasskoe, including Nekrasov, Fet, Polonsky and Aksakov. Lev Tolstoy,

*Turgenev's sleep-inducing sofa
at Spasskoe Lutovinovo*

whose sister lived at Pokrovskoe near by and whose brother lived at Nikolsky-Vyazemsky, paid a visit in 1859. This was the beginning of their mutual disagreement, described by Turgenev in a letter to his friend Botkin: 'We are created at opposite poles. If I eat soup and like it I know from *that very fact* for certain that Tolstoy finds it repulsive – and vice versa.' The room in which Tolstoy stayed is now named after Maria Savina, who acted the part of Verochka in Turgenev's play *A Month in the Country* and spent five days at Spasskoe in 1881. In her memoirs she remembers Turgenev taking her into his study and showing her his desk, saying, 'At this desk I wrote *Fathers and Sons*.' There was also a musical festival arranged in her honour by the serfs on the estate.

The house, now a museum, has been furnished to recreate its appearance when Turgenev lived here. Much of the furniture is Turgenev's own; although there was a second fire in 1906, Turgenev's belongings had by this time been moved for safe-keeping to Orel. Therefore we can see the grandfather clock described in the short story 'Brigadier', the portraits on the wall which inspired the short story 'Three Portraits', as well as the large sofa described in *On the Eve*. 'A dangerous sofa,' wrote Turgenev to Gustave Flaubert, 'you only have to lie down on it and you fall fast asleep. Try to avoid it.' A chessboard in a room called the 'casino' by Turgenev's mother is where Turgenev indulged his habit: 'I am the best chess player of all the writers; and the best writer of all the chess players.' Very little survives from his mother's day and a few pieces of china under a glass case are all that remains of a once large collection. The books in the house are copies of originals from Turgenev's library, many of which originally belonged to the Lutovinov family. The oldest object in the house is an icon supposedly presented to Turgenev's ancestors by Ivan the Terrible.

The park outside, once containing many more trees, still has an oak tree in it planted by Turgenev. The alleyway of lime trees which stretches down to the lake is original. When the park was first laid out the trees were planted to form the roman numerals XIX. The lake is now all that remains of an elaborate cascade of ponds.

The outbuildings include the wooden house where Turgenev spent his exile. There is an exhibition housed here called 'Turgenev and his Native Land' whose eight rooms give a detailed description in pictures and photographs of the history of the estate and of Turgenev's life. In a room dedicated to the *Hunter's Sketches* you can see Turgenev's hunting clothes and gun, and copies of the illustrations to the book. Relics from Turgenev's mother's day include the instruments from her serf orchestra. 'On the eve of her death,' wrote Turgenev to Pauline Viardot, 'and indeed when the rattle of the death agony was beginning, there was – by her orders – an orchestra playing polkas in the neighbouring room.' A map of the Orlov and Tula provinces shows the places mentioned in Turgenev's work.

In the grounds there is a church where Turgenev's parents were married and a chapel built over the Lutovinov burial vault. The Spas Preobrazheniya (Saviour's Transfiguration) Church, built in 1809, replaced an older one which had stood in the centre of the village cemetery. The old walls of the cemetery, by the manor gate, are faintly discernible; they date back to the time of the first Russian settlers. Between the church and the chapel is the grave of a mysterious governess, whose origins are to this day unknown. Neither Turgenev nor his parents are buried on the estate.

The estate suffered much damage during the Second World War, but was restored and opened to visitors in 1976.
Open every day

Penza Region

Belinsky

— *Belinsky Museum* It was in a one-storey wooden house, in the small Russian provincial town of Chembara (named after Belinsky in 1948), which lies in the western part of the province about seventy miles from Penza, that Russia's most famous literary critic spent most of his childhood. It was the first museum about Belinsky to be opened in Russia, and was founded in 1938, thanks to the efforts of Lenin's widow, Nadezhda Krupskaya, among others. Belinsky's surviving relatives handed over items in their possession which had belonged to the critic; others were purchased from long-time residents in Chembara. Full restoration work was completed in 1973, and was carried out through recourse to Belinsky's letters and articles, in which he speaks about his family home. There are nine rooms.

Belinsky was born in 1811, in a town now part of Finland. His father was a doctor, and used to receive his patients in the family home. Although not many of Belinsky's possessions have survived (with the notable exception of his library, purchased by Turgenev from his widow, and now preserved here), the family furniture in the house gives the visitor a good idea of how everything looked in his day. On display in the museum are various personal effects belonging to Belinsky and his family, including a pencil belonging to the critic, as well as a collection of contemporary periodicals with articles by him.

Adjoining the Belinsky family property, in spacious grounds, is a slightly grander nineteenth-century porticoed building, also wooden, which was once the local school where the future radical critic was a pupil in the early 1820s. It also houses a Belinsky Museum now, with an exhibition about his youth. After he left the local school in 1825, Belinsky became a pupil at the Penza Gymnasium, and shared an austerely decorated room on Verkhnaya Peshchaya ul. with a relative, but was expelled four years later for poor attendance. He then set out immediately for Moscow, to enrol in the university (entrance did not require a school-leaving certificate), where all his hopes were focused. The museum contains authentic period school furniture, photographs, school textbooks of the time and autographed manuscripts.

Address: Ul. Barisheva, 2

Narovchat

— *Kuprin Museum* This museum, which opened in 1981, commemorates the prose writer Alexander Kuprin, who was born here into the family of a minor official in 1870. As well as various personal items, the museum's six rooms contain some of the original family furniture, as well as autographed books, correspondence and other memorabilia.

Address: Ul. Kuprina, 2

Tarkhany

— *Lermontov Museum* Situated about one hundred miles to the south-west of Penza is the country estate where Mikhail Lermontov spent much of his childhood. Tarkhany has now become a museum complex occupying 170 acres. The estate is divided in two by the River Miloraik. There is an old park with three

gardens (Dalny – distant; Sredny – middle; and Krugly – round).
It has two complexes of buildings, the first encompassing the
main house and its outbuildings, the second where the poet and
his family are buried.

The estate was acquired in 1794 by Lermontov's grandmother, Mariya Arsenieva, in 1794, who rebuilt some of the
buildings and laid out the park. A strong character, she ran her
estate with great efficiency.

When Lermontov's mother died in 1817, Arsenieva declared
that all her inheritance would pass to her grandson providing
that he was brought up by her, rather than by his father. She
came from the Stolypin family, who, although untitled, occupied
prestigious government, military and court positions. The family
of Lermontov's father were less distinguished, although they
claimed noble descent from the Scottish family of Learmonth.
Lermontov's father had little choice but to accept, particularly as
she offered to extend a loan she had made to him of 25,000
roubles. Lermontov was to visit his father's modest estate at
Kropotovo in the holidays but otherwise was to spend his entire
childhood and adolescence with his over-protective grandmother. From 1818 to 1828, when Lermontov and his grandmother moved to Moscow for the sake of his education, they
lived at Tarkhany. Lermontov had first come to Tarkhany as a
baby with his parents, who had stayed in the old manor house,
which was later dismantled and replaced by the Church of
Mariya Egipetskaya. He now found himself in the yellow
wooden main house, built and designed by his grandmother,
which has been restored and furnished in a manner reminiscent
of Lermontov's time and is described by him in the poem 'How
Frequently Amid . . .': 'The stately manor tall against the sky; /
The garden with its broken greenhouse / and the green-slimed
sleepy water.'

The aim of the displays in the various buildings throughout
the estate is to show how Lermontov lived and to tell the story

of his short life. The family history is told through copies of paintings, books and journals as well as through many of Lermontov's own drawings. Arsenieva's will is on display, reminding us of its great significance in Lermontov's life. Contemporary newspapers provide historical context, including a copy of the *Severnaya pchela* (the Northern Bee), announcing the Decembrist revolt of 1825.

Behind the main house is the Church of Mariya Egipetskaya, which Arsenieva built in honour of her daughter, Lermontov's mother. Peasants came here to worship from Tarkhany and the neighbouring villages, and it was here that they learned of current events throughout Russia. Detailed church records on display reveal information such as disorderly and drunken conduct among certain peasants, and references to a manifesto issued by the government after the Decembrist Rising, to quell any unrest that may have spread from the capital.

Much of the museum is devoted to the life of the surrounding country and its people. The displays in the housemaid's room, the servants' hut and the Dom Klyuchka or housekeeper's house all emphasize Lermontov's supposed sympathy with the countryside and the peasants who lived on it – particularly his faithful servant Andrey Ivanovich Sokolov, who lived to be an old man in the Dom Klyuchka. Like Pushkin, Lermontov was keenly interested in peasant culture and folklore, and the stories told by the peasants on the estate are reflected in his poems such as 'Vadim', 'The Prophecy', 'The Song of the Tsar Ivan Vasilievich, the Oprichnik' and 'Birthplace', all of which are explicitly set in the Penza district.

On the other side of the river is the Church of Mikhail Arkhistratiga, built by Arsenieva in 1840. This is where Lermontov's coffin, which had been brought from the Caucasus, lay for two days and two nights in April 1842. Nearby is the small family chapel where Lermontov was buried on 23 April. He lies next to his grandfather and mother. His mother's grave has a cross and a broken anchor on it, the anchor being a symbol of broken hopes. Arsenieva, who outlived her grandson by three years, is buried here too. In 1974 the remains of Lermontov's father (who died in 1841, at his estate at Kropotovo) were moved here.

The small village of Apalikha lies two miles from Tarkhany and used to belong to relations on Lermontov's mother's side of the family called the Shan-Gireys. The estate was acquired in 1826 and the park was laid out at the end of the eighteenth century. The house no longer stands.

Pskov Region

Pushkinskie Gory

— *Pushkin Museum* Roughly sixty miles south of Pskov amid countryside of great beauty lies an area of about 250 acres made up of three small estates, Mikhailovskoe, Trigorskoe and Petrovskoe, and their neighbouring villages. It is bordered by the River Sorot to the north and the town of Pushkinskie Gory (Pushkin Hills) to the south. It is here, on his family estate at Mikhailovskoe, that the twenty-five-year-old Alexander Pushkin was sent into internal exile in 1824 by the government. He had just completed a term of semi-exile in the south for what the Tsar deemed to be the 'scandalous verse' he had written in St Petersburg in his early twenties; but in the south he had angered the governor general of the region, in part by his flirtation with his wife, and finally by a letter Pushkin wrote to a friend in which he said he was 'taking lessons in pure atheism'. The result was further exile to Mikhailovskoe, where it was hoped that the countryside would still Pushkin's muse.

But living in this quiet country backwater had quite the opposite effect. During the two years Pushkin spent in Mikhailovskoe he was to produce more than 100 works, many of them inspired by the Russian countryside, its people, customs, language and folklore. His enforced absence from St Petersburg was fortunate in another respect: in December 1825 the Decembrist Rising took place, leading to the execution, imprisonment or exile of many of its participants. It is almost certain that Pushkin would have been among them had he been in the capital.

The three estates lie within a few miles of each other. The houses and outbuildings, which were devastated during the Second World War, have all been rebuilt and many new trees have been planted. This represents an attempt to recreate the estates' appearance during Pushkin's day, rather than the early eighteenth century when Pushkin's family's associations with the land began. It was then that it was bequeathed by the Empress Elizabeth to Pushkin's maternal great-grandfather, the Abyssinian Prince Abram Petrovich Hannibal.

— *Mikhailovskoe* This was the modest wooden house belonging to Pushkin's parents which Pushkin once referred to as his izba or hut. On his arrival in Mikhailovskoe he quarrelled with his father, who had agreed to aid the authorities by opening Pushkin's mail. The family left for St Petersburg, leaving Pushkin alone with his nanny, Arina Rodionovna.

The house has been reconstructed to reflect its appearance in Pushkin's day, its rooms being furnished with period furniture such as a copy of the old billiards table on which Pushkin used to play. There is the small wooden study where he wrote Chapters 3–7 of *Eugene Onegin*. These are set in the Russian countryside and draw considerably on his own experiences. In the grounds is the house of Arina Rodionovna, of whom Pushkin wrote: 'in the evenings I listen to the fairy tales of my nanny, the original of Tatyana's nanny ... she is my only female friend – and only with her am I not bored.'

He also enjoyed the company of his neighbours, the Osipov Wolffs, at Trigorskoe. In 1825 a woman named Anna Kern came to stay with her aunt for a few days. On a visit to Mikhailovskoe,

Pushkin walked her down an avenue of lime trees. He had met her six years earlier, but seeing her again rekindled old feelings and inspired one of his finest love poems, 'I Remember the Wondrous Moment'. The avenue of lime trees in the grounds outside the house has been preserved and is now known as the Anna Kern Avenue. Pushkin's poem to Anna Kern – as well as other poems by him – have been put up all over the grounds on signs or boards, particularly where they have a topographical relevance.

— *Trigorskoe* Pushkin tended to shun his country neighbours, who were the objects of his satire in *Eugene Onegin*, but he made an exception with the Osipov Wolff family. Their house became his second home and he particularly enjoyed the large library. He was to do much reading during his exile and, as well as reading Shakespeare, managed to read all twelve volumes of Karamzin's *History of the Russian State*. The house differs greatly in appearance from the manor house at Mikhailovskoe. In the eighteenth century it had been a linen factory, where the family had sought refuge while their own house was being redecorated. But then their own house burned down so they were obliged to stay here. Restored in 1962, it is now a museum with furnished replicas of the rooms in which the family lived. The main house is surrounded by a beautiful park with the famous Onegin bench. This is the spot where in *Eugene Onegin* Onegin sits with Tatyana after he has received a letter from her in which she openly declares her love for him, to which he can only respond coldly.

— *Petrovskoe* The third estate house, Petrovskoe, is where the surviving son of the great Hannibal, Petya Abramovich, Pushkin's great-uncle, came to live in 1783 and is now the house-museum of the Hannibals (rebuilt 1977). Hannibal was an Abyssinian prince, who was found living as a hostage at the house of a Turkish sultan. The Russian envoy who found him decided to take him back to Russia and present him to the Tsar,

Peter the Great. Hannibal went on to live a distinguished career in Russia, attaining the rank of general in Peter's own Preobrazhensky Regiment. Pushkin once met his great-uncle on an earlier visit to Mikhailovskoe, and his family history, of which he was proud, inspired works such as 'The Moor of Peter the Great', 'Dubrovsky' and 'My Genealogy'.

— *Svyatogorsk Monastery* Three miles to the south of Mikhailovskoe, on the outskirts of the village of Pushkinskie Gory, stands the Svyatogorsk Monastery. Pushkin's body was brought here under police surveillance from St Petersburg and he was buried on 5 February 1837. His grave, which stands by the monastery walls, is now a literary shrine, one of the most frequently visited writers' graves in Russia.

Rostov Region

Rostov-on-Don

Rostov, one of the largest cities in the northern Caucasus, is where Alexander Solzhenitsyn came from his birthplace, Kislovodsk, to live as a child. For twelve years he and his mother lived in extreme poverty in a small shack-like building on Per. Khalturina (formerly Per. Soglasie) in the centre of the town. His mother, widowed six months before Solzhenitsyn was born, had to conceal her noble origins in order to find work. When asked about his childhood in an interview, Solzhenitsyn's reply was that it was one of hardship: 'Up to the age of forty I knew nothing but a kind of dignified destitution. From the end of 1918, the year I was born, until 1941, I didn't know what a house was. We lived in huts which were constantly assailed by the cold. Never enough fuel to keep us warm. No water in the room where we lived – we had to go out and fetch it some distance away . . .'

Despite the difficulty of his life there, Solzhenitsyn describes Rostov with affection in his novel *August 1914*:

Sadovaya Street was fresh and clean in the deep shade of the trees as it climbed the hill towards Dolomanovsky ... The trams had long arms with runners instead of hoop-shaped pick-ups, there were special cars for summertime with airy, open sides ... Typical, too, were the special mobile lattice-work bridges, arc-shaped with handrails, which were placed across flooded streets in the southern rainstorms and were kept on the pavements when the weather was dry. From Nikolsky Street onwards the Bolshaya Sadovaya straightened out and ran like a mile-long arrow to the city limits at the suburb of Nakhichevan.

Solzhenitsyn attended the Malevich School in Rostov at Soborny per., 26, and then the university (Ul. Maxima Gorkogo, 100) where he studied physics and mathematics. Both these buildings now have plaques to Solzhenitsyn on the wall. In 1934 he and his mother moved from their shack to a similar but warmer shack at Voroshilov pr., 32 (formerly Bolshoi pr.). In 1940 he married in secret a fellow university student Natalya Reshetovskaya and, after a honeymoon in Moscow and a spell in a cabin in Tarusa, seventy miles to the south of Moscow, they moved into a house on Ul. Chekhova where they both continued their studies at the university. When the Second World War broke out, Solzhenitsyn joined the army and left Rostov. The house on Ul. Chekhova was destroyed by bombardment when Rostov was taken by the Germans in 1942.

Kruzhilin

— *Sholokhov Museums* No other Russian writer has written so vividly of the Don region, its Cossack inhabitants and its landscape as Mikhail Sholokhov. In the work for which he is most famous in the West and for which he won the Nobel Prize for Literature in 1965, *The Quiet Don*, he explores the effect of the Civil War on the region and its people. Sholokhov was not a

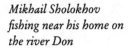

*Mikhail Sholokhov
fishing near his home on
the river Don*

Cossack himself, but was born and spent most of his life living in the Don area.

Although descended from nomadic tribes, the Cossacks are not a race. Rather, they are an order given special privileges and freedoms in return for military service. The primary unit of Cossack organization was the *stanitsa* or village which held its lands communally, but could allow people who were not Cossacks to settle on these lands in return for rent.

It was into one such village farmstead, the *khutor* of Kruzhilin, that Mikhail Sholokhov was born on 24 May 1905. Kruzhilin is a large steppe farmstead situated between the Chir and Don rivers, part of the large village of Vyoshenskaya. The house where Sholokhov was born and spent his first five years stood in the centre of the farmstead on the church square, a small dwelling with a thatched roof. He returned to live in Vyoshenskaya in 1926. The house he moved into was much grander than his childhood dwellings, a large villa with a grand porch. The main Sholokhov museum is on Ul. Rozy Lyuksemburg, 41. There is also a small memorial-house museum in the Kruzhilin farm-stead, a literary–memorial exhibition, his larger estate house and his grave.

In 1910 Sholokhov's family moved to the nearby village of Karginskaya, into a tiny white house, six steps in length and four steps wide. They lived in two crowded rooms with minuscule windows. The walls were adobe, the roof made of reeds. A memorial museum is situated in the village.

Taganrog

— *Chekhov Cottage* It was in this tiny white cottage with green shutters that Chekhov was born in 1860, and where he spent the first year of his life. It is now a four room museum, which was founded in 1929.

Two sons had been born before Anton Chekhov arrived and he was followed by two brothers and a sister. Life here was hardly opulent (the house had no plumbing) and was inevitably some-what cramped. The sitting room, where most of the family slept at night, behind screens, had to double both as the dining room and as Chekhov's father's study, and was less than 100 square feet in size. Chekhov's father had been a serf, and the family was never well off. He had married the daughter of a travelling salesman in 1854 and had started up a grocery shop in Taganrog, paying the necessary dues to join the merchant class, second guild. Although now surrounded by cherry trees, the house used to stand in a very dusty, run-down part of town. Despite the thin veneer of sophis-tication given by the town's maritime location, which attracted Greek and Turkish merchants, Taganrog in the 1860s was other-wise a typical provincial Russian town, of the sort which figures so frequently in Chekhov's fiction. The museum contains books, pictures and china belonging to the Chekhov family, as well as furniture typical of the period.

Address: Ul. Chekhova, 69

— *Chekhov Shop* The two-storey building on the corner of

what used to be Monastyrskaya ul. and Yarmarochny per. was home to the Chekhov family in the mid-1860s, and in 1977 opened as a museum with ten rooms. Downstairs on the ground floor visitors may see the grocer's shop kept by Chekhov's father, and the family dining room. Upstairs are the bedrooms and drawing room.

Chekhov did not particularly enjoy his childhood. His family was very poor and there was a constant struggle to make ends meet. His father was also a strict disciplinarian, and forced his children not only to serve long hours in his shop, but also to sing in the church choir (Chekhov later became an atheist). At the age of seven, Chekhov was sent by his father initially to the local Greek school (on Ul. III Internatsionala, 54), but completed his secondary education at the local high school. The family subsequently moved to Elizavetinskaya ul. (now Ul. Rozy Lyuksemburg, 77), and it was here that Chekhov ended up living by himself for three years to finish his schooling, after his father absconded to Moscow to avoid debtors' prison when his business failed. To earn money for food and winter fuel, Chekhov was forced to give private tuition.

Address: Ul. Sverdlova, 100

— *Chekhov Literary Museum* This building was once the local gymnasium, which from 1868 to 1879 numbered Chekhov among its pupils, and now houses a museum devoted to the writer's life and works. There are eleven rooms, five of which have been restored. The remaining rooms contain an exhibition about the time Chekhov spent in Taganrog.

Although his early years were not particularly happy ones, Chekhov enjoyed himself when he could, especially when opportunities for practical jokes presented themselves (on one occasion he went to visit his uncle dressed as a beggar and was given three copecks). He developed a passion for drama from an early age, and derived much pleasure from going to the local theatre, built in 1866 (Ul. Lenina, 90), and also to the local library on Grecheskaya ul. (now Ul. III Internatsionala, 55), which moved in 1879 to the town's main thoroughfare, Petrovskaya ul. (now Ul. Lenina, 96). Although Chekhov was prone to curse his native town in later life for its philistinism, he at some level retained a deep affection for it; it was thanks to his efforts that the building of a new library took place, for which he provided regular shipments of books, as well as the erection of the statue of Peter the Great and the opening of the town museum.

Address: Oktyabrskaya ul., 9

Ryazan Region

Konstantinovo

— *Esenin Museum* The poet Esenin was born on this site in September 1895. His family was of such humble means that their cottage combined living quarters with a barn and storage facilities on the lower floor. The cottage was so decrepit by the time Esenin was born that in 1910 it was pulled down and in 1930 replaced by the present one-storey wooden dwelling, with ornately carved blue window frames and birch trees on either side.

Esenin's parents were so poor that his father had to leave to find work in Moscow before he was born, and when he stopped sending money the two-year-old child was given to his grandparents to bring up. In 1904, when he was nine, he started to go to the village school here, where he learned to read, and began to develop an enthusiasm for Russian poetry. At the same time, he began to write poetry himself. From 1909 to 1912 Esenin studied in Spas-Klepiki, some thirty-five miles away, at a church school which trained people to teach. From this point, Esenin would return to his native Konstantinovo only for visits, but for the rest of his life made sure he came back at least once a year to stay with his parents and sit at the oak table to write

Sergey Esenin and his mother, Tatyana Fyodorovna

poetry under the green lamp which visitors can still see today. In his parents' modest abode one can also see the trunk in which Esenin used to keep his favourite books. A permanent Esenin exhibition can also be seen at the former estate of local land-owner L. I. Kashina, the heroine of Esenin's poem 'Anna Snegina'. It contains manuscripts, letters, books, memoirs and rare editions.

Solzhenitsyn visited the Esenin Museum while he was living in nearby Ryazan, and it later became the subject of one of the prose poems he wrote in the 1960s:

> Inside the Esenins' cottage, wretched little partitions that do not reach the ceiling divide it up into what are more like cupboards or loose-boxes than rooms. Outside is a little fenced-in yard; here there used to be a bath-house, where Sergey would shut himself in the dark and compose his first poems ... What a thunderbolt of talent the Creator must have hurled into that cottage, into the heart of that quick-tempered country boy, for the shock of it to have opened his eyes to so much beauty – by the stove, in the

pig-sty, on the threshing floor, in the fields; beauty which
for a thousand years others had simply trampled on and
ignored ...

Ryazan

Solzhenitsyn joined his wife Natalya Reshetovskaya in Ryazan
in 1957, after his years spent at the front and in the gulag. Having
found a job as a teacher of physics and astronomy at High
School No. 2, he moved into Reshetovskaya's two-roomed
communal flat on Kasimovsky per. on the outskirts of the city,
where she lived with her mother. The flat was part of a long
wooden house built to accommodate teachers from the Agricultural Institute, where Natalya worked. They shared a kitchen
and lavatory with their neighbours and heated the flat with
wood-burning stoves. Many of the drafts of Solzhenitsyn's
manuscripts were burned in secret in the stove in the kitchen,
after his neighbours had gone to bed. Despite the shortage of
space, Natalya had managed to fit her grand piano into one of
the rooms. The house had its own garden, where Solzhenitsyn
constructed a desk and wrote under an old apple tree. He recalls
the garden in one of his short prose pieces, 'Breathing':

> I stand beneath the apple tree – the blossom not quite faded
> yet – and breathe in ... So what if this is only a postage
> stamp of a garden hemmed in by five-storey monsters? I
> no longer hear the roar of motorcycle exhausts, the whine
> of record players or the tinkling of transistors. Even if you
> or I are constantly made the sport of others, so long as we
> can breathe here under the apple tree after the rain, it will
> still be possible to live.

Such domestic bliss was not to last. Two years later two of
Natalya's aged aunts moved into the flat, and it became even
more cramped. They sought new lodgings, and were offered
accommodation by the City Council in Yablochkov Passazh, a
three-roomed flat in a nineteenth-century building overlooking

a square in the middle of the city. Solzhenitsyn found this unbearably noisy, and almost as cramped as before. (They continued to share the flat with Natalya's mother and the two aunts.) As Solzhenitsyn's fame and notoriety grew, he found Ryazan an unsafe place in which to write. The publication in Russia in 1962 of *A Day in the Life of Ivan Denisovich* had brought him instant fame. But his other work was extremely sensitive in content and he was forced to write in secret. In Ryazan his main literary endeavours had been *Cancer Ward*, *The First Circle* and various short stories including 'An Incident at Krechetovka Station', based on a true incident in Ryazan. He was expelled from the Writers' Union in 1969 and left Ryazan alone that same year for Moscow.

Saratov Region

Saratov

Situated on the River Volga, Saratov is the main town of its province. Vasily Zhukovsky passed through here in 1837 while he was accompanying the future Alexander II, to whom he was tutor, on his tour of Russia. During their stay in Saratov, the Tsarevich and his retinue visited the Vice-Governor and went to a ball at his house, inspected the local gymnasium and attended a military parade. Other writers who visited Saratov include Pushkin, who was here in 1833; Tolstoy, who passed through on his way to the Caucasus in 1851; Ostrovsky, who came on tour in 1865 with an actor from the Maly Theatre in Moscow; and the poet Yakov Polonsky, who came to visit Nikolay Chernyshevsky for a week in 1889, and stayed in the town's central hotel (Kirova pr., 3). Chernyshevsky, author of the political novel *What Is To Be Done?*, is the literary figure most Russians probably associate with Saratov. It was here that the great revolutionary democrat, whose ideas influenced a generation of revolutionaries and who was held in particularly high esteem by

Lenin, was born in 1828. Konstantin Fedin, author of the novel *Cities and Years* (1924), and another writer venerated by the Soviet literary establishment, was born here in 1892. In his capacity as first secretary of the Union of Writers in the 1960s, Fedin later became notorious as the party functionary responsible for banning Solzhenitsyn's *Cancer Ward*.

In retrospect, Saratov should perhaps be best known as the place where Nadezhda Mandelstam was born in 1899. Author of two extraordinary volumes of memoirs about her life with the poet Osip Mandelstam, she later moved with her family to Kiev.

— *Chernyshevsky Museum* The Chernyshevsky Museum is situated in the house where the critic was born in 1828, a wooden building with a mezzanine and wooden balcony overlooking the Volga. It had been built two years earlier by Chernyshevsky's father, who was a priest. Chernyshevsky lived here for twenty years and was educated at home until the age of fourteen by his father, who then enrolled his son in the local church school. This was followed by four years in the Saratov Seminary. Chernyshevsky had no desire to take holy orders, however, and had his heart set on entering St Petersburg University, which he was able to do in 1846.

Chernyshevsky returned to his native city in 1851 to teach in the Saratov Gymnasium, and for the next two years lived once more in his father's house, settling in the mezzanine. In 1853 he married the daughter of a local doctor in the main church here and returned to St Petersburg.

In June 1889, Chernyshevsky was finally allowed to return from exile, having spent six years in Astrakhan. Since his father's house had been let, he settled into a flat on Sobornaya ul., 22 (now Ul. Kommunarnaya, 22), where he continued his activities, but died in October of that year. He is buried here. Other buildings connected to Chernyshevsky in the town include the former seminary where he was a student from 1842 to 1845

(Chelyuskintsev ul., 12) and the former gymnasium where he taught from 1851 to 1853 (Ul. Nekrasova, 17).

The Chernyshevsky Museum opened in 1920, with Lenin's blessing. The house has been restored to look as it did in the nineteenth century. The dining room and drawing room reflect Chernyshevsky's early childhood, while his study on the mezzanine represents a later period, when he taught at the Saratov Grammar School. A permanent exhibition about the critic explores his biography in the context of the times in which he lived, and includes contemporary documents (an example of his handwriting as a child, for example, as well as his arrest warrant), photographs and manuscripts, some of Chernyshevsky's own belongings, and a model of old Saratov. Two outbuildings are part of the museum: the wing where his wife, Olga Sokratovna, lived while he was in exile, and Golubev's house, which belonged to Chernyshevsky's grandfather. The museum was initially run by the Chernyshevskys' younger son. Upon his death, curatorship was handed over to the critic's great-granddaughter, who at the age of seventy fell to her death from the balcony of the house.

Address: Ul. Chernyshevskogo, 142
Closed Fridays
— *Fedin Museum* Founded in 1981, the Fedin Museum is housed in the eighteenth-century building of the religious school where the future author was a pupil. The museum's permanent exhibition traces his life and works, and contains manuscripts, memorabilia and personal effects.
Address: Ul. Chernyshevskogo, 154

Smolensk Region

Khmelita
— *Griboedov Museum* Near Vyazma, at the eastern edge of the Smolensk region, lies the estate of Khmelita, which was the

*The Griboedov mansion at Khmelita, where the dramatist spent
summers during his childhood and early youth*

ancestral home of the aristocratic Griboedov family, and is now
a museum founded in memory of the famed dramatist and
diplomat who spent his summers with his uncle here during his
childhood and early youth.

In Griboedov's time the estate was vast, covering over 10,000
acres and incorporating several villages. Surrounding the central
building of the estate, the palatial fifty-eight-room mansion built
in the Baroque style in the latter part of the eighteenth century,
were extensive formal gardens, a rambling park in the 'English'
style, orchards, stables, workshops (where, among other things,
furniture for the house was made), several churches, barns,
offices and pavilions. But probably the place where the young
Griboedov most enjoyed spending time was the theatre housed
in the southern wing of the main house, run by serf actors and
gypsy musicians.

Griboedov's uncle was the last member of the family to own
the estate. By the end of the nineteenth century, when it was
bought by Count Heiden as a wedding present for his daughter,

the house had fallen into a bad state of disrepair. Grain was to be found drying in the ballroom, and rye growing through the parquet floor. Careful restoration work restored the estate to a semblance of its former glory (by this time some of its original buildings were no longer standing), and major restoration was begun again in the 1980s, when the house was turned into the Griboedov Museum, opening finally in 1995, the bicentenary of the writer's birth.

Address: Vyazemsky region, village of Khmelita

Nikolskoe

In 1916 Mikhail Bulgakov, who had just qualified as a doctor, was sent to this small village in the Smolensk province to serve his apprenticeship. In the normal course of events, he would have served an internship at a large hospital, rather than being sent straight to a remote village. But the experienced doctors had been sent to the front, and there was a shortage of medical personnel in the provinces. His wife, who worked with him as a nurse, recalls their arrival at Nikolskoe:

> We went to the town council ... we were given a pair of horses and a 'drozhky' as it was called – fairly comfortable. There was terrible mud, we travelled 40 versts in one day. We arrived late in Nikolskoe, and, of course, nobody met us. There was a two-floored doctor's house. It was closed; a doctor's assistant arrived, bringing keys and showed us to the door. 'Here's your house.' The house consisted of two halves, with separate entrances: It was designed for two doctors, serving the hospital. But the second doctor wasn't there.
>
> Upstairs was a bedroom, a study, and downstairs – a dining room and a kitchen. We occupied the two rooms, and began to unpack. That first night a woman giving birth was brought in! I went to the hospital with Mikhail. The woman was in the operating theatre; in great pain of course; the baby was lying incorrectly. I looked at the woman, she

had lost consciousness. I stayed at a distance, searching in the medical text book for the necessary place, and Mikhail left her for a moment, came and took a look: 'Open up at that page!' The woman's husband had said to him as he brought her in: 'If she dies, you won't live either – I'll kill you.'

Bulgakov described his experiences in his semi-fictional, semi-autobiographical book of short stories, *Notes of a Country Doctor*, in which he vividly recreates the difficult conditions in which he worked. In the stories we read of how the young doctor has to travel in horse-drawn sleighs through blizzards, fighting off wolves, in order to see a patient. Bulgakov was particularly struck by the ignorance of the peasantry he treated. His short story 'Morphine' illustrates the isolation that he must have felt and is based on his own short-lived morphine addiction.

In 1917 Bulgakov was transferred to nearby Vyazma, which, with three doctors instead of two serving a smaller population, was a great relief. In Vyazma he lived near the hospital, on Moskovskaya ul.

Tambov Region

Lebedyan

Lebedyan is the birthplace of Evgeny Zamyatin, who spent the first eighteen years of his life in a town which he described as 'famed for its cardsharpers, gypsies, horse fairs, and the most vivid Russian speech'. The house where he was born in 1884 remains on Pokrovskoi ul. Zamyatin left Lebedyan to study in St Petersburg at the Polytechnic Institute. In a short autobiographic sketch he describes Lebedyan:

And so you insist on my autobiography. But you will have to content yourself with a purely external view, with perhaps a fleeting glance into darkened windows: I rarely invite anyone to come inside. And from the outside you will not see much. You will see a very lonely child, without companions of his own age, on the sofa, on his stomach, over a book, or under the piano, on which his mother is playing Chopin. Two steps away from Chopin, and you are in the midst of provincial life: windows with geraniums, a piglet tied to a stake, in the middle of the street, and hens bathing in the dust. If you want geography, it's this: Lebedyan, the most Russian of towns . . .

Zamyatin's experience of the provinces found expression in his stories such as 'The Provinces' and 'Out in the Sticks'. He returned to Lebedyan in the spring of 1906 after he had been in the Shpalernaya Prison in St Petersburg, only to find the boredom of provincial life unbearable. He returned illegally to St Petersburg that summer.

Nearby Tambov, the centre of the province, is satirized by Mikhail Lermontov in his poem on provincial life, 'Lady of Tambov'. Lermontov passed through Tambov in December 1835 on his way to his grandmother's estate at Tarkhany, where he was seeing in the new year.

Mara

Mara, in the eastern corner of the province, was originally an estate which belonged to the Imperial family; it was then given to the Baratynsky family. The poet Evgeny Baratynsky spent much of his childhood here, and came here to spend several months at a time in the early 1830s, when it became necessary to look after the running of the estate.

Tatarstan Republic

Chistopol

— *Boris Pasternak Memorial Room* Chistopol, a river port on the River Kama, is some 600 miles east of Moscow. At Ul. Lenina (formerly Volodarskogo ul.), 81, kv. 2, is the room where

Boris Pasternak spent two years as an evacuee during the Second World War, now open to the public as a 'memorial room'. The building, a turn-of-the-century private residence which once belonged to a family by the name of Vavilov, stands on a street where the same lime and poplar trees, of which Pasternak wrote in his poetry, grow. By the nearby River Kama there is a wide alley of old trees where Pasternak used to walk.

Other writers were evacuated to Chistopol together with Pasternak, many of whom lived in considerably more luxurious circumstances than his. The playwright Alexander Gladkov left a valuable record of his *Meetings with Pasternak* during these years. 'Chistopol,' he writes, 'a small, run-of-the-mill provincial town, took on a strange appearance with the arrival of evacuees from Moscow and Leningrad. An odd touch was added by the writers, of whom there must have been several dozen. In their stylish overcoats and soft felt hats they wandered through the streets – which were covered with good Russian mud – as though they were still in the corridors of their building on Vorovsky Street.'

A steep wooden staircase leads to the small second-floor room where Pasternak lived with his wife and child. Before the war, it was used as a nursery, and a border of black and red swallows decorates the walls. The furniture from Pasternak's time remains – most importantly the desk where he would sit translating Shakespeare. Some copies of original pages of his translation of *Romeo and Juliet* decorate the work surface.

Pasternak's life here was not 'a sweet bread-roll', in the words of Gladkov. The winters were particularly harsh, but nevertheless Pasternak is said to have braved the cold: 'Entering the canteen where the temperature was the same as out on the street and where no one took their coats off, Pasternak always took off his coat and hung his hat up on a nail. He would bring his work with him: an Anglo-Russian dictionary, a miniature volume of Shakespeare, and the next page of the translation.'

One witness of the time recalls Pasternak being jeered at in the street by children, because of his unusual and humorous surname – Pasternak in Russian means 'Parsnip'.

While in Chistopol Pasternak heard of the suicide of one of his friends, the poet Marina Tsvetaeva, in nearby Elabuga.

Elabuga

The town of Elabuga, near Chistopol, is where Marina Tsvetaeva lived for ten days in the summer of 1941, before committing suicide at the age of forty-nine.

In early summer of 1941, when the Soviet Union became involved in the Second World War, Tsvetaeva joined a group of writers being evacuated to the Tatar republic, after it became clear that she would not be able to stay with Pasternak in Peredelkino, outside Moscow. Having left the capital on 8 August 1941 with her son Mur, she arrived almost two weeks later, on the 21st, but they were unable to reside with the better-placed writers in Chistopol, as her husband and daughter, who had been arrested two years before, were 'enemies of the people'. Tsvetaeva was reduced to renting a room in a house in the neighbouring town of Elabuga. The house, on a quiet street (Ul. Zhdanova, 20), was clean and peaceful. Apart from the kitchen there were two rooms, separated by partitions: one taken by Tsvetaeva and Mur (which was about thirty square feet in size, and looked out on to the fields and woods at the back), and another lived in by their landlords.

Tsvetaeva found it impossible to make ends meet in Elabuga, and travelled back to Chistopol on 30 August to look for work. Despite the help and support of Lydia Chukovskaya and her friends, she went home and hanged herself the day after she came back, while her landlords and her son were out. She was buried in an unmarked grave on a spot on which now stands a small white cross placed by her sister Anastasia.

Kazan

In 1841, the thirteen-year-old Lev Tolstoy moved with his brothers and sister to Kazan, where they took up residence at Poperechno-Kazanskaya ul., 9, following the deaths of their father and grandmother (their mother had died much earlier). The Tolstoy children had been adopted by their aunt and uncle, the Yushkovs, with whom they were to live for the next few years.

Tolstoy's grandfather had once been Governor of Kazan, and the house of Count Yushkov and his wife, Pelageya (sister to Tolstoy's father), was the centre of aristocratic life in the city at that time. The Tolstoy children were swept up into the round of parties, balls and trips to the theatre during their time here, and were generally well looked after by their aunt and uncle.

When Tolstoy and his three brothers became students at Kazan University in the 1840s, they began to live independently for the first time, renting a house at Bolshaya Krasnaya ul., 68. Tolstoy joined the university in 1844, first as a student in oriental languages, and then in law. He was not an outstanding student and never actually graduated. In retrospect, the most significant event during Tolstoy's short time as an undergraduate was perhaps his contraction of venereal disease (having been introduced to brothels by his elder brothers) – significant in that it was while he was recuperating in the clinic that he began to write his famous diary, which he would keep on and off until his death and which would become an important laboratory for his writing.

Tolstoy probably dropped out of university because in April 1847 he came into his inheritance. In his case this meant the acquisition of Yasnaya Polyana, the estate where he had been born and had spent his early childhood. At this time Tolstoy regularly changed his mind about what he wanted to do with his life, and the prospect of becoming lord of the manor was clearly more inviting than finishing his degree.

Tolstoy is not the only famous Russian writer to have studied at Kazan University. In 1903, the poet Velimir Khlebnikov became an undergraduate there, and like his forebear, not only switched subjects – from mathematics (which included the study of non-Euclidean geometry founded there in the previous century by Lobachevsky) to natural science – but also never graduated. Unlike Tolstoy, however, Khlebnikov was sent to prison for a month for taking part in anti-tsarist demonstrations.

Khlebnikov had moved with his family to Kazan in 1898, and before attending university had begun to refine the drawing skills he had developed at an early age. He was tutored by a student from Kazan Art School, then a well-established graphic artist. Khlebnikov was a keen naturalist, and liked to sketch birds and animals. In 1905 he undertook a five-month ornithological expedition to the northern Urals with his brother, during which they gathered specimens for their father's collection.

— *Baratynsky Museum* This small two-room museum, founded in 1975, contains personal effects and literary memorabilia pertaining to the time Baratynsky spent both here and at his father-in-law's estate at Kaimara, about fifteen miles from Kazan. Exhibits include furniture from the poet's study here, as well as books from his library, and etchings by Vasily Zhukovsky.

Baratynsky first came to Kazan in 1831, for business reasons, and settled for a few months with his family on Gruzinskaya ul., in his father-in-law's town house. He found cultural life here primitive and did not enjoy himself very much. In 1833 he was compelled to come back again to take care of the Kaimara estate, and his melancholy state of mind was dispelled only by a chance meeting with Pushkin, who was travelling round Russia collecting materials on Pugachov.

Address: Ul. Korolenko, 26

— *Gorky Museum* Gorky lived in Kazan from 1884 to 1888, and hoped to go to university here. He held a succession of jobs while he was living in Kazan, and between 1886 and 1887 he worked as an apprentice at the Derenkov bakery. It is here, on its former site on the corner of Malaya and Bolshoi Lyadsky streets, that a museum about his experiences was founded in 1940. The bakery has been recreated in the cellar of the building, where Gorky used to sleep on sacks. Although he never matriculated, Gorky nevertheless referred to the four years he spent in Kazan as his 'universities'.

The nine rooms of the museum have been arranged chronologically to tell the story of Gorky's life and works, and contain a collection of his personal belongings, including books and clothes, as well as letters and photographs. In 1968, on the centenary of Gorky's birth, two additional floors were added to include exhibitions on the first floor about the writer's relationship with Chaliapin (who was born here and became a close friend), and the productions of his plays in Kazan.

Address: Ul. Gorkogo, 10
Closed Fridays

Krasnovidovo
— *Gorky Museum* On the right bank of the Volga river, about forty miles from Kazan, a distance which takes an hour by boat, is the village of Krasnovidovo, where Gorky lived in 1888. The small museum which opened here contains three rooms. Loneliness, unrequited love and harsh living conditions had led Gorky to attempt suicide in 1887, but after a stay in hospital he took himself off to Krasnovidovo to distribute revolutionary propaganda among the local peasant population. It was the first time he had found himself in a really rural area, and many of his negative ideas about the political stance of peasants were formed here. The museum contains personal letters, clothing and books from the library of Gorky's descendants. The museum, which opened in 1979, holds an exhibition which tells the story of what

brought Gorky to Krasnovidovo at this particular time, and documents his local activities (also described in his fictionalized autobiography *My University*).

Tula Region

Darovoe

In 1831 and 1832 Fyodor Dostoevsky's father acquired two small properties outside Moscow, Darovoe and Cheremoshnya, totalling 1,200 acres and 170 serfs. The estates were within easy reach of Moscow, where the family – and his job – were based at the time. Of a morose and suspicious nature, Dostoevsky's father was often tyrannical towards his servants. After his wife's death in 1837, he gave himself up to a life of drink and debauchery. When his body was found mutilated in 1839 on the road from Darovoe to Cheremoshnya, his exasperated serfs were inevitably the prime suspects. The young Dostoevsky drew inspiration from this incident for Karamazov's murder in *The Brothers Karamazov*, and both villages are mentioned in the novel. A memorial plaque decorates Dostoevsky's father's house in Darovoe.

Serebryanny Kolodez

In 1898 Bely's father bought a small estate at Serebryanny Kolodez (Silver Well), not far from the town of Efremov, in the southernmost part of the region, where subsequent summers were spent until 1908, when it was sold. The old house with its nine windows, surrounded by poplars, stood on a hill, at the bottom of which was a river. To one side was a dark avenue of limes, and beyond the garden were fields of rye. Bely later alleged that the place had played an important role in his literary destiny. 'All my *Symphonies* had their origin here – in this place: in the azure of the heavens, in the noisy gold of the rye...'

Yasnaya Polyana

— *Tolstoy Museum* One of the most famous literary landmarks in the whole of Russia, Tolstoy's estate Yasnaya Polyana (Clear Glade) lies some eight miles south of Tula, and approximately 125 miles south of Moscow. It is where the great writer was born in 1828, where he spent most of his eighty-two years, and where he was buried in 1910.

The main house of the estate today was originally a wing of the larger home built at the beginning of the nineteenth century by Prince Nikolay Volkonsky, Tolstoy's maternal grandfather, who also erected the famous white gateposts at the entrance to the estate, and several other buildings. This house, where Tolstoy was born, no longer stands. Having inherited it in 1847, Tolstoy was forced to sell it in 1854 to cover his gambling debts (after which it was taken apart and moved to a nearby village and subsequently demolished), and it was at this time that he moved into one of the two separate wings which his grandfather had built earlier. Tolstoy spent the first nine years of his life at Yasnaya Polyana, before moving in 1837 with his widowed father, sister and three brothers to Moscow (see *Childhood* for a fictionalized account of his early years). The death of both his father and grandmother soon afterwards, however, resulted in the children moving in 1841 to Kazan, to live with their aunt. Tolstoy returned here in 1847, at the age of nineteen, upon inheriting the property, and for the next three years tried, under the influence of Rousseau and other writers he was reading at the time, to become simultaneously a model farmer, painter, musician and scholar, who would also be fluent in the major modern languages, and an upholder of impossibly high moral and ethical standards, which he invariably failed to live up to. In 1850 Tolstoy gave up trying to lead the life of an exemplary landowner and out of boredom moved to Moscow, to go into society. Of this, too, he soon tired, and headed off to the Caucasus with his brother, who was stationed there as an officer with the Russian army. For the next few years, during which time he fought in the Crimean War and began his literary career, Tolstoy's stays at Yasnaya Polyana were sporadic; in 1859 he began a school here for the peasant children, then went on a lengthy trip abroad to study the educational systems in Germany and England. In 1862, however, he settled here again for good in the northern wing with his young wife Sofya Behrs, daughter of the Kremlin physician. This was to be their main residence for the next fifty years, and many extensions were added to it as the family grew: the Tolstoys had thirteen children over the course of their stormy life together (three of whom did not live to adulthood).

Tolstoy had begun his literary career in the Caucasus in the early 1850s, and was already a famous author by the time he returned to Yasnaya Polyana a decade later. It was here, however, that he wrote his two great novels, *War and Peace* and *Anna Karenina*, the former a reflection of the happy early years of his marriage, and the latter an equally accurate mirror of more troubled times in the 1870s, which were to result in Tolstoy experiencing a spiritual crisis, following which he (temporarily) renounced the writing of fiction in favour of the propagation of his religious views. In the latter part of his life, Tolstoy devoted much time to the study of philosophy and religion (his library here contains 22,000 volumes in thirty-five different languages), the fruits of which were published in numerous essays and pamphlets, some of which were distributed through the non-profit press he set up with his chief disciple Vladimir Chertkov.

The room which Tolstoy used as his study changed many times. He wrote the first part of *War and Peace* in the room 'under the arches', looking out into the garden, but *Anna Karenina* was written in one of the rooms in the extension built in 1871. All Tolstoy's works were written at his father's desk, however, and it was on the leather couch behind the desk, also a permanent fixture of his study, that his mother had given birth

Tolstoy playing tennis at Yasnaya Polyana

to him. Tolstoy would always go for a walk before settling down to work each day (he was also fond of horse-riding), and maintained a regular routine of spending several hours each morning at his desk. Sofya assumed the thankless task of writing out his manuscripts in fair hand in preparation for publication.

Visitors were entertained in the dining room, which was the largest room of the house, and was lined with family portraits. Coffee was drunk here at nine in the morning, lunch generally taken between two and three, supper was held at six in the evening, followed by tea from the samovar at nine. As well as a fondness for chess, Tolstoy greatly enjoyed listening to music in the evening, and the family pianos were played regularly, sometimes by members of the family, including Tolstoy himself, sometimes by family friends (the composer Taneev, for example), and sometimes by guests such as Wanda Landowska. Writers who came to see Tolstoy here include Turgenev, Leskov, Gorky, Chekhov and Rilke. The 'sage of Yasnaya Polyana' also attracted hundreds of disciples each year, who came to consult him on all matters.

In 1881, the Tolstoys began spending their winters in

Moscow, for the sake of their children's education, but would return to Yasnaya Polyana each summer. Tolstoy settled back here permanently in 1902, following his excommunication from the Orthodox church, but relations with Sofya were by this time so strained that he became gradually resolved of the need to leave, which he finally did secretly at night in 1910. On 28 October he left Yasnaya Polyana at dawn so as not to be followed and travelled west by train from Shchekino (the nearest railway station) to the monastery at Optina Pustyn, near Kozelsk, in neighbouring Kaluga province. The next day he visited the nearby Shamardino Convent to see his sister Marya, who was a nun. By this time his departure had made the world's newspapers.

Tolstoy's body was brought back here for burial ten days later, followed by a 700-strong choir and thousands of mourners, who paid their last respects to the writer in the house, before attending the first civil burial in Russia. Tolstoy was buried in the grounds of his estate on the edge of a ravine, at the spot where his brother had once buried a green stick, on which was written the secret for human happiness.

The house was turned into a museum in 1921, and has been open to visitors since then, except for a brief period during the war when it was occupied briefly by the Nazis (fortunately the majority of its contents had already been evacuated to Tomsk). *Closed Mondays and the last Wednesday of every month*

Tver Region

Tver

The ancient city of Tver, known as Kalinin in Soviet times, lies on the River Volga, ninety-three miles north-west of Moscow. In the thirteenth and fourteenth centuries it was an important centre of the Tver principality, competing with Moscow. Over the centuries much of old Tver was destroyed and it was only under Catherine the Great that the city enjoyed its second stage of development. Catherine had much of the city rebuilt by Moscow architects as well as having her own palace designed by Matvei Kazakov and later Carlo Rossi. As Tver falls on the main Moscow to St Petersburg route, it has always been the main stopping-off place for the traveller.

Between 1826 and 1836 Pushkin broke off his journeys at Tver, staying at the Hotel Galyan (Pushkinskaya/Galyanskaya ul., 1), whose Italian cooking he praised in his poetry. The building remains, but it is no longer a hotel. Pushkin also visited the poet Fyodor Nikolaevich Glinka, cousin of the famous composer, in 1830. His house still stands on Kozmodemyanskaya/Zhelyabova ul., 30. A statue of Pushkin by the sculptor O. K. Komov stands in the grounds of Catherine the Great's palace, put up in 1974.

— *Saltykov-Shchedrin Museum* The stone house where Mikhail Saltykov-Shchedrin lived in the centre of Tver opened as a museum in 1976. Saltykov-Shchedrin worked here in 1860 as a vice-governor of the Tver province. In his bureaucratic career he found much inspiration for the satire for which his work is famous.

The exhibition concentrates not only on the two-year period the writer spent in Tver, but on his life as a whole, and contains manuscripts, books, documents and portraits as well as reconstructed interiors such as his study. Some of the furniture from his family home has been donated to the museum by relatives.

Saltykov-Shchedrin's arrival at his new post coincided with the preparation for the emancipation of the serfs of 1861. He devoted much of his energy to the measure, which he strongly supported, but was frustrated by the fact that his position was not of sufficient influence to push for the changes he wanted. He left government service in 1862 to devote his energies to journalism in St Petersburg.

Address: Ul. Rybatskaya, 11/37
Closed Mondays and Tuesdays

Torzhok

— *Pushkin Museum* Pushkin had many friends living on small country estates in the Tver principality and his travels can be followed in a ring to the west of Tver. In the old trading town of Torzhok, forty miles from Tver, he stayed at the Pozharsky *traktir* or tavern (Yamskaya ul./Ul. Dzerzhinskogo, 48), where he praised the 'wonderful kvas and wonderful cutlets' prepared by the innkeeper's wife. Also on Yamskaya ul. at number 71, is a Pushkin museum, opened in 1972, dedicated to Pushkin's travels in the Tver region. This house is thought to have belonged to the Olenin family, great friends of Pushkin.

The Olenin family married into the Lvov family and lived on small estates in this district. One of these was Mitino, situated six versts from Torzhok. A mile away at Priyutino is their family graveyard, where Anna Kern is buried. Anna Kern was immortalized by Pushkin's poem 'I Remember the Wondrous Moment', written while he was in exile at Mikhailovskoe. Although no written evidence exists that Pushkin ever visited the Mitino estate, both the park at Mitino and the graveyard can be recognized in one of his many drawings of this period. He also drew arched bridges such as the one that survives at Gruzini, the estate of Anna Kern's grandmother. The house, designed by Rastrelli, can still be seen on the road to Vernovo.

Vernovo

— *Pushkin Museum* In the years 1828–33 Pushkin stayed at the estates of the Osipov-Wolff family. The largest of these was at the ancient village of Vernovo, about four miles from Mitino. The house at Vernovo was built at the end of the eighteenth century in the Empire style and is well preserved. There is a Pushkin museum here containing many portraits of the poet's Tver friends.

Praskovya Alexandrovna Osipov-Wolff, Pushkin's great friend and neighbour at Mikhailovskoe, also had a small estate at nearby Malinniki (Raspberries), where Pushkin stayed in 1828. Here he wrote his dedication to 'Poltava' and completed work on the seventh chapter of *Eugene Onegin*. Now only the park with its many overgrown raspberry bushes remains.

Pavlovskoe

Pushkin enjoyed the company of Pavel Ivanovich Wolff at Pavlovskoe, about five miles from Malinniki, where he wrote the unfinished *Novel in Letters* and poems such as 'Winter Morning' and 'It Is Winter. What Shall We Do in the Country?'. *Novel in Letters* describes the house at Pavlovskoe as an 'old house on a hill, a garden, a lake, pine trees all around ...'. Pushkin wrote a large part of the chapter 'Onegin's Journey' in *Eugene Onegin* at Pavlovskoe and began work on *Prose Tales of Belkin*. Only the foundations of the house remain.

The last town in the Pushkin 'ring' before returning to Tver is the ancient Staritsa on the Volga. Pushkin met Katenka Belyasheva here in 1829, a cousin of the Osipov-Wolffs. He dedicated a poem to her, inspired by her blue eyes.

Gradnitsy

The former Gumilyov family estate at Slepnyovo, near the town of Bezhetsk in the northern part of the region, was where Nikolay Gumilyov and his young wife Anna Akhmatova spent their summers from 1911 to 1917. The main house, located in the nearby village of Gradnitsy, now houses a museum dedicated to the memory of both poets. The house, a typical Russian provincial home, a wooden one-storey building with a mezzanine, belonged to Gumilyov's mother and sisters, who had inherited it from their elder brother.

Works by Akhmatova written here include poems published in her first two collections, *Rosary* and *The White Flock*. They include 'July 1914' – her reaction to the outbreak of the First World War – and 'Slepnyovo' – her reaction to the October

Revolution, written during her only winter visit to the house. After the Revolution, Gumilyov's mother Anna Ivanovna left the estate, and settled in the town of Bezhetsk with the child of her son and daughter-in-law, Lev.

Museum exhibits include early editions of Akhmatova's and Gumilyov's poetry, some of their letters, and photographs and other contemporary documents.

Ulyanovsk Region

Before Sergey Aksakov's family moved to the Orenburg region, the area he was to celebrate in his novels, the Aksakov family estate was based in the Simbirsk region. After the Revolution this was renamed the Ulyanovsk region after Lenin (born Vladimir Ulyanov), who was born in the town of Simbirsk/ Ulyanovsk. The Aksakov family's former estate at Staro-Aksakovo in the Maininsky region now houses the Historico-Cultural Centre. Aksakov's *Chronicle of a Russian Family* begins with a description of his reasons for moving:

> When my grandfather lived in the province of Simbirsk, on the ancestral estate granted to his forefathers by the Tsars of Muscovy, he felt cramped and confined. Not that there was really want of room; for he had arable land and pasture, timber and other necessities in abundance; but the trouble was, that the estate which his great grandfather had held in absolute possession, had ceased to belong to one owner. This happened quite simply: for three successive generations the family consisted of one son and several daughters; and, when some of these daughters were married, their portions took the shape of a certain number of serfs and a certain amount of land. Though their shares were not large, yet, as the land had never been properly surveyed, at this time four intruders asserted their right to share in the management of it. To my grandfather, life under these conditions was intolerable: there was no patience in his

passionate temperament; he loved plain dealing and hated complications and wrangles with his kith and kin.

Simbirsk

— *Goncharov Museum* The town of Simbirsk is the birthplace of Ivan Goncharov, author of the famous novel *Oblomov*, and there is now a Goncharov museum situated in the house where he grew up. When Goncharov was born in 1812, Simbirsk was a small provincial Volga town, once described by Lermontov in his poem 'Sashka': 'Sleep and idleness have taken complete hold of Simbirsk.' Both 'sleep' and 'idleness' are important themes in *Oblomov*, whose hero leads a life of inactivity and boredom.

Goncharov was the son of a prosperous grain merchant who owned a large stone house on Bolshaya ul. The house stood out among the other modest wooden town houses, resembling a large country mansion transplanted to the town. The house is well described by a contemporary:

> The furnishings were gentrified; a big room with a chandelier, a formal drawing room with a portrait of the master of the house and the inevitable ottoman; the landlord's study, the lady of the house's bedroom and a big, light children's room looked out onto a courtyard. Ivan Alexandrovich [Goncharov] said that his father's courtyard was packed full of buildings, it couldn't have been otherwise: the two main servants lived there ... guinea fowl, peacocks etc. roamed. An old employee of the Goncharovs told me that each servant had some amusement of his own: someone looked after the doves, someone else the dogs, someone else reared crows and sparrow hawks – in short, everyone to his own taste; and the rare little birds, the canaries or nightingales which flew around in the grand rooms of the house, soothed the landlord.

As a child in Simbirsk, Goncharov saw two juxtaposed lifestyles: the enterprising and efficient homesteads run by members of the merchant class such as his father, and the rural stagnation of the traditional country estate. The latter is described in *Oblomov*. Though the novel is largely set in St Petersburg, Goncharov takes us back to the fictional country estate of his hero's childhood in Chapter 9, 'Oblomov's Dream':

> Everything in the village is quiet and sleepy: the doors of the silent cottages are wide open; not a soul is to be seen; only the flies swarm in clouds and buzz in the stuffy air. On entering the cottage, you will call in vain in a loud voice: dead silence will be your answer; very seldom will some old woman, who is spending her remaining years on the stove, reply with a painful sigh or a sepulchral cough; or a three year old child, long-haired, barefoot, and with only a torn shirt on, will appear from behind a partition, stare at you in silence, and hide himself again.

Address: corner of Ul. Goncharova and Ul. Lenina
Closed Mondays

Vladimir Region

Alexandrov
— *Tsvetaeva Museum* Tsvetaeva's younger sister Anastasia used to rent a summer dacha before the Revolution in this fourteenth-century town in the north-eastern part of the region, about sixty miles from Moscow. Tsvetaeva spent the summer of 1916 here, and a small museum has been founded in the house.
Address: Voenny per., 5

Torfoprodukt
Torfoprodukt is situated some 100 miles east of Moscow, on the road to Ryazan. Alexander Solzhenitsyn came here in 1956 after he had been released from exile to look for teaching work. He found a room with an old woman named Matryona in a small hamlet named Miltsevo. His story 'Matryona's Place' is about his experiences here and, above all, about Matryona:

We came to an understanding on the price and on the peat which the school would supply. I learned only later that year after year, for many years, Matryona Vasilyevna had not earned a ruble from any source, because they didn't pay her a pension. Occasionally her relatives helped her out a little. In the kolkhoz she used to work, not for money, but for 'credits' in the dog-eared account books. So I lodged in Matryona's house. We didn't divide off a room. Her bed was near the stove in the corner by the door. I fixed myself a primitive cot by one window, and pushed aside Matryona's beloved rubber trees to set up a small table in the light from another. There was electric lighting in the village – it had already been extended from Shatury in the twenties. At the time the newspapers wrote about little Ilyich [Lenin] lamps and the peasants, their eyes goggling, called them, 'The Tsar's lights!' Perhaps to one of the more wealthy villagers, Matryona's izba may not have seemed habitable; nevertheless, for that autumn and winter with her it was fine. It didn't leak from the rains, and the cold wind did not blow the warmth from the stove at once but only towards morning, especially when it blew from the other side. Other things lived in the izba besides Matryona and myself, such as a cat, mice, and cockroaches.

This was Solzhenitsyn's first experience of the real Russian countryside, which he had missed so deeply since camp life.

Vologda Region

Danilovskoe
— *Batyushkov and Kuprin Museum* This small museum, in an eighteenth-century building, commemorates the lives and works of two former residents, Kuprin and Batyushkov, both writers who spent time in Danilovskoe, a village not far from Ustyuzhna, in the western part of the region. A century separates the poet Batyushkov from the prose writer Kuprin. There are two rooms

in the museum, the second of which contains various articles linked to Batyushkov's life here.

Vologda
— *Shalamov Museum* The two-storey building across from the church, overlooking the river, used to be the rectory for the Cathedral of St Sophia, and it was the childhood home at the beginning of the twentieth century of the writer Varlam Shalamov, whose father was a priest. The building currently houses part of the local art gallery, but, when it was discovered in the late 1980s that Shalamov had grown up here, two rooms were sectioned off and turned into a small museum dedicated to his memory. Now located in the Shalamov House, and run by the director of the art gallery, the museum has a permanent exhibition of copies of Shalamov's manuscripts, rare photographs of the writer and a collection of biographical materials and KGB documents. Shalamov is not the only writer associated with Vologda. The town was a popular destination for political exiles before the Revolution, and Alexey Remizov, Anatoly Lunacharsky and Nikolay Berdyaev were among the hundreds of political activists exiled here in the early years of the twentieth century.
Address: Kremlevskaya ul., 6

Vytegra
Although Fyodor Sologub is best known as a Symbolist poet and novelist, he began his career as a teacher in the Russian provinces. In 1885, he had taken his family from Novgorod to Velikie Luki, in Pskov province, and in 1889 they moved to Vytegra in Vologda province. Vytegra's chief literary association, however, is with the 'peasant poet' Nikolay Klyuev, who spent part of his childhood and adolescence here during the 1890s and 1900s. A memorial plaque can be found on the wall of his family's previous house in the village of Makachevo in Vologda province (the house was moved from its original site in

Zhelvachevo). Best known as a poet steeped in Russian folklore and peasant beliefs, Klyuev was nevertheless a supporter of the Bolsheviks in his youth. In 1906 he was arrested and spent some time in the local jail here. Klyuev returned to Vytegra after the death of his father in 1918, and remained here until his arrest in 1923, having only the previous year received his own apartment in an old merchant house on Voskresensky pr.

Voronezh Region

Voronezh

The city of Voronezh, some 300 miles to the south-east of Moscow, is situated on a tributary of the River Don, which flows into the Sea of Azov. It was of strategic importance to Russia in the time of Peter the Great, who had his flotilla built in the shipyards and gained access to the Azov Sea by defeating the Turks in 1696.

The city, in the words of Nadezhda Mandelstam, 'is located on the boundary line between forest and steppe'. This is the heart of provincial Russia, famous for its rich black soil. Alexander Pushkin remembers in his *Journey to Arzrum* how 'at last I saw the Voronezh steppes and we travelled smoothly through a green valley'.

It was in a relatively large house, with a wooden first floor, at Pr. Revolyutsii, 3 (then Bolshaya Dvoryanskaya ul.), that Ivan Bunin was born in October 1870, into a gentry family of good ancestry, that had become decidedly impoverished by the late nineteenth century. The family had country estates not far away to the north, in Orel province, but moved here temporarily for the sake of the education of Bunin's elder brothers.

Zamyatin and Mandelstam, two of the great twentieth-century writer, who spent time in the city were not natives of Voronezh. Evgeny Zamyatin studied at the red-brick Voronezh Gymnasium on Bol. Dvoryanskaya ul. between 1893 and 1902, where his achievements (particularly the high marks in his essays) were rewarded by a gold medal. But his enjoyment of his prize was short-lived. In a short autobiographical sketch in *A Soviet Heretic* he recalls how 'In 1902 I discarded my grey school uniform. My gold medal was soon pawned for 25 roubles in a Petersburg pawnshop and remained there.'

Osip Mandelstam and his wife Nadezhda lived as exiles here between 1935 and 1937, after Osip's arrest and torture in the Lubyanka prison in Moscow and brief exile at Cherdyn in the Urals. His arrest had followed his 'Stalin Epigram', written in 1933, a poem which denounced Stalin. During their stay in Voronezh they moved flats five times, often renting rooms from suspicious and inhospitable landlords, a time that is reinvoked most clearly in Chapter 30 of Nadezhda Mandelstam's memoir *Hope against Hope*. The couple's reactions to living in the city are keenly felt in both their writings, which express great pain illuminated by moments of joy. Another valuable record of their time is a book by a great friend of the Mandelstams, Natasha Shtempel, a teacher who lived and worked in Voronezh.

It is clear that the Mandelstams lived in great poverty. 'Future generations,' writes Nadezhda, 'will never understand what living space means to us.' Osip wrote, 'I sleep badly in strangers' homes, and my own life is not near me.' He found it hard to live in a place with little culture, although he obtained some work in the local theatre and frequented Voronezh's one concert hall.

After his torture at the Lubyanka, Mandelstam had stopped writing poetry. It is said that, following a concert given in the city in 1935, he felt moved to start writing again. There followed a period of creativity and in the three years spent here he wrote a quarter of his entire literary output. Nadezhda Mandelstam writes that her husband was keenly affected by the landscape, and the black earth of the steppe is often referred to in his verse of the time, just as he writes, too, of the city: 'Let me go, return me, Voronezh: / you will drop me or lose me, / you will let me fall or give me back. / Voronezh, you are a whim, / Voronezh, you are a raven and a knife.' *Voron* in Russian means 'crow' and *vor* means 'robber'.

The Mandelstams were visited by their friend Anna Akhmatova from 5 to 11 February 1936. She wrote a poem about the city and about Mandelstam, which sums up very succinctly the way in which he lived:

> *And the town stands locked in ice:*
> *A paperweight of trees, walls, snow.*
> *Gingerly I tread on glass;*
> *the painted sleighs skid in their tracks.*
> *Peter's statue in the square points to*
> *crows and poplars, and a verdigris dome*
> *washed clean, seeded with the sun's dust.*
> *Here the earth still shakes from the old battle*
> *where the Tartars were beaten to their knees.*
> *Let the poplars raise their chalices*
> *for a sky-shattering toast,*
> *like thousands of wedding-guests drinking*
> *in jubilation at a feast.*
> *But in the room of the banished poet*
> *Fear and the Muse stand watch by turn,*
> *and the night falls,*
> *without the hope of dawn.*

The Mandelstams first lived in a 'glassed-over veranda in a large tumbledown house that belonged to the best cook in town'. The house can no longer be found. They moved out in the autumn of 1934 because of the cold, to a flat in the same region whose address was 2-aya Lineinaya, 4. Its present name is Per. Shveinkov, house 4–6. Mandelstam uses the old address 'Lineinaya' in one of his poems, making a wordplay on its meaning, 'Straight line': 'What street is this? / Mandelstam Street. / What a devil of a name! / However you turn it / it sounds crooked, not straight. / There was little of the straight line in him, / his morals were not lily-white / and so this street, / or rather this pit, / is named after this Mandelstam.' Nadezhda Mandelstam comments on the poem in *Hope Abandoned*: 'There is no house on which it would be possible to put up a plaque saying "Mandelstam lived here", there is no grave on which to put a cross ... It is thus a good thing that he had the foresight to name a street in his own honour.'

Their third flat stood on the spot now occupied by a toyshop at Ul. 25 Oktyabrya, 45. Their fourth address is on the central street of the town, Ul. Fridrikha Engelsa, 11, known before the Revolution as Malo-Dvoryanskaya ul. Its street address when the Mandelstams stayed there was Ul. Fridrikha Engelsa, 13, fifth doorway, second floor, flat 39. This is the only flat rented by the Mandelstams which still survives, in a big corner block which, against Nadezhda Mandelstam's predictions, now bears a plaque: 'In this house lived the poet Osip Mandelstam in 1936.' Their last flat was on Ul. 27 Fevralya, 50, flat 1, in a well-situated one-storeyed house, small and built of stone, which has now been demolished. 'It seemed like heaven to us, a dream from a vanished past, a reward for all our tribulations. M. had taken them all quite calmly, but living at the seamstress' house, he came back to life.'

Andrey Platonov was born on the outskirts of Voronezh in the Yamskaya Settlement (Yamskaya Sloboda) in 1899 and his first book *Electrification* was published in Voronezh in 1921. The conflict between the rural and industrial world became a growing theme in his novels and short stories. Significantly, Platonov was born on the edge of these two worlds, a railroad separating the industrial settlement where he lived from the open Russian countryside:

> Only ten years ago Yamskaya was barely distinguishable from a village ... It had wattle fences, vegetable gardens,

vacant, weed-filled lots, huts instead of houses, chickens, boot-makers, and lots of peasants on the road to Zadonsk. The bell of the 'iron' church was the settlement's only music, and on quiet summer evenings it was listened to with emotion by old women, beggars, and me ... Apart from the field, the village, my mother, and the tolling of the bell, I loved (and the longer I live the more I love) locomotives, machines, the moaning of the factory whistle, and sweaty work ... Between the weeds, beggar women, the song of the fields and electricity, the locomotive, and the factory whistle which shakes the earth, there is a link, a native connection; the one and the other bear the same birthmark. What it is I do not yet know. But I know that the pitiful peasant plowing his field could tomorrow get on a five-axle locomotive and run the controls so well, looking like such a master of the thing, that you wouldn't recognize him. The growth of grass and the swirling of [a locomotive's] steam demand equal mechanics.

Platonov first worked as an electrical engineer in Voronezh before moving to Moscow to take up a serious career as a writer in 1927. He fell out of favour under Stalin, and many of his works were published posthumously.

Vyatka Region

Vyatka

— *Saltykov-Shchedrin Museum* The satirist Mikhail Saltykov-Shchedrin spent a seven-year term of exile in Vyatka (known in Soviet times as Kirov) from 1848 to 1855 for his radical political views, expressed in two stories published in St Petersburg. Surprisingly, he was allowed to work in Vyatka as a government official. The house where he lived on Ul. Lenina (formerly Ul. Voznesenskaya), 93, has been opened as a museum. Its appearance has changed little since Saltykov-Shchedrin lived here and it has been furnished with contemporary furniture and artefacts

– such as goose quills, candlesticks and embroidery – to recreate
its nineteenth-century appearance.

'The road ends at this town, as if this were the end of the
world,' Saltykov-Shchedrin wrote of Vyatka. His experiences are
recorded in his *Provincial Sketches*, where he directs his satire at
the bureaucrats among whom he worked. He was able to leave
Vyatka after the death of Nicholas I. One of the men who played
a large part in this was General Adjutant Peter Petrovich Lansky,
who arrived in Vyatka with his wife, Natalya Nikolayevna.
Natalya Nikolayevna's first husband was Alexander Pushkin.

Alexander Herzen was exiled to Vyatka via Perm in 1835
for his involvement in revolutionary circles while a student in
Moscow. During his two-year sentence he shared accommodation with another exile, Alexander Vitberg, and worked as a
government clerk in an office full of 'dirty companions, low
ideals and coarse feelings'. His hatred of his office life is
described in his memoirs, *My Past and Thoughts*: 'When I
remembered that I must go back there in the afternoon and back
again tomorrow, I sometimes fell into such fits of rage and
despair that I drank wine and spirits for consolation.' However,
not all his experiences there were bad ones: 'In that dreary
distant backwater of exile, separated from all I loved, surrounded
by the unclean horde of officials, and exposed without defence
to the tyranny of the Governor, I met nevertheless with many
warm hearts and friendly hands, and there I spent many happy
hours which are sacred in recollection.' When the Crown Prince
(Alexander II) visited Vyatka he was surprised to find 'an official
who could speak like a gentleman'. He intervened on Herzen's
behalf, which resulted in Herzen's subsequent transfer to exile
in Vladimir. This pleased him as Vladimir was situated '700
versts nearer to Moscow'.

— *Alexander Grin Museum* This small museum, founded in
1980, is located on the site of the wooden house Grin's family
lived in at the end of the nineteenth century. Its four rooms

contain family photographs, memorabilia and personal items belonging to the writer.

Address: Ul. Volodarskogo, 44

Yaroslavl Region

Yaroslavl

— *Lay of Prince Igor Museum* The ancient city of Yaroslavl on the Upper Volga is famous in literary terms because of the discovery of a twelfth-century manuscript in the Spasso-Preobrazhensky Cathedral here. *The Lay of Prince Igor* is considered to be the most important early work of Russian literature. It was first discovered in 1795 by Count Musin-Pushkin, a great collector of antiquities, who purchased several documents from the Archimandrite of the cathedral, among which was the valuable manuscript. The manuscript perished in the Fire of Moscow in 1812, but it was saved from complete extinction as a copy of it had been taken for Catherine the Great's private library. It was first published in Russia in 1800. An exhibition in the Spasso-Preobrazhensky Cathedral (Pl. Podbelskogo, 25) traces the manuscript's history, discovery and publication. Objects from Musin-Pushkin's estate are included in the exhibition, together with his portrait.

Yaroslavl is where the poet Nekrasov spent the early part of his childhood, from 1832 to 1837, and although he was born in Nemirov in the Ukraine he considered Yaroslavl to be his birthplace. Many buildings in the town bear Nekrasov's name and a statue (1958) stands on the river bank. His father's house stands at Vlasevskaya ul., 61 (known as Ul. Svobody in Soviet times), and the two-storeyed stone building of the school Nekrasov attended between 1832 and 1837 stands at Revolut-sionnaya ul., 11.

His father owned an estate at Greshnevo (now Nekrasovo) to the north-east of Yaroslavl, where Nekrasov lived from the

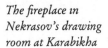

The fireplace in Nekrasov's drawing room at Karabikha

age of three. In his long narrative poem *Who Is Happy in Russia?*, the seven peasants set off from Greshnevo on their wanderings throughout Russia in their quest for a happy man. The estate burned down in the poet's lifetime.

Karabikha

— *Nekrasov Museum* In 1861, the year of the emancipation of the serfs, Nekrasov acquired his own estate, Karabikha, situated nine miles south of Yaroslavl on the Moscow road in the village of Krasnye Tkany. The large manor house had stables, an orangerie, ponds and formal gardens, set within a park. When Nekrasov bought the estate, he was now the distinguished editor of Russia's leading literary journal, *Otechestvennye zapiski* (National Annals). He lived in great style, hunting and entertaining guests during the summer months until 1875. Many of the poems written here such as 'Red Nosed Frost', 'Orina, a Soldier's Mother' and 'Railroad' were all about the plight of the Russian peasant, including his most famous poem, *Who Is Happy in Russia?*.

The house opened to the public in 1946. It has ten rooms dedicated to the poet's life and work, as well as reconstructions of the rooms in which Nekrasov lived.

Closed Mondays and the last Wednesday of the month

THE CAUCASUS

Caucasus

The Caucasus became part of the Russian Empire when it was annexed in 1801. In Pushkin's and Lermontov's lifetime it was seen as an area of unrest as the hill tribes fought against the expansionist Russians. The Russian army had frontier-posts and forts which stretched across the Caucasus from the Black Sea to the Caspian. Despite the constant unrest, the Caucasian mineral waters, with their curative properties, made towns such as Pyatigorsk fashionable nineteenth-century resorts.

Today, the northern part of the Caucasus still belongs to European Russia. To the south are the republics of Georgia, Armenia and Azerbaijan. Although varied within itself, the Caucasus is quite un-Russian in character: its mountainous grandeur has inspired Russians to write some of their finest literature, especially in the nineteenth century. The first Russian authors of international status to celebrate the Caucasus were Pushkin and Lermontov. Tolstoy came here a few decades later.

Pushkin travelled through the Caucasus twice in his life and was brought here by inspiration rather than necessity. From an early age he had heard romantic tales about the area. Later, he came to visit his Decembrist friends who had been exiled to the south, and to see his brother, who was a soldier in the Russian army, involved in the wars against both Persia (1826–7) and Turkey (1828–9). He made the journey with some cunning, as his motives were always under question from the secret police. His *Journey to Arzrum* records his second trip. The Caucasus also inspired his poetry; his 'Prisoner of the Caucasus' became an indispensable literary companion for subsequent travellers.

Lermontov made several visits to the Caucasus as a child and was later exiled to the region twice, first in 1837 for writing an outspoken poem about Pushkin's death, 'The Death of a Poet', and secondly in 1840 following a duel. He too was to

Lermontov's lithograph of a Caucasian landscape

celebrate the Caucasus in verse, but is remembered chiefly for his novel *A Hero of Our Time*, whose action takes place near the spa town of Pyatigorsk. The novel, as well as Lermontov's death in a duel fought near Pyatigorsk, has connected his name more strongly with the area than Pushkin's. Pushkin and Lermontov never met each other in the Caucasus.

Chechnya

Starogladkovskaya

— *Tolstoy Museum* For want of anything better to do, and desperate for adventure, the twenty-three-year-old Tolstoy decided to accompany his brother Nikolay back down to the Caucasus at the end of his home leave in the spring of 1851, where he was serving in the Russian army. Their destination was Starogladkovskaya, a Cossack village on the banks of the River Terek, situated among stunning mountainous scenery on the borders with Chechnya, where Nikolay's regiment was stationed. There is now a small museum here, where the lodgings of a Russian officer (such as Tolstoy would have lived in) and the house of a Grebensk Cossack have been recreated. It also houses an exhibition about the time Tolstoy spent in the area.

Tolstoy idled away his summer in the Caucasus gambling and womanizing before deciding to join the army himself, which he did when he went to Tiflis that autumn. It was there, while recuperating from treatment for venereal disease, that he began seriously writing and revising what would become his first piece of published fiction, *Childhood*, which appeared in Russia's most prestigious literary journal, *Sovremennik* (the Contemporary), in September 1852, two months after it was submitted as an unsolicited manuscript. This work drew heavily on Tolstoy's own childhood in Yasnaya Polyana and in Moscow, but his next published work, a story entitled 'The Raid', was directly inspired by his experiences as a volunteer with a detachment from his brother's regiment when they sacked a Chechen village in the summer of 1851. The story was published in 1853, and it is clear from the beginning that, much as he was awed by his surroundings, Tolstoy would not go in for the kind of romantic evocations so favoured by Lermontov a decade or so earlier:

> Right in front of us, sharp against the dark blue of the horizon, the gleaming white snowy mountains rose with amazing clarity, their shadows uncanny and yet harmonious in every detail. Crickets, grasshoppers, and thousands of other insects woke up in the tall grass and filled the air with varied and continual noises. It seemed as if thousands of little bells were ringing inside our very ears. The air smelled of water, grass and fog – the smell of a beautiful summer morning...

The same powers of description inform Tolstoy's first masterpiece, the short novel *The Cossacks*, written ten years later, and set in the area of Chechnya inhabited by the Grebensk Cossacks, who settled, according to the narrator:

beyond the Terek among the Chechens on the Greben, the
first range of wooded mountains of Chechnya. Living
among the Chechens the Cossacks intermarried with them
and adopted the manners and customs of the hill tribes,
though they still retained the Russian language in all its
purity, as well as their Old Faith.

Like most of Tolstoy's fiction, *The Cossacks* is autobiographical,
and tells the story of a Russian nobleman who has joined the
Caucasian army as a cadet, and yearns to lead the simple life of
the Cossacks with whom he is billeted. Tolstoy's realistic style
does not just stop with the ethnographic accuracy of his descriptions of Cossack life, but extends to his anti-romantic treatment
of the battle against the Chechens with which the work ends:

The bodies of the red-bearded Chechens with their clipped
mustaches lay on the ground, slashed and mauled. Only
the one who had shot Luke was still alive, though he too
was slashed. He looked like a wounded hawk, bleeding all
over – blood gushing from his right eye, his teeth clenched,
pale and sinister-looking, and he gazed around him with
huge angry eyes as he squatted, dagger in hand, ready to
continue fighting. The Cossack lieutenant went toward
him, as if to pass by him, then suddenly bent over and
shot him in the ear. The Chechen jerked violently and
collapsed.

North Ossetian Republic

Vladikavkaz

Mikhail Bulgakov lived in Vladikavkaz (formerly Ordzhoni-
kidze) in 1919 when he was attached to the Terek Cossack forces
of the White Army as a doctor. During his two-year stay here,
he decided to devote himself to writing full time. He abandoned
his medical career and worked as a journalist and playwright. He
wrote five plays; *The Days of the Turbins* was premièred at the
Vladikavkaz Theatre. In a letter to his brother, he could only

express disappointment: 'You cannot imagine the deep sorrow I felt that the play was being put on in the back of beyond.'

Bulgakov and his wife rented accommodation from an ataman or Cossack chief; his wife remembers that the atmosphere in the town was fairly lively and that 'there were cafés on the streets playing music'.

Stavropol Territory

Kislovodsk

The name of the town means 'bitter water' in Russian and it is the source of the famous Narzan mineral water. Like Pyatigorsk, the town is strongly connected with Lermontov, who writes in *A Hero of Our Time*, 'It's not for nothing that they call Narzan "the champion's spring". The local people claim that the air in Kislovodsk puts one in the mood for love, and that love affairs that begin at the foot of Mashuk reach happy endings here.' The town is smaller and quieter than Pyatigorsk, the capital of the spa towns. The fortress that stood here in Lermontov's day and which is mentioned in the novel no longer exists. A sanatorium now stands in its place.

The two-floored house with a wooden gallery at Ul. Kominterna, 3, is known as Rebrov's House and is where both Pushkin and Lermontov stayed at different times. Pushkin's visit was in 1829 and Lermontov's in 1837. After the publication of *A Hero of Our Time* it became known as Princess Mary's House, as this is where she is supposed to have stayed in the novel. The house has been rebuilt.

The Lermontovskaya ploshchadka (small square) in the town was where the wooden Restoratsiya (the local restaurant) stood. People would eat and drink here and hold balls and other spectacles, such as the magic show mentioned in the novel. Pechorin and Grushnitsky meet here in the encounter which leads to their duel. The building no longer remains, but a stone marks the place on which it stood. Lermontov stayed in this quarter of town with his grandmother when he was a boy.

Two and a half miles to the south-east of Kislovodsk is the place where Pechorin and Grushnitsky fight their duel in the novel. It is now known as the Lermontovskaya Skala (the Lermontov Cliff) and lies in the valley of the Olkhovka river. On the road from Pyatigorsk to Kislovodsk, there is an outcrop of rock known as the Koltso Gora (Ring Mountain), where a large patch of sky is visible through a ring of rock. It is described in Lermontov's novel: 'Two or three versts from Kislovodsk, in the gorge of the Podkumok, there's a rock called The Ring. It stands high on a hill and forms a natural gateway, through which the setting sun casts a last fiery glance at the world. A large party of us rode out to watch the sunset through this stone window, though, in fact, nobody gave much thought to the sun.' A railway line runs near by and when the train reaches the bridge across the Podkumok the passengers all crowd to the window.

Alexander Solzhenitsyn was born in Kislovodsk in 1918. Plans to open a museum have not yet been realized, in part because it is against the author's wishes to have a museum or exhibition opened during his lifetime. Solzhenitsyn was born in his uncle Shcherbak's house, which stood on Ul. Semashko. The street's name has changed frequently and has been known as Sheremetevskaya, Kaganovicha and Bukharina. In the 1970s, many of the old houses on this street were pulled down but the Gorin House, belonging to relations on his mother's side, where he lived as a child from 1920 to 1924, still remains. The church where Solzhenitsyn was christened, the church of St Panteleimon, was destroyed at the beginning of the 1960s. There are plans to rebuild it.

Pyatigorsk

The largest of the five spa towns, Pyatigorsk is situated at the foot of Mount Mashuk on the River Podkumok and its suburbs extend to Mount Beshtau to the north-west. On a clear day, it is within sight of Mount Elbrus. The town grew up around the Constantine Fortress built in 1740 and the springs that served it, and until 1830 it was known simply as Goryachie Vody (Hot Springs).

Alexander Pushkin first came to Pyatigorsk in June 1820 with the Raevsky family, who had met him in Ekaterinoslav in the Ukraine. His friend General N. N. Raevsky had obtained special permission to take him with them on their travels to the south and on to the Crimea. The town had not yet been modernized into the fashionable resort it was to become and the conditions were fairly primitive. The first visitors to the springs stayed in *kibitkas* (tents) or *balagandas* (wooden booths). 'The baths,' wrote Pushkin, 'are in small hastily built shacks. The steaming waters gush down from the mountains leaving white and reddish traces. We draw the water with scoops made of bark, or the bottom of broken bottles.' In a letter to his brother he praises the curative effect of the waters, particularly the sulphurous ones. The wild grandeur of the Caucasian scenery, the varied tenor of the lives of the Cossacks and hill tribes, the danger of a sudden encounter with a Circassian – all greatly appealed to Pushkin's romantic nature. He describes his first impression of the Caucasus in the epilogue to his narrative poem *Ruslan and Ludmilla*, written in 1820. The poem 'Prisoner of the Caucasus', written in 1820–1 and much influenced by Byron, was inspired by Pushkin's meeting with a soldier who had been kept captive by the Circassians. 'I placed my hero in one of the monotonous plains where I had lived for two months,' wrote Pushkin, who had first intended to set the poem further south, in Georgia.

He undertook his second journey to Arzrum in Turkey between May and September 1829 and again stopped off in Pyatigorsk. He was astonished and somewhat saddened by the changes to the town, which had by then become a smart resort.

'There are clean paths everywhere, little green benches, tidy flower beds, little bridges, pavilions. The springs are tidied up and faced in stone; Instructions from the police are nailed up on the walls of the baths; there is order and cleanliness everywhere ... I must admit: The Caucasian waters are now much more convenient; but I miss their former wild state...'

Lermontov was exiled to the Caucasus in 1837 and there are many places connected with his life and prose in the district. Part Two of *A Hero of Our Time* opens in Pyatigorsk as the 'hero', Pechorin, describes the view from his lodgings in the outskirts at the foot of Mount Mashuk:

> I have magnificent views on three sides – to the west lies Beshtau with its five blue peaks, like 'the last cloud of the dying storm', to the north Mashuk towers like a shaggy Persian cap, filling the whole horizon; to the east the view is gayer – below me, in a splash of colour, lies the little town, all neat and new, with the babbling of medicinal springs and the clamour of the multilingual throng ... It's a delight to live in a place like this. Every fibre of my body tingles with joy.

A fine view of the town can be had from the Ayolova Arfa (Aeolus' Harp), a small pavilion built on the slope of Mount Mashuk, once a Cossack lookout post. The pavilion was built in 1830 and is described in *A Hero of Our Time*. Inside was a real harp, but now its chords are electronic.

Beneath it is the Grot Lermontova (Lermontov's Cave), where Pechorin unexpectedly meets Vera in the novel. Near by is the Academic Gallery, which was built in 1851 to house the Elizavetinsky Istochnik (Elizabeth's Spring). Pechorin and Grushnitsky meet here for the first time, and later Grushnitsky becomes acquainted with Princess Mary here. A fifteen-minute walk from here takes you to the *proval* (chasm) visited by Pechorin and Princess Mary: 'When we reached the chasm, the ladies separated from their escorts, but she didn't leave my arm.

She was unamused by the quips of the local dandies and unalarmed by the steepness of the drop beneath us, though the other girls squealed and shut their eyes.'

'The Boulevard' where Pechorin takes his first walk runs up Pr. Kirova from the Academic Gallery to Andzhievsky ul. Pr. Kirova, 12, is known as Princess Mary's House, after a picture painted of it by M. A. Zichi in the 1880s. It depicts a scene described in the novel where Pechorin spites Princess Mary: 'She was haggling over the price of a Persian rug and pleading with Mama not to begrudge her it, as it would look so nice in her study. I offered forty roubles more and bought it from under her nose. I was rewarded with a superb look of fury. Near dinner time I had my horse walked specially past her windows with the rug draped over him.' One of the finest buildings in the town is the Restoratsiya, the scene of a ball in the novel: 'The restaurant-saloon turned into the Assembly Rooms.' Lermontov is comparing it to the Blagorodnoe Sobranie or Club of the Nobility in Moscow.

Also on Pr. Kirova, at number 19, is the Officers' House, a storey higher than it would have been in Lermontov's day, and next door are the Lermontov (formerly Nikolaevsky) Baths. Lermontov stayed here when he came to take the waters, and the building remains. The statue of Lermontov which stands in a park adjoining Ul. Andzhievskogo is the work of the sculptor A. M. Opekushin, who also designed the famous Pushkin Monument in Moscow. Near it stands a statue of Tolstoy.

— *Lermontov Museum* At Ul. Lermontova, 4, is the small Lermontov Museum, a modest, thatched building where in 1841 Lermontov and his friend Stolypin rented rooms from Captain Chilaev 'for 100 roubles'. This was to be Lermontov's last visit to the town before his death. Chilaev, who was still living here in 1870, described Lermontov's visit to the writer P. K. Martyanov, who has left a written description of each room. The Pyatigorsk Duma (Parliament) bought the building in 1912 and

*The Lermontov Museum
in Pyatigorsk*

it was given to the state after the October Revolution. Its four rooms have been reconstructed to reflect an officer's humble quarters. It also displays copies of pictures by Lermontov, showing his talent as a watercolourist. Ul. Lermontova and the surrounding streets (Karl Marx, Buachidze, and Andzhievsky) all make up the Lermontov quarter.

Closed on Tuesdays and the last Thursday of the month

The nearby Grot Diany (Diana's Grotto) in the Tsvetnik Park was where Lermontov organized a ball on 8 July 1841, a week before he was killed in the duel. The events that led to the duel took place on Ul. Buachidze, 9, one of the oldest quarters of the town, in the so-called Dom Verzilinikh (the Verzilin House), now a six-roomed museum. Lermontov was a frequent guest at this house, then known as the Temple of the Graces after the three unmarried daughters of its owner. The dining room has been arranged in an attempt to recreate its appearance on that day, and it was in this room that Lermontov offended Martynov and provoked their duel.

Martynov, a retired major, whom Lermontov had known for some time, was often the butt of the writer's jokes. Lermontov saw him across the room and called him the 'ferocious highlander with the big dagger'. Just before he had delivered his sentence the music stopped and the word 'dagger' resounded through the room. Martynov came over to Lermontov and said, 'How many times have I asked you to abandon your jokes, at least when ladies are present?' What Lermontov thought was a friendly misunderstanding turned into something much more serious. The two men met in the hall on the way out and Martynov made it clear he was still not happy. Lermontov asked, jokingly, 'Are you going to get really angry and challenge me to a duel for this?' Martynov's answer was 'Yes', and the day for a duel was arranged.

At the foot of Mount Mashuk, an hour's walk from the town, is the place where the duel was fought, now marked by a stone obelisk. It took place on 5 July 1841 between 6 and 7pm. The two men walked towards each other until they reached the barrier from where they could fire. It is said that Lermontov never intended to shoot, although the opinions of witnesses vary, some saying he fired into the air. Lermontov was killed immediately. The place of the duel was left unmarked until 1881, when a monument was erected. This was destroyed and another erected in 1915. Lermontov was initially buried in the Pyatigorsk Cemetery on the slopes of Mashuk. His body was moved to Tarkhany in accordance with his grandmother's wishes in spring 1842. Ironically, the duel described in *A Hero of Our Time* was mimicked by his own. He was only twenty-seven years old when he died.

Zheleznovodsk

The appearance of Zheleznovodsk (Iron Waters) has changed dramatically since the nineteenth century when Lermontov was here. As well as taking the waters of Zheleznovodsk, Lermontov

spent the last day of his life here. The town influenced his poem
'Ismail Bey', based on a real character of that name who was
instrumental in opening the spring, around which the town grew.
Karpov's House, where Lermontov stayed in 1841, is at Ul.
Semashko, 9. A relative of Lermontov's, Ekaterina Grigorievna
Bikhovetz, visited him on the eve of the duel. As he kissed her
hand when she was leaving, he said, 'I will never again have a
happier hour than this.' The last hours before the duel were
spent in the village of Inozemtseva, a small German colony
formerly known as Shotlandka (little Scotland) or Karras. It is
five miles from Zheleznovodsk. The village is also recalled in
Pushkin's poem 'Tazit', inspired by a group of Scottish mission-
aries who lived here.

SIBERIA

Altai Territory

Srostki

— *Shukshin Museum* The remote village of Srostki, near the town of Biisk, is where the writer, film director and actor Vasily Shukshin was born in 1929. With the proceeds of his first major literary success, the novel *The Lyubavins* (1965), he bought a house here for his mother, who lived in it for seven years. He had become a student at the Moscow Film School in 1954, and lived in the capital thereafter (until his untimely death twenty years later at the age of forty-five), but came back to Srostki as often as he could to work on the house. The bath-house and 'summer kitchen' in its grounds were built by Shukshin himself.

The small one-storey dwelling, built in 1958 of simple design by the local singing teacher, opened as a museum in 1978, and by 1989 had attracted over 300,000 visitors. It was the first museum of its kind to open in the area. Three of its rooms have been restored, while the largest room houses an exhibition about Shukshin's life and works. The plain decor of the house reflects his humble origins. On the walls of the white-washed room where he slept during his visits are simple portraits of his grandparents, painted from photographs, and the interior of the kitchen has not changed since the 1960s. Over the years, the museum has accumulated a wealth of exhibits to add to its collection, including letters to his children and photographs of the author taken by friends. Visitors can inspect Shukshin's typewriter and pipe, and various pages from his manuscripts. They can also walk outside in the garden among the fruit trees and bushes where the writer once hid secretly to film his mother, who did not like to have her photograph taken.

Irkutsk Region

Bratsk

In this town north of Irkutsk the Archpriest Avvakum, leader of the Old Believers, and author of the first Russian autobiography, was imprisoned for a time in the winter of 1656. Avvakum later described his living conditions in his autobiography in the most lurid detail: 'Like a little dog I lay on my lump of straw. Sometimes they fed me, sometimes not. The mice were plentiful ... I lay on my belly all the time; my back was rotting. Plentiful too were the fleas and lice...'

Avvakum's autobiography is remarkable not only for its use of the vernacular, but also for its descriptions of the landscape and wildlife of Siberia, which had not hitherto been described by a Russian writer. Having been exiled to Siberia with his family (initially to Tobolsk) by the Russian Patriarch Nikon, whose reforms Avvakum opposed, he was then attached to a colonizing expedition in eastern Siberia, which took him to Lake Baikal, whose natural wonders are also described in detail in the autobiography: 'There's no end to the birds, to the geese and swans – like snow they swim on the lake. In it are fish, sturgeon and taimen salmon, sterlet and omul salmon, whitefish, and many other kinds. The water is fresh, but huge seals and sea lions live in it.'

Irkutsk

Chekhov stopped in Irkutsk for a few days before crossing Lake Baikal by steamer on his way to Sakhalin Island in May 1890. Of all the Siberian cities he had travelled through so far, it made the most favourable impression on him. While he was here, he sold the carriage he had bought in Tomsk, wrote letters, went to the local bath-house ('the soap-suds that flowed down from my head weren't white, but an ashy-grey and reddy-brown sort of colour, as if I'd been scrubbing down a horse'), and caught up with his sleep ('it's only now that I understand what sleep means').

Tobolsk
The poet Küchelbecker died here in 1846, having been exiled to Siberia following his involvement in the Decembrist Rising twenty years earlier.

Kemerovo Region

Novokuznetsk
— *Dostoevsky Museum* This is the Siberian town where Dostoevsky married his first wife, Mariya Dmitrievna Isaeva. Dostoevsky met and fell in love with Isaeva while he was serving a five-year exile in Semipalatinsk in Kazakhstan, as a private in the army. Isaeva was then married to a drunken official and Dostoevsky tutored their son, Pasha. In 1855, the Isaevs left Semipalatinsk for Novokuznetsk, their departure being described by Dostoevsky's companion Vrangel: 'In order to allow Dostoevsky to make tender farewells to Marie Dmitrievna, I plied her husband with vast quantities of Champagne ... then I carried him to my equipage where he slept like a log ... The moment came for us to part. My doves embraced again one last time, both of them wiping away their tears while I dragged the dead drunk Isaev into his carriage.' The separation from Mariya caused Dostoevsky much grief, seemingly alleviated in August 1855 when he received news of her husband's death. Dostoevsky was convinced Mariya would now marry him, but she wrote of marrying a young friend of her husband. Eventually Dostoevsky's persistence, which included visits and letters, persuaded her to agree to the marriage, which took place on 6 February 1857, with the chief of police of Novokuznetsk and his wife as witnesses.

Mariya Isaeva was Dostoevsky's first great love: 'she was the

The house (first left) in which Dostoevsky lived after his marriage to Mariya Isaeva in 1857

light of my life. She appeared to me at the saddest moment of my fate and resurrected my spirit ...' he wrote to Vrangel in 1856. But the marriage was short-lived and tortuous. Mariya suffered from hysteria and tuberculosis and died in 1864. The complications of the relationship led Dostoevsky to write: 'Oh Lord, don't let anyone suffer this frightening, terrible feeling. The joy of love is great, but the suffering is so terrible, that it is better never to have loved.' Isaeva's house, where she had lived before marrying Dostoevsky, is open as a memorial museum (Ul. Dostoevskogo, 40). The Dostoevskys lived here for two weeks after their marriage – and the wooden house opposite (Ul. Dostoevskogo, 29) is also open as a museum.
Closed Sundays. Closed Saturdays and Sundays in the summer months

Krasnoyarsk Territory

Krasnoyarsk

For Chekhov, who travelled through Siberia on his way to the island of Sakhalin in 1890, Krasnoyarsk was 'the best and most beautiful of all Siberian towns' (until he arrived in Irkutsk, at any rate). It was in Krasnoyarsk that Chekhov first encountered the Yenisey river, about whose beauty he speaks in his travel notes:

> I have never in my life seen a more magnificent river than the Yenisey. A beautifully dressed, melancholy beauty the Volga may be, but at the other extreme, the Yenisey is a mighty, raging Hercules, who does not know what to do with his power and youth. On the Volga a man starts out with spirit, but finishes up with a groan which is called a song; his radiant golden hopes are replaced by an infirmity which it is the done thing to term 'Russian pessimism', whereas on the Yenisey life commences with a groan and finishes with the kind of high spirits which we cannot even dream about...

Magadan Region

Kolyma

Among the millions of Soviet citizens sent to the notorious concentration camps in the gold-mining area of Kolyma, in the freezing wastes of this remote north-eastern part of Siberia, only a few lived to write about their experiences (most perished – the literary critic Dmitry Mirsky, for example, passed away in a camp hospital in 1939). Evgeniya Ginzburg was sent here for a ten-year sentence from Kazan in 1937, and remained in exile in Magadan afterwards until she was rehabilitated following Stalin's death. Her finely written autobiographical works *Into the Whirlwind* (1967) and *Within the Whirlwind* (1981), neither of which could be published in her lifetime, but which circulated in Russia in samizdat, document her life following her arrest.

Varlam Shalamov spent sixteen years in Kolyma, from 1938 to 1953, the year of Stalin's death. One of his 'crimes' was to have praised the Paris-based émigré writer Ivan Bunin, the first

Russian writer to receive the Nobel Prize for Literature, as a 'classic' author. His remarkable stories, *Kolyma Tales*, which are both fictional and factual, describe what it was like to live through that experience. When the stories were published in the West in the early 1970s, the Soviet authorities forced Shalamov to renounce them.

Omsk Region

Omsk

— *Dostoevsky Museum* This ten-room museum opened in 1982 commemorates the many writers who have been exiled to Omsk. It is housed in a building of 1790, the oldest in Omsk, which before the Revolution was the official residence of the prison governor. The prison's most famous inmate was Dostoevsky, to whom most of the space in the museum is devoted.

Dostoevsky was exiled to the prison fortress of Omsk from St Petersburg in 1850 for his involvement in the Petrashevsky Circle, a group of young intellectuals whose theories were deemed too radical by the Tsar. Dostoevsky and his fellow prisoners made the 2,000-mile journey to Omsk from St Petersburg in a closed sledge in freezing temperatures. En route, they stopped for six days in a transit prison in Tobolsk. Here they were met by four of the wives of the Decembrists, who had followed their husbands into exile. These women gave the prisoners copies of the gospels containing ten rouble notes. From Tobolsk they travelled three more days on to Omsk.

Dostoevsky spent four years as a convict. 'I consider those four years as a time during which I was buried alive and shut up in a coffin,' he wrote to his brother Andrey. But in another letter to his brother Mikhail he praised his fellow prisoners: 'What a wonderful people. My time has not been wasted. Even if I have not come to know Russia, I have come to know the Russian people better than many know it, perhaps.' Dostoevsky recorded his experiences in notebooks which he used extensively in 1859 for his novel *The House of the Dead*. He also used his prison experience for the final chapters of *Crime and Punishment*, whose denouement takes place in Siberia on the banks of the River Irtysh:

> Raskolnikov went out of the shed right down to the bank, sat down on the logs that were piled near the shed and began to look out at the wide, lonely river. From the high river-bank a broad panorama opened out. From the far-off opposite bank he could just make out the sound of someone singing. Over there, in the boundless steppe awash with sunlight, he could see the yurts of the nomad tribesmen like barely perceptible black dots. Over there was freedom, over there lived other people, quite different from those who lived here, over there time itself seemed to have stopped, as though the days of Abraham and his flocks had never passed. Raskolnikov sat gazing motionlessly, without cease; his thoughts moved away into dreams, into contemplation; he had not a thought in his head, but a sense of weariness tormented him.

In March 1854 Dostoevsky was dispatched to serve as a private soldier in the Seventh Siberian Battalion of the Line stationed at Semipalatinsk in Kazakhstan.

The town's other literary associations are with the poet Annensky, born here in 1855 (his civil servant father was posted here), and with Solzhenitsyn. Almost exactly 100 years after Dostoevsky, Solzhenitsyn passed through Omsk on his way to the gulag in Ekibastuz, Kazakhstan. He was struck by the solidity of the prison, which was not 'any old Gulag transit prison hastily knocked together from matchwood', and felt that little had changed since the time of Catherine the Great, when it was built: 'It was a formidable jail ... and its dungeons were particularly terrible ... The small square windows gave onto the well of an oblique shaft that rose to ground level. The thickness

of the window's sides – three metres – gave you an idea of what the walls were like ...'
Address: Ul. Dostoevskogo, 1
Closed Mondays

Primorsk Territory

Vladivostok

In May 1938 Osip Mandelstam was sentenced to five years in a labour camp. His wife saw him for the last time at Samatikha, 125 miles to the south of Moscow, where they had been granted permission to stay in a rest home for writers. But no sooner had they arrived than Osip was arrested and driven away in a lorry. It is now almost certain that he died of heart failure on 27 December 1938 in a transit camp on the way to Vladivostok.

Chuguevka

— *Fadeev Museum* Alexander Fadeev grew up in this remote town to the east of Arseniev after his family moved here from Tver in 1908, when he was seven years old. In 1960 a museum was founded in the house in which he spent his childhood. Miles from the nearest railway station, the primitive house with a tin roof, which has now been restored, had no electricity and was situated deep in the taiga (forest) beneath the Sikhote-Alin Mountains.

Fadeev went to school in Vladivostok before joining the Communist Party and moving to Moscow in the early 1920s. A talented but complex figure, Fadeev compromised himself hideously by becoming a hard-line party figure in order to ensure his own survival. He took a leading role in the persecution of writers during the Stalinist regime, and became head of the Union of Writers in 1946, but (in Pasternak's eyes) redeemed himself by committing suicide in 1956, when his crimes were made public. Akhmatova also had sympathy for him, as he helped release her son Lev from prison.

The museum contains two rooms. Downstairs is a literary exhibition about Fadeev and his times, while upstairs visitors can see furniture from his dacha in Peredelkino, as well as books from his library and other personal items.

Address: Ul. 50-Letiya Oktyabrya, 124

Sakhalin Region

Alexandrovsk-Sakhalinsky

— *Chekhov Museum* It was in this small wooden one-storey house that Chekhov stayed in Alexandrovsk in the summer of 1890, during his momentous three-month tour of the penal colony on Sakhalin Island conducting a detailed census of its population. The results were published in the remarkable study he spent the next few years writing, *The Island of Sakhalin*, which appeared in 1895.

Having arrived on the northern coast by steamer from Nikolaevsk on the mainland, Chekhov slowly worked his way round the island (twice the size of Greece), but began in Alexandrovsk, its main town (the 'Sakhalin Paris'), and the residence of the Governor. Some 3,000 people were living here in 1890, in dwellings constructed entirely out of wood. Chekhov has left us a description of the house he first stayed in outside the town when he first arrived:

> There was a small yard, paved in the Siberian fashion, with logs around an awning, and, in the house, five clean and spacious rooms with a kitchen, but not a stick of furniture. The landlady, a young peasant woman, fetched a table, then, about five minutes later, a stool ... through the window could be seen beds of cabbage seedlings, around them unsightly ditches, and, in the distance, gaunt, withered larch-trees loomed indistinctly ...

Chekhov (second from right) visiting the Japanese consul on Sakhalin Island in 1890

The next day, Chekhov moved into the house of the local doctor on the main street, which now houses the Chekhov Museum. Each morning he would hear the 'most diverse sounds':

> Through the open windows could be heard the rhythmical clanking of prisoners in irons passing down the street; opposite our quarters, in the army barracks, soldier instrumentalists were rehearsing their marches for the visit of the Governor General, and, as the flute was playing a part from one piece, the trombone a part from another and the bassoon a part from a third, the result was indescribable chaos; while, in our own rooms, there was the tireless whistling of canaries, and my host the doctor walking from corner to corner, leafing through law-books while on the move, and thinking aloud...

Officials were allowed to employ any number of convicts as domestic servants, a state of affairs Chekhov found distasteful, to judge from his comment about the two cooks, a caretaker and a maid who attended on his landlord and his son: 'for a junior prison surgeon this is very opulent'.

When the surgeon moved back to the mainland, Chekhov took lodgings with an official who had only one elderly servant, as well as a convict, Yegor, who carried out heavy-duty jobs and is described with much affection in *The Island of Sakhalin*: 'You would be sitting and reading, or writing something, when suddenly you would hear a sort of rustling and panting, and something weighty would be moving around underneath the table by your leg; you would glance down – and see Yegor, barefoot, gathering up bits of paper or wiping away the dust beneath the table.' Chekhov's accommodation in the rest of Sakhalin was less salubrious. In one place he slept on hay on the floor, and at Derbinskoie, due to lack of space, he stayed in a granary next to the prison, and would hear its inmates whispering in despair during the night.

Address: Ul. Chekhova, 19

Tomsk Region

Tomsk

Chekhov stopped here for a few days on his way to Sakhalin in 1890. It did not impress him as much as Krasnoyarsk, which was his next port of call ('not worth a brass farthing' was his verdict on Tomsk), and the journey between the two cities was memorable only for the quantities of mud to be endured. In general, Chekhov did not find this part of the trip very interesting, as he recorded in his travel notes:

> If, while you are travelling, the countryside possesses any significance at all for you, then going from Russia to Siberia you could have a very boring time from the Urals right up the Yenisei. The chilly plain, the twisted birch-trees, the pools, the occasional islands, snow in May, and the barren,

bleak banks of the tributaries of the Ob – these are all that
the memory succeeds in retaining from the first 2,000
versts ...

Over the centuries, numerous Russian citizens have spent time
in Tomsk serving sentences of exile. Among them was the
peasant poet Nikolay Klyuev. After depicting the Soviet authorities as the devil and other evil mythical creatures in a
succession of long poems written after the Revolution, Klyuev
was exiled in 1934 to Kolpashovo, in the Narym region, to the
north-west of Tomsk. He was transferred to Tomsk later that
year, and lived at Per. Krasnogo Pozharnika, 12, until his arrest
in 1937. A memorial plaque has now been fixed to the wall of
the house. Klyuev was shot a few months following his arrest,
having been accused of participating in a Monarchist plot.
The long autobiographical poem, 'Song of the Great Mother',
which he wrote during his Siberian exile, was long thought
to have been lost, but was miraculously published in 1991,
having been discovered in a KGB archive by the critic Vitaly
Shentalinsky.

Tyumen Region

Tyumen

Anton Chekhov arrived in this city in May 1890. He was two
weeks into his epic journey from Moscow to the island of
Sakhalin. Until now he had travelled partly by train, and partly
by boat, along the Volga and Kama rivers from Yaroslavl. River
travel would have been the most comfortable method of continuing his journey (the Trans-Siberian Railway was not completed
until many decades later), but since the River Ob was still frozen
Chekhov now faced two gruelling months travelling by horse-
driven carriage to cover the remaining few thousand miles to the
port of Nikolaevsk.

It was at Tyumen, the first Siberian town beyond the Urals,

that Chekhov began his travel notes, which were published in his friend Suvorin's newspaper *Novoe vremya* (New Time):

> Yes, it is May now, and by this time in European Russia the woods are turning green and the nightingales are pouring out their songs, while in the south the acacia and lilac have been in blossom for ages already, yet here, along the road from Tyumen to Tomsk, the earth is brown, the forests are bare, there is dull ice on the lakes, and snow still lying on the shores and in the gullies.
>
> But, to make up for this, never in my life have I seen such a vast number of wildfowl. I catch sight of wild ducks walking on the ground, swimming in the pools and roadside ditches, constantly fluttering almost right up to my carriage, and flying lazily off into the birch-woods. Amidst the silence a familiar melodious sound rings out, you glance up and see high above your head a pair of cranes, and for some reason you are overcome by melancholy . . .

Yakutsk Region

Vilyuisk

— *Chernyshevsky Museum* In 1864 Nikolay Chernyshevsky was sentenced to seven years' hard labour in Siberia, which he spent in the Tobolsk Prison, working in the salt mines of Usol'e and the silver mines in the Irkutsk region. This was followed by twelve years of exile in the arctic village of Vilyuisk, situated on a tributary of the River Lena, to the north-west of Yakutsk. His wife and their eight-year-old son had made the 4,000-mile journey to be with him in 1866. When his sentence finally came to an end in 1870, Chernyshevsky was not allowed to go back to European Russia; until 1889 Astrakhan became the family's new place of exile. There is also a Chernyshevsky museum in Alexandrovsky zavod (factory), where the critic lived from 1866 to 1871.
Address: Ul. Chernyshevskogo, 1

THE
UKRAINE

Kiev

— *Bulgakov Museum* Bulgakov was born in Kiev, and his family moved to this two-storey house on this steep street in 1906, when the future writer was 15 years old. When Bulgakov's father, a Professor at the Kiev Theological Academy, died in 1907, his mother was left to care for seven children, and the house remained in their possession until 1922. The family lived in seven rooms on the first floor of the building, and this is where Bulgakov later housed the Turbins, the heroes of his novel *The White Guard*. Ever since the writer Nekrasov published an important article about it in the magazine *Novy mir* in 1967, the building has been known as the "Turbins' House". In Soviet times the building was turned into communal flats and fell into disrepair, but restoration work began in the late 1980s, when Bulgakov's reputation as a major Russian writer was rightfully restored. The house opened as a museum in 1991, attached to the Museum of the History of Kiev, and remains the only Bulgakov museum in the world, as its curators are proud to relate. Its exhibits simultaneously tell the story of Bulgakov's childhood, and *The White Guard*.
Address: Andreyevsky spusk, 13
Closed Wednesdays

Crimea

1) YALTA
— *Chekhov Museum* Like many sufferers from tuberculosis, when Chekhov moved to Yalta in 1898, it was for health reasons. A year later he moved into a newly built villa on the outskirts of the resort which was immediately christened the "White Dacha". His mother moved down from Moscow to join him, with the family's retired cook, and his sister Masha came down during vacations. Chekhov immediately started to cultivate a very fine (and well preserved) garden, which helped him while away long days of boredom, as did the

mongrel dogs and pet crane who became part of his Crimean menagerie. The five and a half years Chekhov spent in Yalta were not happy ones. Despite the beauties of the Crimean riviera (Yalta was regarded as Russia's Nice), and hordes of inquisitive visitors, Chekhov pined for Moscow, particularly when his illness worsened and he was housebound. He nevertheless managed to write several fine stories in Yalta, including "The Lady with a Little Dog", and his two last plays, *Three Sisters* and *The Cherry Orchard*. His loneliness was alleviated by the relationship by correspondence which he developed with Olga Knipper, a leading actress with the Moscow Art Theatre, which toured Yalta in 1900. The couple married in 1901, and Knipper made several long visits, but continued her acting career in Moscow. The museum was opened to the public the year after Chekhov died, in 1905 and became a state museum in 1921. Its custodian became Chekhov's sister Masha, who lived in the house for 56 years, until her death in 1957. She took care to preserve its interiors, and refused to let German officers move into her brother's rooms during the Nazi occupation of Yalta.

Address: Ul. Kirova, 12
Closed Monday

II) GURZUF (GREATER YALTA)

— *Chekhov Museum* The seaside dacha Chekhov bought in this picturesque Tatar village a few miles down the coast from Yalta in 1900 came with its own little bay. Partly Chekhov wanted to get away from the streams of visitors to his Yalta house, and partly he wanted to be able to spend some time alone with his sweetheart Olga Knipper, away from the prying eyes of his mother and sister. The tiny house with the red tiled roof was rather decrepit when Chekhov bought it, but its three rooms came with a shady veranda and a short flight of steep steps leading down the cliff to the pebbly beach below. The miniature garden contained just one tree: a mulberry, which probably inspired Chekhov's quotation of lines from Pushkin's poem *Ruslan and Lyudmila* in his play *Three Sisters*, begun here, supposed themselves to have been inspired by a famous tree in Taganrog. Pushkin spent three weeks in Gurzuf in 1820 staying in the spacious house built by the Duc de Richelieu in the middle of a beautiful park. A small *Pushkin Museum* was opened in the house in 1989, but public access has been severely restricted since 2003. *Address: Ul. Chekhova, 22*

III) PLANERSKOE (KOKTEBEL)

— *Voloshin Museum* The writer and artist Maximilian Voloshin's house in the former Koktebel is situated some 14 miles south-west of Feodosia on the eastern shore of the Crimean peninsula. Marina Tsvetaeva, who worshipped Voloshin, made her first visit here in 1911, and wrote several breathless and typically eliptical articles inspired by her experiences. It was during her first visit that she met her future husband Sergey Efron. Before and after the Revolution, the balconied house by the sea became an artistic mecca in the spring and summer for nearly every writer of note. Voloshin lived here permanently from 1917 and died here in 1932, after which time the house became a creative retreat for Moscow writers. Osip Mandelstam stayed here during his visit to the Crimea in 1933, and used the pebbles he collected on the beach as a way of making sense of the structure of Dante's *Divine Comedy*. The house opened as a museum in 1975.

Sorochintsy (Poltava region)

— *Gogol Museum* Founded in 1929, this five-room museum commemorates the Russian-Ukrainian writer Nikolay Gogol, who was born here in 1809. The original house was destroyed during World War II, but was reconstructed, and re-opened as a museum in 1951. *Address: Ul. Gogolya, 32*

Odessa

— *Literature Museum*   The 27 rooms of this museum, which opened in 1977, trace the literary history of Odessa, with exhibits relating to the lives and works of Pushkin, Gogol, Chekhov, Tolstoy and Gorky.
Address: Vulitsya Lanzheronovska, 2
Closed Monday

— *Pushkin Museum*   This small, three-room museum, founded in 1960, commemorates Pushkin's stay in Odessa in the city during his period of exile from July 1823 to August 1824. Pushkin wrote two chapters of *Eugene Onegin* while living in Odessa, as well as a number of poems. His corner room in the Hotel Rainaud overlooked the sea, and only a few minutes walk from the theatre, the casino and Odessa's best restaurant, famed for its oysters. The street in which the museum is located is named after Pushkin, and the poet's stay in the city was commemorated by the erection of a statue in 1889.
Address: Vulitsya Pushkinska, 13

Sumy

— *Chekhov Museum*   This museum, in north-east Ukraine on the banks of the River Psel, was opened in 1960, on the centenary of Chekhov's death. It is located in the annexe of the former gentry estate owned by the Lintvaryov family which Chekhov rented in 1888 and 1889 as a summer dacha. Sumy was a town of 25,000 in 1888 when Chekhov first arrived, initially with his mother and sister, to spend an idyllic few months fishing and enjoying the fine weather and beautiful scenery. The Lintvaryov family became good friends. The second summer spent at Luka, as the estate was called, was a miserable one for the Chekhovs, as it was here that Nikolai (Chekhov's elder brother) died from tuberculosis. His grave is in the local cemetery.

MAPS

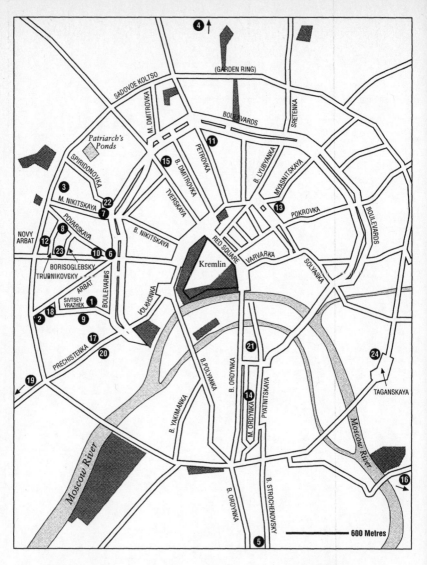

1 Aksakov Museum	9 Herzen Museum	17 Pushkin Museum
2 Bely Museum	10 Lermontov Museum	18 Pushkin Museum
3 Chekhov Museum	11 Literary Museum	19 Tolstoy Museum
4 Dostoevsky Museum	12 Literary Museum	20 Tolstoy Museum
5 Esenin Museum	13 Mayakovsky Museum	21 Tolstoy Museum (annexe)
6 Gogol Museum	14 A. Ostrovsky Museum	22 Alexey Tolstoy Museum
7 Gorky Museum	15 N. Ostrovsky Museum	23 Tsvetaeva Museum
8 Gorky Museum	16 Paustovsky Museum	24 Vysotsky Museum

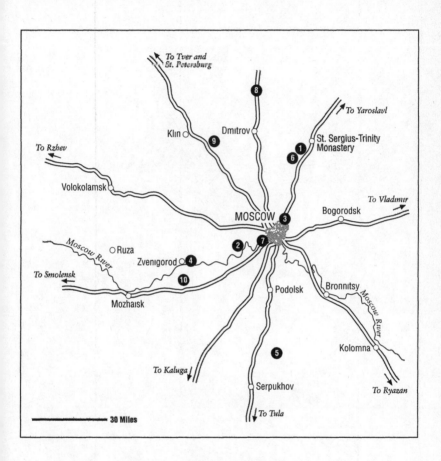

1 Abramtsevo

2 Arkhangelskoe

3 Bolshevo: Tsvetaeva Museum

4 Dunino: Prishvin Museum

5 Melikhovo: Chekhov Museum

6 Muranovo: Tyutchev Museum

7 Peredelkino: Chukovsky Museum; Pasternak Museum

8 Spas Ugol (near Taldom): Saltykov-Shchedrin Museum

9 Tarakanovo: Blok Museum

10 Zakharovo: Pushkin Museum

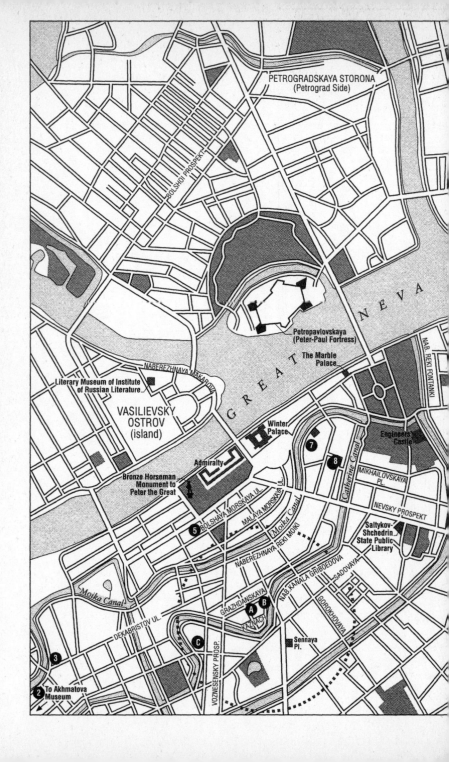

PETROGRADSKAYA STORONA
(Petrograd Side)

BOLSHOI PROSPEKT

N E V A

G R E A T

Petropavlovskaya
(Peter-Paul Fortress)

The Marble
Palace

NABEREZHNAYA MAKAROVA

NAB. REKI FONTANKI

Literary Museum of Institute
of Russian Literature

VASILIEVSKY
OSTROV
(island)

Winter
Palace

Engineers
Castle

Admiralty

7

8

MIKHAILOVSKAYA
PL.

Bronze Horseman
Monument to
Peter the Great

5

BOLSHAYA MORSKAYA UL.

MALAYA MORSKAYA UL.

Moika Canal

NEVSKY PROSPEKT

Catherine Canal

Saltykov-
Shchedrin
State Public
Library

NABEREZHNAYA REKI MOIKI

Moika Canal

NAB. KANALA GRIBOEDOVA

SADOVAYA

GRAZHDANSKAYA

A B

KAZNACH.

BOROKHOVAYA

DEKABRISTOV UL.

C

VOZNESENSKY PROSP.

Sennaya
Pl.

3

2 To Akhmatova
Museum

1 Akhmatova Museum
2 Akhmatova Museum
3 Blok Museum
4 Dostoevsky Museum
5 Nabokov Museum
6 Nekrasov Museum
7 Pushkin Museum
8 Zoshchenko Museum

The section marked by the circle is the region
described by Dostoevsky in *Crime and Punishment*:

A Stolyarny Per: The street where Raskolnikov lived
B The house where Sonya Marmeladov lived
C The scene of the murder

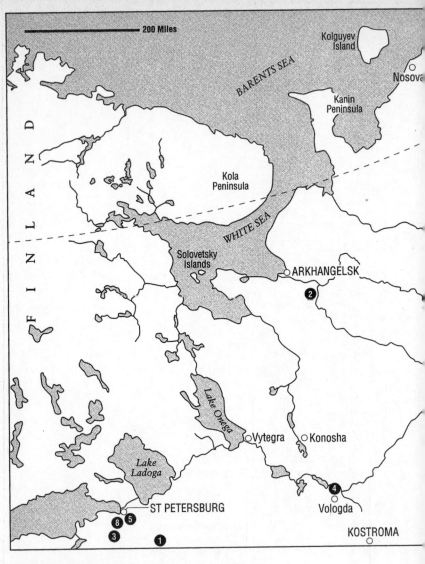

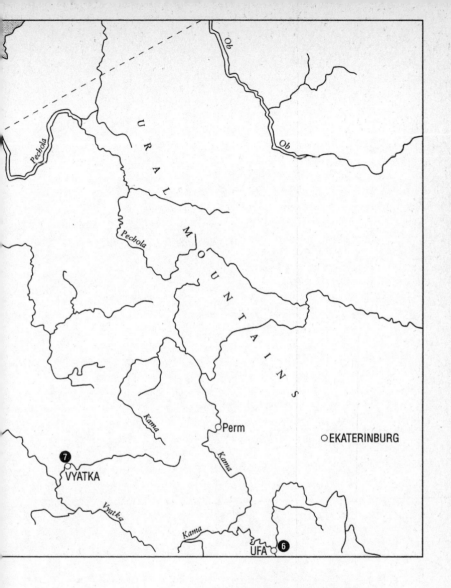

1 Chudovo: Nekrasov Museum
2 Lomonosovo: Lomonosov Museum
3 Rozhdestveno: Nabokov Family Museum
4 Vologda Shalamov Museum
5 Tsarskoe Selo: Pushkin Museums
6 Ufa: Aksakov Museum
7 Vyatka: Saltykov-Shchedrin Museums and Grin
  Museums
8 Vyra· Postmaster's Cottage Museum

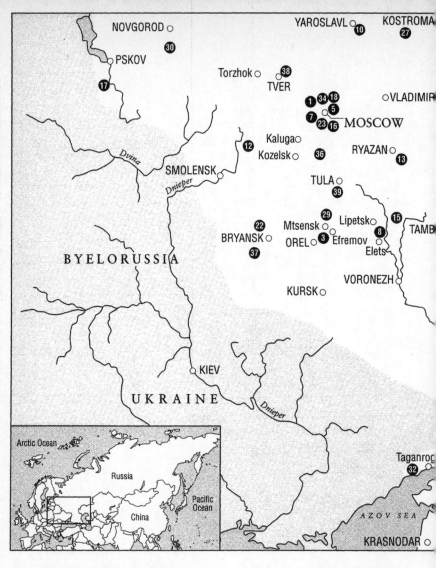

1 Abramtsevo: Aksakov & Gogol Museums

2 Aksakovo: Aksakovo Museum

3 Orel: Andreev, Bunin, Leskov & Turgenev Museums

4 Belinsky: Belinsky Museum

5 Bolshevo: Tsvetaeva Museum

6 Bolshoe Boldino: Pushkin Museum

7 Dunino: Prishvin Museum

8 Elets: Bunin Museum

9 Gelendzhik: Korolenko Museum

10 Karabıkha: Nekrasov Museum

11 Kazan: Baratynsky & Gorky Museums

12 Khmelita: Griboedov Museum

13 Konstantinovo: Esenin Museum

14 Kruzhilin: Sholokhov Museum

15 Lev Tolstoy: Tolstoy Museum

16 Melikhovo: Chekhov Museum

17 Mikhailovskoe: Pushkin Museum

18 Muranovo: Tyutchev Museum

19 Narovchat: Kuprin Museum

20 Nizhny Novgorod: Gorky Museums

21 Novorossusk: Gladkov Museum
22 Ovstug: Tyutchev Museum
23 Peredelkıno: Pasternak & Chukovsky Museums
24 Pyatıgorsk: Lermontov Museum
25 Samara: A.N. Tolstoy Museum
26 Saratov: Chernyshevsky & Fedın Museums
27 Shchelykovo: A. Ostrovsky Museum
28 Sımbırsk: Goncharov Museum
29 Spasskoe Lutovınovo: Turgenev Museum
30 Staraya Russa: Dostoevsky Museum

31 Starogladkovskaya: Tolstoy Museum
32 Taganrog: Chekhov Museums
33 Taman: Lermontov Museum
34 Tarakanovo: Blok Museum
35 Tarkhany: Lermontov Museum
36 Tarusa: Tsvetaeva Museum
37 Krasny Rog: A. K. Tolstoy Museum
38 Tver: Saltykov-Shchedrın Museum
39 Yasnaya Polyana: Tolstoy Museum

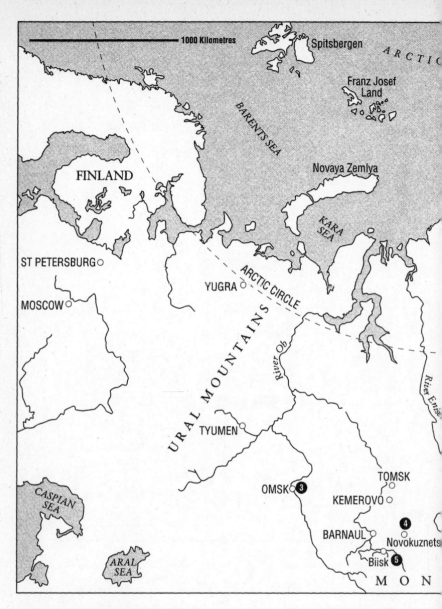

1 Alexandrovsk-Sakhalınsky: Chekhov Museum
2 Chuguevka: Fadeev Museum
3 Omsk: Dostoevsky Museum
4 Novokuznetsk: Dostoevsky Museum
5 Srostkı: Shukshın Museum
6 Vılyuısk: Chernyshevsky Museum

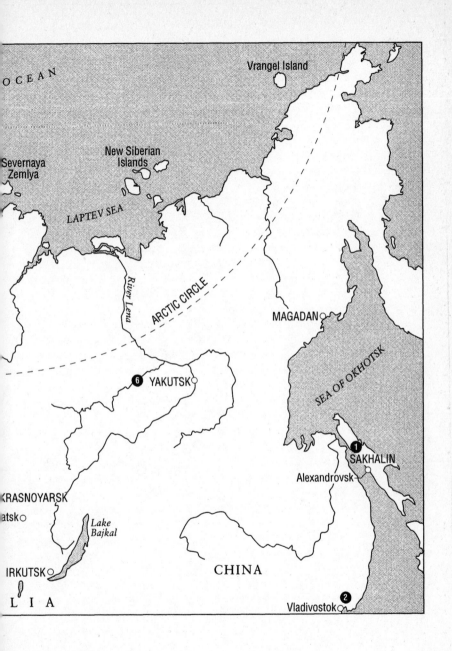

Further Reading

Aleksandrov, A., *Blok v Peterburge-Petrograde*, Leningrad, 1987

Antsiferov, N. P., *Moskva Pushkina*, Moscow, 1950

——, *Dusha Peterburga*, Leningrad, 1991

——, *Peterburg Dostoevskogo*, Leningrad, 1991

——, *Nepostizhimii gorod*, Leningrad, 1991

Aronson, M. and Reiser, S., *Literaturnye kruzhki i salony*, Leningrad, 1929

Avdeev, Y., *Po chekhovskim mestam podmoskov'ya*, Moscow, 1959

Azarova, N., Kostyukovskaya, N. and Strizhneva, S., *Tolstoi v Moskve*, Moscow, 1985

Balabanovich, E., *Dom A. P. Chekhova v Moskve*, Moscow, 1958

Belozerskaya, L. E., *O, med vospominanii*, Ann Arbor, 1977

Biron, V., *Peterburg Dostoevskogo*, Leningrad, 1991

Bonch-Bruevich, V., ed., *Literaturnye ekskursii po Moskve*, Moscow, 1948

Byaliy, G. A. and Muratov, A. B., *Turgenev v Peterburge*, Leningrad, 1970

Bychkov, Y., *Techenie melikhovskoi zhizni*, Moscow, 1989

Bykovtseva, L., *Russkie pisateli v Moskve*, 3rd edn, Moscow, 1987

Chebotarevskaya, Y., Bokk, Z. and Khitrovo, N., *Tolstoy's Moscow Home*, Moscow, 1957

Chekhova, M. P., *Dom-muzei A. P. Chekhova v Yalte*, Moscow, 1958

Chudakova, M., *Zhizneopisanie Mikhaila Bulgakova*, Moscow, 1988

Chudnova, L. G., *Leskov v Peterburge*, Leningrad, 1975

Dits, V. F., *Esenin v Petrograde-Leningrade*, Leningrad, 1990

Dokusov, A. M., ed., *Literaturnye pamyatnye mesta Leningrada*, Leningrad, 1968

Eventov, I., *Gorky v Peterburge-Leningrade*, Leningrad, 1956

Fet, A., *Moi vospominaniya*, Moscow, 1890

Fomichev, S., *Griboedov v Peterburge*, Leningrad, 1982

Gaynor, E., Goldstein, D. and Haavisto, K., *Russian Houses*, New York, 1991

Gillelson, M., Manuilov, V. and Stepanov, A., *Gogol v Peterburge*, Leningrad, 1961

Gollerbakh, E., *Gorod muz. Tsarskoe selo v poezii*, St Petersburg, 1993

Gordeev, N., *Tambovskaya tropinka k Pushkinu*, Voronezh, 1969

Grigoriev, N., *Mayakovsky v Vladimire*, Vladimir, 1959

Iezuitova, R., *Zhukovsky v Peterburge*, Leningrad, 1976

Kagan, I., *Marina Tsvetaeva v Moskve: Put' v gibelyu*, Moscow, 1992

Khrenkov, D., *Anna Akhmatova v Peterburge-Petrograde-Leningrade*, Leningrad, 1989

Kochetkova, N. D., *Fonvizin v Peterburge*, Leningrad, 1984

Kuz'mina, L., *Lev Tolstoy v Peterburge*, Leningrad, 1986

Levinson, N. R., *Pushkinskaya Moskva*, Moscow, 1937

Likhotkin, G. A., *Lomonosov v Peterburge*, Leningrad, 1981

Loman, O. V., *Nekrasov v Peterburge*, Leningrad, 1985

Mamaev, A., *Astrakhan Velimira Khlebnikogo*, Astrakhan, 1993

Manuilov, V. and Nazarova, L. N., *Lermontov v Peterburge*, Leningrad, 1984

Manuilov, V. and Semenova, G., *Belinsky v Peterburge*, Leningrad, 1979

Mikitich, L. D., *Literaturnyi Peterburg, Petrograd*, Moscow, 1991

Miller, O. V., Manuilov, V. A. and Lentsova, V. B., *Po lermontovskim mestam*, Moscow, 1989

Muraviev, V., *Gorod chudnyi, gorod drevnyi: Moskva v russkoi poezii XVII-nachala XX vekov*, Moscow, 1985

Myagkov, B., *Bulgakovskaya Moskva*, Moscow, 1993

Otradin, M., *Peterburg v russkoi poezii*, Leningrad, 1988

Ovchinnikova, S. T., *Pushkin v Moskve: lętopis' zhizni A. S. Pushkina s 5 dekabrya 1830 po 15 maya 1830*, Moscow, 1984

Pini, O., *Chernyshevsky v Peterburge*, Leningrad, 1978

Popova, N. and Popov, I., *Moskva Alekseya Remizova*, Moscow, 1996

Puzin, N., *Yasnaya Polyana. Dom-muzei L. N. Tolstogo*, Moscow, 1982

Roosevelt, P., *Life on a Russian Country Estate*, New York, 1995

Sarukhanyan, E. P., *Dostoevsky v Peterburge*, Leningrad, 1970

Shiroky, V. F., *Pushkin v Peterburge: pushkinskie mesta v Leningrade*, Leningrad, 1937

Shkolnik, B. A., *Peterburg Mandelshtama*, Leningrad, 1991

Shtempel, N., *Mandelshtam v Voronezhe*, Moscow, 1992.

Smirnov, A. E., *Tverskoi venok Pushkinu*, Kalinin, 1989

Starodub, K. et al., *Ya lyublyu etot gorod vyazevyi: putevoditel' po literaturnym mestam Moskvy*, Moscow, 1990

Sytin, P., *Iz istorii moskovskikh ulits*, Moscow, 1958

Tomashevsky, Y. V., *Litso i maska Mikhaila Zoshchenko*, Moscow, 1994

Vanslova, E. et al., *Literaturnie mesta Rossii*, Moscow, 1987

Veis, Z. and Grechnev, V., *S Mayakovskim po Sankt-Peterburgu*, St Petersburg, 1993

Vinogradova, K., *Chekhov v Melikhove*, Moscow, 1956

Yatsevich, A., *Pushkinskii Peterburg*, St Petersburg, 1993

Zemenkov, B., *Pamyatnye mesta v Moskve*, Moscow, 1959

Zhelvakova, I. A., *Togda ... v Sivtsevom*, Moscow, 1992

List of Authors Mentioned

AKHMATOVA, Anna (1889–1966): poet; author of *Rosary* (1917), *The White Flock* (1921), 'Requiem' (1935–40), 'Poem without a Hero' (1966)

AKSAKOV, Sergey (1791–1859): prose writer; author of *Family Chronicle* (1856), *Childhood Years of Bagrov the Grandson* (1858)

ANDREEV, Leonid (1871–1919): prose writer, dramatist; author of *The Story of Seven Who Were Hanged* (1908), *He Who Gets Slapped* (1915)

ANNENSKY, Innokenty (1856–1909): poet, playwright, critic, translator; author of *Quiet Songs* (1904), *The Cypress Chest* (1910)

AVVAKUM, Petrovich (1620–82): archpriest, leader of the Old Believers; author of the first Russian autobiography, *The Archpriest Avvakum: The Life Written by Himself* (1669–76)

BABEL, Isaak (1894–1940): prose writer; author of *Red Cavalry* (1926)

BAGRITSKY, Eduard (1897–1934): poet; author of 'The Lay about Opanas', *Victors* (1932), *The Last Night* (1932)

BAKHTIN, Mikhail (1895–1975): critic, literary theorist; author of *Problems of Dostoevsky's Poetics* (1929), *Rabelais and His World* (1965)

BALMONT, Konstantin (1867–1942): poet, novelist, translator, essayist; author of *Let Us Be Like the Sun* (1903)

BARATYNSKY, Evgeny (1800–44): poet; author of *Poems* (1827), *Twilight* (1842)

BATYUSHKOV, Konstantin (1787–1855): lyric poet and essayist; author of 'A Vision on the Banks of Lethe' (1809) and 'My Penates' (1811)

BEDNY, Demyan, pseudonym of Efim Pridvorov (1883–1945): poet; author of 'New Testament without Flaw of Demyan the Evangelist' (1925)

BELINSKY, Vissarion (1811–48): critic; contributor to *Otechestvennye zapiski* (National Annals) and *Sovremennik* (the Contemporary); author of 'Letter to Gogol' (1847)

BELY, Andrey, pseudonym of Boris Bugaev (1880–1934): poet, novelist, critic, theorist; author of *Gold in Azure* (1904), *Petersburg* (1916), *The First Encounter* (1921)

BLOK, Alexander (1880–1921): poet, playwright, essayist; author of *Verses about the Beautiful Lady* (1904), 'The Twelve' (1918)

BRIK, Osip (1888–1945): literary theorist; author of 'Sound Repetitions' (1917), 'Rhythm and Syntax' (1927). Husband of Lili Brik, lyric heroine of much of Mayakovsky's early poetry

BRODSKY, Joseph (1940–96): poet, essayist, critic; author of *Part of Speech* (1977), *The End of a Beautiful Era* (1977), *Less Than One* (1986)

BRYUSOV, Valery (1873–1924): poet, novelist, critic; author of *The Russian Symbolists* (1894), *Chefs D'oeuvre* (1895), editor of *Vesy* (the Scales) (1904–9)

BULGAKOV, Mikhail (1891–1940): writer and playwright; author of *The Master and Margarita* (1967)

BUNIN, Ivan (1870–1953): prose writer; author of 'The Gentleman from San Francisco' (1911), *The Life of Arseniev* (1952)

CHAADAEV, Pyotr (1794–1856): philosopher; author of *Philosophical Letters* (1829–31)

CHEKHOV, Anton (1860–1904): short-story writer and dramatist; author of 'The Lady with a Little Dog' (1899), *The Seagull* (1895), *Uncle Vanya* (1900), *The Three Sisters* (1901), *The Cherry Orchard* (1904)

CHERNYSHEVSKY, Nikolay (1828–89): political thinker and novelist; author of *What Is To Be Done?* (1963)

CHUKOVSKY, Korney, pseudonym of Nikolay Korneichuk-hov (1882–1969): writer, critic, translator, essayist

CHULKOV, Georgy (1879–1939): essayist, critic; author of 'On Mystical Anarchism' (1906)

DELVIG, Anton (1798–1831): poet; author of 'The Bathing Women' (1825)

DERZHAVIN, Gavrila (1743–1816), poet; author of 'On the Death of Prince Meshchersky' (1779), 'God' (1784), 'The Waterfall' (1798)

DOBROLYUBOV, Nikolay (1836–61): literary critic; contributor to *Sovremennik* (the Contemporary)

DOSTOEVSKY, Fyodor (1821–81): novelist; author of *Memoirs from the House of the Dead* (1861–2), *Crime and Punishment* (1866), *The Idiot* (1868), *Devils* (1871), *The Brothers Karamazov* (1880)

EHRENBURG, Ilya (1891–1967): novelist, journalist; author of *The Thaw* (1954)

EROFEEV, Venedikt (1938–88): prose writer; author of *Moscow–Petushki* (1969)

ESENIN, Sergey (1895–1925): poet; author of 'Moscow of the Taverns' (1924)

FADEEV, Alexander (1901–56): novelist, literary administrator, head of the Union of Writers (1946–54); author of *The Young Guard* (1945)

FEDIN, Konstantin (1892–1977): novelist; author of *Cities and Years* (1924)

FET, Afanasy (1820–92): poet; author of *Evening Fires* (1883)

FONVIZIN, Denis (1745–92): playwright; author of *The Brigadier* (1769)

FORSH, Olga (1873–1961): novelist; author of *The Mad Ship* (1931)

GINZBURG, Evgeniya (1906–77): novelist; author of *Into the Whirlwind* (1967)

GIPPIUS, Zinaida (1867–1945): poet, critic, novelist; author of 'The Green Ring' (1914)

GLADKOV, Fyodor (1883–1958): prose writer; author of *Cement* (1925)

GOGOL, Nikolay (1809–52): short-story writer, novelist, playwright; author of 'The Nose' (1836), 'The Overcoat' (1842), *The Government Inspector* (1836), *Dead Souls* (1842)

GONCHAROV, Ivan (1812–91): novelist; author of *Oblomov* (1859)

GORKY, Maxim, pseudonym of Alexey Peshkov (1868–1936): prose writer, playwright; author of *Twenty-Six Men and a Girl* (1899), *The Lower Depths* (1902), *My Universities* (1923)

GORODETSKY, Sergey (1884–1967): poet; author of *Sap* (1907)

GRIBOEDOV, Alexander (1795–1829): playwright; author of *Woe from Wit* (1822–4)

GRIN, Alexander (1880–1932): prose writer; author of *Crimson Sails* (1923)

GROSSMAN, Vasily (1905–64): novelist; author of *Life and Fate* (1980)

GUMILYOV, Nikolay (1886–1921): poet; author of *Pearls* (1910), *The Pyre* (1918)

HERZEN, Alexander (1812–70): writer, journalist, editor; author of autobiographical memoirs *My Past and Thoughts* (1868)

ILF, Ilya (1897–1937) and PETROV, Evgeny (1903–42), a team of satirical writers and journalists, authors of *The Twelve Chairs* (1928) and *The Golden Calf* (1931)

IVANOV, Vyacheslav (1866–1949): poet, critic, philosopher; author of *Pilot Stars* (1903), *Eros* (1907), *Cor Ardens* (1911)

KAMENSKY, Vasily (1884–1961): poet; author of *The Mud Hut* (1910)

KANTEMIR, Antiokh (1709–44): poet and satirist; author of nine satires modelled on Horace and Boileau (1762)

KARAMZIN, Nikolay (1766–1826): poet, short-story writer, historian; author of twelve-volume *History of the Russian State* (1818–26)

KATAEV, Valentin (1897–1986): novelist; author of *Time, Forward!* (1932)

KHARMS, Daniil, pseudonym of Daniil Yuvachev (1905–42): poet, prose writer, dramatist; author of *Elizaveta Bam* (1927)

KHLEBNIKOV, Velimir (1885–1922): poet, theorist; author of *Incantation by Laughter* (1910)

KHODASEVICH, Vladislav (1886–1939): poet, critic; author of *The Heavy Lyre* (1922)

KLYUEV, Nikolay (1884–1937): poet; author of 'Lenin' (1924), 'My Country, I Am Guilty' (1924), 'Lament for Esenin' (1926), 'The Village' (1927)

KOROLENKO, Vladimir (1853–1921): prose writer; author of 'Makar's Dream' (1895)

KRUCHONYKH, Alexey (1886–1969): poet, theorist; author of *Victory over the Sun* (1913)

KRYLOV, Ivan (1769–1844): journalist, playwright, fabulist; translator of La Fontaine and author of numerous fables

KÜCHELBECKER, Wilhelm (1797–1846): poet; author of 'They Will Not Understand My Suffering' (1839), 'Ahasuerus' (1832–46)

KUPRIN, Alexander (1870–1938): novelist and short-story writer; author of 'The Garnet Bracelet' (1911)

LERMONTOV, Mikhail (1814–41): poet, novelist; author of *A Hero of Our Time* (1840)

LESKOV, Nikolay (1831–95): short-story writer; author of 'Lady Macbeth of Mtsensk' (1865)

LOMONOSOV, Mikhail (1711–65): man of science and letters;

author of *A Short Guide to Rhetoric* (1748) and the poem 'Evening Meditation upon the Greatness of God' (1743)

LUNACHARSKY, Anatoly (1875–1933): administrator, critic

MANDELSTAM, Nadezhda (1899–1980): wife of Osip Mandelstam; author of *Hope against Hope* (published abroad 1970), *Hope Abandoned* (published abroad 1974)

MANDELSTAM, Osip (1891–1938): poet; author of *Stone* (1913), *Tristia* (1922), *The Voronezh Notebooks* (1935–7)

MARIENGOF, Anatoly (1897–1962): poet, friend of Esenin; author of *A Novel without Lies* (1927)

MARSHAK, Samuil (1887–1964): children's writer, editor

MAYAKOVSKY, Vladimir (1893–1930): poet, dramatist; author of *Vladimir Mayakovsky: A Tragedy* (1914), *Vladimir Ilyich Lenin* (1924), *The Bedbug* (1928), *The Bath-House* (1929)

MEREZHKOVSKY, Dmitry (1865–1941): writer and religious philosopher; author of *Death of the Gods* (trans. 1902), *Tolstoy as Man and Artist* with an essay on Dostoevsky (trans. 1902)

MIRSKY, Dmitry (1890–1939): critic; author of *A History of Russian Literature* (1926)

NABOKOV, Vladimir (1899–1977): novelist, short-story writer, poet; author of *The Gift* (1938), *Lolita* (1955), *Pnin* (1957)

NEKRASOV, Nikolay (1821–78): poet, publisher; editor of *Sovremennik* (the Contemporary) and *Otechestvennye zapiski* (National Annals); author of epic poem *Who Is Happy in Russia?* (1878)

ODOEVSKY, Vladimir (1804–69): short-story writer, critic; author of *Russian Nights* (1844)

OSTROVSKY, Alexander (1823–86): dramatist; author of *The Storm* (1859)

OSTROVSKY, Nikolay (1904–36): novelist; author of *How the Steel Was Tempered* (1932–4)

PASTERNAK, Boris (1890–1960): poet, prose writer; author of *Doctor Zhivago* (1959)

PAUSTOVSKY, Konstantin (1892–1968): prose writer; author of *Sea Sketches* (1925)

PAVLOVA, Karolina (1807–93): poet, prose writer; author of *A Double Life* (1848)

PILNYAK, Boris (1894–1937): novelist and short-story writer, author of *The Volga Falls to the Caspian Sea* (1930)

PLATONOV, Andrey (1899–1951): novelist; author of *The Foundation Pit* (written 1930s, published abroad 1973)

POGODIN, Mikhail (1800–75): historian, journalist; editor of *Moskvityanin* (the Muscovite) (1841–56)

PRISHVIN, Mikhail (1873–1954): prose writer; author of *In the Land of Unfrightened Birds* (1907), *Calendar of Nature* (1935)

PRUTKOV, Kozma: fictitious writer invented by A. K. Tolstoy and his cousins, the Zhemchuzhnikovs, in the 1850s; 'author' of *Fantasia* (1851)

PUSHKIN, Alexander (1799–1837): poet; author of *Eugene Onegin* (1833), 'The Bronze Horseman' (1833)

RADISHCHEV, Alexander (1749–1802): prose writer, poet and political thinker; author of *A Journey from Petersburg to Moscow* (first published anonymously in Russia 1790)

REMIZOV, Alexey (1877–1957): prose writer; author of *The Pond* (1907), *The Fifth Pestilence* (1912)

RYBAKOV, Anatoly (1911–): novelist; author of *Children of the Arbat* (1987)

SALTYKOV-SHCHEDRIN, Mikhail (1826–89): satirist; author of *The Golovlyovs* (1870s)

SHALAMOV, Varlam (1907–82): prose writer; author of *Kolyma Tales* (1978)

SHKLOVSKY, Viktor (1893–1984): literary scholar, critic; author of *A Sentimental Journey* (1923)

SHOLOKHOV, Mikhail (1905–84): Soviet novelist; author of four-volume *The Quiet Don* (1928–40)

SHUKSHIN, Vasily (1929–74): prose writer; author of *Country Folk* (1963)

SOLLOGUB, Count Vladimir (1813–82): prose writer; author of *Tarantas* (1845)

SOLOGUB, Fyodor, pseudonym of Fyodor Teternikov (1863–1927): prose writer, poet; author of *The Petty Demon* (1907)

SOLZHENITSYN, Alexander (1918–): novelist; author of *One Day in the Life of Ivan Denisovich* (1962), *The Gulag Archipelago* (1973–5)

SUMAROKOV, Alexander (1718–77): poet, dramatist, journalist, critic; author of *Chorus to a Perverse World* (1762)

TOLSTOY, A. K. (1817–75): poet, dramatist, satirist; author of 'The Vampire' (1841), *The Silver Prince* (1863), *Tsar Fyodor Ivanovich* (1868)

TOLSTOY, A. N. (1883–1945): novelist; author of *Nikita's Childhood* (1921), *Aelita* (1924), *Road to Calvary* (1921–41)

TOLSTOY, Lev (1828–1910): prose writer; author of *War and Peace* (1865–8), *Anna Karenina* (1873–7)

TRIFONOV, Yury (1925–81): novelist, short-story writer; author of *The House on the Embankment* (1976)

TSVETAEVA, Marina (1892–1941): poet; author of *Evening Album* (1910), *Mileposts* (1922)

TURGENEV, Ivan (1818–83): novelist; author of *Rudin* (1855), *A Nest of the Gentry* (1858), *Fathers and Sons* (1861), *Sketches from a Hunter's Album* (1852)

TVARDOVSKY, Alexander (1910–71): poet; editor of *Novy mir* (New World) (1950–4, 1958–70)

TYUTCHEV, Fyodor (1803–73): poet; author of 'A Vision' (1829), 'Silentium!' (1830), 'Holy Night' (1849)

VENEVITINOV, Dmitry (1805–27); poet and philosopher; author of 'On the State of Enlightenment in Russia' (1833)

VOLOSHIN, Maximilian (1877–1932): poet, translator; author of *Mute Demons* (1919)

VYAZEMSKY, Pyotr (1792–1878): polemicist, poet and prose writer; author of sketches 'Griboedov's Moscow', 'An Old-fashioned Moscow Family' (1877) and 'The Russian God' (1854)

VYSOTSKY, Vladimir (1938–80): poet, singer, actor, composer

ZABOLOTSKY, Nikolay (1903–58): poet; author of *A Celebration of Agriculture* (1929–30)

ZAMYATIN, Evgeny (1884–1937): novelist, short-story writer, essayist; author of *We* (1924)

ZHUKOVSKY, Vasily (1783–1852): poet, translator; author of *Lyudmila* (1808)

ZOSHCHENKO, Mikhail (1895–1958): satirical writer; author of *Before Sunrise* (1943)

Index